THRASHED

Also by Jerry Scott and Jim Borgman

Zits: Sketchbook 1
Growth Spurt: Zits Sketchbook 2
Don't Roll Your Eyes at Me, Young Man!: Zits Sketchbook 3
Are We an "Us"?: Zits Sketchbook #4
Zits Unzipped: Sketchbook Number 5
Busted!: Zits Sketchbook 6
Road Trip: Zits Sketchbook No. 7
Teenage Tales: Zits Sketchbook No. 8

Treasuries
Humongous Zits
Big Honkin' Zits
Zits: Supersized
Random Zits

THRASHED

Zits® Sketchbook No. 9

by JERRY SCOTT and JIM BORGMAN¨

**Andrews McMeel
Publishing**

Kansas City

Zits® is syndicated internationally by King Features Syndicate, Inc. For information, write King Features Syndicate, Inc., 300 West Fifty-Seventh Street, New York, New York 10019.

07 08 09 BBG 10 9 8 7 6 5 4 3 2

ISBN-13: 978-0-7407-5117-2
ISBN-10: 0-7407-5117-4

Library of Congress Control Number: 2004114452

Zits® may be viewed online at
www.kingfeatures.com.

——— **ATTENTION: SCHOOLS AND BUSINESSES** ———

Andrews McMeel books are available at quantity discounts with bulk purchase for educational, business, or sales promotional use. For information, please write to: Special Sales Department, Andrews McMeel Publishing, LLC, 4520 Main Street, Kansas City, Missouri 64111.

For Sarah Jewler.

—J.B. & J.S.

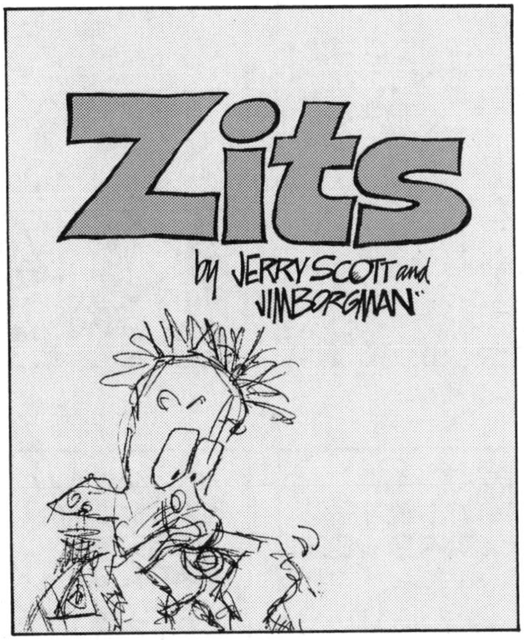
Zits
by JERRY SCOTT and JIM BORGMAN

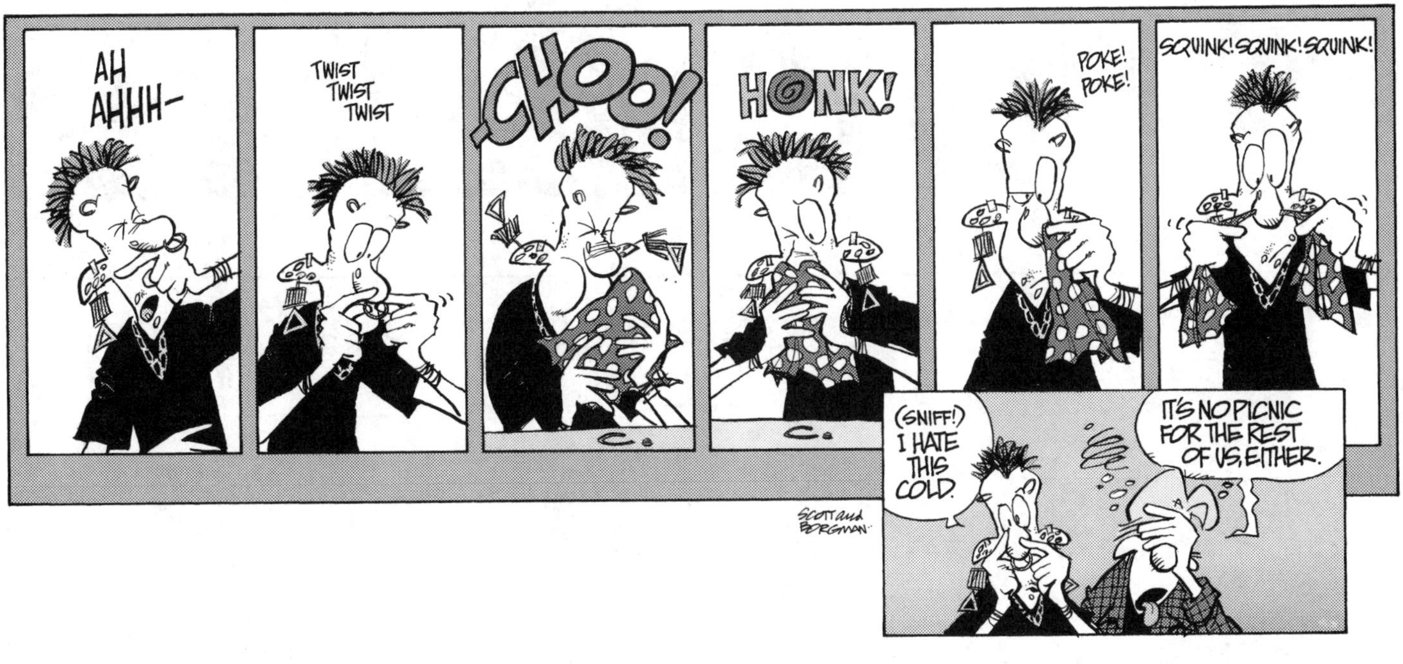
AH AHHH-
TWIST TWIST TWIST
-CHOO!
HONK!
POKE! POKE!
SQUINK! SQUINK! SQUINK!
(SNIFF!) I HATE THIS COLD.
IT'S NO PICNIC FOR THE REST OF US, EITHER.
SCOTT and BORGMAN

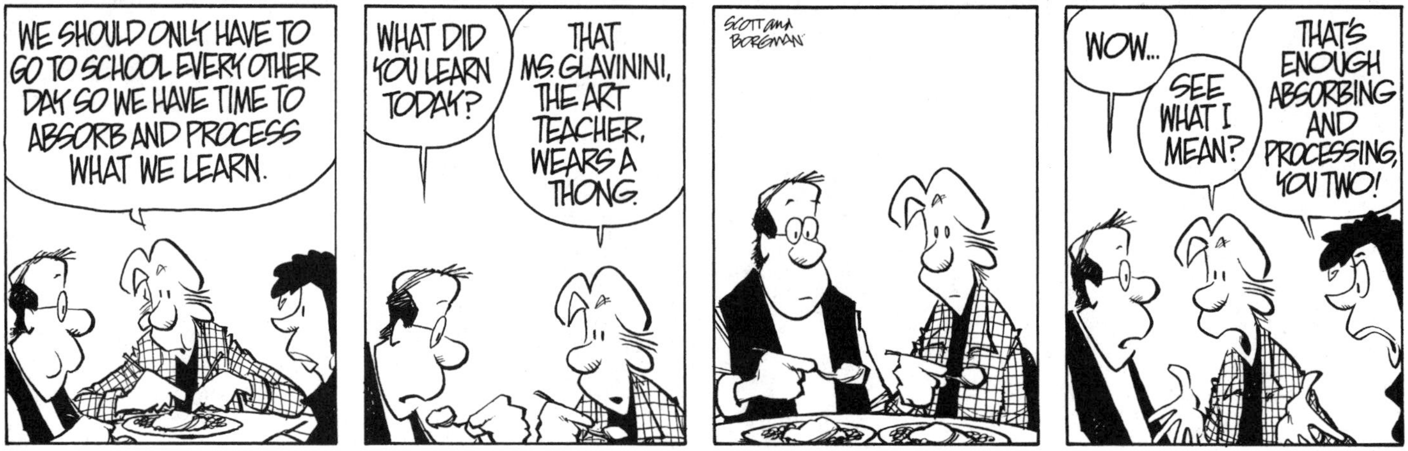
WE SHOULD ONLY HAVE TO GO TO SCHOOL EVERY OTHER DAY SO WE HAVE TIME TO ABSORB AND PROCESS WHAT WE LEARN.
WHAT DID YOU LEARN TODAY?
THAT MS. GLAVININI, THE ART TEACHER, WEARS A THONG.
WOW...
SEE WHAT I MEAN?
THAT'S ENOUGH ABSORBING AND PROCESSING, YOU TWO!

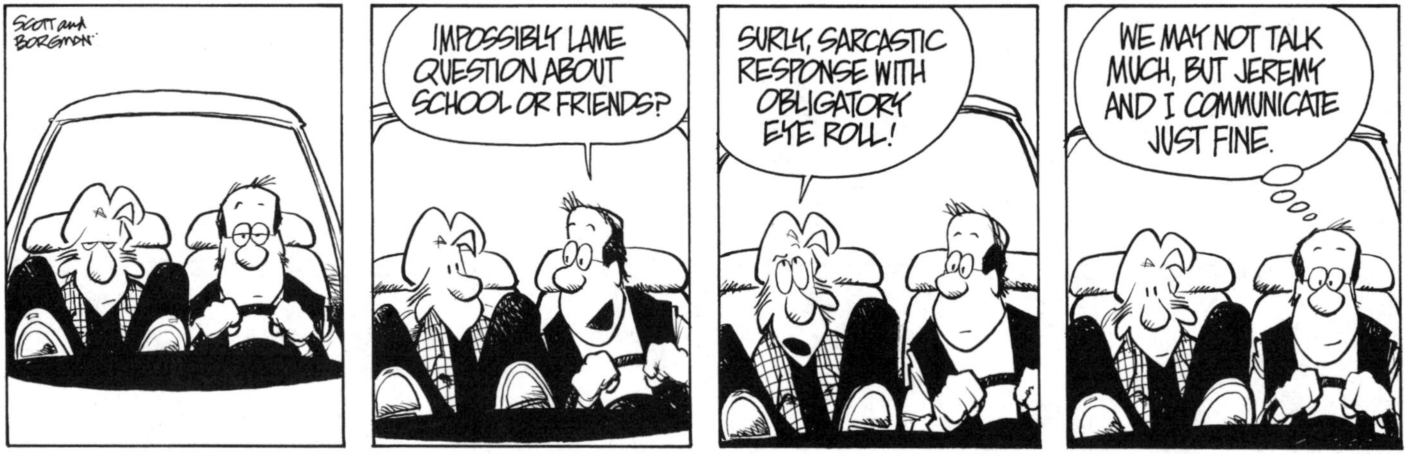
IMPOSSIBLY LAME QUESTION ABOUT SCHOOL OR FRIENDS?
SURLY, SARCASTIC RESPONSE WITH OBLIGATORY EYE ROLL!
WE MAY NOT TALK MUCH, BUT JEREMY AND I COMMUNICATE JUST FINE.

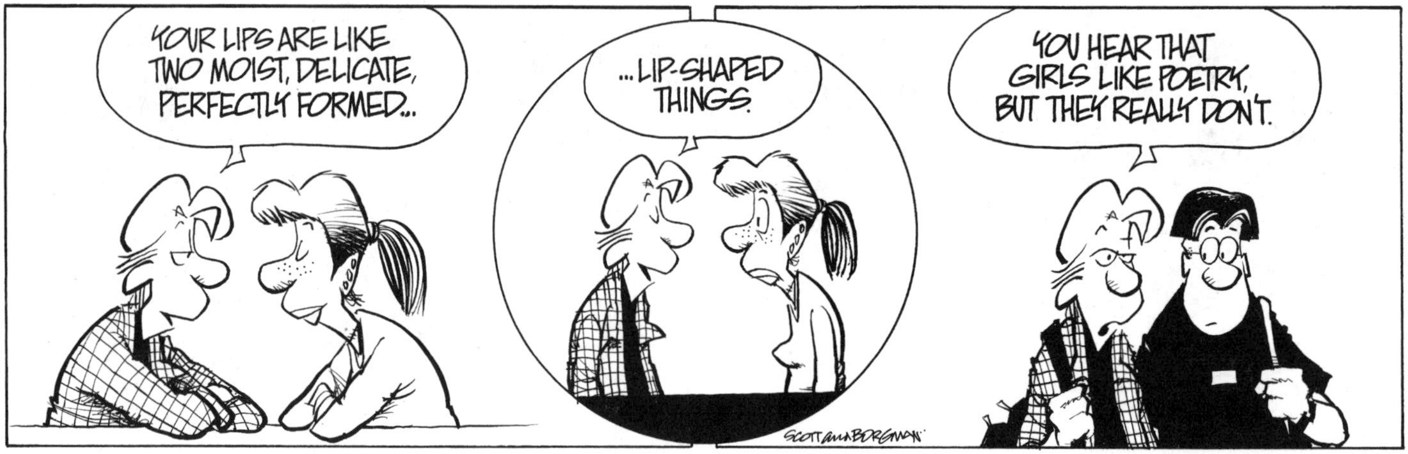
YOUR LIPS ARE LIKE TWO MOIST, DELICATE, PERFECTLY FORMED...
...LIP-SHAPED THINGS.
YOU HEAR THAT GIRLS LIKE POETRY, BUT THEY REALLY DON'T.

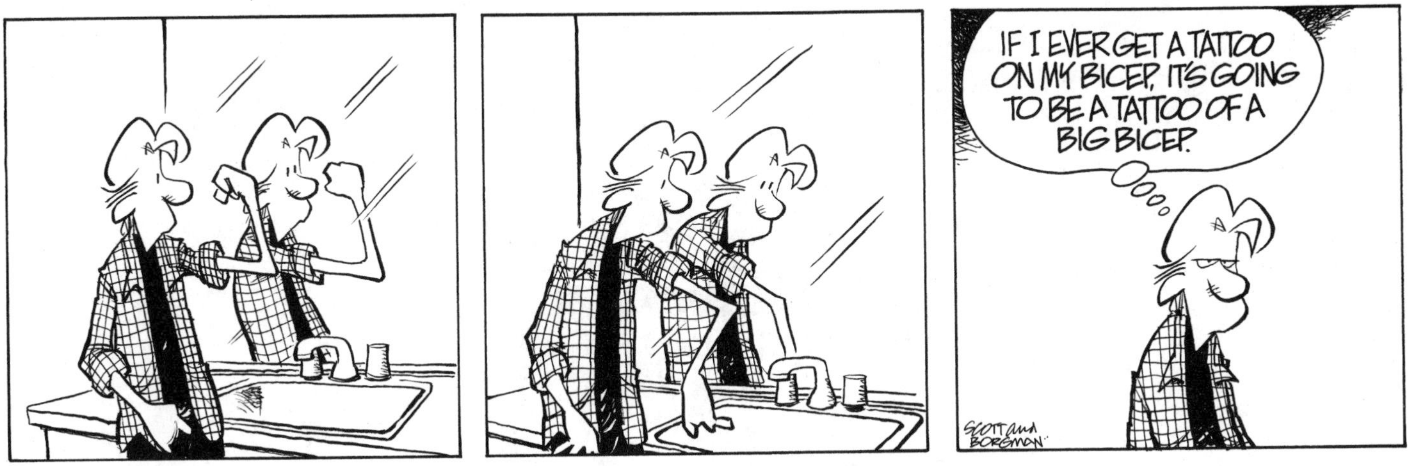
IF I EVER GET A TATTOO ON MY BICEP, IT'S GOING TO BE A TATTOO OF A BIG BICEP.
SCOTT AND BORGMAN

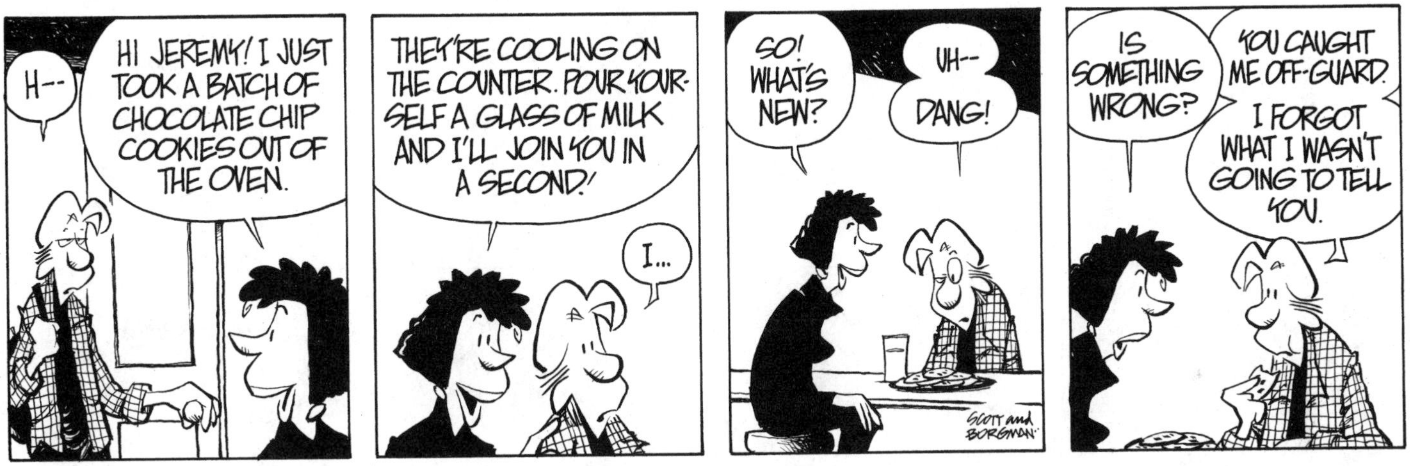
H--
HI JEREMY! I JUST TOOK A BATCH OF CHOCOLATE CHIP COOKIES OUT OF THE OVEN.
THEY'RE COOLING ON THE COUNTER. POUR YOURSELF A GLASS OF MILK AND I'LL JOIN YOU IN A SECOND!
I...
SO! WHAT'S NEW?
UH--
DANG!
SCOTT AND BORGMAN
IS SOMETHING WRONG?
YOU CAUGHT ME OFF-GUARD.
I FORGOT WHAT I WASN'T GOING TO TELL YOU.

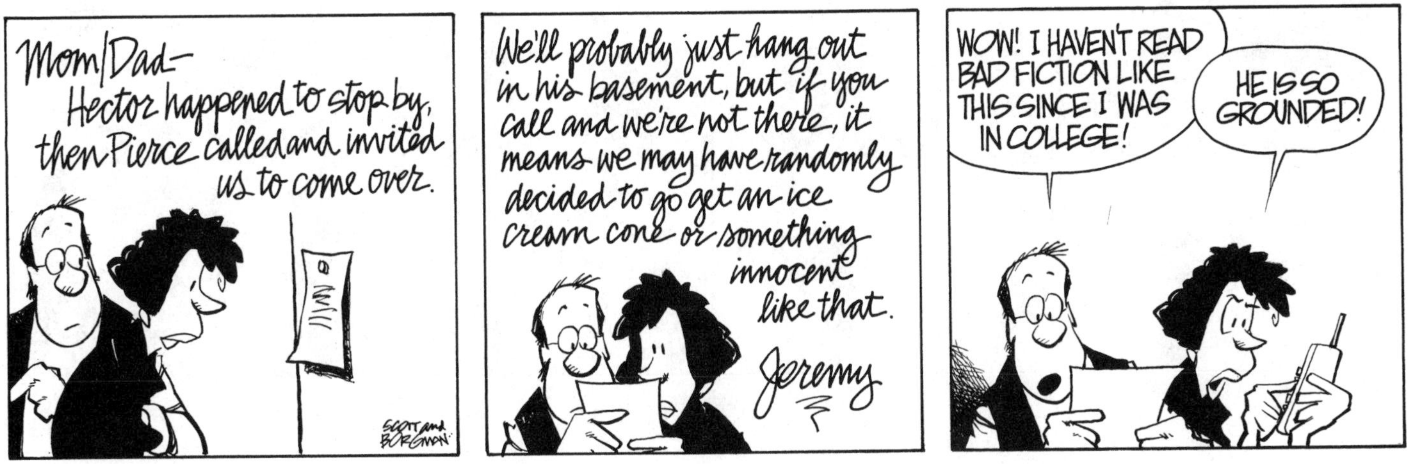
Mom/Dad-
Hector happened to stop by, then Pierce called and invited us to come over.
SCOTT AND BORGMAN
We'll probably just hang out in his basement, but if you call and we're not there, it means we may have randomly decided to go get an ice cream cone or something innocent like that.
Jeremy
WOW! I HAVEN'T READ BAD FICTION LIKE THIS SINCE I WAS IN COLLEGE!
HE IS SO GROUNDED!

Zits
by JERRY SCOTT and JIM BORGMAN

YOU'RE HOME!
YUP.
SCOTT AND BORGMAN
(AHEM!)
WE NEED TO TALK
ABOUT ANYTHING SPECIFICALLY?

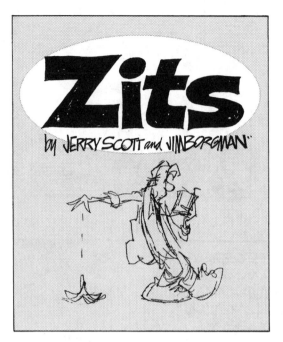

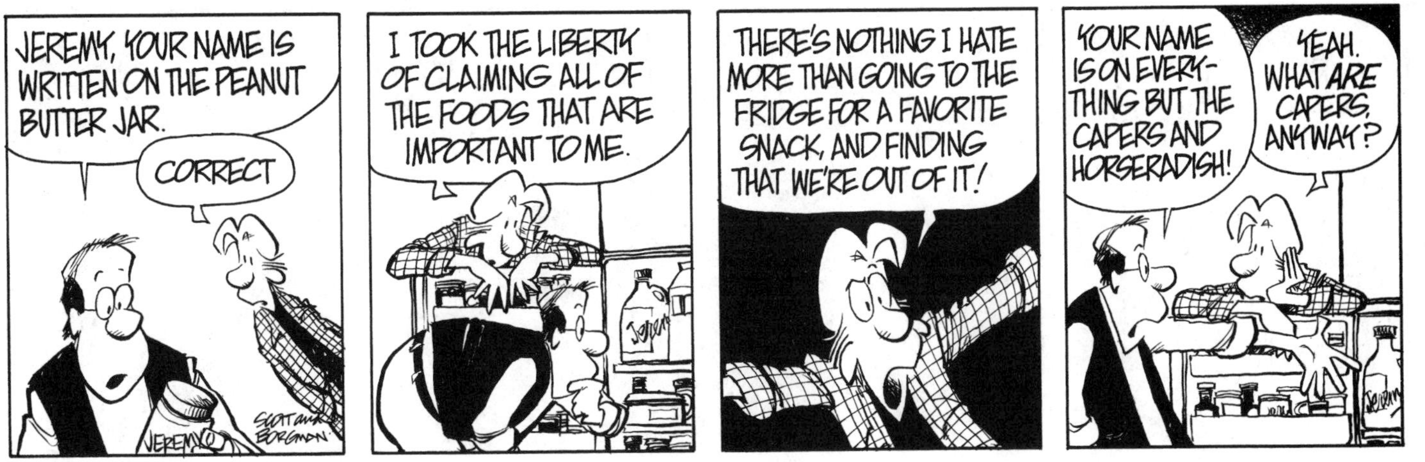
JEREMY, YOUR NAME IS WRITTEN ON THE PEANUT BUTTER JAR.
CORRECT
JEREMY
SCOTT and BORGMAN
I TOOK THE LIBERTY OF CLAIMING ALL OF THE FOODS THAT ARE IMPORTANT TO ME.
THERE'S NOTHING I HATE MORE THAN GOING TO THE FRIDGE FOR A FAVORITE SNACK, AND FINDING THAT WE'RE OUT OF IT!
YOUR NAME IS ON EVERYTHING BUT THE CAPERS AND HORSERADISH!
YEAH. WHAT **ARE** CAPERS, ANYWAY?

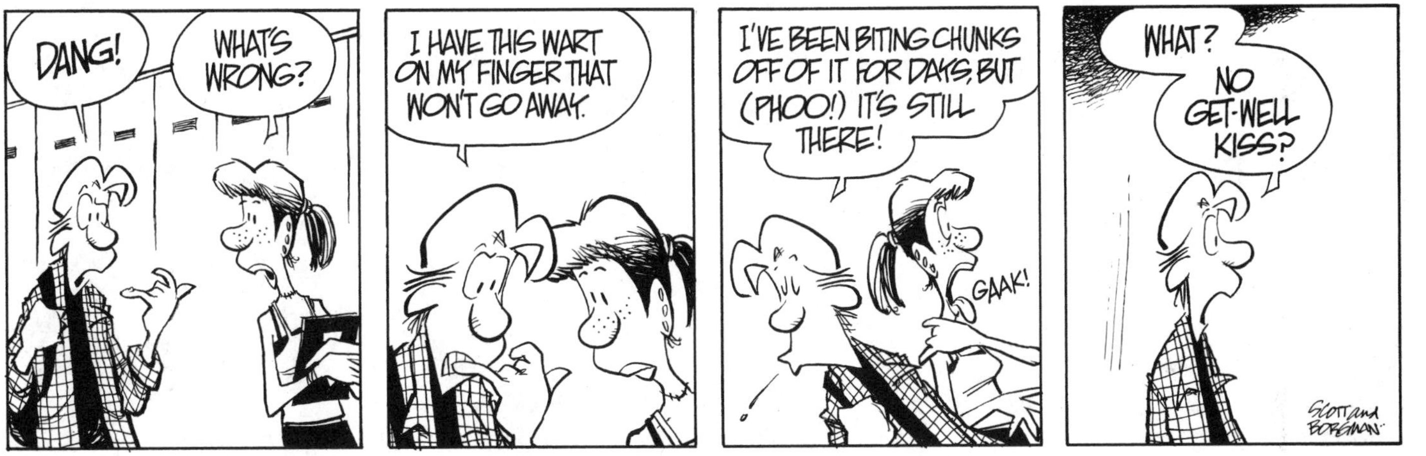
DANG!
WHAT'S WRONG?
I HAVE THIS WART ON MY FINGER THAT WON'T GO AWAY.
I'VE BEEN BITING CHUNKS OFF OF IT FOR DAYS, BUT (PHOO!) IT'S STILL THERE!
GAAK!
WHAT?
NO GET-WELL KISS?
SCOTT and BORGMAN

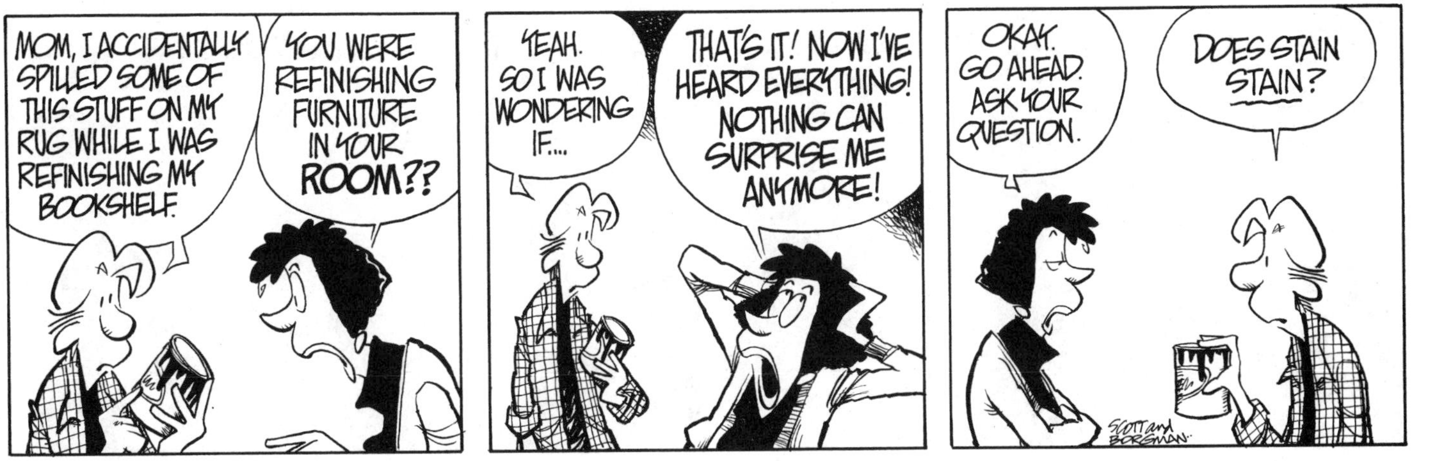
MOM, I ACCIDENTALLY SPILLED SOME OF THIS STUFF ON MY RUG WHILE I WAS REFINISHING MY BOOKSHELF.
YOU WERE REFINISHING FURNITURE IN YOUR **ROOM**??
YEAH. SO I WAS WONDERING IF....
THAT'S IT! NOW I'VE HEARD EVERYTHING! NOTHING CAN SURPRISE ME ANYMORE!
OKAY. GO AHEAD. ASK YOUR QUESTION.
DOES STAIN STAIN?
SCOTT and BORGMAN

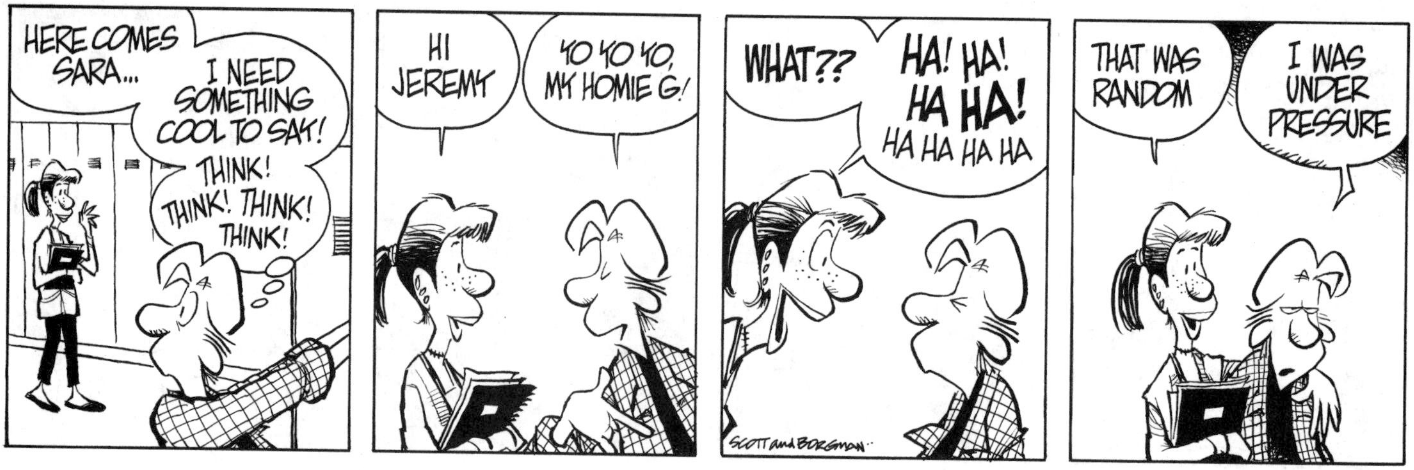
HERE COMES SARA...
I NEED SOMETHING COOL TO SAY!
THINK! THINK! THINK! THINK!
HI JEREMY
YO YO YO, MY HOMIE G!
WHAT??
HA! HA! HA HA! HA HA HA HA
SCOTT and BORGMAN
THAT WAS RANDOM
I WAS UNDER PRESSURE

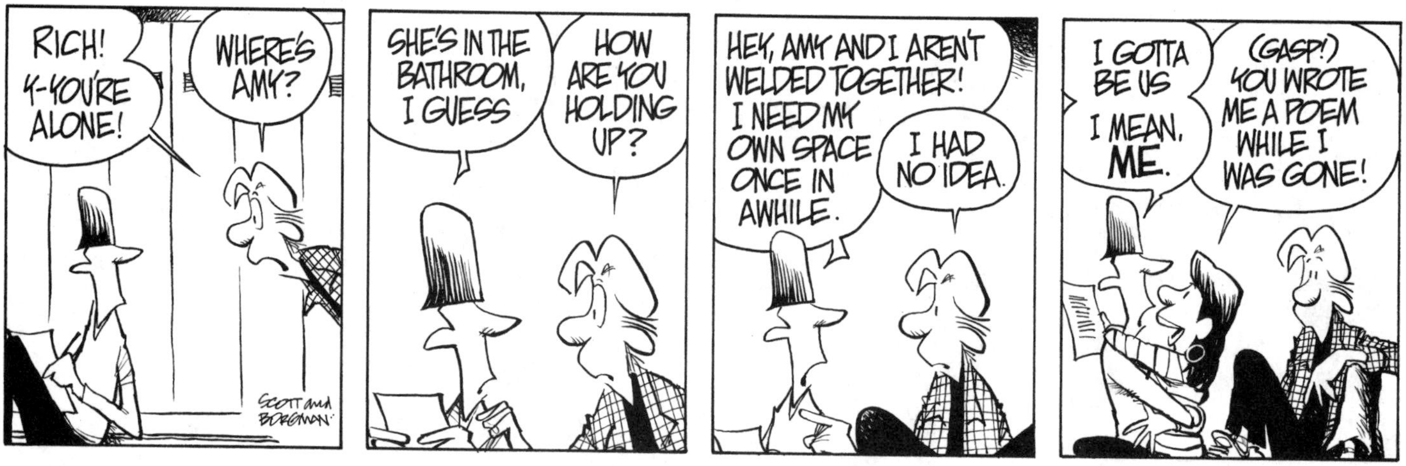
RICH! Y-YOU'RE ALONE!
WHERE'S AMY?
SCOTT and BORGMAN
SHE'S IN THE BATHROOM, I GUESS
HOW ARE YOU HOLDING UP?
HEY, AMY AND I AREN'T WELDED TOGETHER! I NEED MY OWN SPACE ONCE IN AWHILE.
I HAD NO IDEA.
I GOTTA BE US
I MEAN, ME.
(GASP!) YOU WROTE ME A POEM WHILE I WAS GONE!

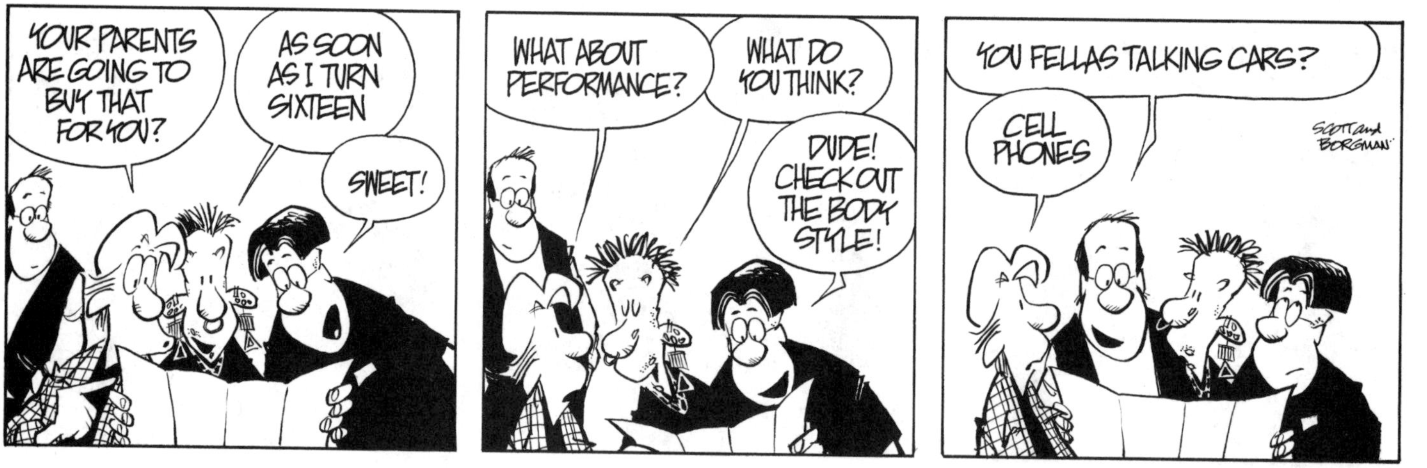
YOUR PARENTS ARE GOING TO BUY THAT FOR YOU?
AS SOON AS I TURN SIXTEEN
SWEET!
WHAT ABOUT PERFORMANCE?
WHAT DO YOU THINK?
DUDE! CHECK OUT THE BODY STYLE!
YOU FELLAS TALKING CARS?
CELL PHONES
SCOTT and BORGMAN

Zits
by JERRY SCOTT and JIM BORGMAN

JEREMY, I'VE BEEN REFLECTING BACK ON THE DAY, AND I SEE A DISTURBING PATTERN OF EVENTS.
OH?
THIS MORNING I SUGGESTED YOU WEAR YOUR GREEN SHIRT WITH THOSE PANTS, AND YOU WORE THE PURPLE ONE.
THEN I SAID YOU SHOULD TAKE AN UMBRELLA, AND YOU REFUSED.
I REMINDED YOU TO WRITE A PERSONAL THANK YOU NOTE TO GRANDMA, BUT YOU SENT HER AN E-MAIL.
SEE? IT SEEMS LIKE NO MATTER WHAT I SAY OR THINK, YOU COMPLETELY DISAGREE WITH ME!
YEAH, I'VE NOTICED IT, TOO.
DON'T YOU EVER GET TIRED OF BEING WRONG?

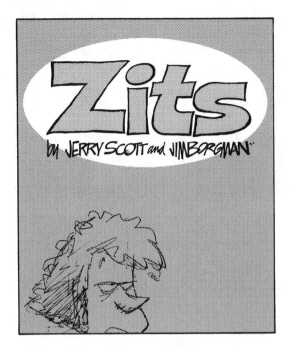

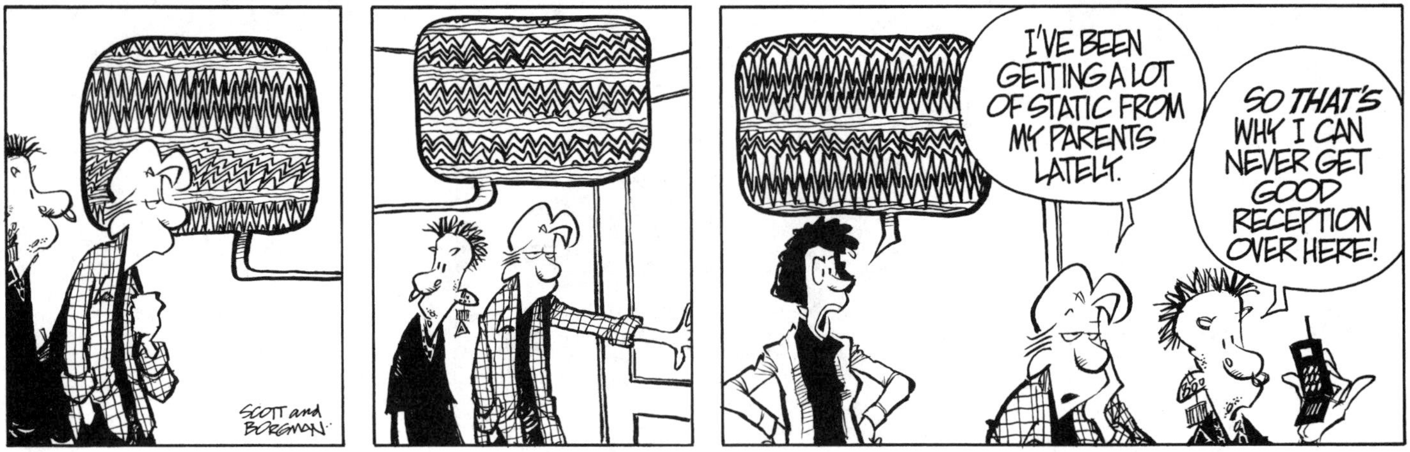
SCOTT and BORGMAN
I'VE BEEN GETTING A LOT OF STATIC FROM MY PARENTS LATELY.
SO THAT'S WHY I CAN NEVER GET GOOD RECEPTION OVER HERE!

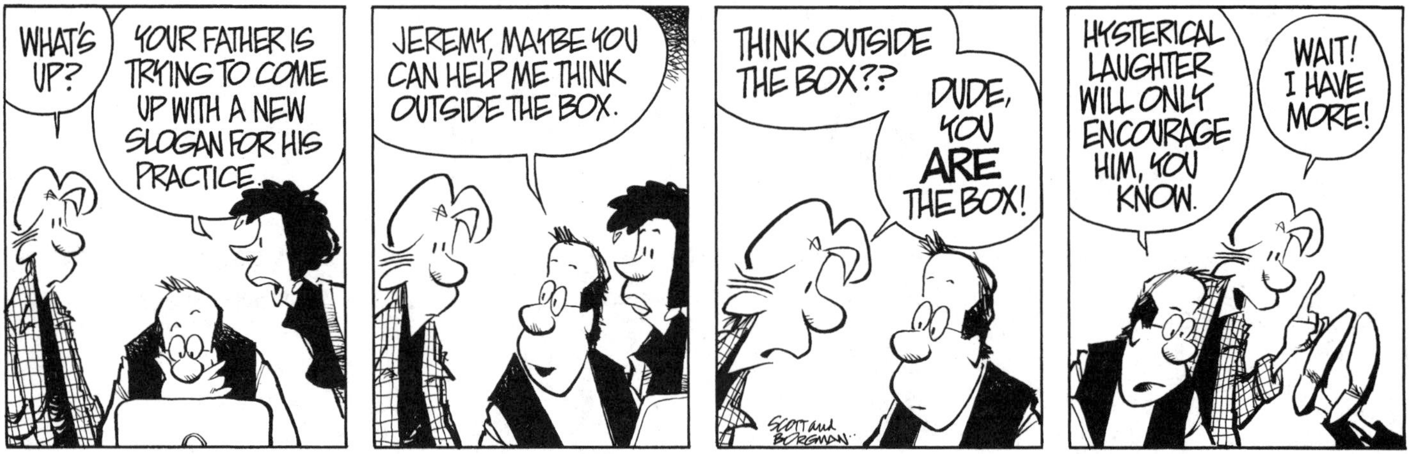
WHAT'S UP?
YOUR FATHER IS TRYING TO COME UP WITH A NEW SLOGAN FOR HIS PRACTICE.
JEREMY, MAYBE YOU CAN HELP ME THINK OUTSIDE THE BOX.
THINK OUTSIDE THE BOX??
DUDE, YOU ARE THE BOX!
SCOTT and BORGMAN
HYSTERICAL LAUGHTER WILL ONLY ENCOURAGE HIM, YOU KNOW.
WAIT! I HAVE MORE!

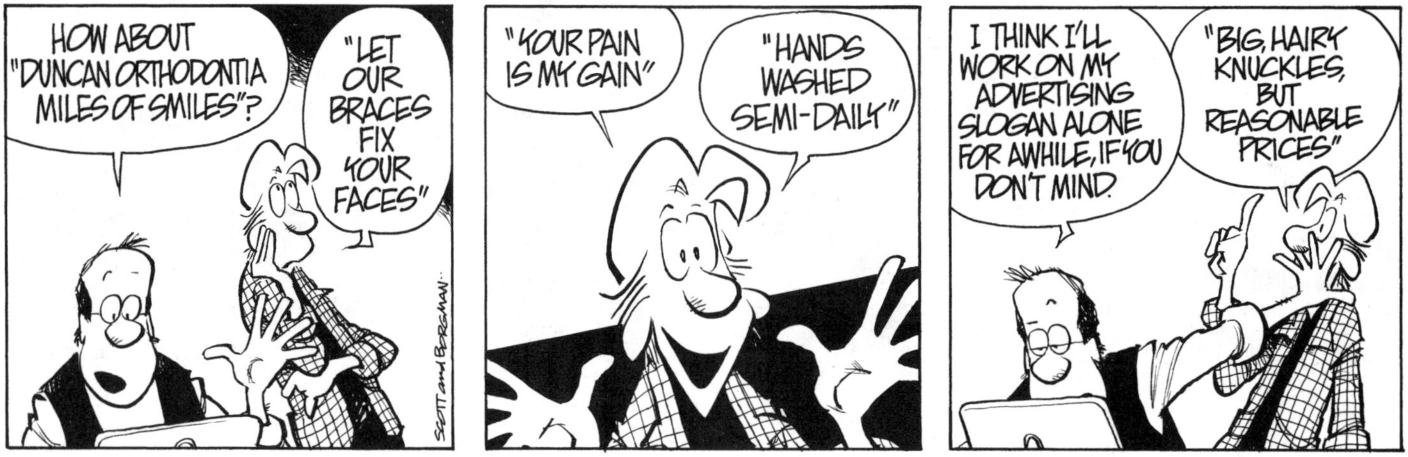
HOW ABOUT "DUNCAN ORTHODONTIA MILES OF SMILES"?
"LET OUR BRACES FIX YOUR FACES"
SCOTT and BORGMAN
"YOUR PAIN IS MY GAIN"
"HANDS WASHED SEMI-DAILY"
I THINK I'LL WORK ON MY ADVERTISING SLOGAN ALONE FOR AWHILE, IF YOU DON'T MIND.
"BIG, HAIRY KNUCKLES, BUT REASONABLE PRICES"

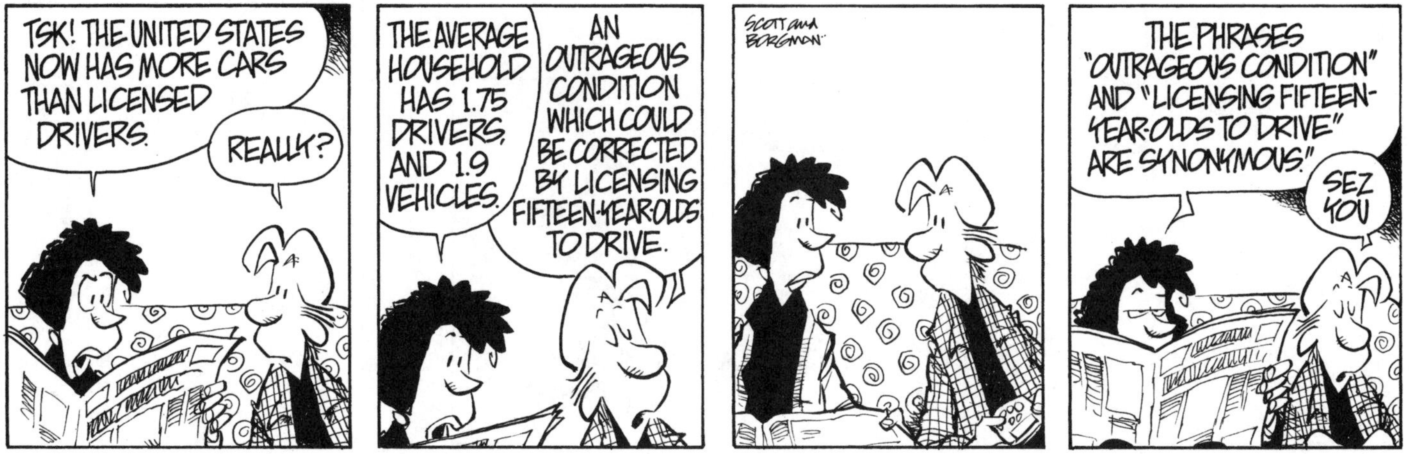
TSK! THE UNITED STATES NOW HAS MORE CARS THAN LICENSED DRIVERS.
REALLY?
THE AVERAGE HOUSEHOLD HAS 1.75 DRIVERS, AND 1.9 VEHICLES.
AN OUTRAGEOUS CONDITION WHICH COULD BE CORRECTED BY LICENSING FIFTEEN-YEAR-OLDS TO DRIVE.
SCOTT and BORGMAN
THE PHRASES "OUTRAGEOUS CONDITION" AND "LICENSING FIFTEEN-YEAR-OLDS TO DRIVE" ARE SYNONYMOUS."
SEZ YOU

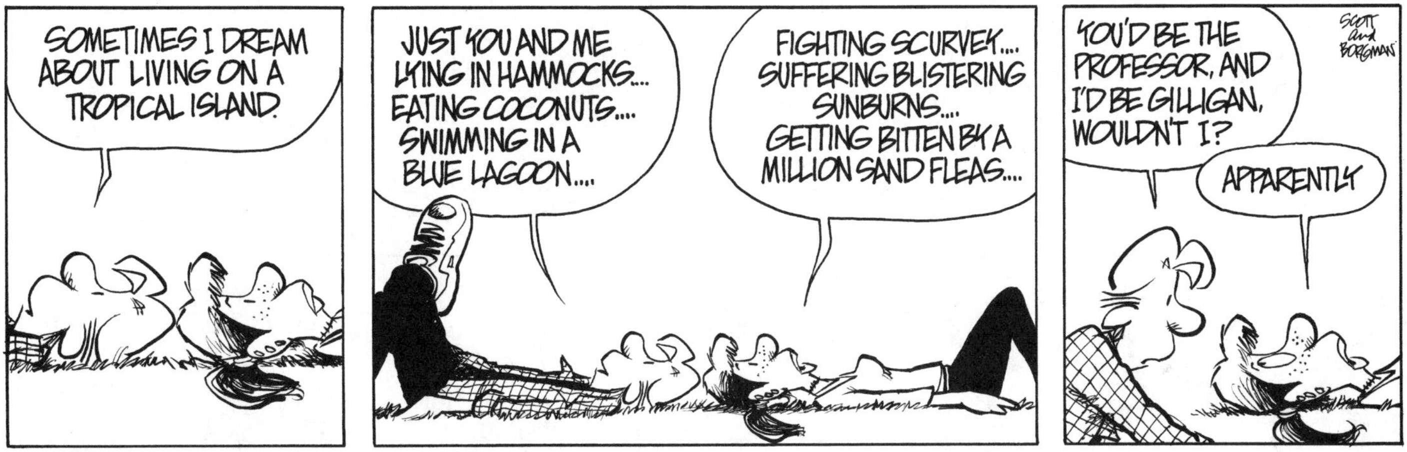
SOMETIMES I DREAM ABOUT LIVING ON A TROPICAL ISLAND.
JUST YOU AND ME LYING IN HAMMOCKS.... EATING COCONUTS.... SWIMMING IN A BLUE LAGOON....
FIGHTING SCURVEY.... SUFFERING BLISTERING SUNBURNS.... GETTING BITTEN BY A MILLION SAND FLEAS....
YOU'D BE THE PROFESSOR, AND I'D BE GILLIGAN, WOULDN'T I?
APPARENTLY
SCOTT and BORGMAN

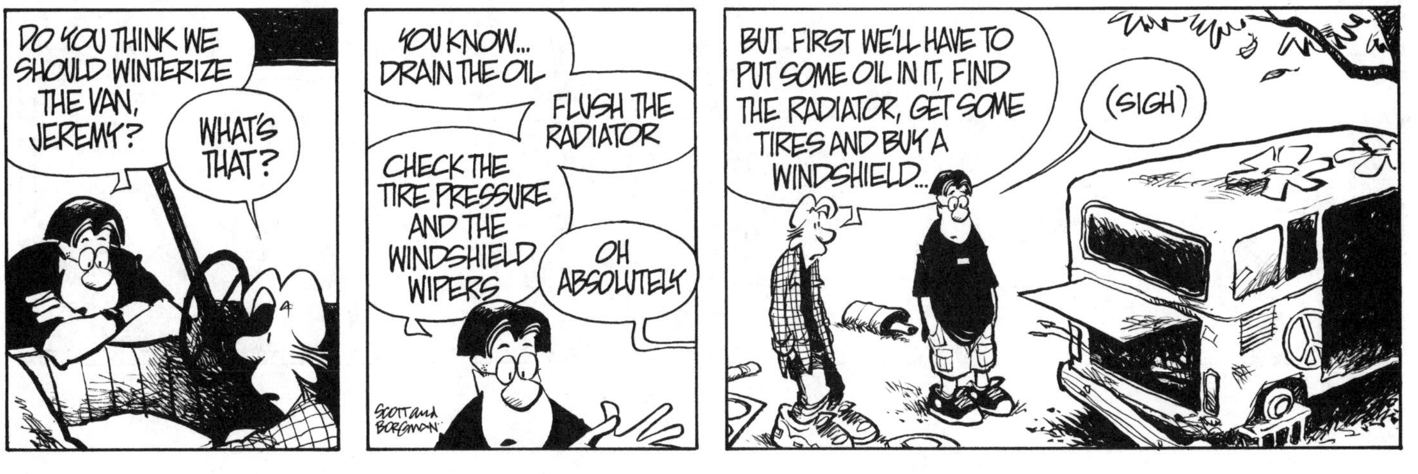
DO YOU THINK WE SHOULD WINTERIZE THE VAN, JEREMY?
WHAT'S THAT?
YOU KNOW... DRAIN THE OIL
FLUSH THE RADIATOR
CHECK THE TIRE PRESSURE AND THE WINDSHIELD WIPERS
OH ABSOLUTELY
SCOTT and BORGMAN
BUT FIRST WE'LL HAVE TO PUT SOME OIL IN IT, FIND THE RADIATOR, GET SOME TIRES AND BUY A WINDSHIELD...
(SIGH)

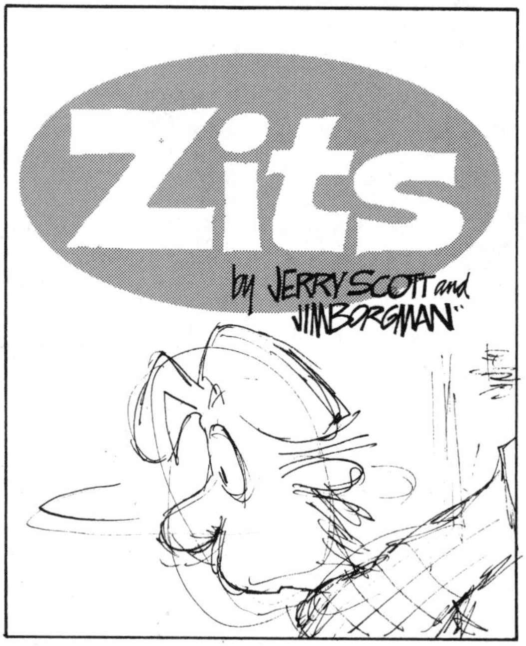
Zits
by JERRY SCOTT and
JIM BORGMAN

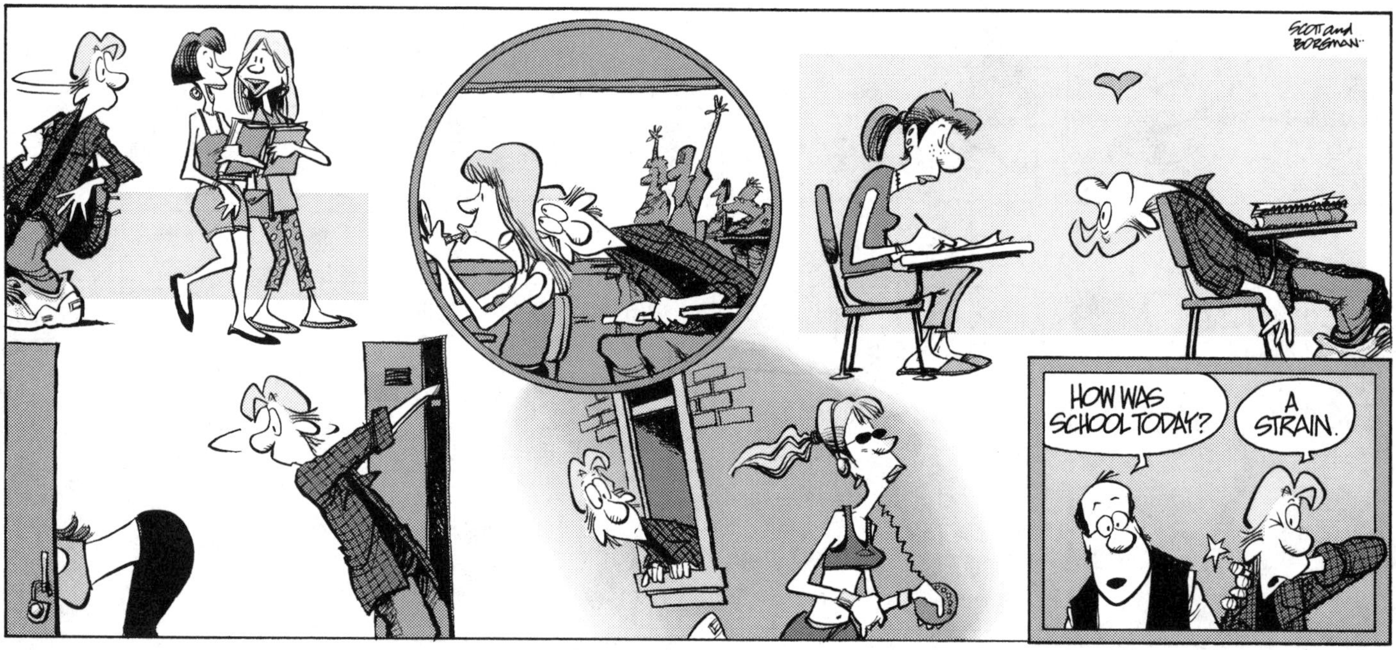
SCOTT and BORGMAN
HOW WAS SCHOOL TODAY?
A STRAIN.

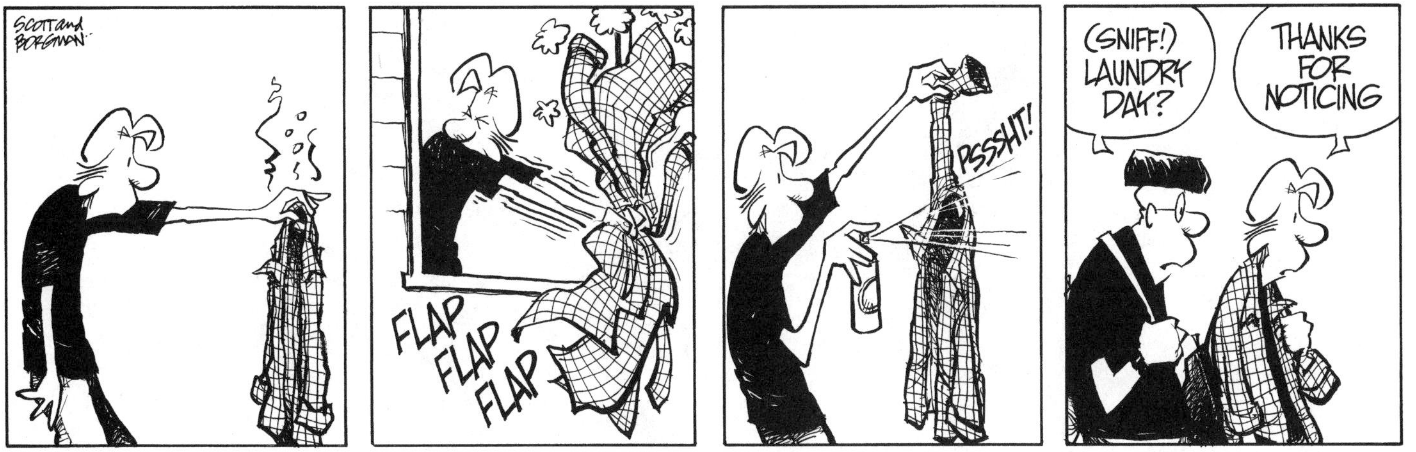
SCOTT and BORGMAN
FLAP FLAP FLAP
PSSSHT!
(SNIFF!) LAUNDRY DAY?
THANKS FOR NOTICING

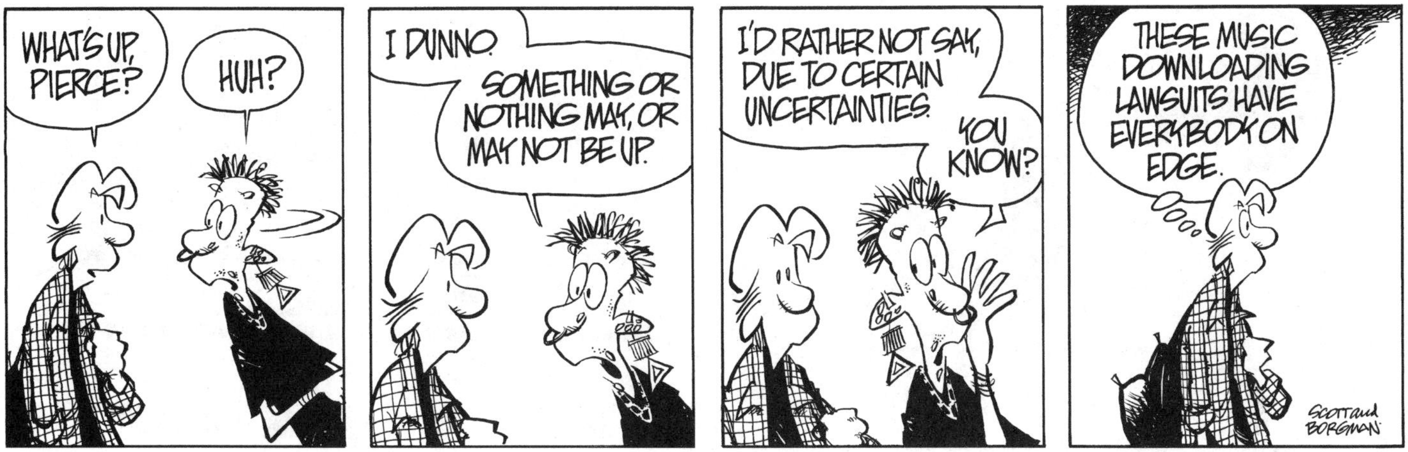
WHAT'S UP, PIERCE?
HUH?
I DUNNO.
SOMETHING OR NOTHING MAY, OR MAY NOT BE UP.
I'D RATHER NOT SAY, DUE TO CERTAIN UNCERTAINTIES.
YOU KNOW?
THESE MUSIC DOWNLOADING LAWSUITS HAVE EVERYBODY ON EDGE.
SCOTT and BORGMAN

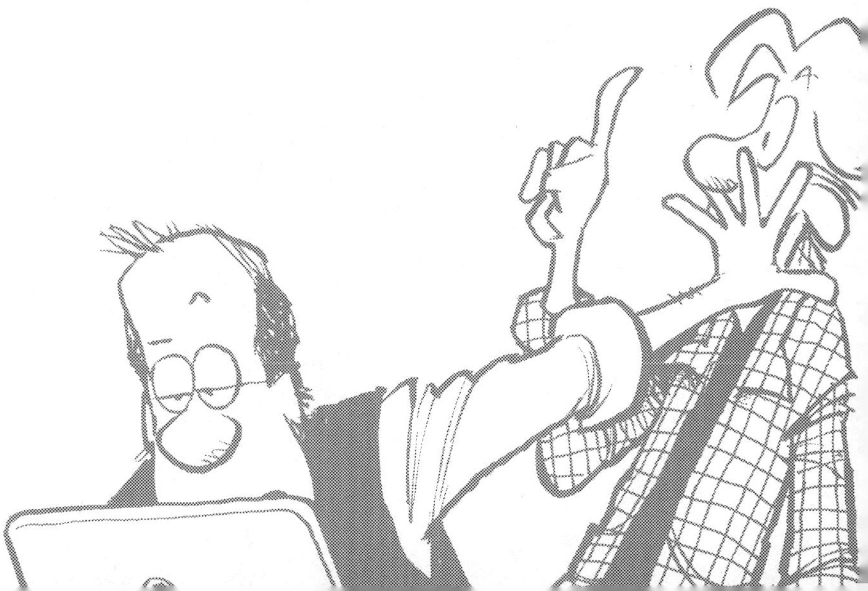

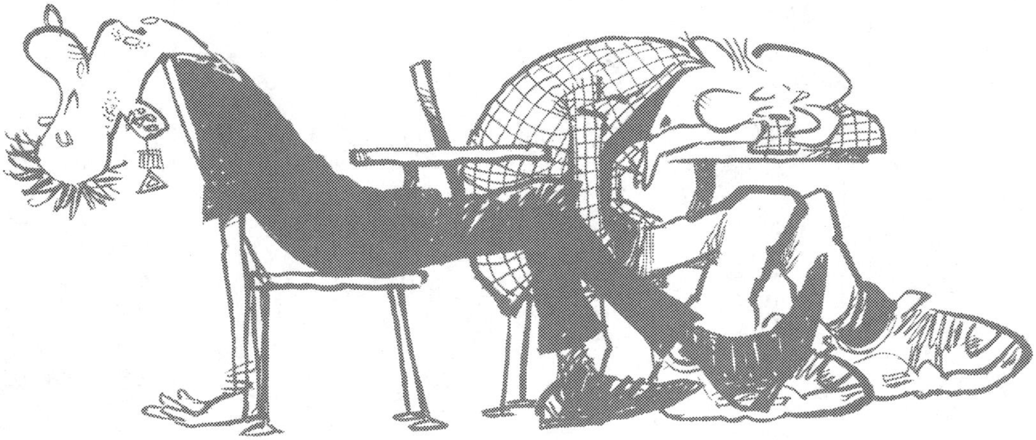

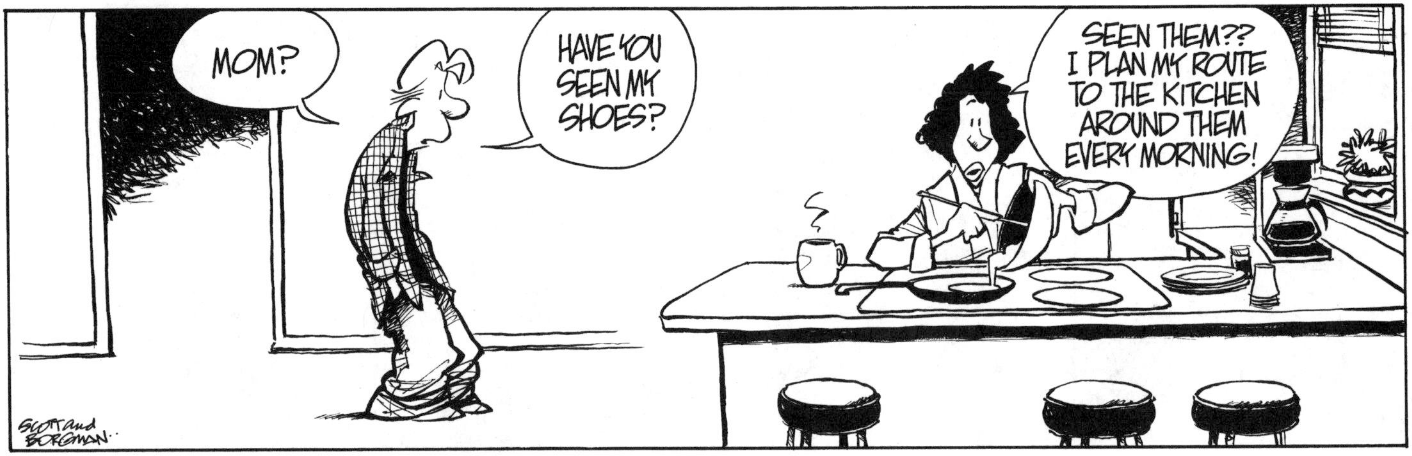
MOM?
HAVE YOU SEEN MY SHOES?
SEEN THEM?? I PLAN MY ROUTE TO THE KITCHEN AROUND THEM EVERY MORNING!
SCOTT and BORGMAN

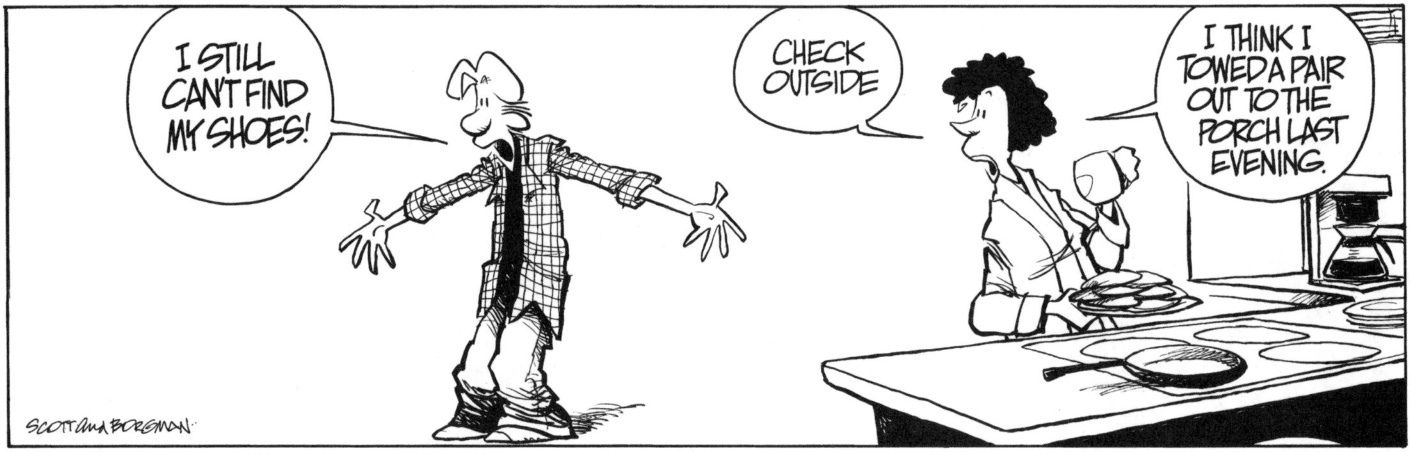
I STILL CAN'T FIND MY SHOES!
CHECK OUTSIDE
I THINK I TOWED A PAIR OUT TO THE PORCH LAST EVENING.
SCOTT and BORGMAN

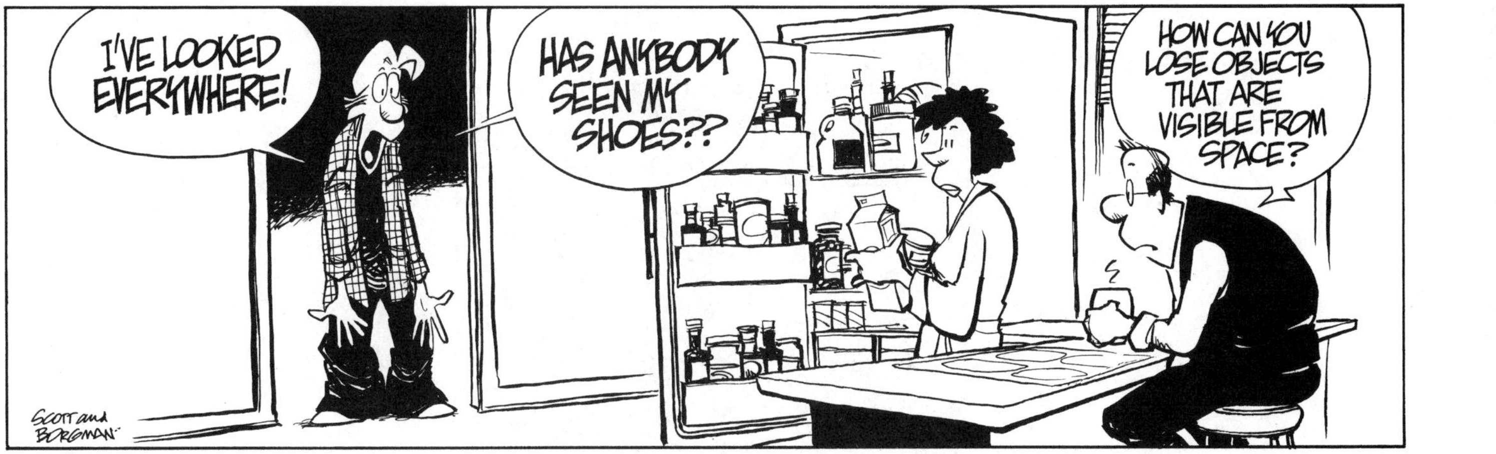
I'VE LOOKED EVERYWHERE!
HAS ANYBODY SEEN MY SHOES??
HOW CAN YOU LOSE OBJECTS THAT ARE VISIBLE FROM SPACE?
SCOTT and BORGMAN

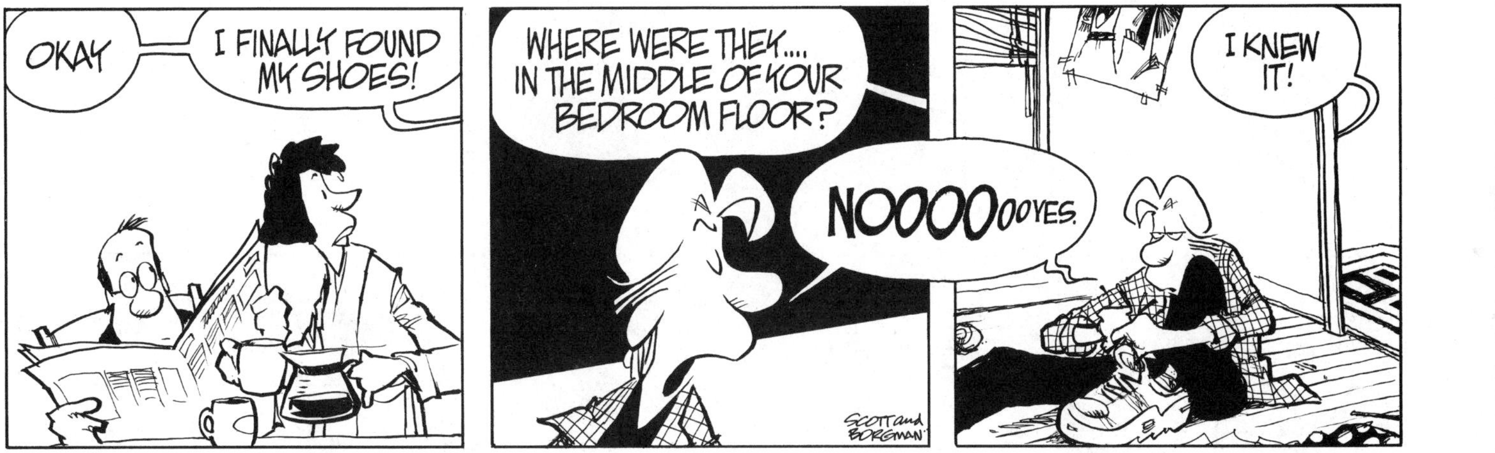
I FINALLY FOUND MY SHOES!
OKAY
WHERE WERE THEY.... IN THE MIDDLE OF YOUR BEDROOM FLOOR?
NOOOOOOYES.
I KNEW IT!
SCOTT and BORGMAN

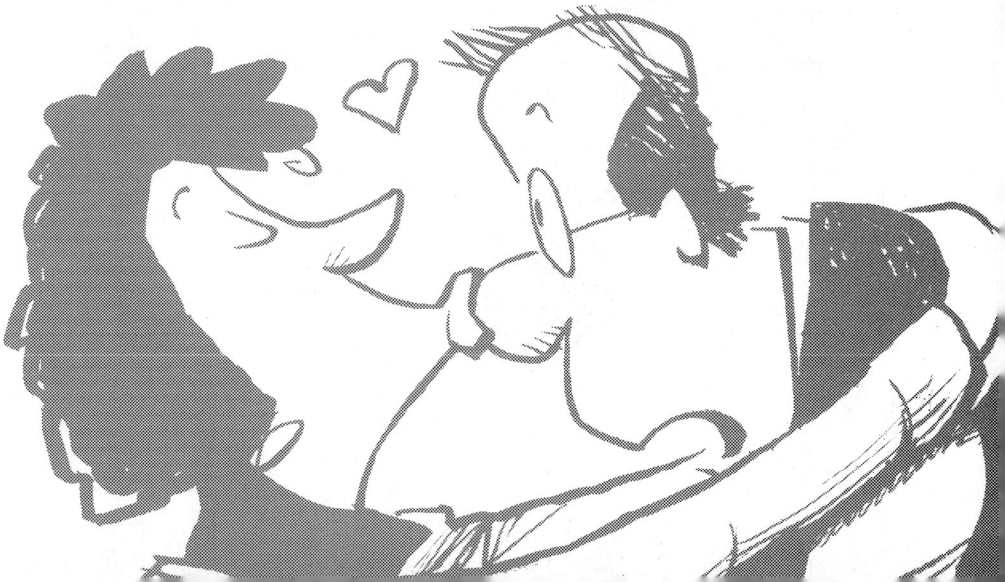

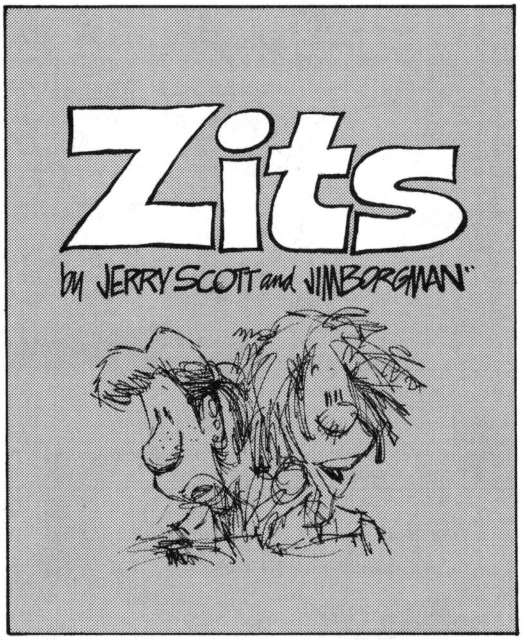
Zits
by JERRY SCOTT and JIM BORGMAN

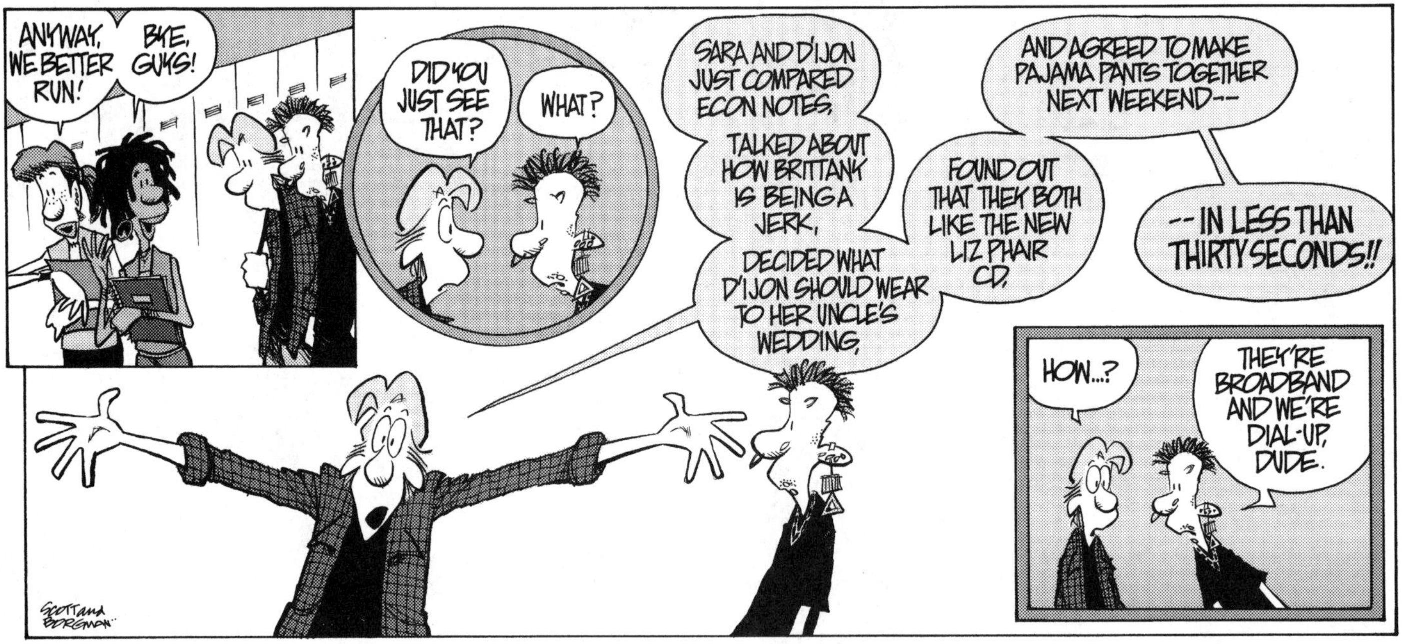
ANYWAY, WE BETTER RUN!
BYE, GUYS!
DID YOU JUST SEE THAT?
WHAT?
SARA AND D'JON JUST COMPARED ECON NOTES,
TALKED ABOUT HOW BRITTANY IS BEING A JERK,
DECIDED WHAT D'JON SHOULD WEAR TO HER UNCLE'S WEDDING,
FOUND OUT THAT THEY BOTH LIKE THE NEW LIZ PHAIR CD,
AND AGREED TO MAKE PAJAMA PANTS TOGETHER NEXT WEEKEND--
-- IN LESS THAN THIRTY SECONDS!!
HOW...?
THEY'RE BROADBAND AND WE'RE DIAL-UP, DUDE.
SCOTT and BORGMAN

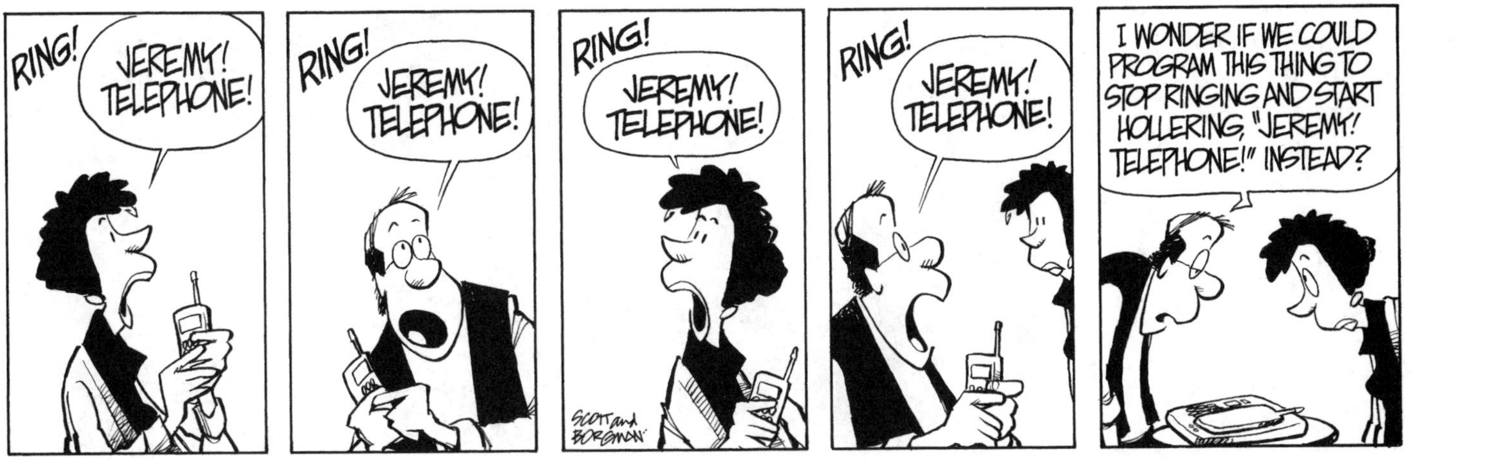
RING!
JEREMY! TELEPHONE!
RING!
JEREMY! TELEPHONE!
RING!
JEREMY! TELEPHONE!
RING!
JEREMY! TELEPHONE!
I WONDER IF WE COULD PROGRAM THIS THING TO STOP RINGING AND START HOLLERING, "JEREMY! TELEPHONE!" INSTEAD?

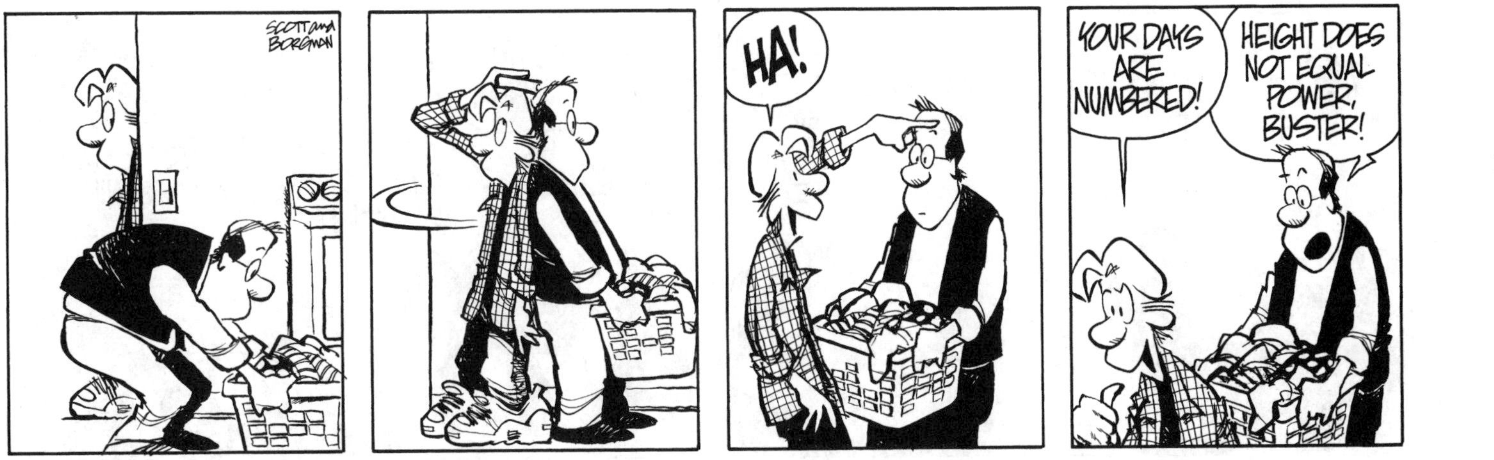
HA!
YOUR DAYS ARE NUMBERED!
HEIGHT DOES NOT EQUAL POWER, BUSTER!

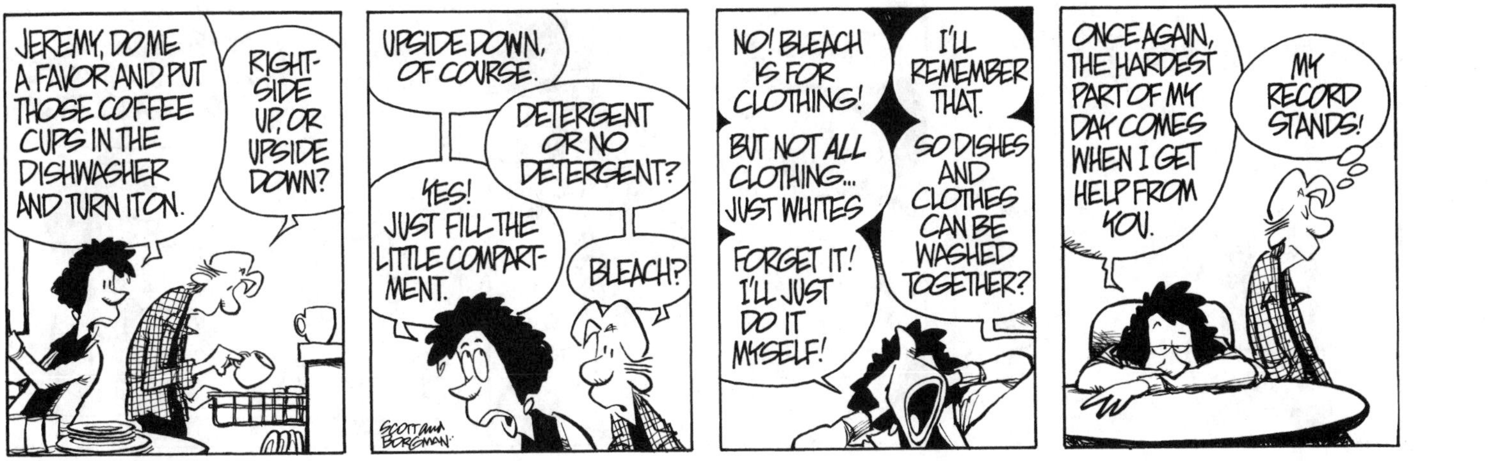
JEREMY, DO ME A FAVOR AND PUT THOSE COFFEE CUPS IN THE DISHWASHER AND TURN IT ON.
RIGHT-SIDE UP, OR UPSIDE DOWN?
UPSIDE DOWN, OF COURSE.
DETERGENT OR NO DETERGENT?
YES! JUST FILL THE LITTLE COMPARTMENT.
BLEACH?
NO! BLEACH IS FOR CLOTHING!
I'LL REMEMBER THAT.
BUT NOT ALL CLOTHING... JUST WHITES
SO DISHES AND CLOTHES CAN BE WASHED TOGETHER?
FORGET IT! I'LL JUST DO IT MYSELF!
ONCE AGAIN, THE HARDEST PART OF MY DAY COMES WHEN I GET HELP FROM YOU.
MY RECORD STANDS!

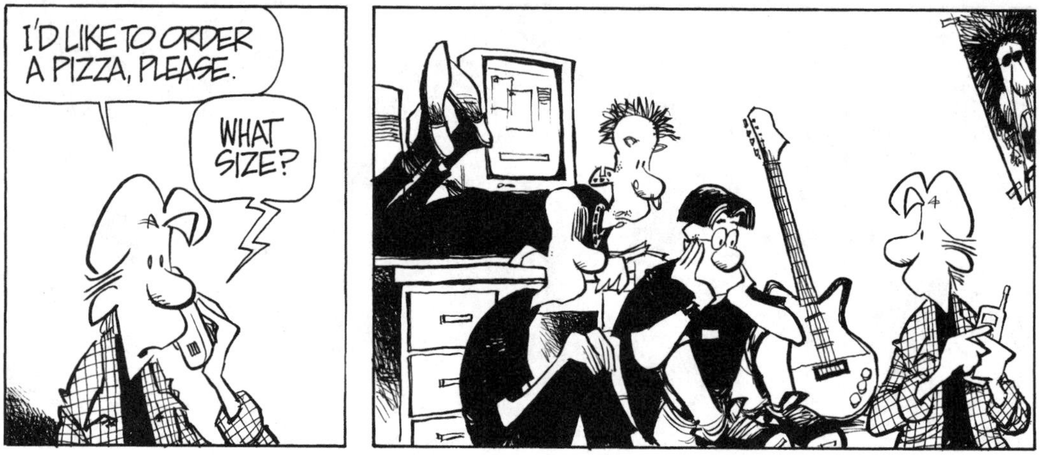
I'D LIKE TO ORDER A PIZZA, PLEASE.
WHAT SIZE?
HOW BIG IS YOUR DELIVERY GUY'S CAR?
SCOTT and BORGMAN

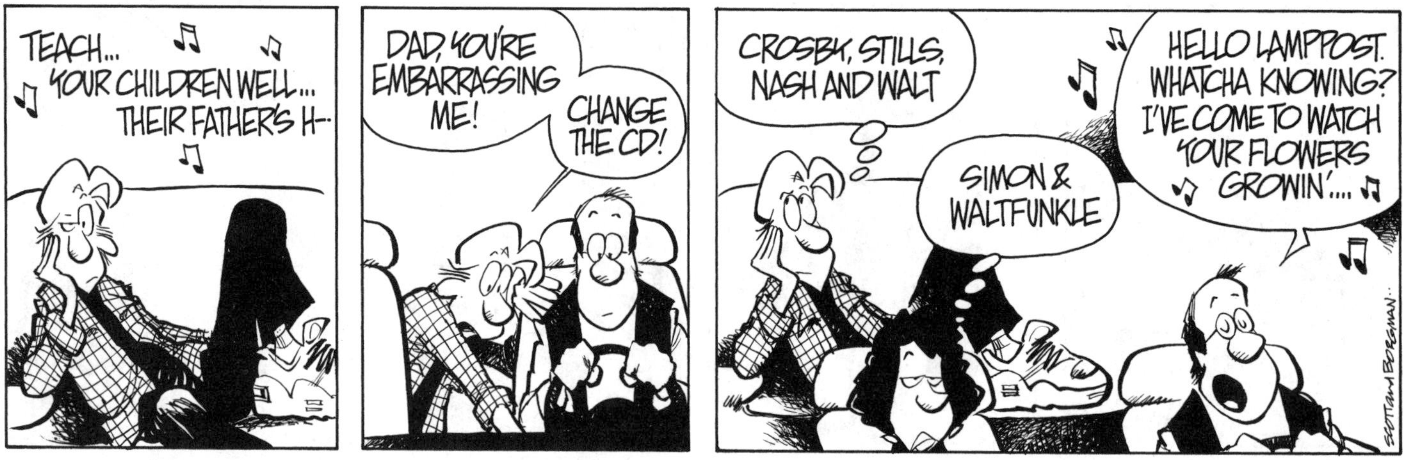
TEACH... YOUR CHILDREN WELL... THEIR FATHER'S H--
DAD, YOU'RE EMBARRASSING ME!
CHANGE THE CD!
CROSBY, STILLS, NASH AND WALT
SIMON & WALTFUNKLE
HELLO LAMPPOST. WHATCHA KNOWING? I'VE COME TO WATCH YOUR FLOWERS GROWIN'....
SCOTT and BORGMAN

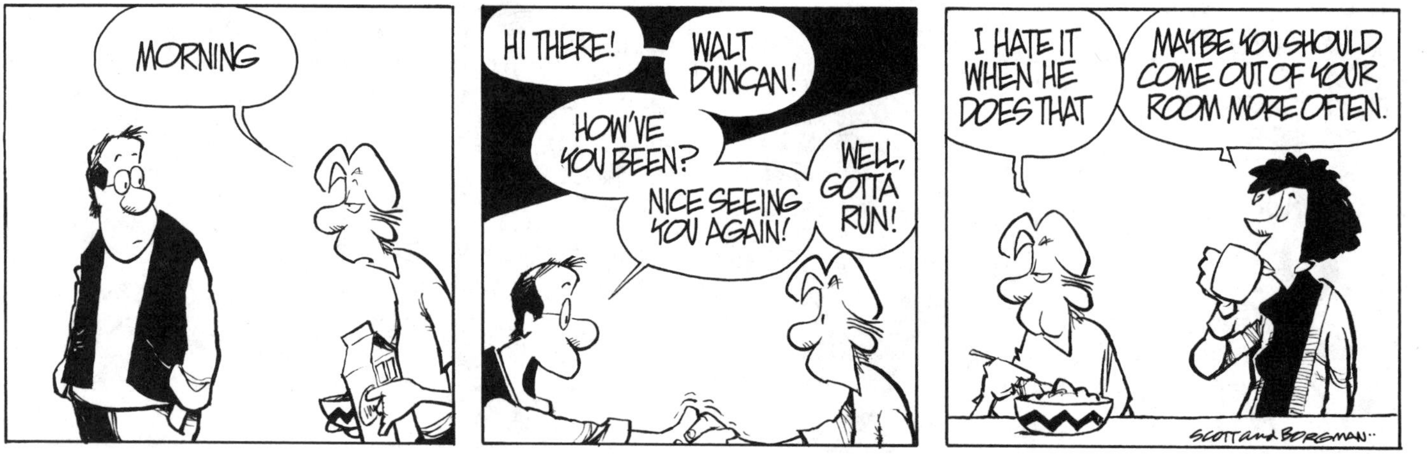
MORNING
HI THERE!
WALT DUNCAN!
HOW'VE YOU BEEN?
NICE SEEING YOU AGAIN!
WELL, GOTTA RUN!
I HATE IT WHEN HE DOES THAT
MAYBE YOU SHOULD COME OUT OF YOUR ROOM MORE OFTEN.
SCOTT and BORGMAN

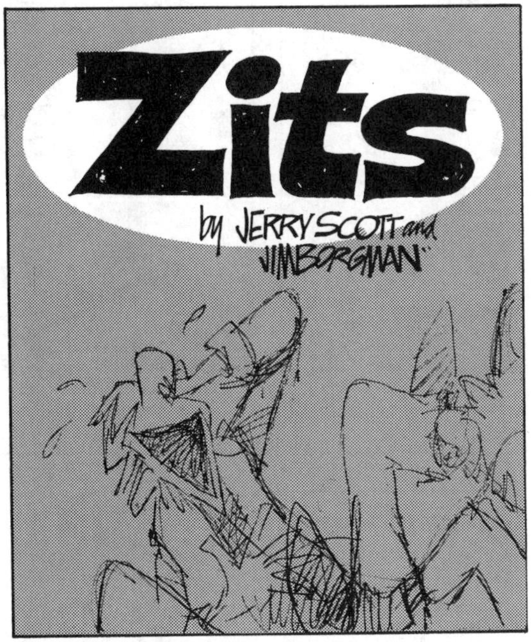
Zits
by JERRY SCOTT and JIM BORGMAN

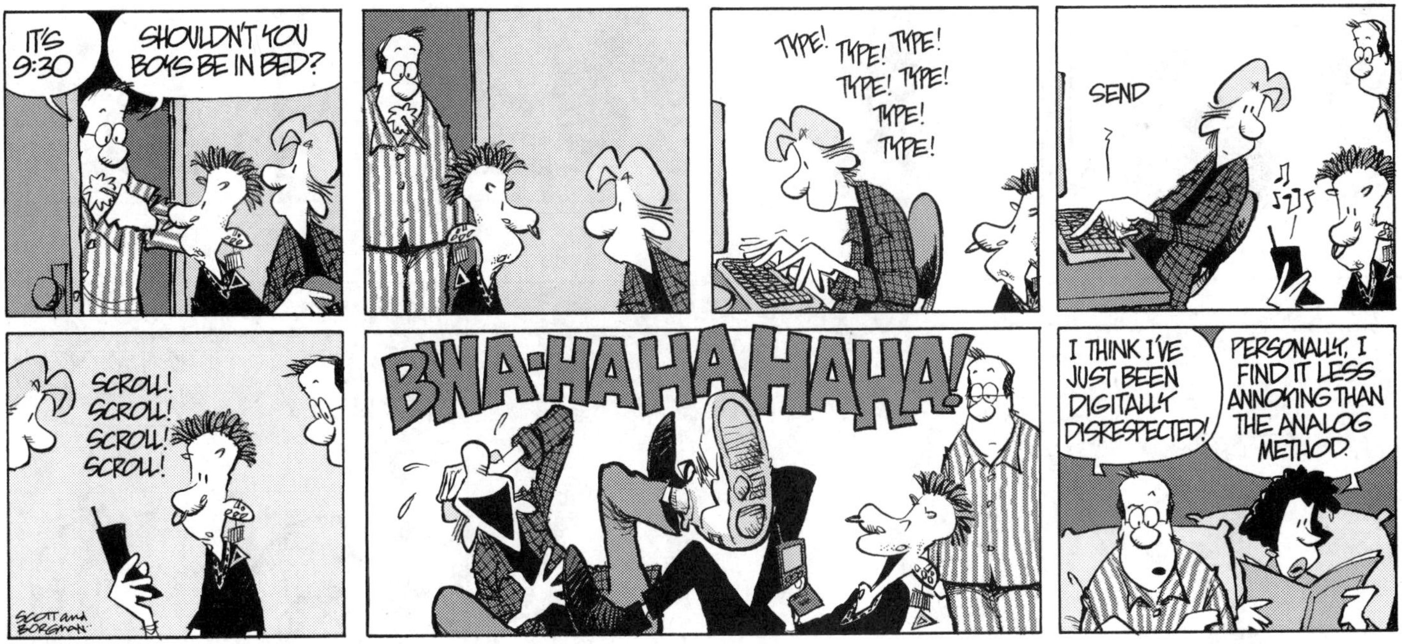
IT'S 9:30
SHOULDN'T YOU BOYS BE IN BED?
TYPE! TYPE! TYPE! TYPE! TYPE! TYPE! TYPE!
SEND
SCROLL! SCROLL! SCROLL! SCROLL!
SCOTT AND BORGMAN
BWA-HAHAHAHAHA!
I THINK I'VE JUST BEEN DIGITALLY DISRESPECTED!
PERSONALLY, I FIND IT LESS ANNOYING THAN THE ANALOG METHOD.

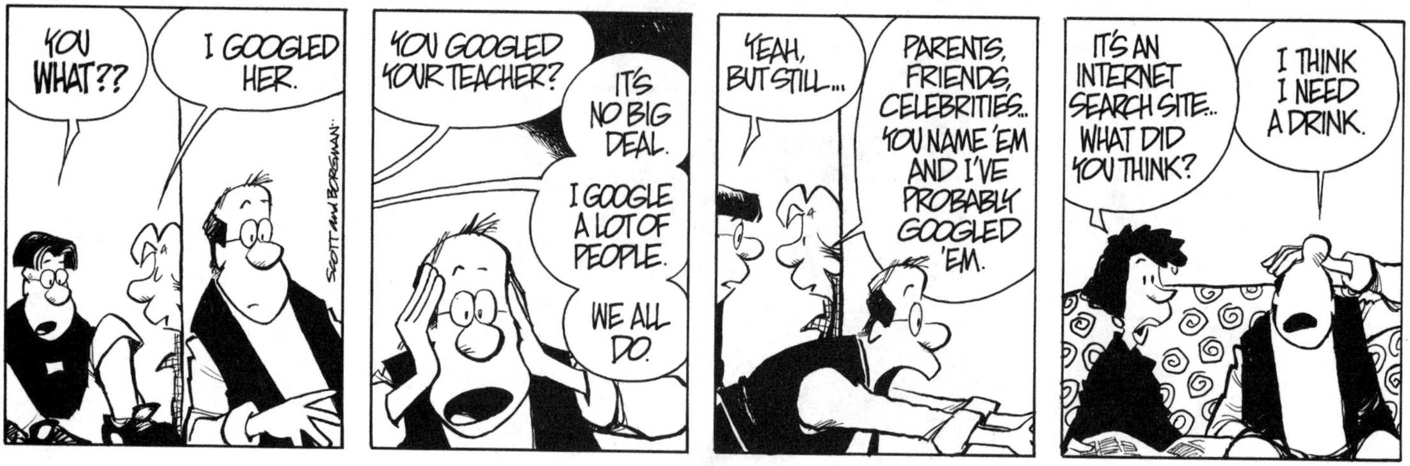
YOU WHAT??
I GOOGLED HER.
SCOTT and BORGMAN
YOU GOOGLED YOUR TEACHER?
IT'S NO BIG DEAL.
I GOOGLE A LOT OF PEOPLE.
WE ALL DO.
YEAH, BUT STILL...
PARENTS, FRIENDS, CELEBRITIES... YOU NAME 'EM AND I'VE PROBABLY GOOGLED 'EM.
IT'S AN INTERNET SEARCH SITE... WHAT DID YOU THINK?
I THINK I NEED A DRINK.

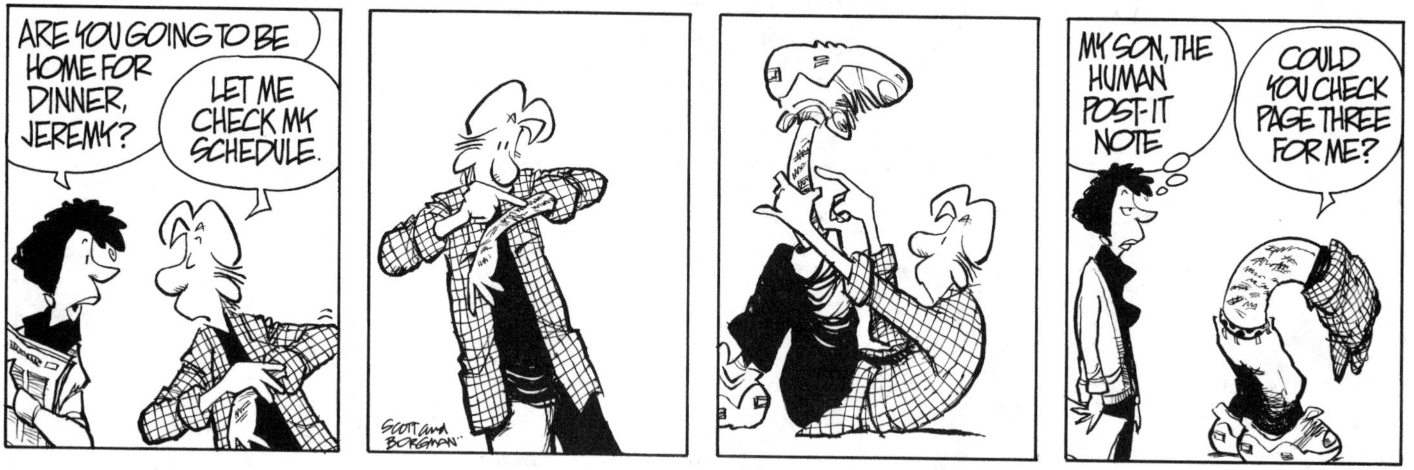
ARE YOU GOING TO BE HOME FOR DINNER, JEREMY?
LET ME CHECK MY SCHEDULE.
SCOTT and BORGMAN
MY SON, THE HUMAN POST-IT NOTE
COULD YOU CHECK PAGE THREE FOR ME?

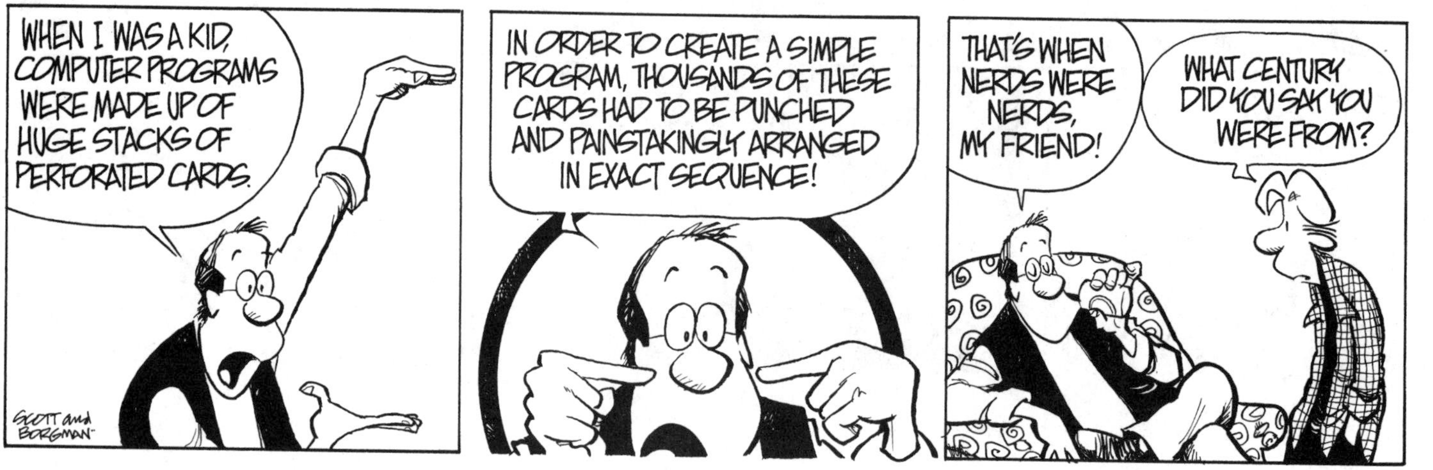
WHEN I WAS A KID, COMPUTER PROGRAMS WERE MADE UP OF HUGE STACKS OF PERFORATED CARDS.
SCOTT and BORGMAN
IN ORDER TO CREATE A SIMPLE PROGRAM, THOUSANDS OF THESE CARDS HAD TO BE PUNCHED AND PAINSTAKINGLY ARRANGED IN EXACT SEQUENCE!
THAT'S WHEN NERDS WERE NERDS, MY FRIEND!
WHAT CENTURY DID YOU SAY YOU WERE FROM?

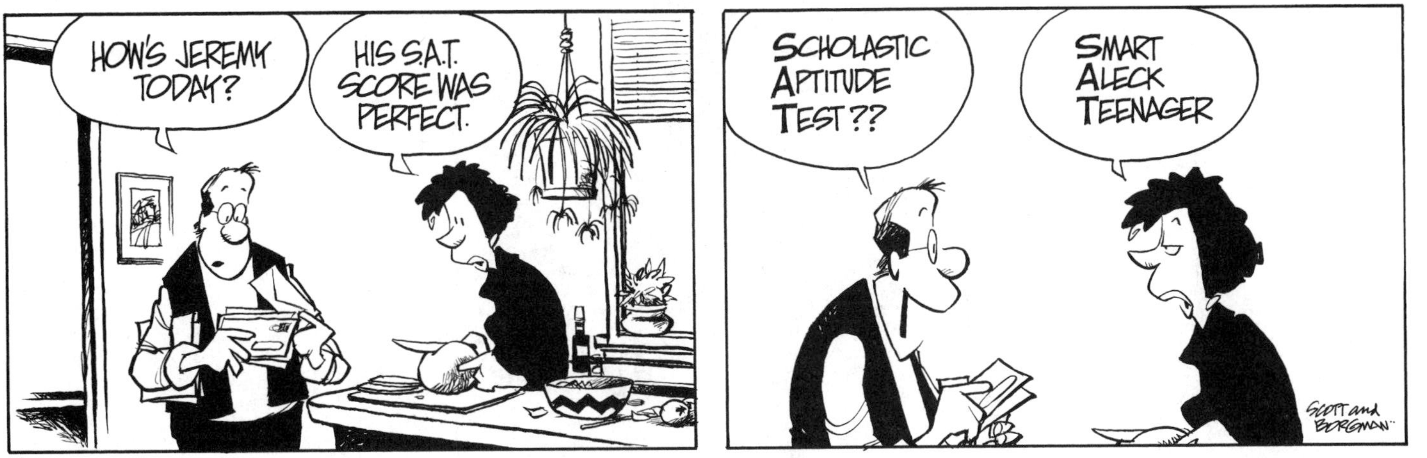
HOW'S JEREMY TODAY?
HIS S.A.T. SCORE WAS PERFECT.
SCHOLASTIC APTITUDE TEST??
SMART ALECK TEENAGER
SCOTT and BORGMAN

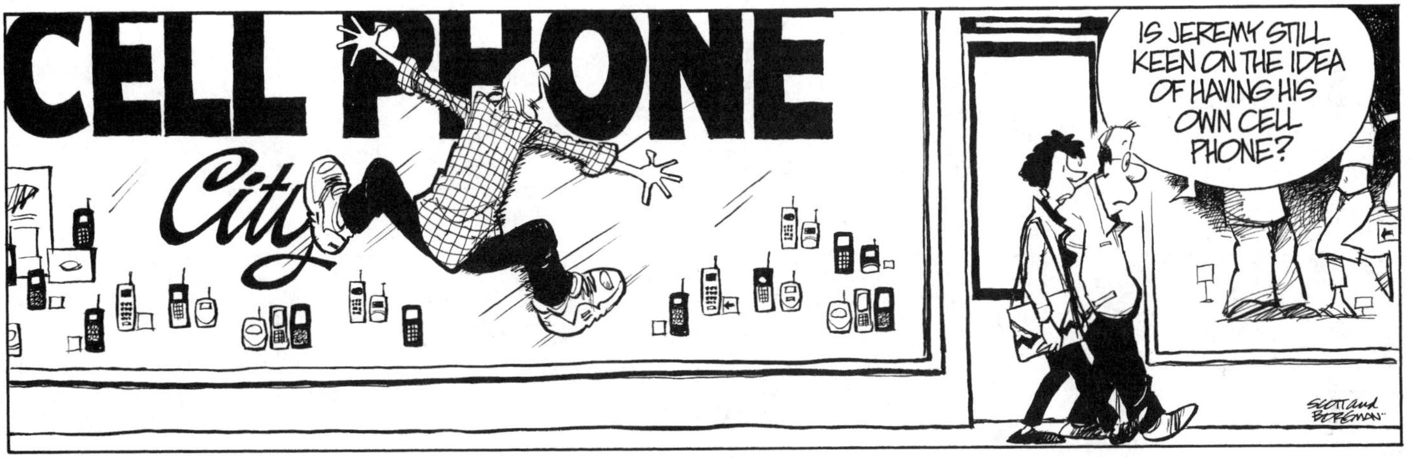
CELL PHONE City
IS JEREMY STILL KEEN ON THE IDEA OF HAVING HIS OWN CELL PHONE?
SCOTT and BORGMAN

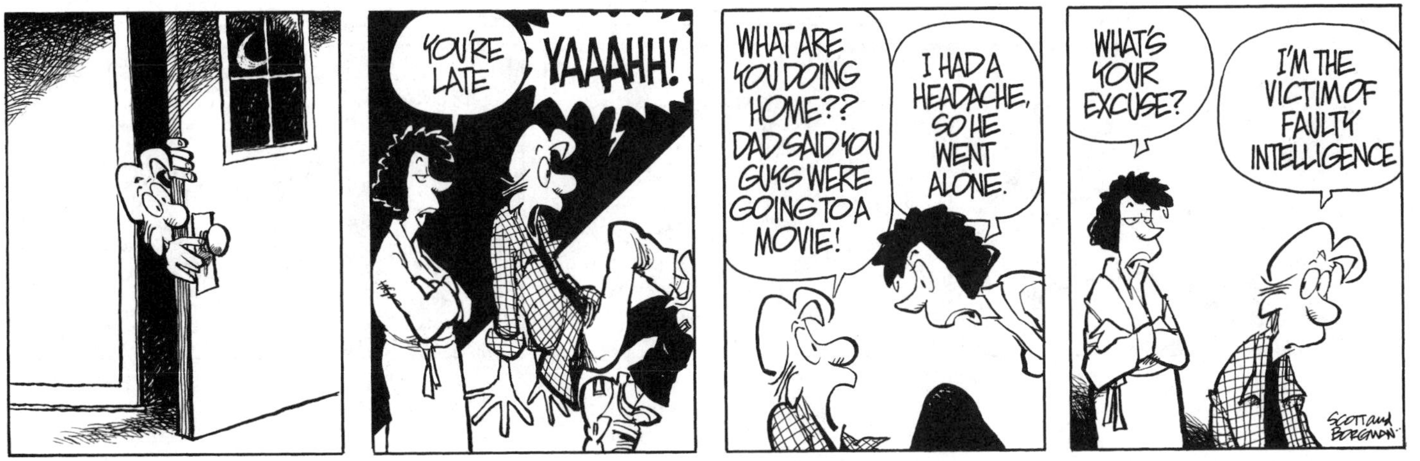
YOU'RE LATE
YAAAHH!
WHAT ARE YOU DOING HOME?? DAD SAID YOU GUYS WERE GOING TO A MOVIE!
I HAD A HEADACHE, SO HE WENT ALONE.
WHAT'S YOUR EXCUSE?
I'M THE VICTIM OF FAULTY INTELLIGENCE
SCOTT and BORGMAN

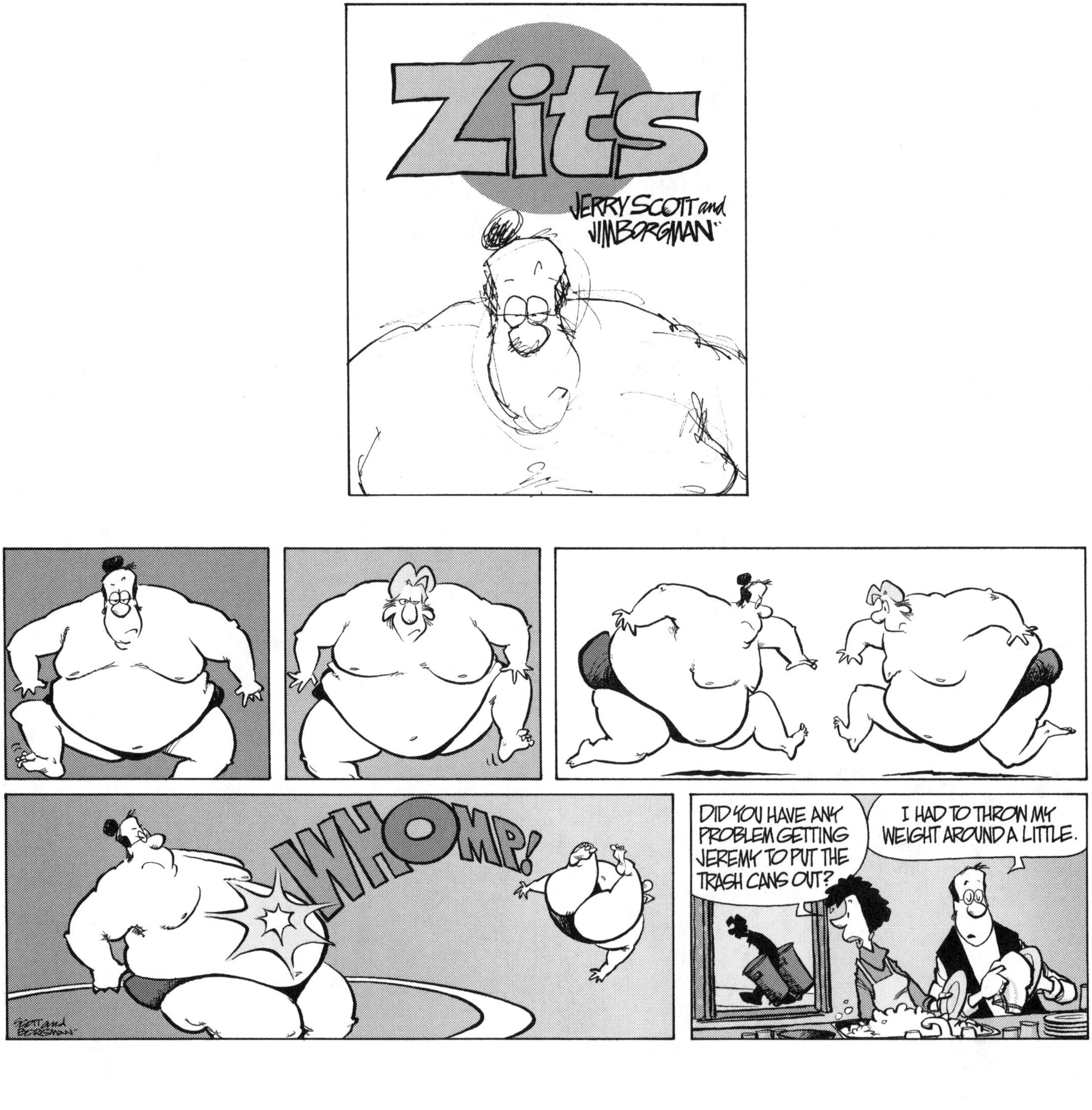
Zits
JERRY SCOTT and JIM BORGMAN
WHOMP!
SCOTT AND BORGMAN
DID YOU HAVE ANY PROBLEM GETTING JEREMY TO PUT THE TRASH CANS OUT?
I HAD TO THROW MY WEIGHT AROUND A LITTLE.

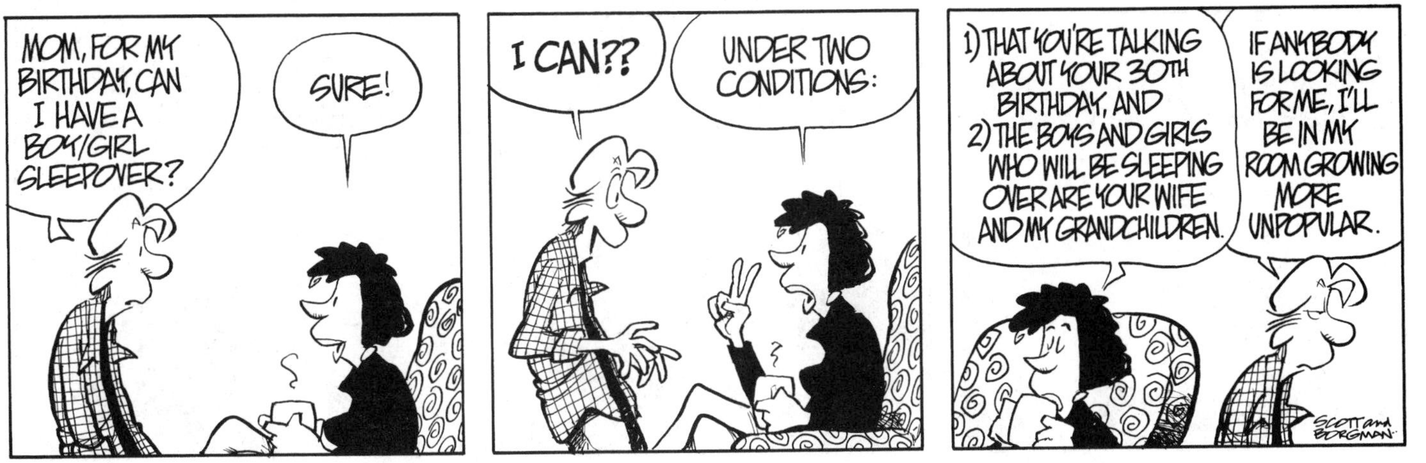
MOM, FOR MY BIRTHDAY, CAN I HAVE A BOY/GIRL SLEEPOVER?
SURE!
I CAN??
UNDER TWO CONDITIONS:
1) THAT YOU'RE TALKING ABOUT YOUR 30TH BIRTHDAY, AND
2) THE BOYS AND GIRLS WHO WILL BE SLEEPING OVER ARE YOUR WIFE AND MY GRANDCHILDREN.
IF ANYBODY IS LOOKING FOR ME, I'LL BE IN MY ROOM GROWING MORE UNPOPULAR.
SCOTT and BORGMAN

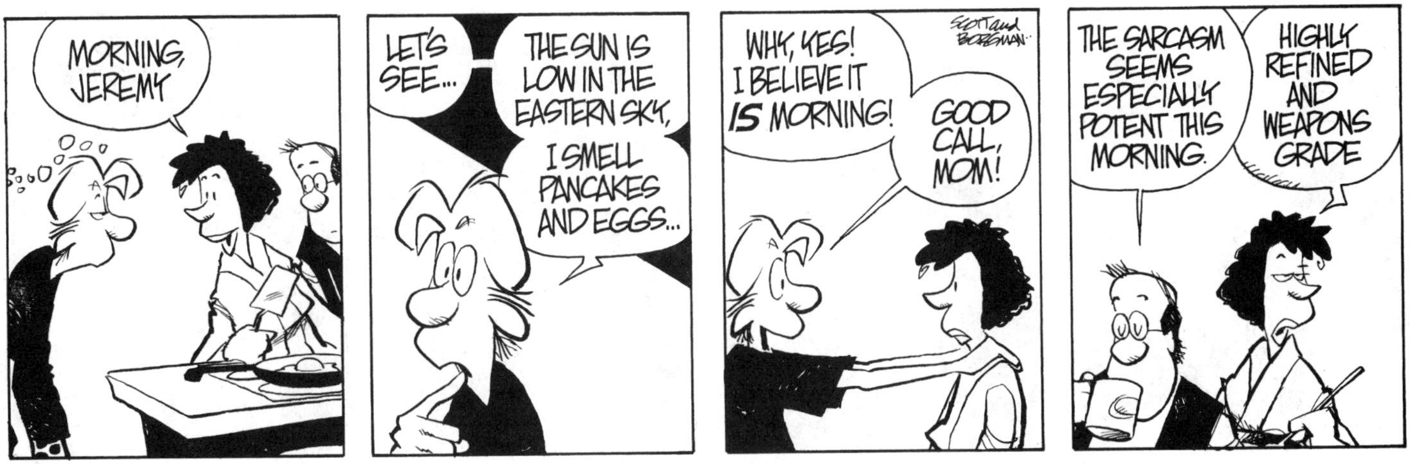
MORNING, JEREMY
LET'S SEE...
THE SUN IS LOW IN THE EASTERN SKY,
I SMELL PANCAKES AND EGGS...
WHY, YES! I BELIEVE IT IS MORNING!
GOOD CALL, MOM!
SCOTT and BORGMAN
THE SARCASM SEEMS ESPECIALLY POTENT THIS MORNING.
HIGHLY REFINED AND WEAPONS GRADE

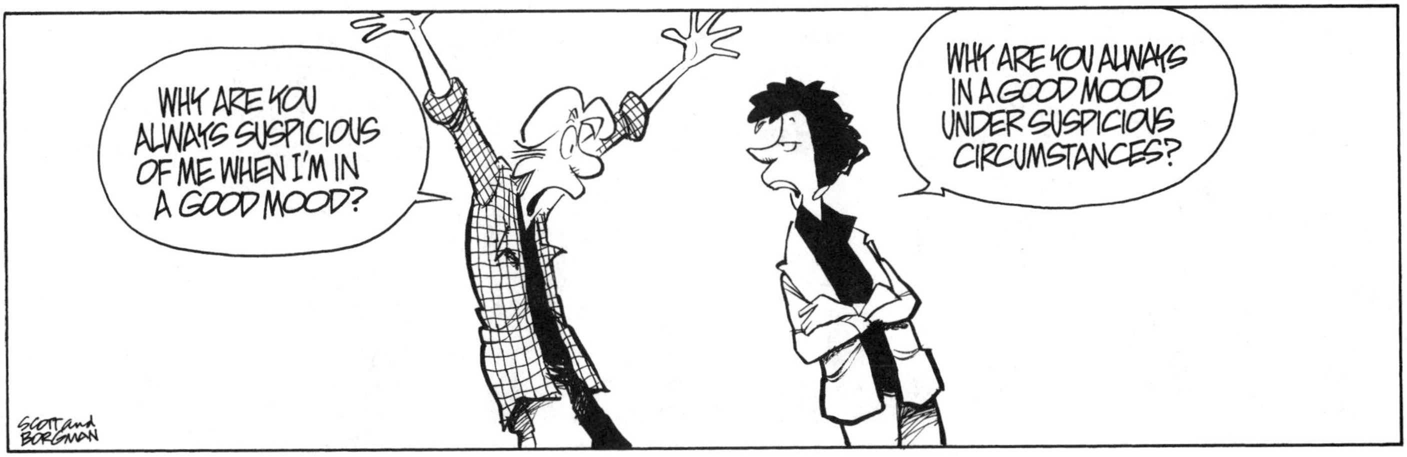
WHY ARE YOU ALWAYS SUSPICIOUS OF ME WHEN I'M IN A GOOD MOOD?
WHY ARE YOU ALWAYS IN A GOOD MOOD UNDER SUSPICIOUS CIRCUMSTANCES?
SCOTT and BORGMAN

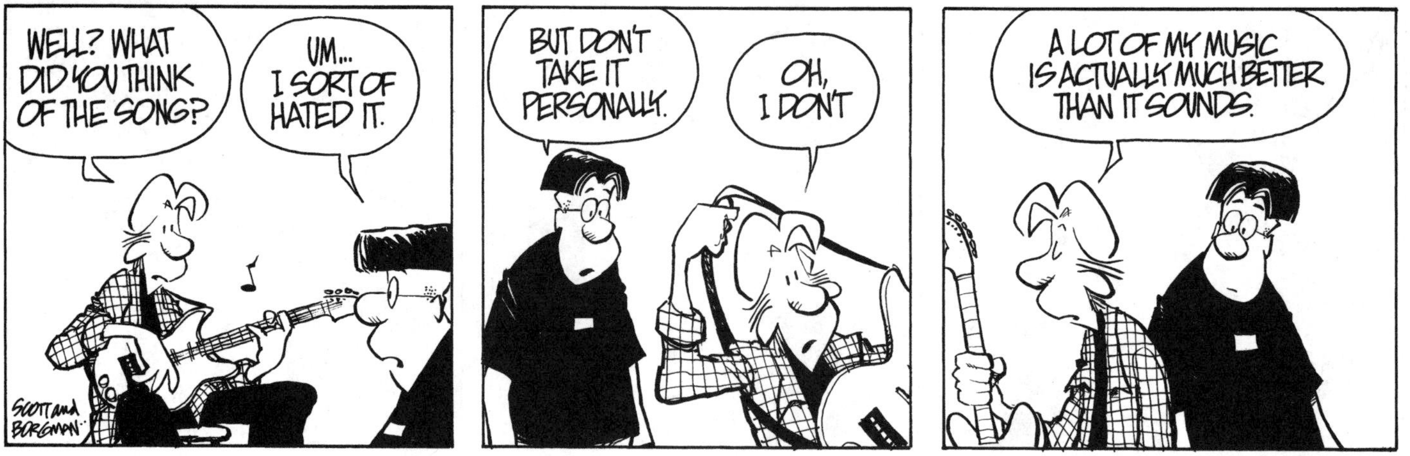
WELL? WHAT DID YOU THINK OF THE SONG?
UM... I SORT OF HATED IT.
BUT DON'T TAKE IT PERSONALLY.
OH, I DON'T
A LOT OF MY MUSIC IS ACTUALLY MUCH BETTER THAN IT SOUNDS.
SCOTT and BORGMAN

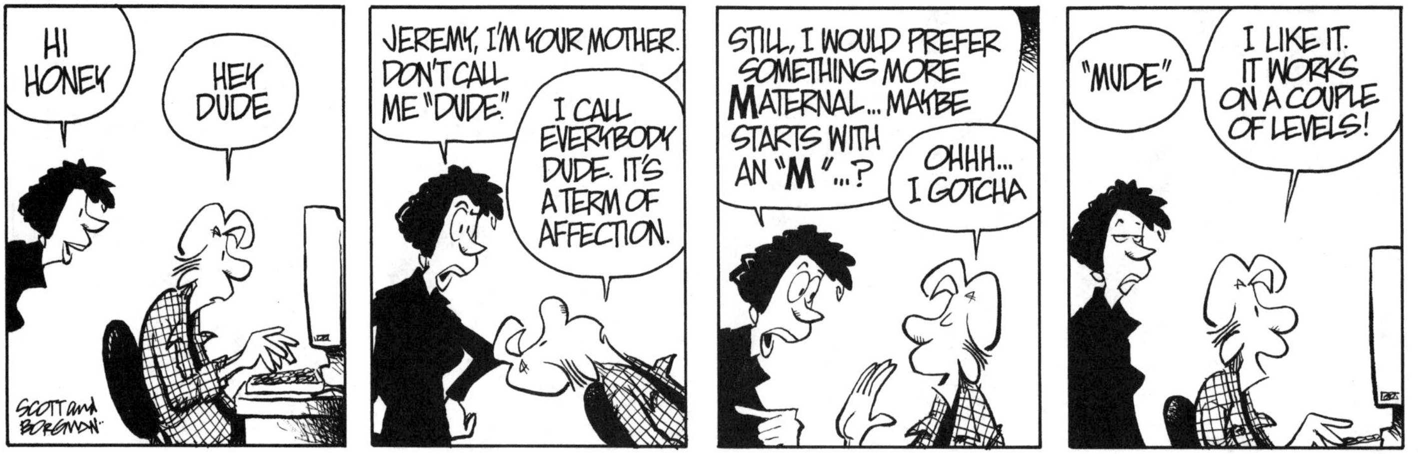
HI HONEY
HEY DUDE
JEREMY, I'M YOUR MOTHER. DON'T CALL ME "DUDE."
I CALL EVERYBODY DUDE. IT'S A TERM OF AFFECTION.
STILL, I WOULD PREFER SOMETHING MORE MATERNAL... MAYBE STARTS WITH AN "M"...?
OHHH... I GOTCHA
"MUDE"
I LIKE IT. IT WORKS ON A COUPLE OF LEVELS!
SCOTT and BORGMAN

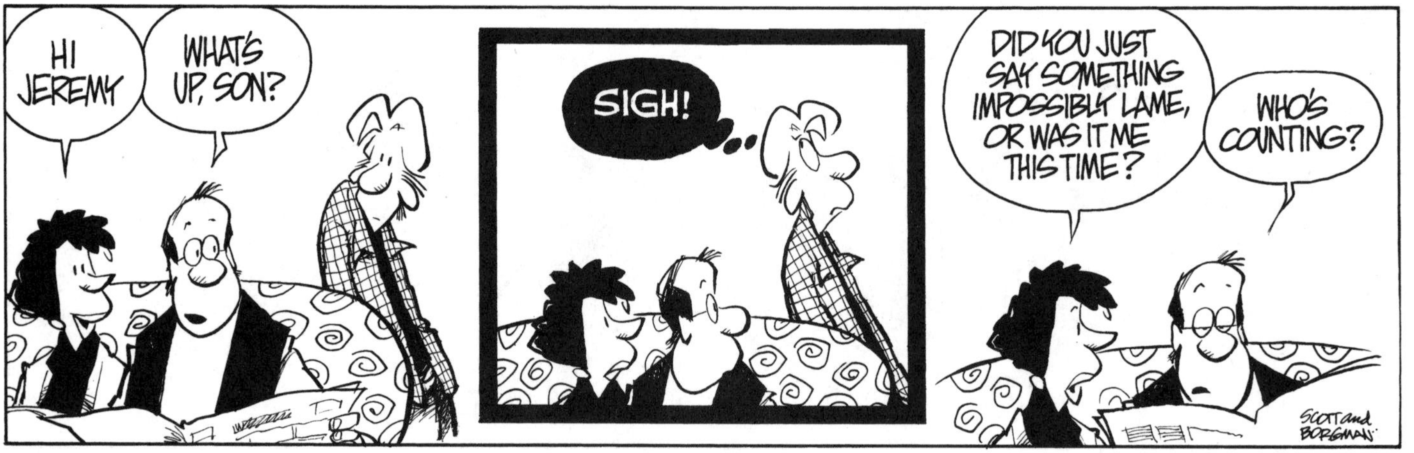
HI JEREMY
WHAT'S UP, SON?
SIGH!
DID YOU JUST SAY SOMETHING IMPOSSIBLY LAME, OR WAS IT ME THIS TIME?
WHO'S COUNTING?
SCOTT and BORGMAN

Zits
by
JERRY SCOTT and
JIM BORGMAN

HEY DAD- CAN I WEAR YOUR OLD ARMY JACKET?
I GUESS SO.
BOY! I'LL BET THIS THING HOLDS A LOT OF MEMORIES, DOESN'T IT?
SURE DOES
MOSTLY BAD MEMORIES, I'M AFRAID.
MEMORIES I'D LIKE TO FORGET
BUT CAN'T
I UNDERSTAND, DAD
THANKS
WHAT BAD MEMORIES?? YOU BOUGHT THAT THING AT A SURPLUS STORE WHEN WE WERE IN COLLEGE!
THE TRAFFIC WAS HORRIBLE THAT DAY....

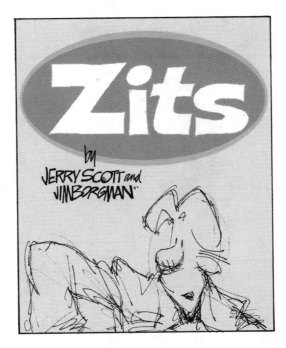

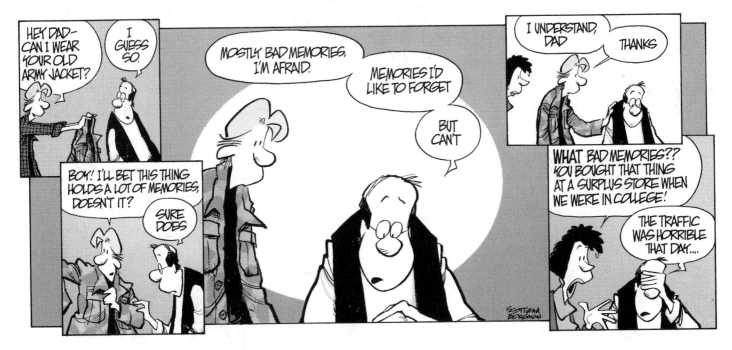

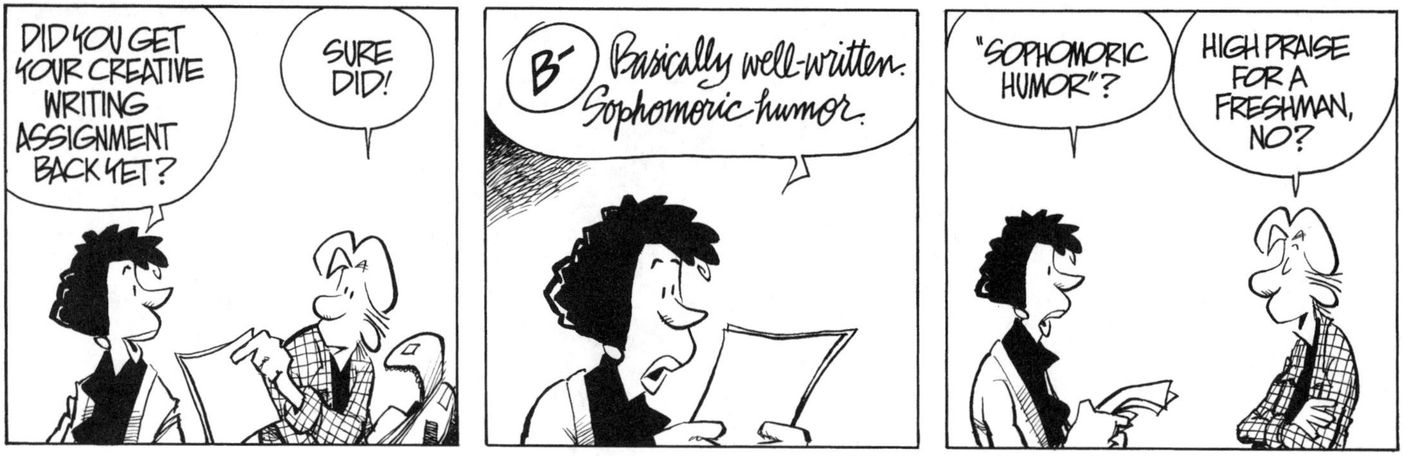
DID YOU GET YOUR CREATIVE WRITING ASSIGNMENT BACK YET?
SURE DID!
B-
Basically well-written. Sophomoric humor.
"SOPHOMORIC HUMOR"?
HIGH PRAISE FOR A FRESHMAN, NO?

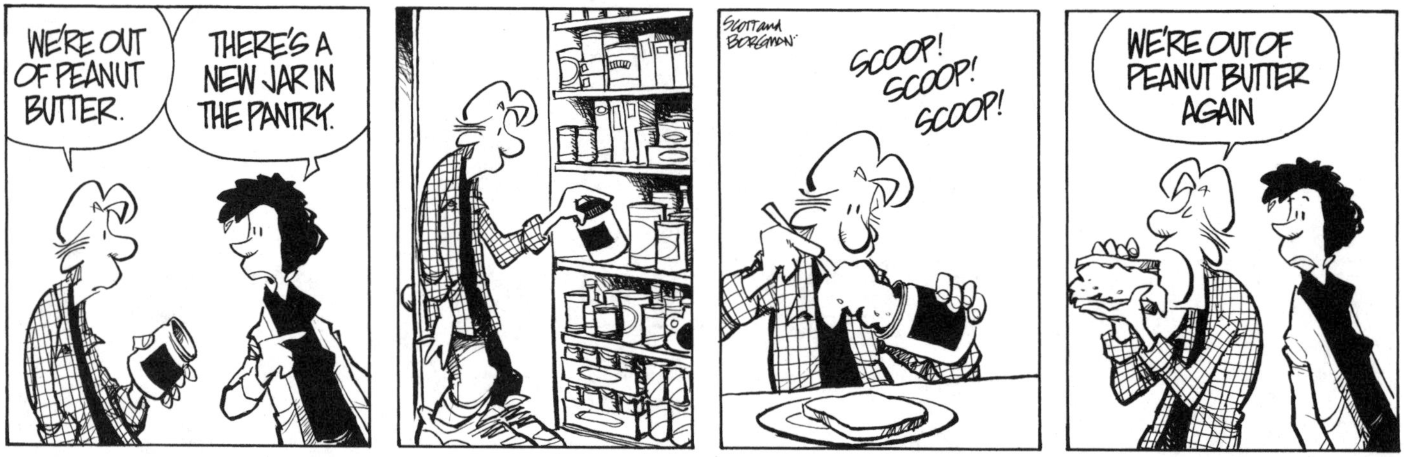
WE'RE OUT OF PEANUT BUTTER.
THERE'S A NEW JAR IN THE PANTRY.
SCOTT and BORGMAN
SCOOP! SCOOP! SCOOP!
WE'RE OUT OF PEANUT BUTTER AGAIN

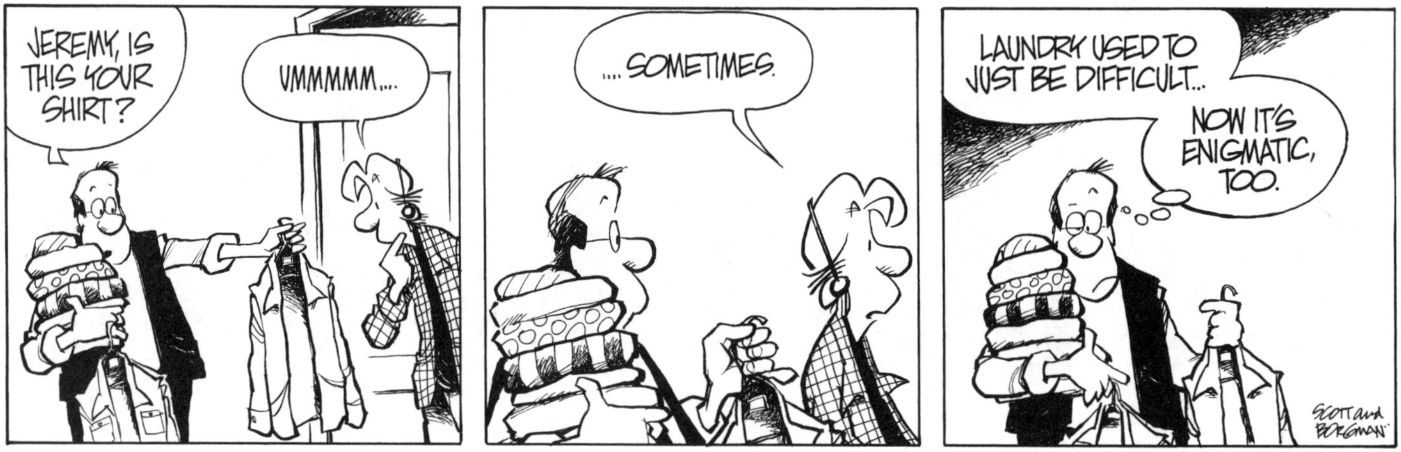
JEREMY, IS THIS YOUR SHIRT?
UMMMMM....
.... SOMETIMES.
LAUNDRY USED TO JUST BE DIFFICULT...
NOW IT'S ENIGMATIC, TOO.
SCOTT and BORGMAN

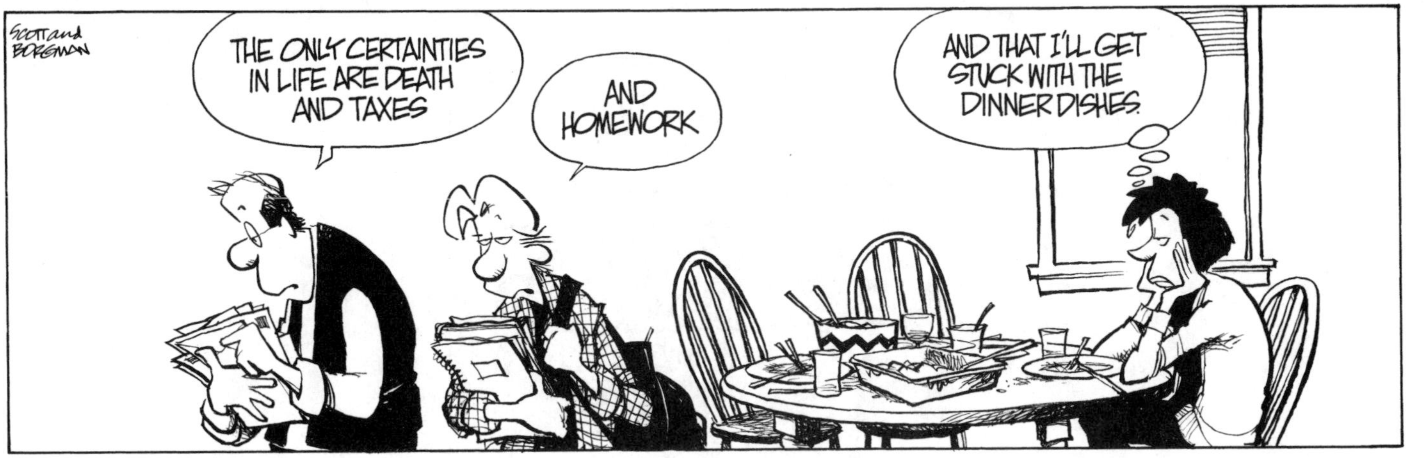
SCOTT and BORGMAN
THE ONLY CERTAINTIES IN LIFE ARE DEATH AND TAXES
AND HOMEWORK
AND THAT I'LL GET STUCK WITH THE DINNER DISHES.

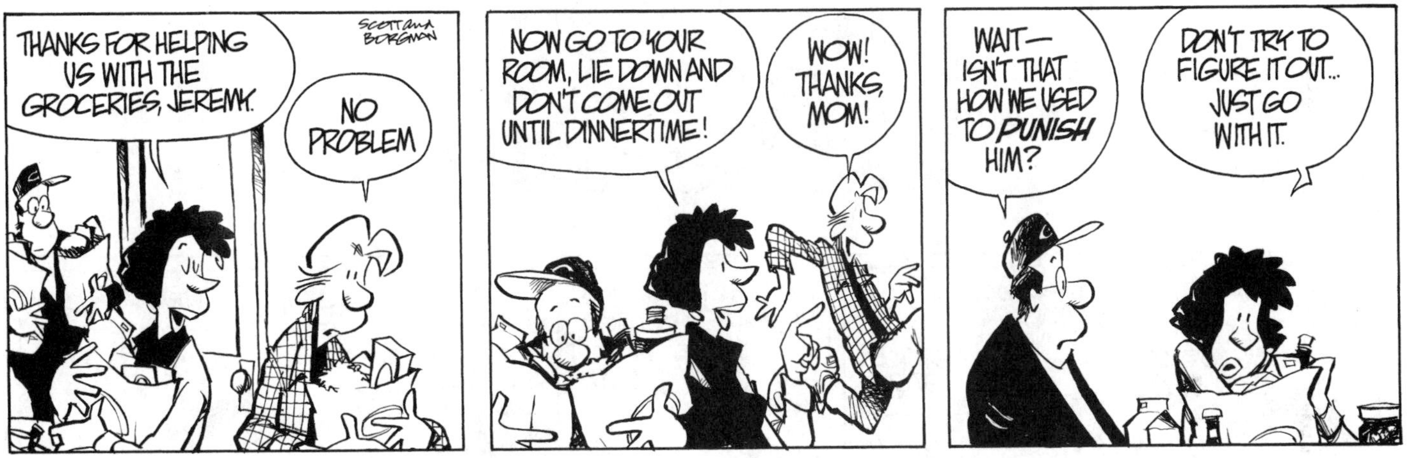
THANKS FOR HELPING US WITH THE GROCERIES, JEREMY.
SCOTT and BORGMAN
NO PROBLEM
NOW GO TO YOUR ROOM, LIE DOWN AND DON'T COME OUT UNTIL DINNERTIME!
WOW! THANKS, MOM!
WAIT— ISN'T THAT HOW WE USED TO PUNISH HIM?
DON'T TRY TO FIGURE IT OUT... JUST GO WITH IT.

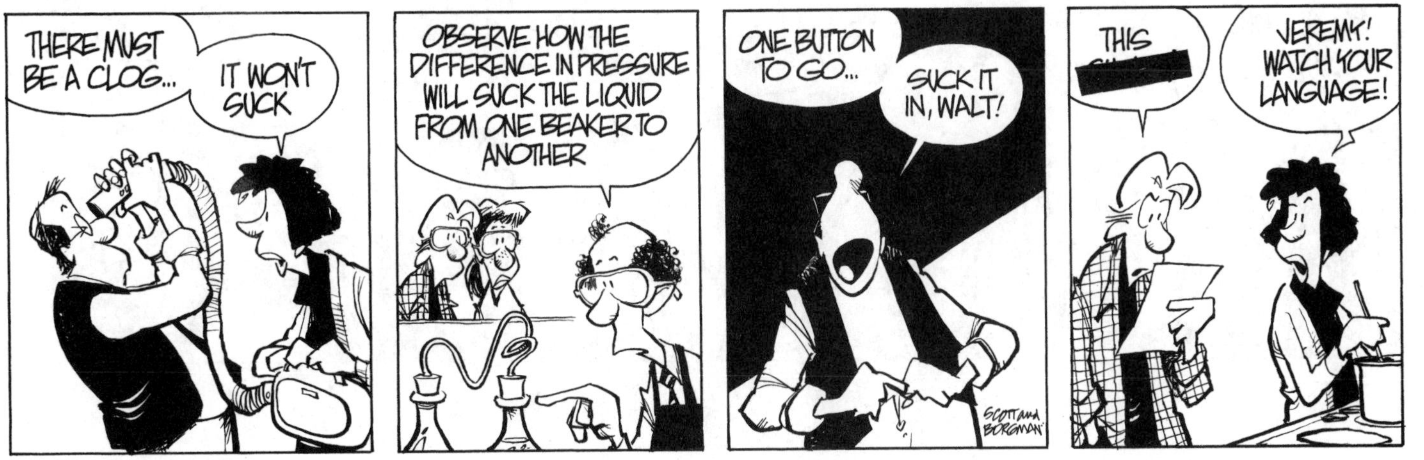
THERE MUST BE A CLOG...
IT WON'T SUCK
OBSERVE HOW THE DIFFERENCE IN PRESSURE WILL SUCK THE LIQUID FROM ONE BEAKER TO ANOTHER
ONE BUTTON TO GO...
SUCK IT IN, WALT!
SCOTT and BORGMAN
THIS [redacted]
JEREMY! WATCH YOUR LANGUAGE!

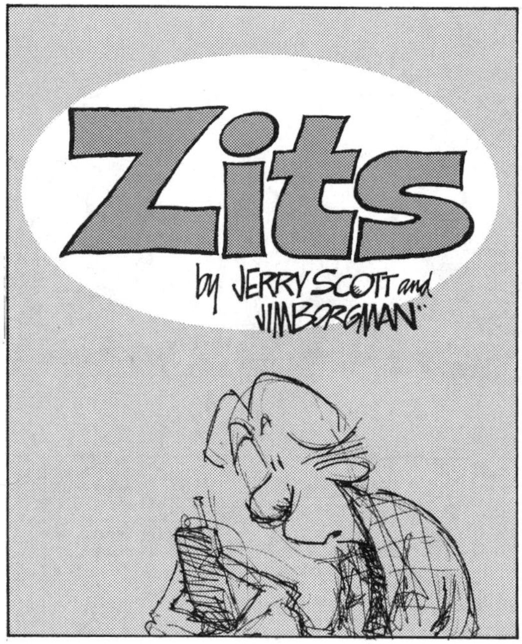
Zits
by JERRY SCOTT and JIM BORGMAN

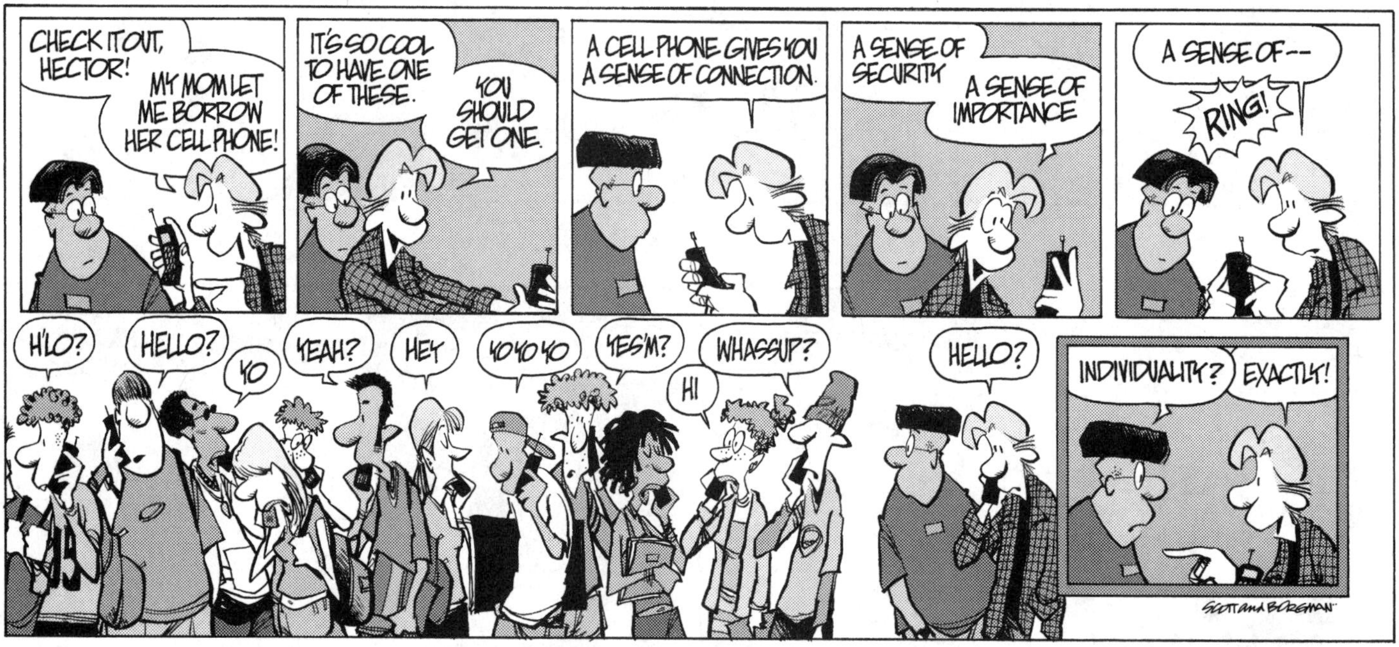
CHECK IT OUT, HECTOR!
MY MOM LET ME BORROW HER CELL PHONE!
IT'S SO COOL TO HAVE ONE OF THESE.
YOU SHOULD GET ONE.
A CELL PHONE GIVES YOU A SENSE OF CONNECTION.
A SENSE OF SECURITY
A SENSE OF IMPORTANCE
A SENSE OF--
RING!
H'LO?
HELLO?
YO
YEAH?
HEY
YO YO YO
YES'M?
HI
WHASSUP?
HELLO?
INDIVIDUALITY?
EXACTLY!
SCOTT and BORGMAN

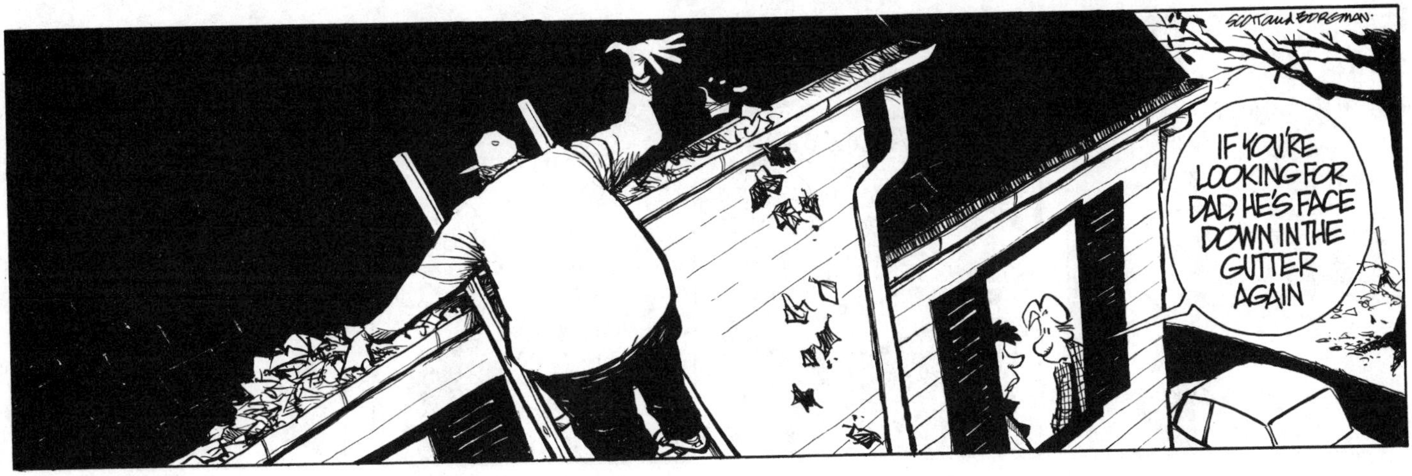
IF YOU'RE LOOKING FOR DAD, HE'S FACE DOWN IN THE GUTTER AGAIN

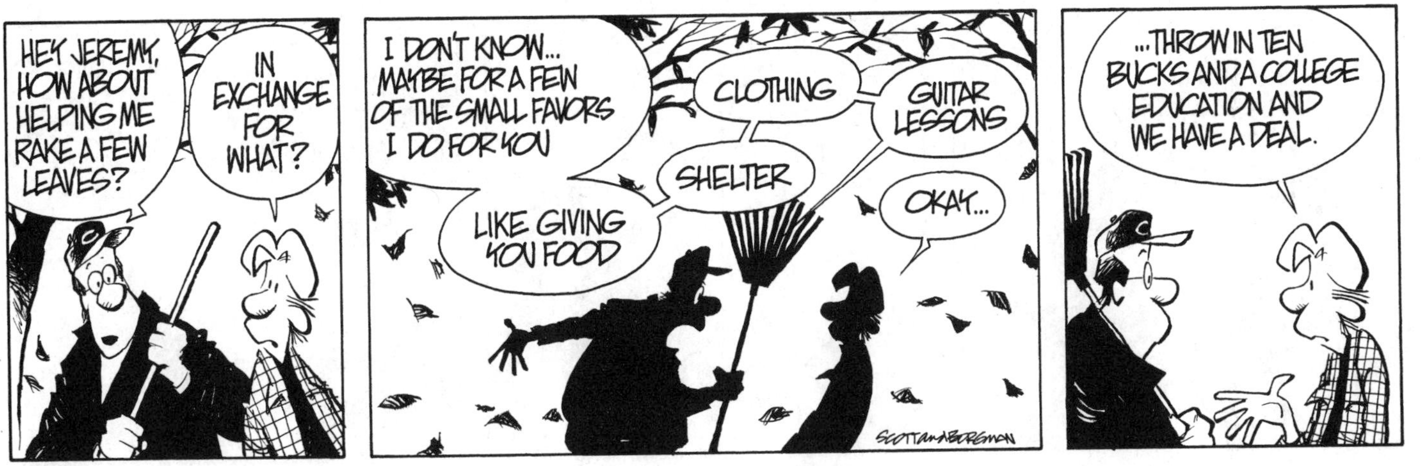
HEY JEREMY, HOW ABOUT HELPING ME RAKE A FEW LEAVES?
IN EXCHANGE FOR WHAT?
I DON'T KNOW... MAYBE FOR A FEW OF THE SMALL FAVORS I DO FOR YOU
LIKE GIVING YOU FOOD
SHELTER
CLOTHING
GUITAR LESSONS
OKAY...
...THROW IN TEN BUCKS AND A COLLEGE EDUCATION AND WE HAVE A DEAL.

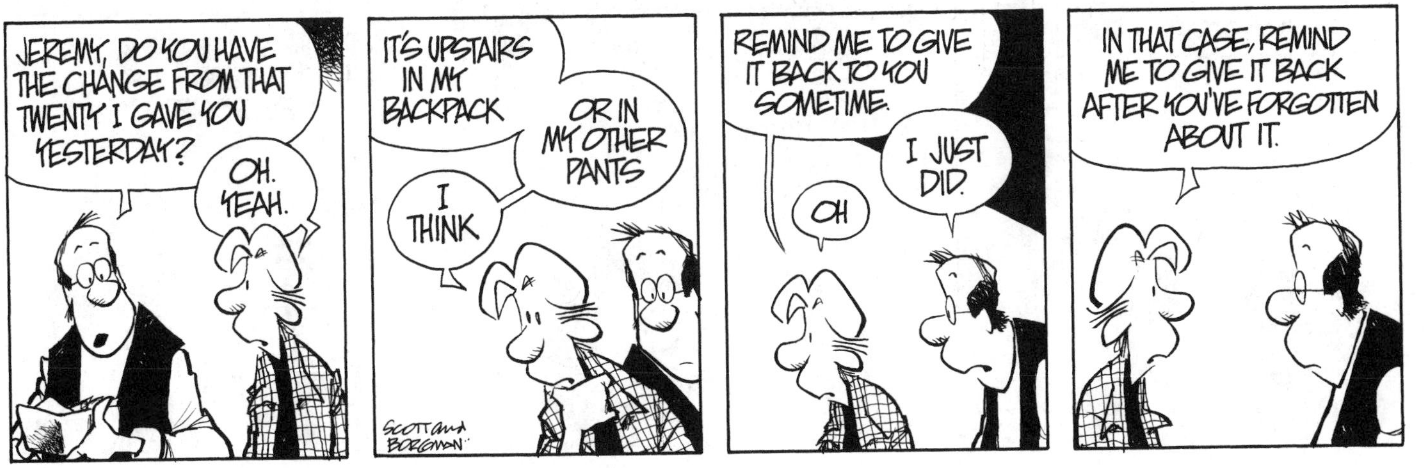
JEREMY, DO YOU HAVE THE CHANGE FROM THAT TWENTY I GAVE YOU YESTERDAY?
OH. YEAH.
IT'S UPSTAIRS IN MY BACKPACK
OR IN MY OTHER PANTS
I THINK
REMIND ME TO GIVE IT BACK TO YOU SOMETIME.
OH
I JUST DID.
IN THAT CASE, REMIND ME TO GIVE IT BACK AFTER YOU'VE FORGOTTEN ABOUT IT.

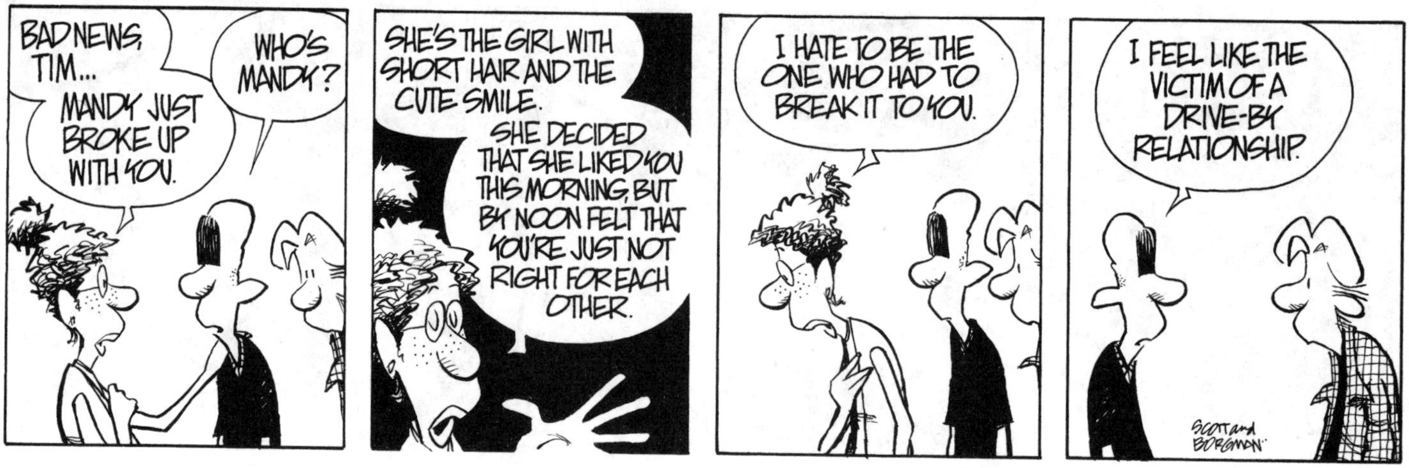
BAD NEWS, TIM...
MANDY JUST BROKE UP WITH YOU.
WHO'S MANDY?
SHE'S THE GIRL WITH SHORT HAIR AND THE CUTE SMILE.
SHE DECIDED THAT SHE LIKED YOU THIS MORNING, BUT BY NOON FELT THAT YOU'RE JUST NOT RIGHT FOR EACH OTHER.
I HATE TO BE THE ONE WHO HAD TO BREAK IT TO YOU.
I FEEL LIKE THE VICTIM OF A DRIVE-BY RELATIONSHIP.
SCOTT and BORGMAN

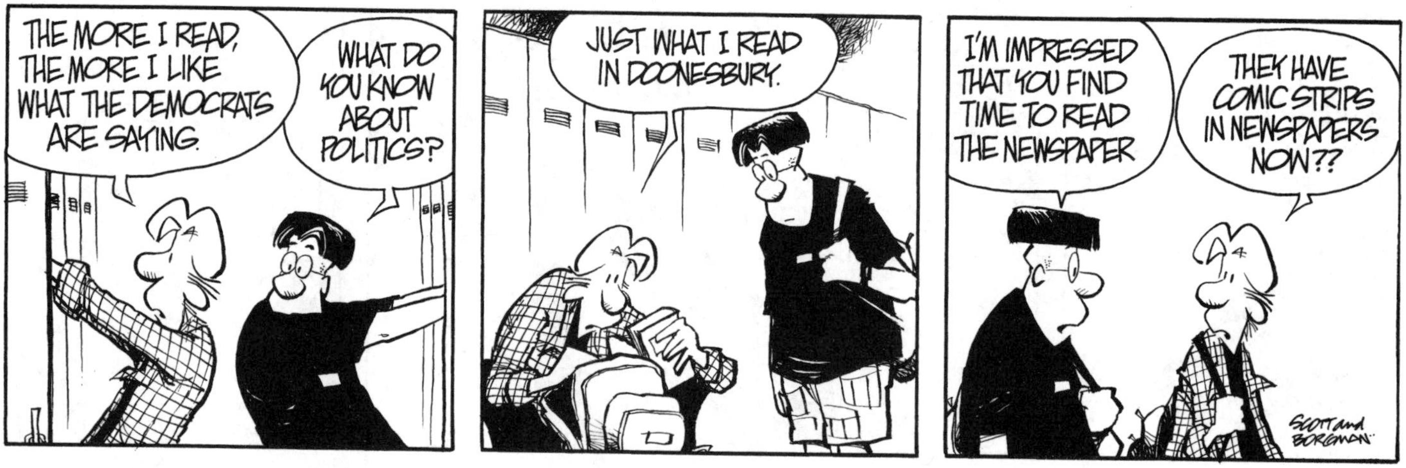
THE MORE I READ, THE MORE I LIKE WHAT THE DEMOCRATS ARE SAYING.
WHAT DO YOU KNOW ABOUT POLITICS?
JUST WHAT I READ IN DOONESBURY.
I'M IMPRESSED THAT YOU FIND TIME TO READ THE NEWSPAPER
THEY HAVE COMIC STRIPS IN NEWSPAPERS NOW??
SCOTT and BORGMAN

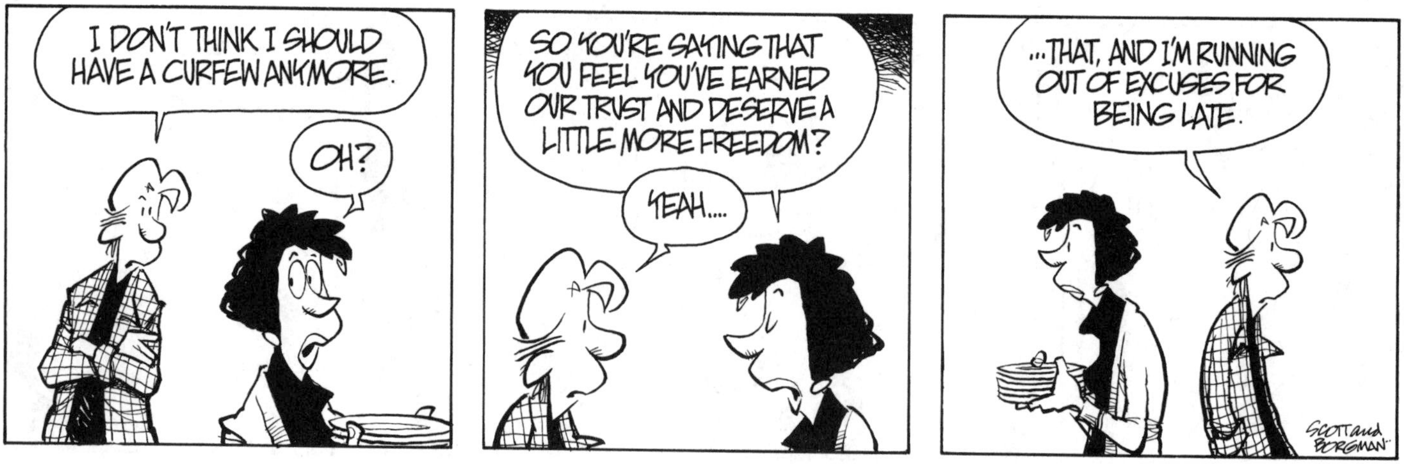
I DON'T THINK I SHOULD HAVE A CURFEW ANYMORE.
OH?
SO YOU'RE SAYING THAT YOU FEEL YOU'VE EARNED OUR TRUST AND DESERVE A LITTLE MORE FREEDOM?
YEAH....
...THAT, AND I'M RUNNING OUT OF EXCUSES FOR BEING LATE.
SCOTT and BORGMAN

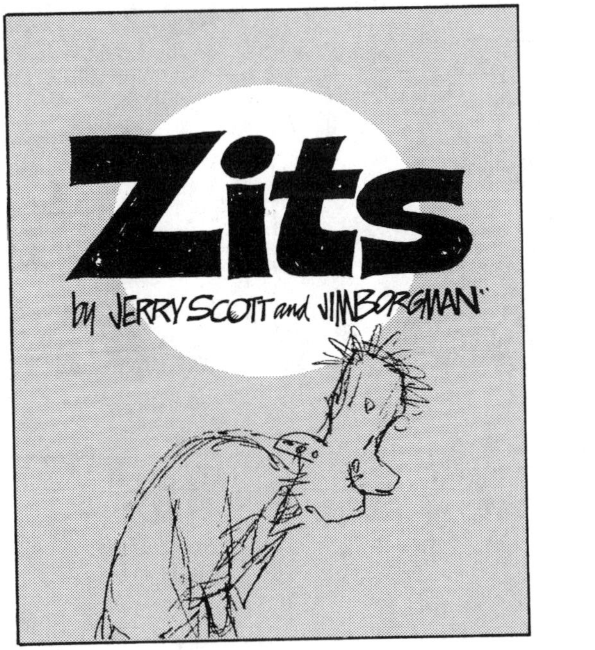
Zits
by JERRY SCOTT and JIM BORGMAN

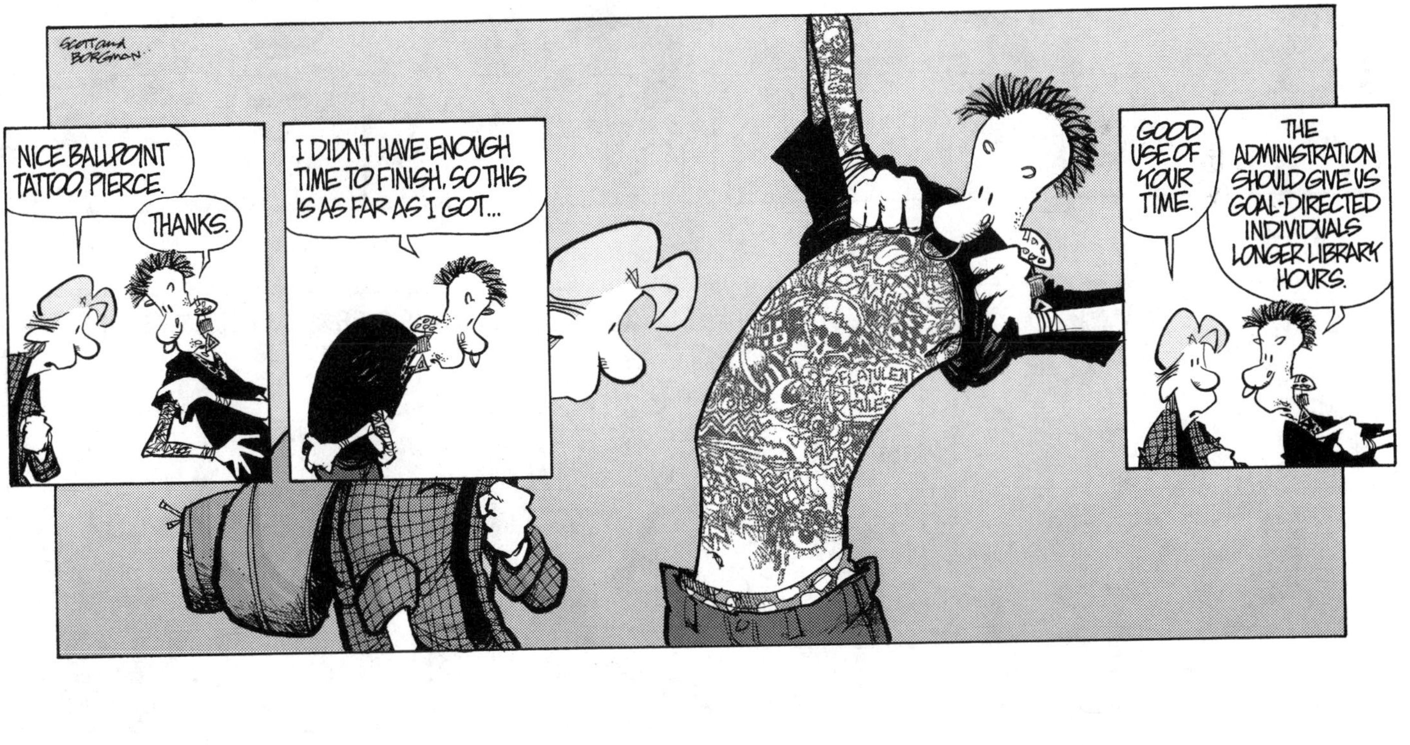
SCOTT and BORGMAN
NICE BALLPOINT TATTOO, PIERCE.
THANKS.
I DIDN'T HAVE ENOUGH TIME TO FINISH, SO THIS IS AS FAR AS I GOT...
FLATULEN RAT RULES
GOOD USE OF YOUR TIME.
THE ADMINISTRATION SHOULD GIVE US GOAL-DIRECTED INDIVIDUALS LONGER LIBRARY HOURS.

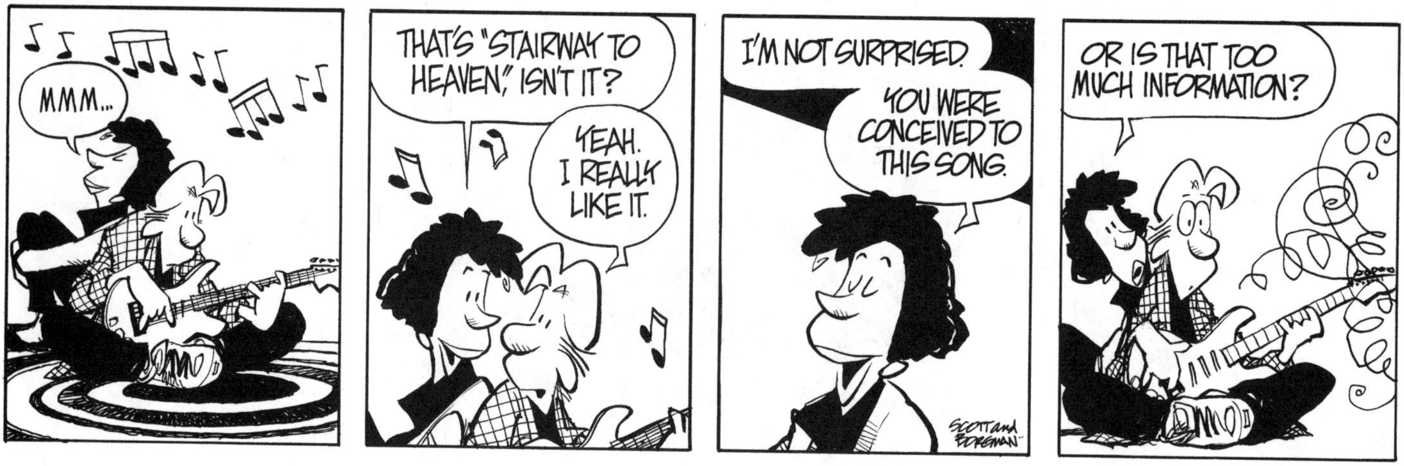
MMM...
THAT'S "STAIRWAY TO HEAVEN," ISN'T IT?
YEAH. I REALLY LIKE IT.
I'M NOT SURPRISED.
YOU WERE CONCEIVED TO THIS SONG.
SCOTT and BORGMAN
OR IS THAT TOO MUCH INFORMATION?

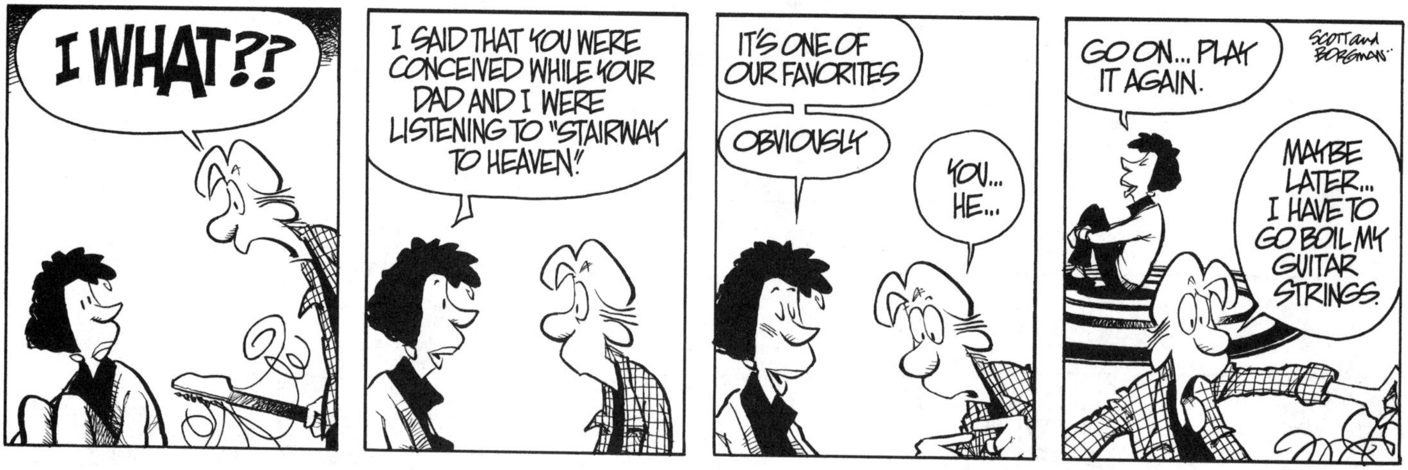
I WHAT??
I SAID THAT YOU WERE CONCEIVED WHILE YOUR DAD AND I WERE LISTENING TO "STAIRWAY TO HEAVEN."
IT'S ONE OF OUR FAVORITES
OBVIOUSLY
YOU... HE...
SCOTT and BORGMAN
GO ON... PLAY IT AGAIN.
MAYBE LATER... I HAVE TO GO BOIL MY GUITAR STRINGS.

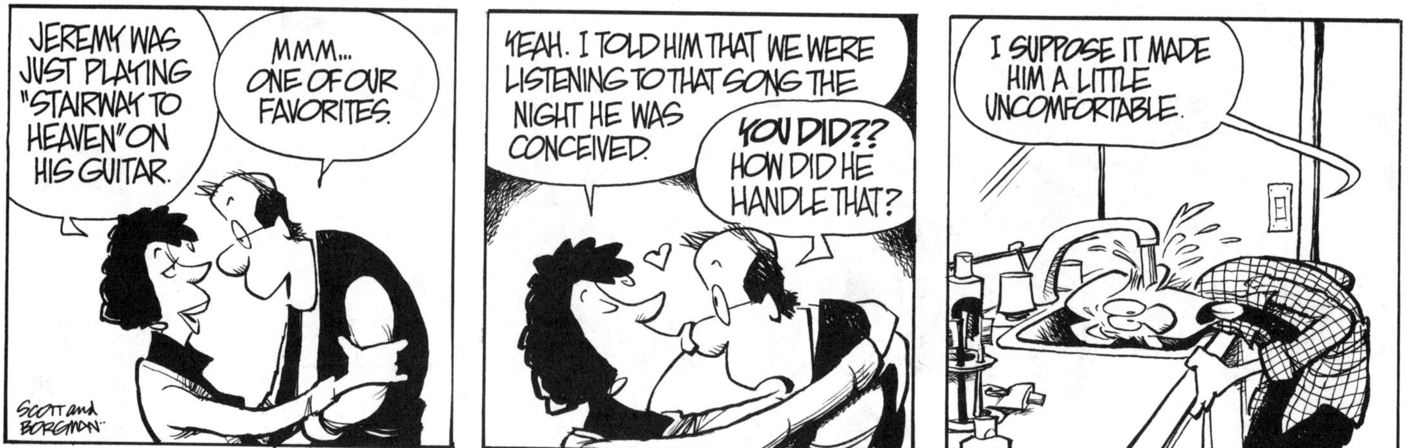
JEREMY WAS JUST PLAYING "STAIRWAY TO HEAVEN" ON HIS GUITAR.
MMM... ONE OF OUR FAVORITES.
SCOTT and BORGMAN
YEAH. I TOLD HIM THAT WE WERE LISTENING TO THAT SONG THE NIGHT HE WAS CONCEIVED.
YOU DID?? HOW DID HE HANDLE THAT?
I SUPPOSE IT MADE HIM A LITTLE UNCOMFORTABLE.

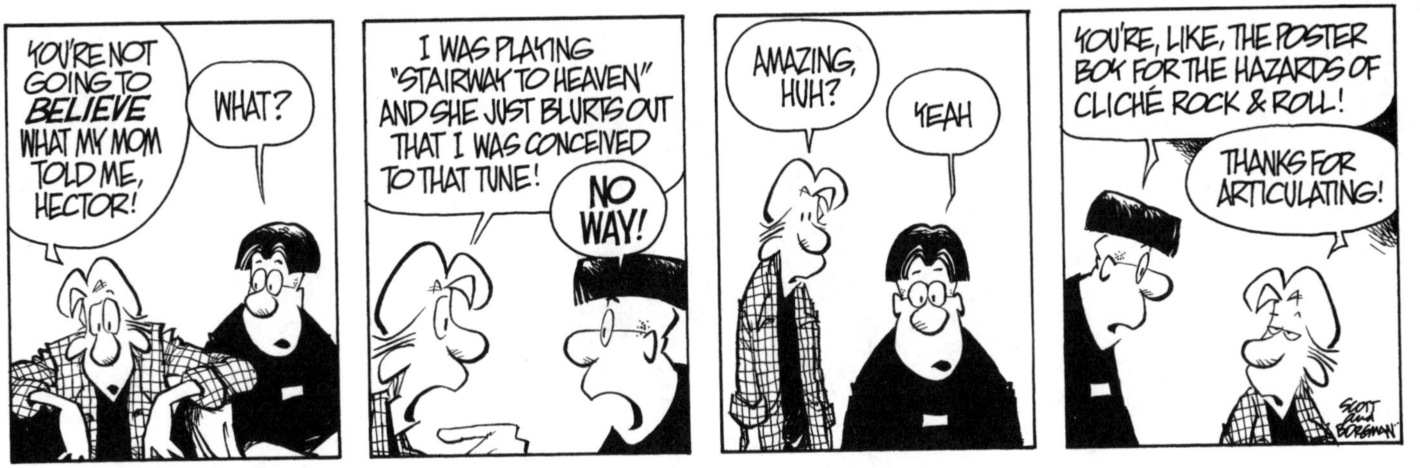
YOU'RE NOT GOING TO BELIEVE WHAT MY MOM TOLD ME, HECTOR!
WHAT?
I WAS PLAYING "STAIRWAY TO HEAVEN" AND SHE JUST BLURTS OUT THAT I WAS CONCEIVED TO THAT TUNE!
NO WAY!
AMAZING, HUH?
YEAH
YOU'RE, LIKE, THE POSTER BOY FOR THE HAZARDS OF CLICHÉ ROCK & ROLL!
THANKS FOR ARTICULATING!
SCOTT and BORGMAN

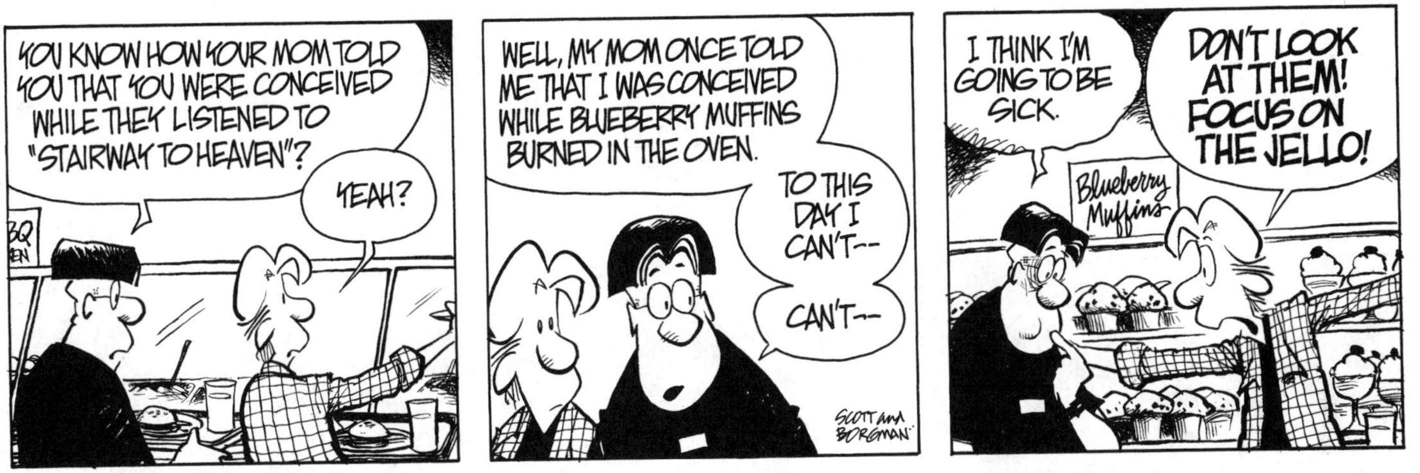
YOU KNOW HOW YOUR MOM TOLD YOU THAT YOU WERE CONCEIVED WHILE THEY LISTENED TO "STAIRWAY TO HEAVEN"?
YEAH?
WELL, MY MOM ONCE TOLD ME THAT I WAS CONCEIVED WHILE BLUEBERRY MUFFINS BURNED IN THE OVEN.
TO THIS DAY I CAN'T--
CAN'T--
SCOTT and BORGMAN
I THINK I'M GOING TO BE SICK.
DON'T LOOK AT THEM! FOCUS ON THE JELLO!
Blueberry Muffins

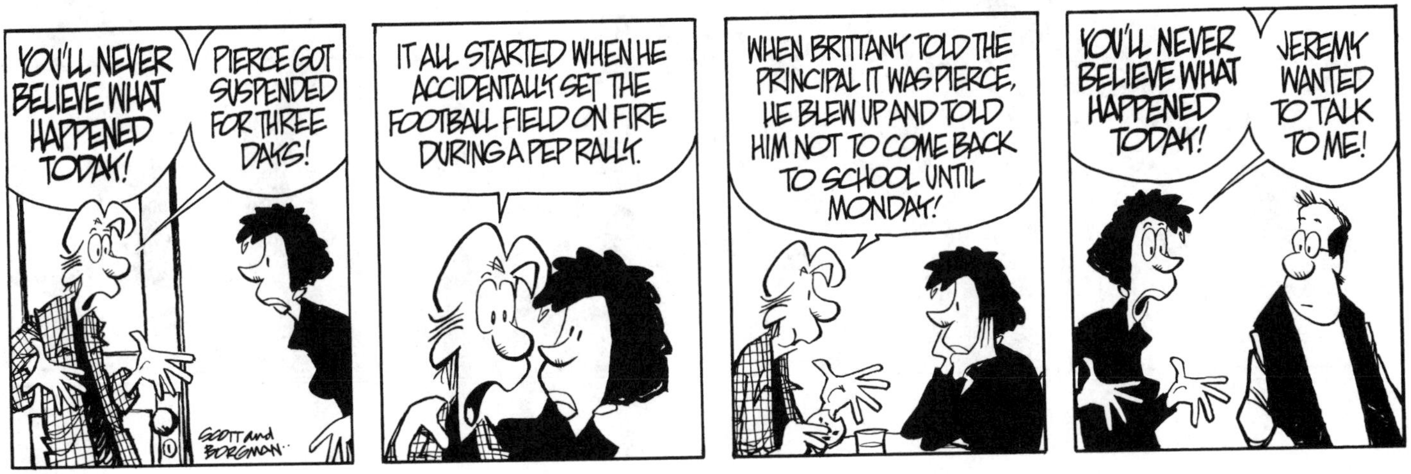
YOU'LL NEVER BELIEVE WHAT HAPPENED TODAY!
PIERCE GOT SUSPENDED FOR THREE DAYS!
SCOTT and BORGMAN
IT ALL STARTED WHEN HE ACCIDENTALLY SET THE FOOTBALL FIELD ON FIRE DURING A PEP RALLY.
WHEN BRITTANY TOLD THE PRINCIPAL IT WAS PIERCE, HE BLEW UP AND TOLD HIM NOT TO COME BACK TO SCHOOL UNTIL MONDAY!
YOU'LL NEVER BELIEVE WHAT HAPPENED TODAY!
JEREMY WANTED TO TALK TO ME!

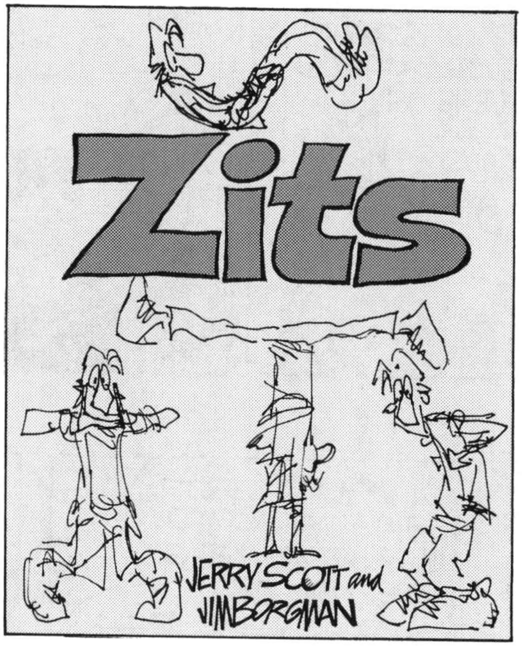
Zits
JERRY SCOTT and
JIM BORGMAN

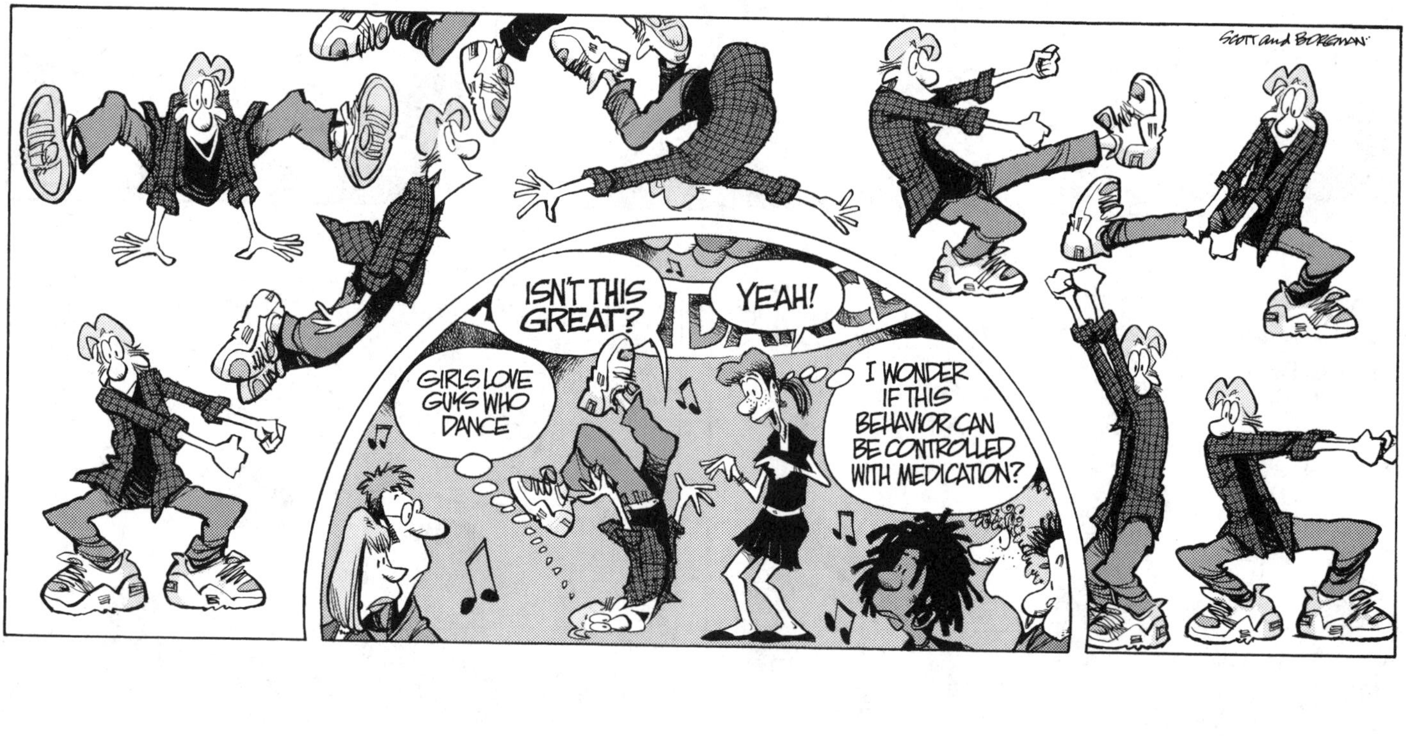
SCOTT and BORGMAN
ISN'T THIS GREAT?
YEAH!
GIRLS LOVE GUYS WHO DANCE
I WONDER IF THIS BEHAVIOR CAN BE CONTROLLED WITH MEDICATION?

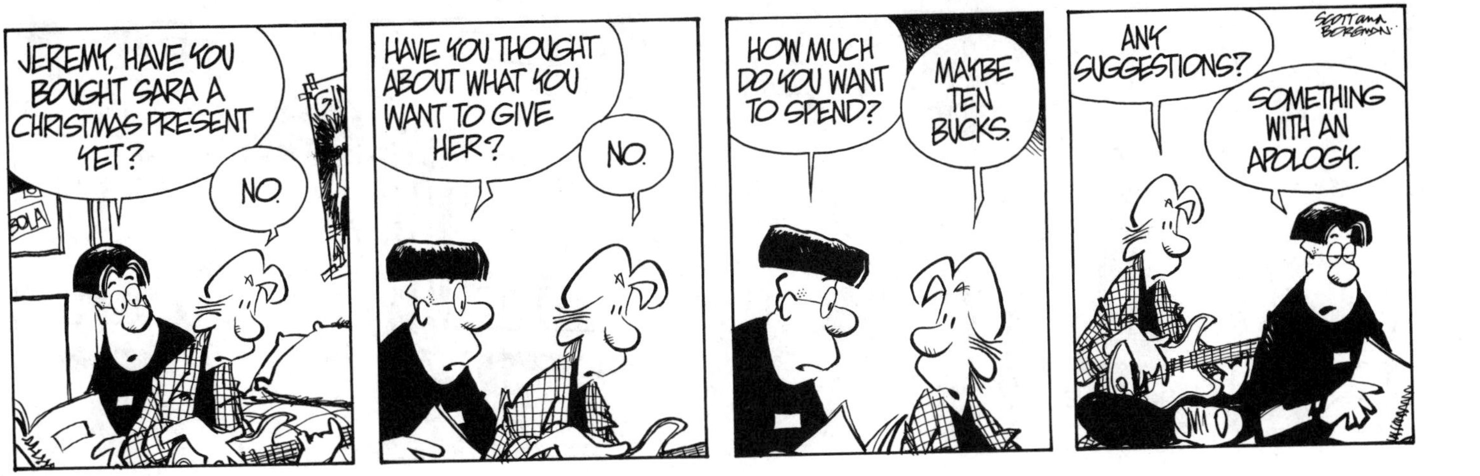
JEREMY, HAVE YOU BOUGHT SARA A CHRISTMAS PRESENT YET?
NO.
HAVE YOU THOUGHT ABOUT WHAT YOU WANT TO GIVE HER?
NO.
HOW MUCH DO YOU WANT TO SPEND?
MAYBE TEN BUCKS.
ANY SUGGESTIONS?
SOMETHING WITH AN APOLOGY.
SCOTT and BORGMAN

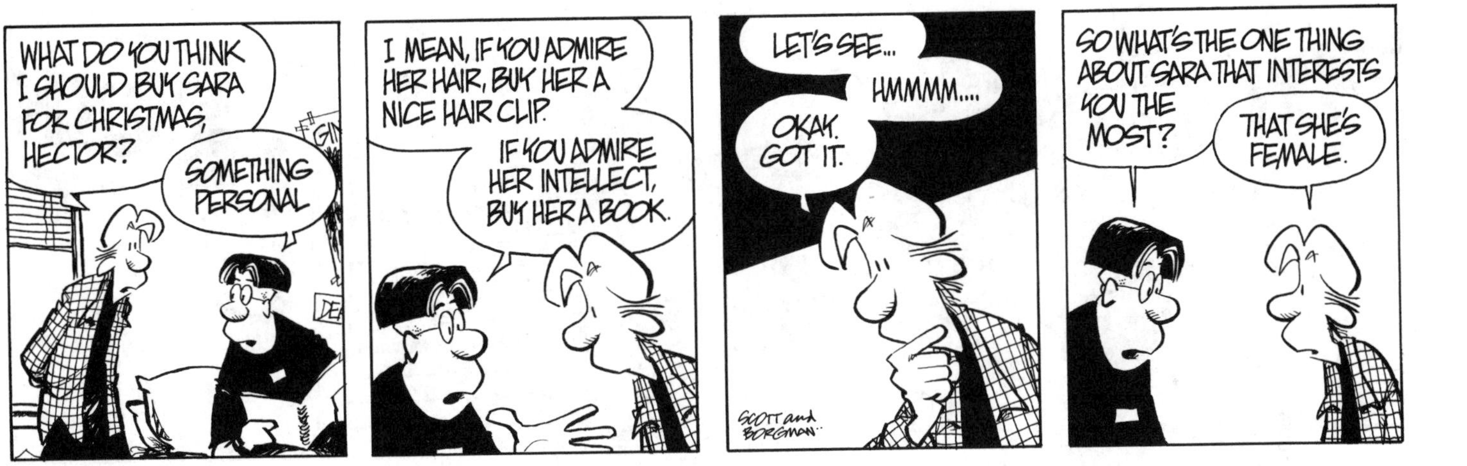
WHAT DO YOU THINK I SHOULD BUY SARA FOR CHRISTMAS, HECTOR?
SOMETHING PERSONAL
I MEAN, IF YOU ADMIRE HER HAIR, BUY HER A NICE HAIR CLIP.
IF YOU ADMIRE HER INTELLECT, BUY HER A BOOK.
LET'S SEE...
HMMMM....
OKAY. GOT IT.
SCOTT and BORGMAN
SO WHAT'S THE ONE THING ABOUT SARA THAT INTERESTS YOU THE MOST?
THAT SHE'S FEMALE.

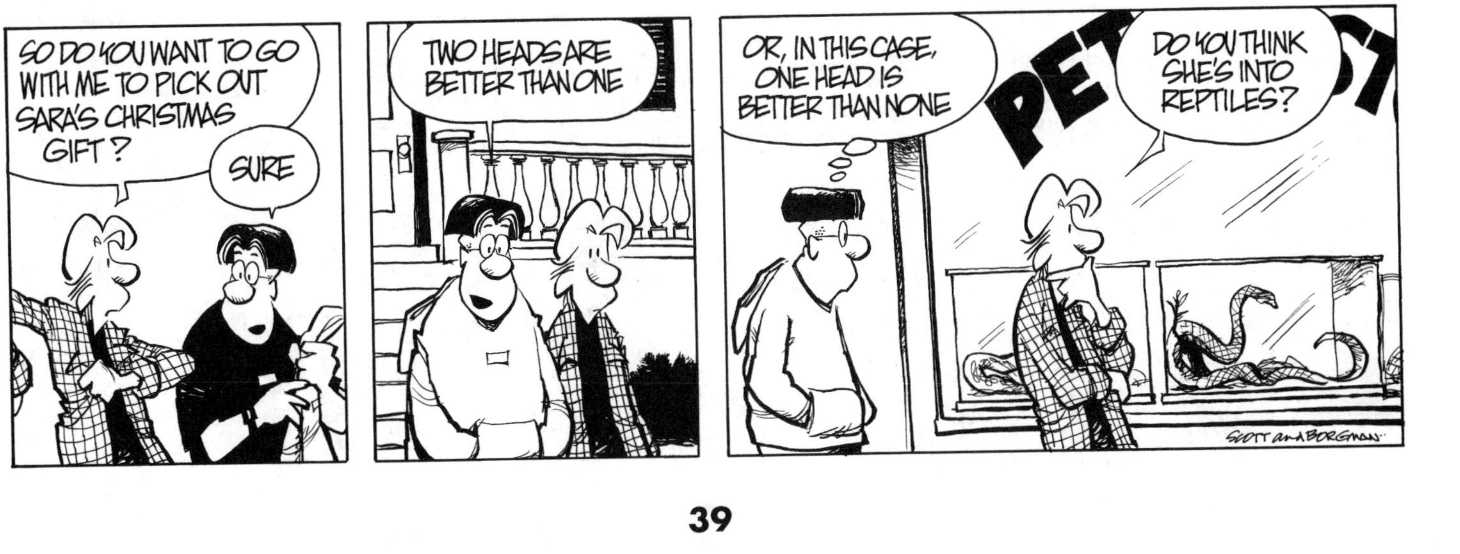
SO DO YOU WANT TO GO WITH ME TO PICK OUT SARA'S CHRISTMAS GIFT?
SURE
TWO HEADS ARE BETTER THAN ONE
OR, IN THIS CASE, ONE HEAD IS BETTER THAN NONE
PET
DO YOU THINK SHE'S INTO REPTILES?
SCOTT and BORGMAN

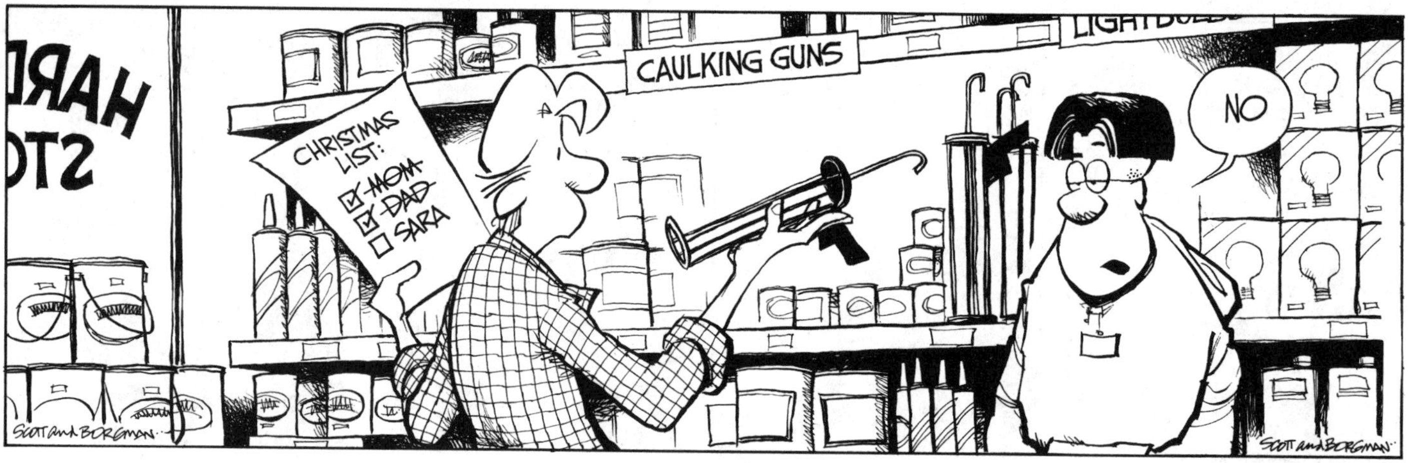
CAULKING GUNS
CHRISTMAS LIST:
MOM
DAD
SARA
NO
SCOTT and BORGMAN

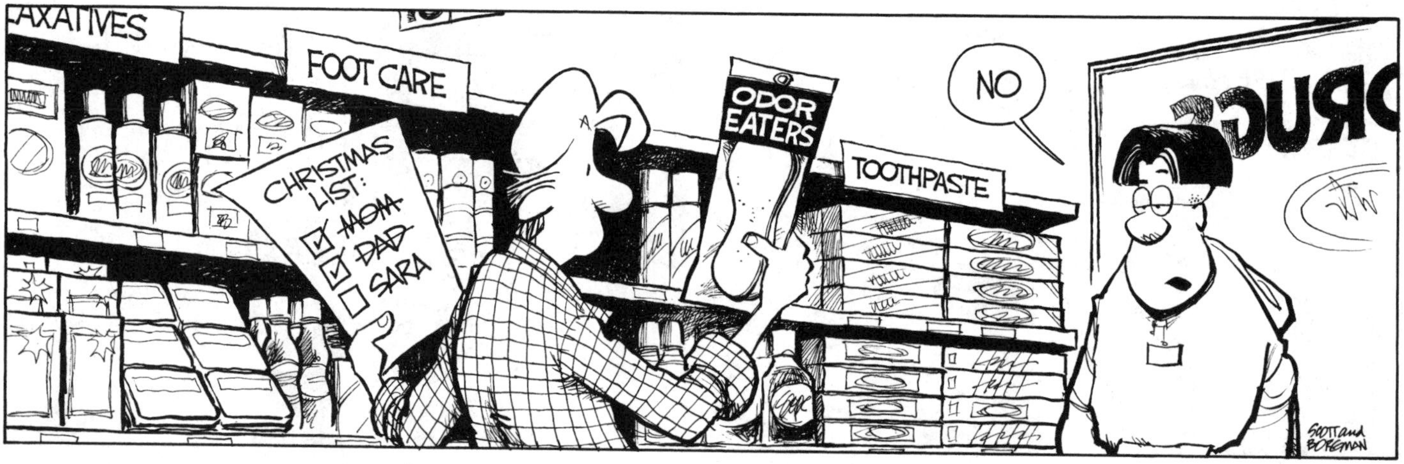
FOOT CARE
CHRISTMAS LIST:
MOM
DAD
SARA
ODOR EATERS
TOOTHPASTE
NO
SCOTT and BORGMAN

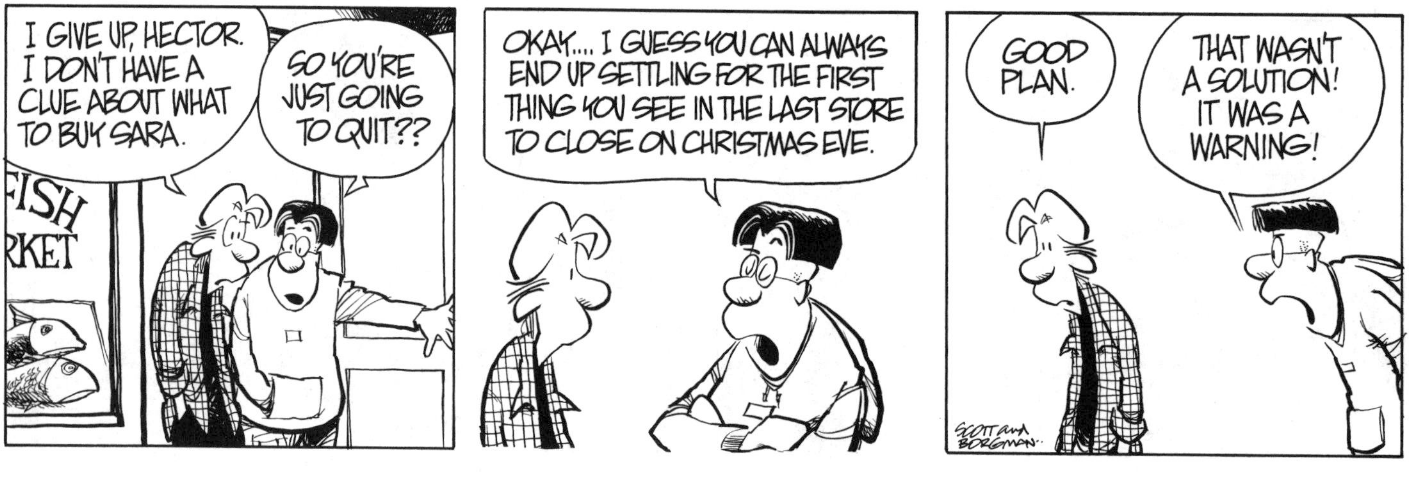
I GIVE UP, HECTOR. I DON'T HAVE A CLUE ABOUT WHAT TO BUY SARA.
SO YOU'RE JUST GOING TO QUIT??
OKAY.... I GUESS YOU CAN ALWAYS END UP SETTLING FOR THE FIRST THING YOU SEE IN THE LAST STORE TO CLOSE ON CHRISTMAS EVE.
GOOD PLAN.
THAT WASN'T A SOLUTION! IT WAS A WARNING!
SCOTT and BORGMAN

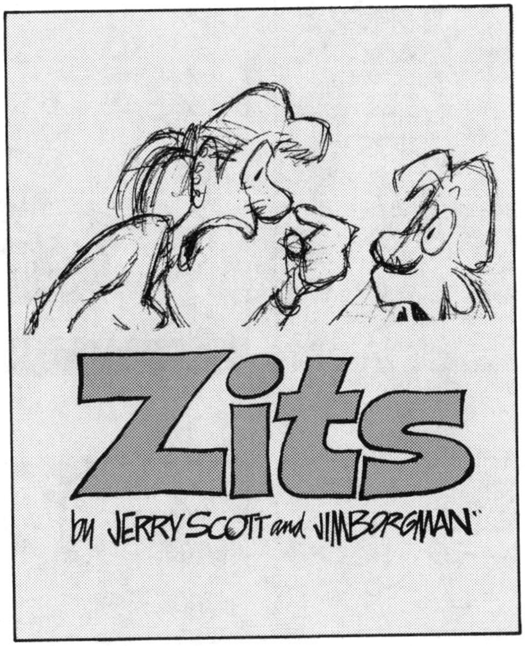
Zits
by JERRY SCOTT and JIM BORGMAN

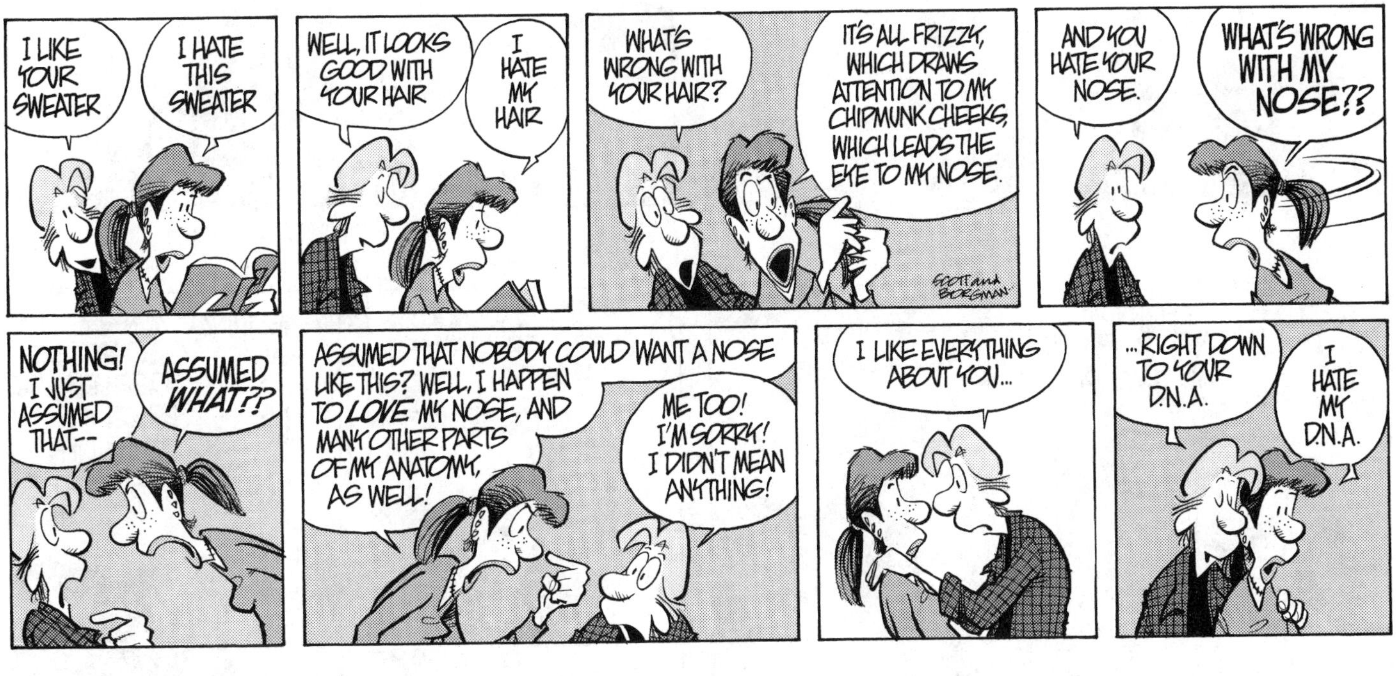
I LIKE YOUR SWEATER
I HATE THIS SWEATER
WELL, IT LOOKS GOOD WITH YOUR HAIR
I HATE MY HAIR
WHAT'S WRONG WITH YOUR HAIR?
IT'S ALL FRIZZY, WHICH DRAWS ATTENTION TO MY CHIPMUNK CHEEKS, WHICH LEADS THE EYE TO MY NOSE.
SCOTT and BORGMAN
AND YOU HATE YOUR NOSE.
WHAT'S WRONG WITH MY NOSE??
NOTHING! I JUST ASSUMED THAT--
ASSUMED WHAT??
ASSUMED THAT NOBODY COULD WANT A NOSE LIKE THIS? WELL, I HAPPEN TO LOVE MY NOSE, AND MANY OTHER PARTS OF MY ANATOMY, AS WELL!
ME TOO! I'M SORRY! I DIDN'T MEAN ANYTHING!
I LIKE EVERYTHING ABOUT YOU...
...RIGHT DOWN TO YOUR D.N.A.
I HATE MY D.N.A.

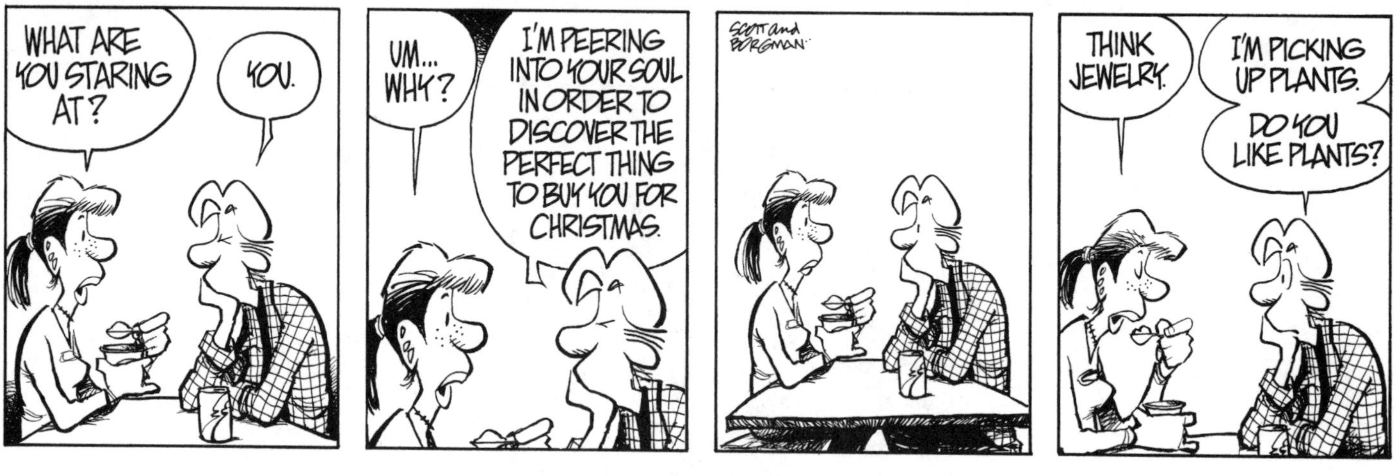
WHAT ARE YOU STARING AT?
YOU.
UM... WHY?
I'M PEERING INTO YOUR SOUL IN ORDER TO DISCOVER THE PERFECT THING TO BUY YOU FOR CHRISTMAS.
SCOTT and BORGMAN
THINK JEWELRY.
I'M PICKING UP PLANTS.
DO YOU LIKE PLANTS?

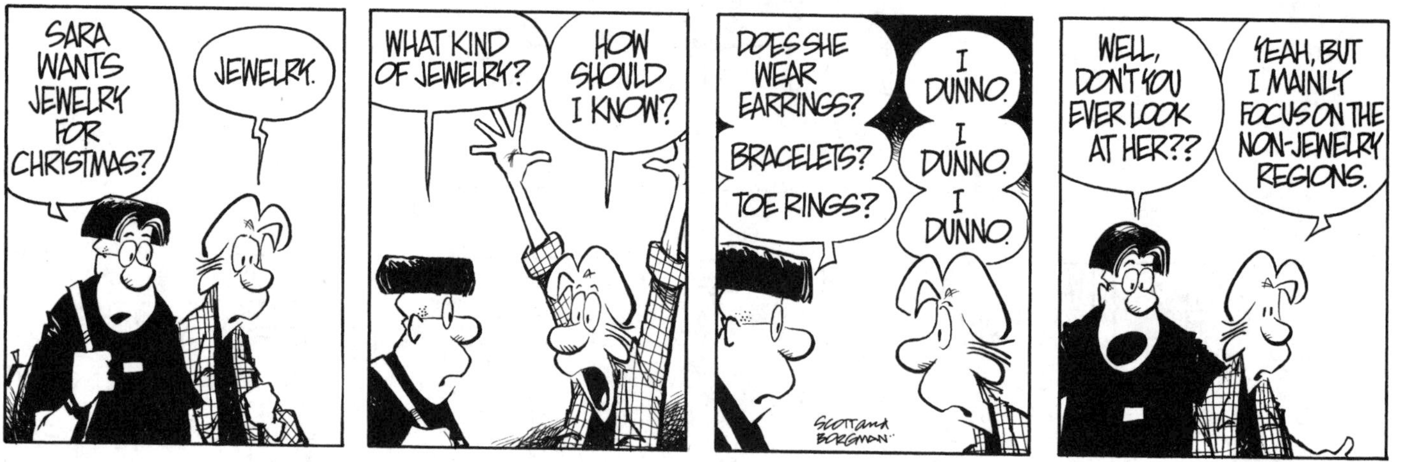
SARA WANTS JEWELRY FOR CHRISTMAS?
JEWELRY.
WHAT KIND OF JEWELRY?
HOW SHOULD I KNOW?
DOES SHE WEAR EARRINGS?
I DUNNO.
BRACELETS?
I DUNNO.
TOE RINGS?
I DUNNO.
SCOTT and BORGMAN
WELL, DON'T YOU EVER LOOK AT HER??
YEAH, BUT I MAINLY FOCUS ON THE NON-JEWELRY REGIONS.

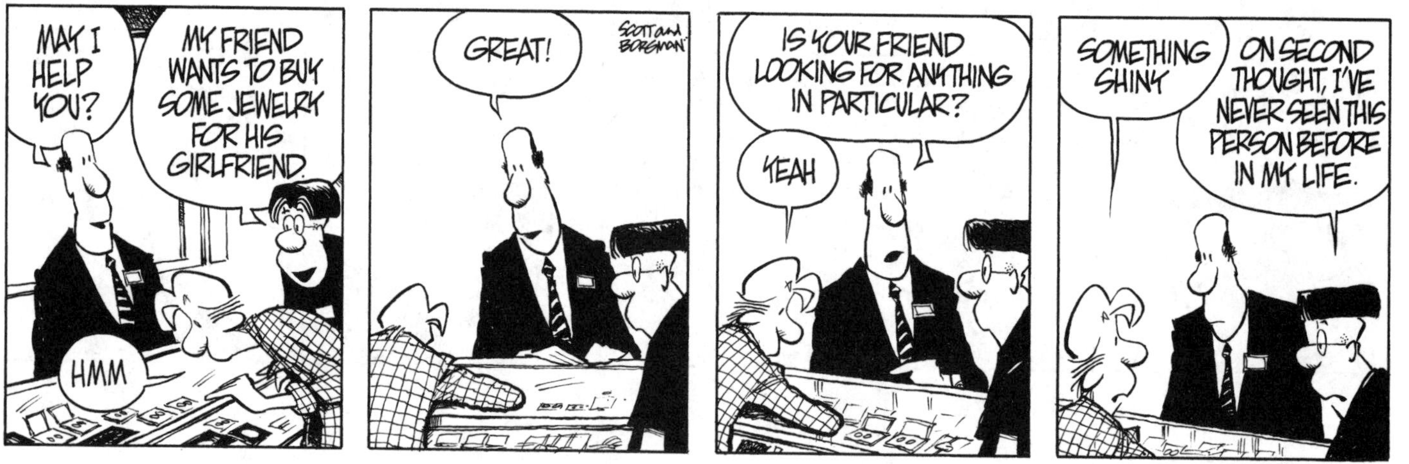
MAY I HELP YOU?
MY FRIEND WANTS TO BUY SOME JEWELRY FOR HIS GIRLFRIEND.
HMM
GREAT!
SCOTT and BORGMAN
IS YOUR FRIEND LOOKING FOR ANYTHING IN PARTICULAR?
YEAH
SOMETHING SHINY
ON SECOND THOUGHT, I'VE NEVER SEEN THIS PERSON BEFORE IN MY LIFE.

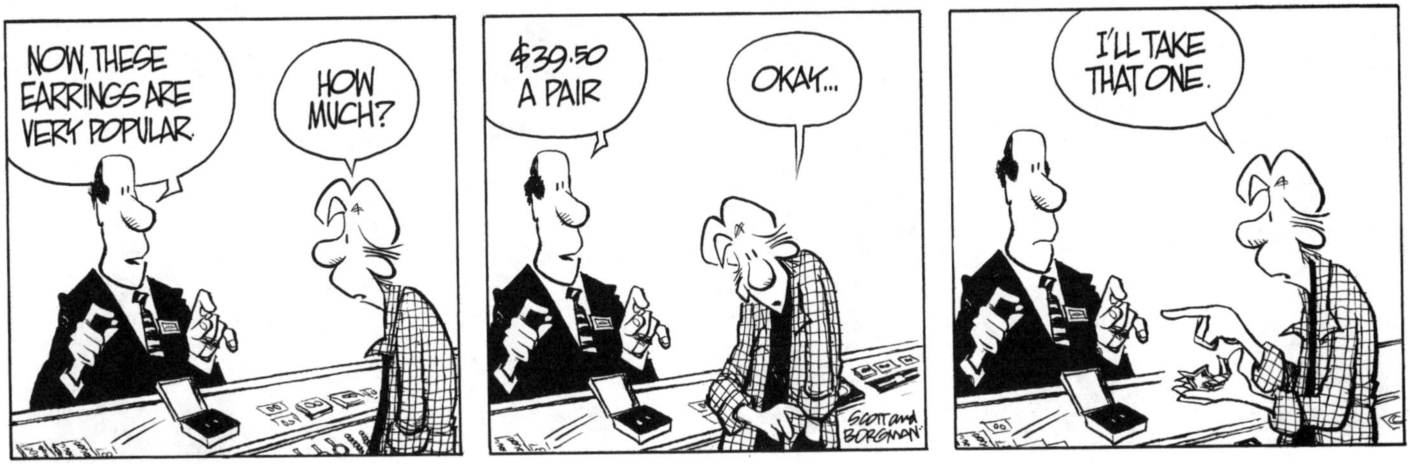
NOW, THESE EARRINGS ARE VERY POPULAR.
HOW MUCH?
$39.50 A PAIR
OKAY...
SCOTT and BORGMAN
I'LL TAKE THAT ONE.

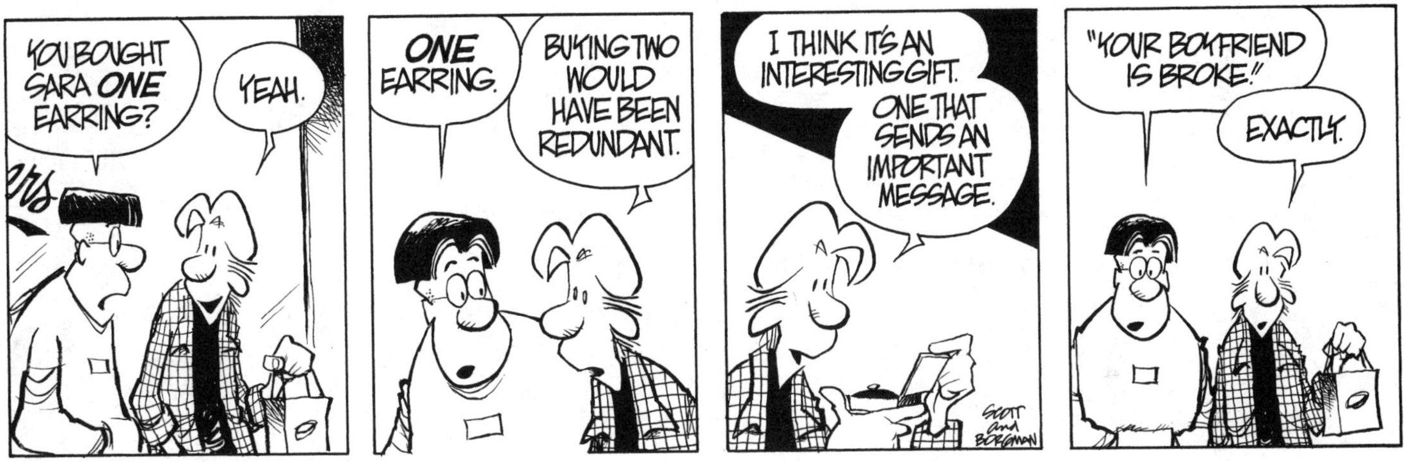
YOU BOUGHT SARA **ONE** EARRING?
YEAH.
ONE EARRING.
BUYING TWO WOULD HAVE BEEN REDUNDANT.
I THINK IT'S AN INTERESTING GIFT.
ONE THAT SENDS AN IMPORTANT MESSAGE.
SCOTT and BORGMAN
"YOUR BOYFRIEND IS BROKE."
EXACTLY.

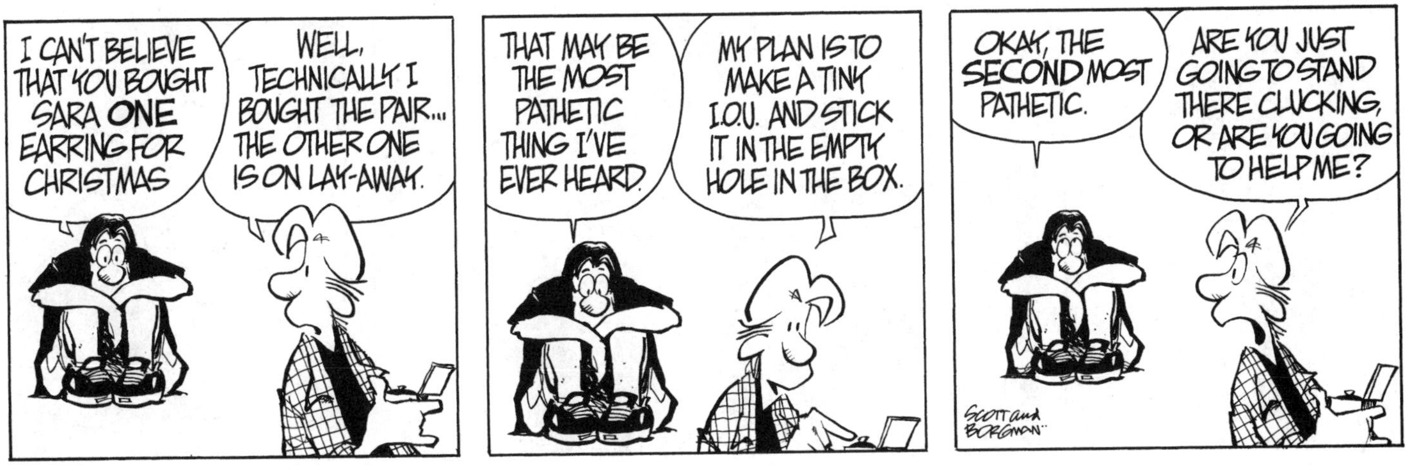
I CAN'T BELIEVE THAT YOU BOUGHT SARA **ONE** EARRING FOR CHRISTMAS
WELL, TECHNICALLY I BOUGHT THE PAIR... THE OTHER ONE IS ON LAY-AWAY.
THAT MAY BE THE MOST PATHETIC THING I'VE EVER HEARD.
MY PLAN IS TO MAKE A TINY I.O.U. AND STICK IT IN THE EMPTY HOLE IN THE BOX.
OKAY, THE **SECOND** MOST PATHETIC.
ARE YOU JUST GOING TO STAND THERE CLUCKING, OR ARE YOU GOING TO HELP ME?
SCOTT and BORGMAN

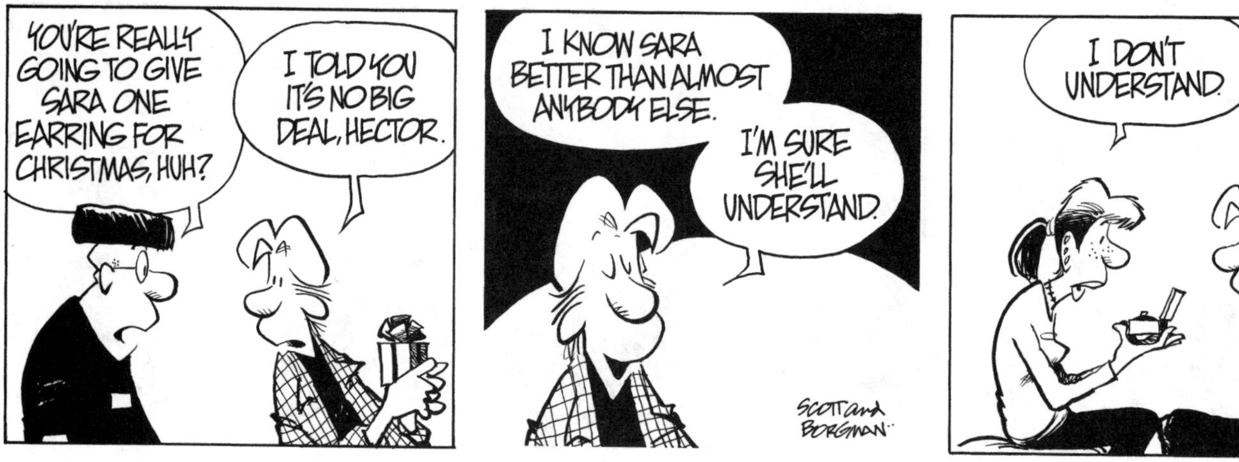
YOU'RE REALLY GOING TO GIVE SARA ONE EARRING FOR CHRISTMAS, HUH?
I TOLD YOU IT'S NO BIG DEAL, HECTOR.
I KNOW SARA BETTER THAN ALMOST ANYBODY ELSE.
I'M SURE SHE'LL UNDERSTAND.
SCOTT and BORGMAN
I DON'T UNDERSTAND.

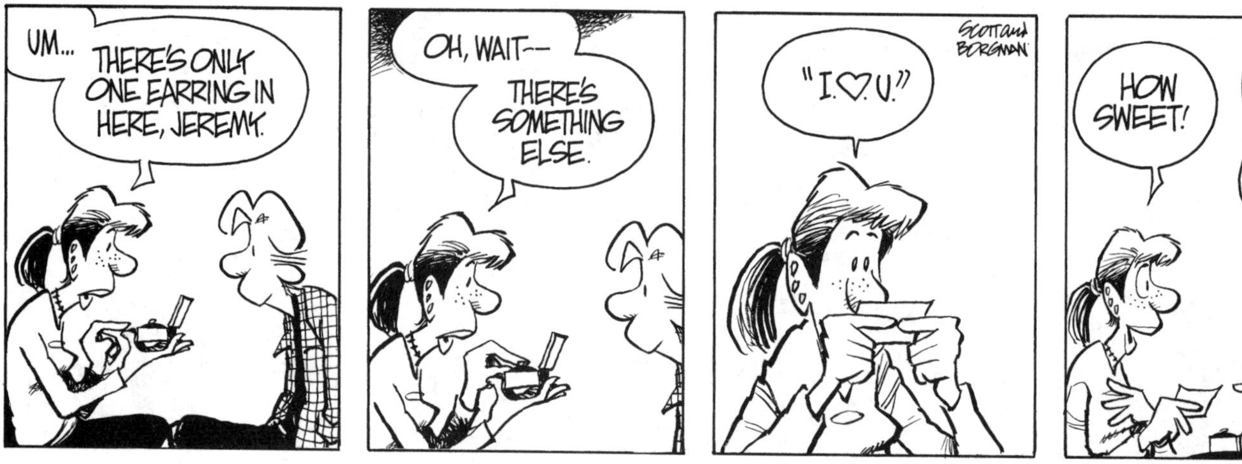
UM...
THERE'S ONLY ONE EARRING IN HERE, JEREMY.
OH, WAIT--
THERE'S SOMETHING ELSE.
SCOTT and BORGMAN
"I.♡.U."
HOW SWEET!
ACTUALLY, IT SAYS "I.O.U."
THE PEN SLIPPED.

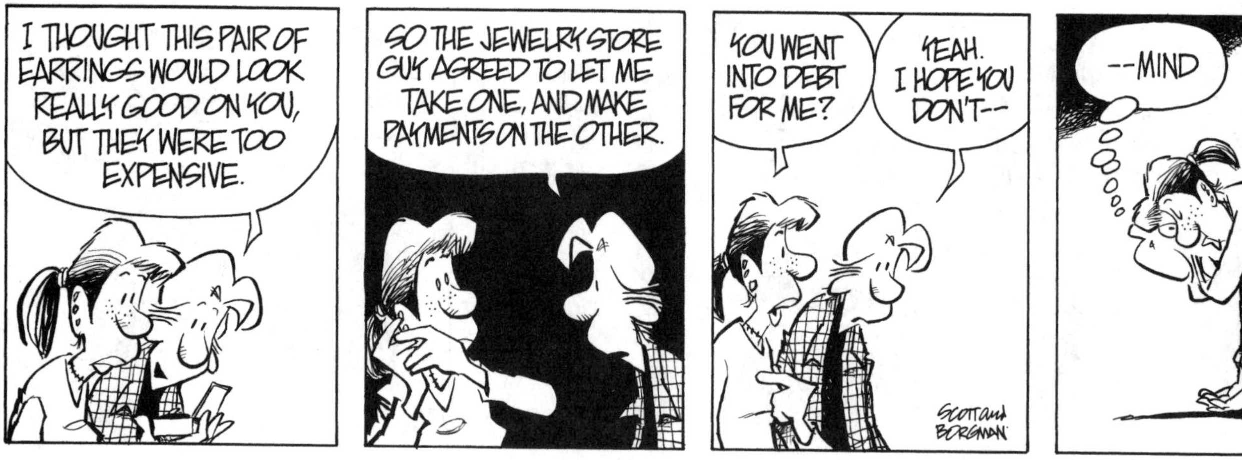
I THOUGHT THIS PAIR OF EARRINGS WOULD LOOK REALLY GOOD ON YOU, BUT THEY WERE TOO EXPENSIVE.
SO THE JEWELRY STORE GUY AGREED TO LET ME TAKE ONE, AND MAKE PAYMENTS ON THE OTHER.
YOU WENT INTO DEBT FOR ME?
YEAH. I HOPE YOU DON'T--
SCOTT and BORGMAN
--MIND

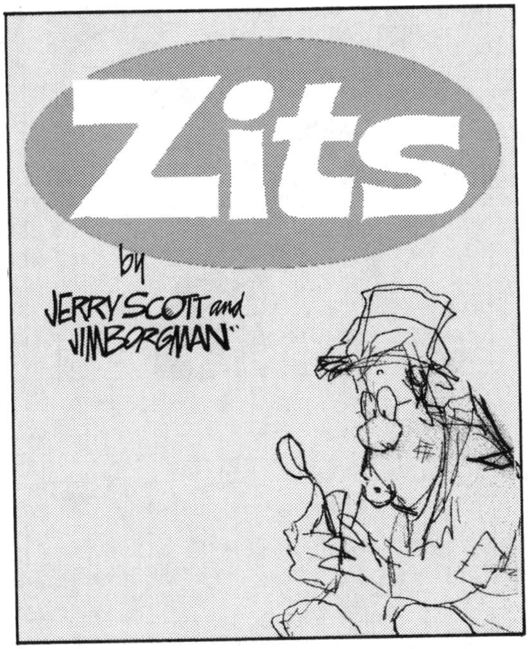
Zits
by
JERRY SCOTT and
JIM BORGMAN

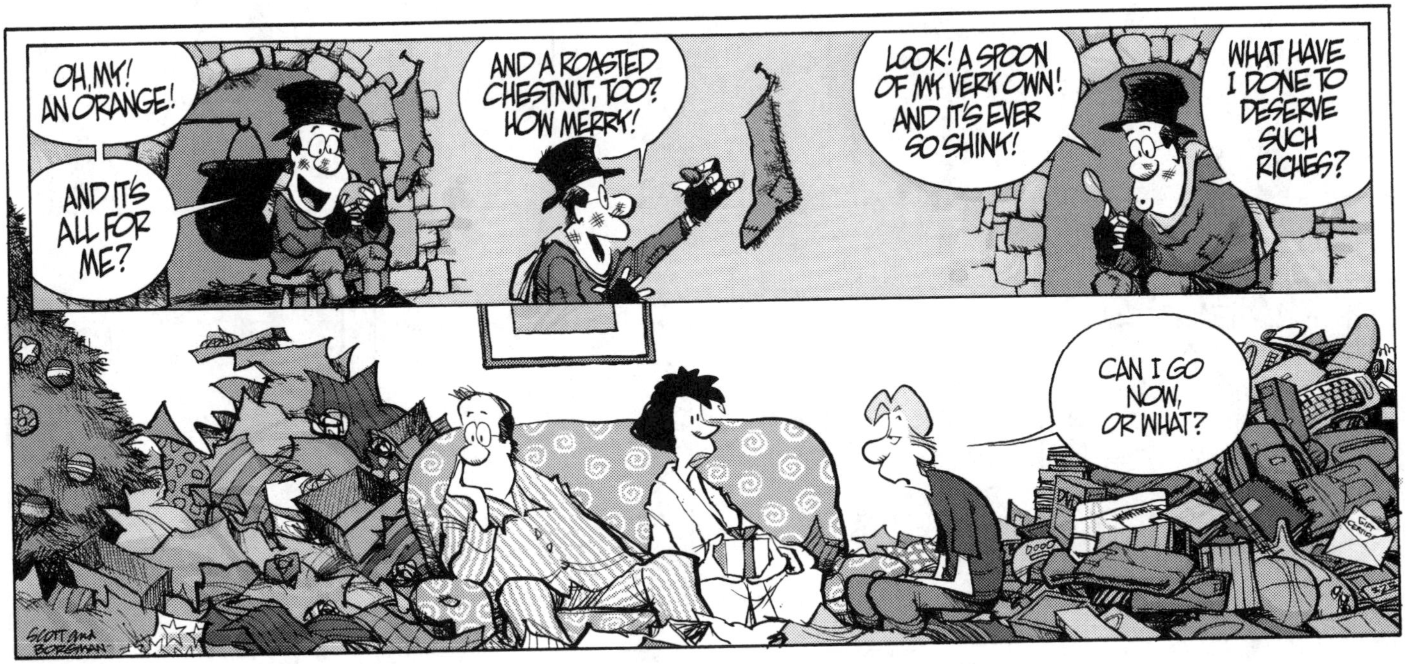
OH, MY! AN ORANGE!
AND IT'S ALL FOR ME?
AND A ROASTED CHESTNUT, TOO? HOW MERRY!
LOOK! A SPOON OF MY VERY OWN! AND IT'S EVER SO SHINY!
WHAT HAVE I DONE TO DESERVE SUCH RICHES?
CAN I GO NOW, OR WHAT?
SCOTT AND BORGMAN

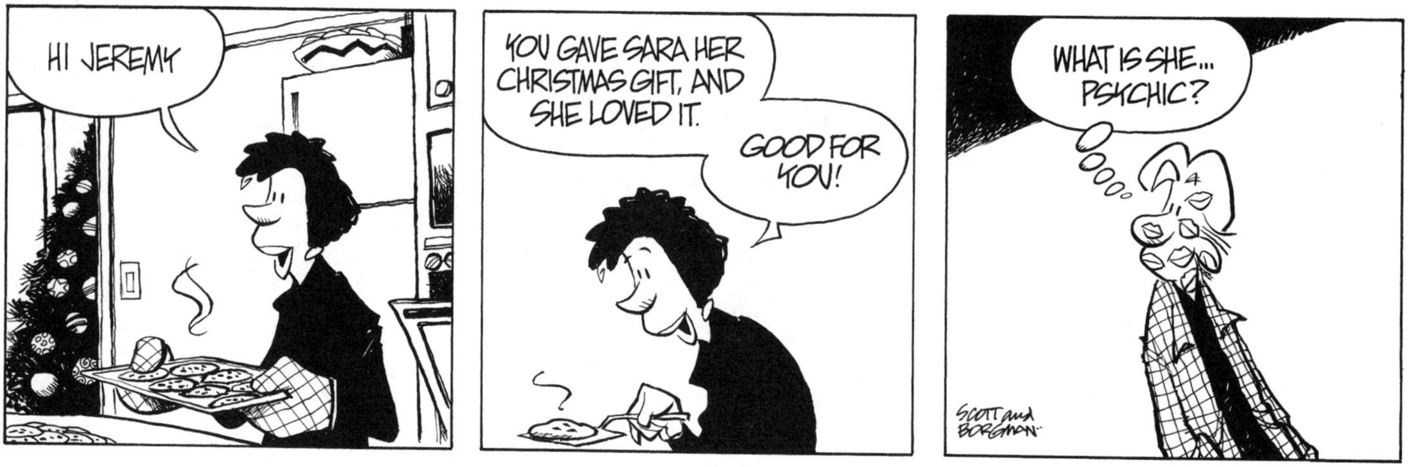
HI JEREMY
YOU GAVE SARA HER CHRISTMAS GIFT, AND SHE LOVED IT.
GOOD FOR YOU!
WHAT IS SHE... PSYCHIC?
SCOTT and BORGMAN

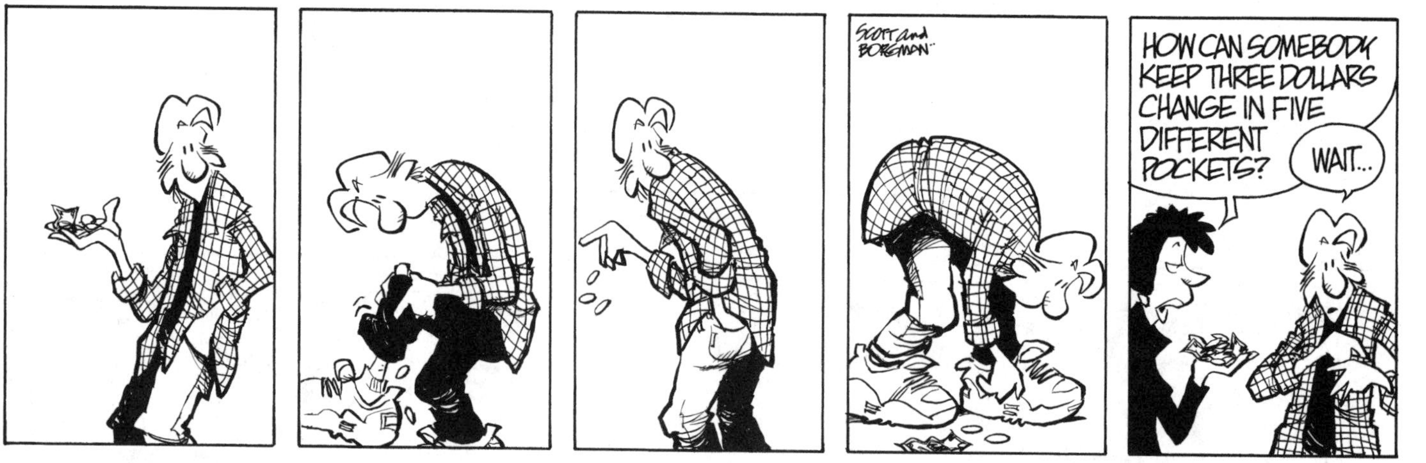
SCOTT and BORGMAN
HOW CAN SOMEBODY KEEP THREE DOLLARS CHANGE IN FIVE DIFFERENT POCKETS?
WAIT...

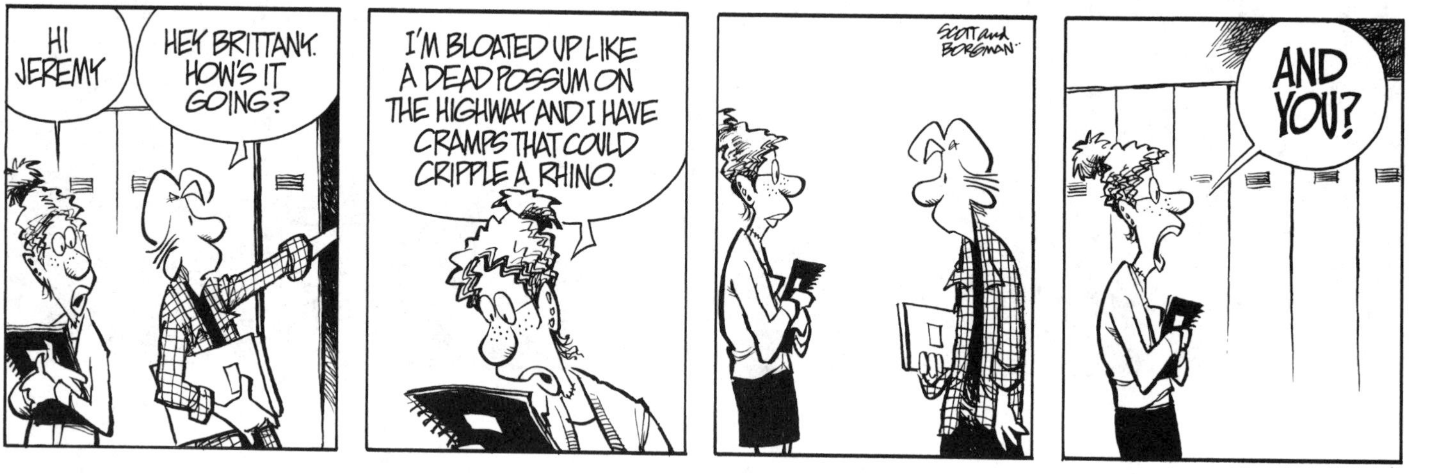
HI JEREMY
HEY BRITTANY. HOW'S IT GOING?
I'M BLOATED UP LIKE A DEAD POSSUM ON THE HIGHWAY AND I HAVE CRAMPS THAT COULD CRIPPLE A RHINO.
SCOTT and BORGMAN
AND YOU?

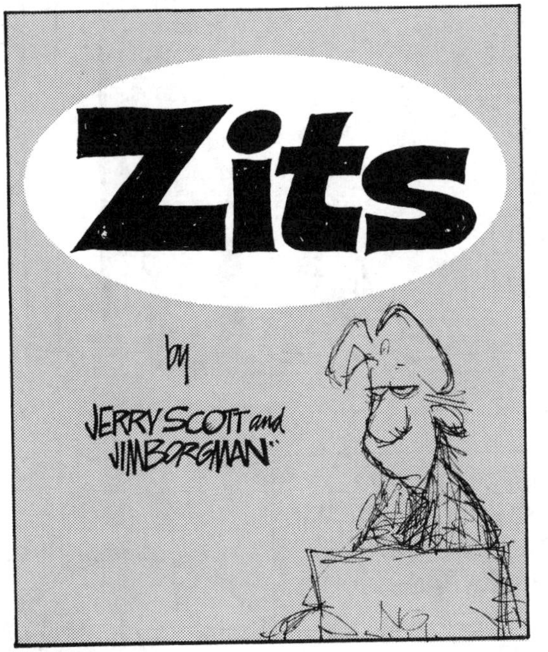
Zits
by
JERRY SCOTT and
JIM BORGMAN

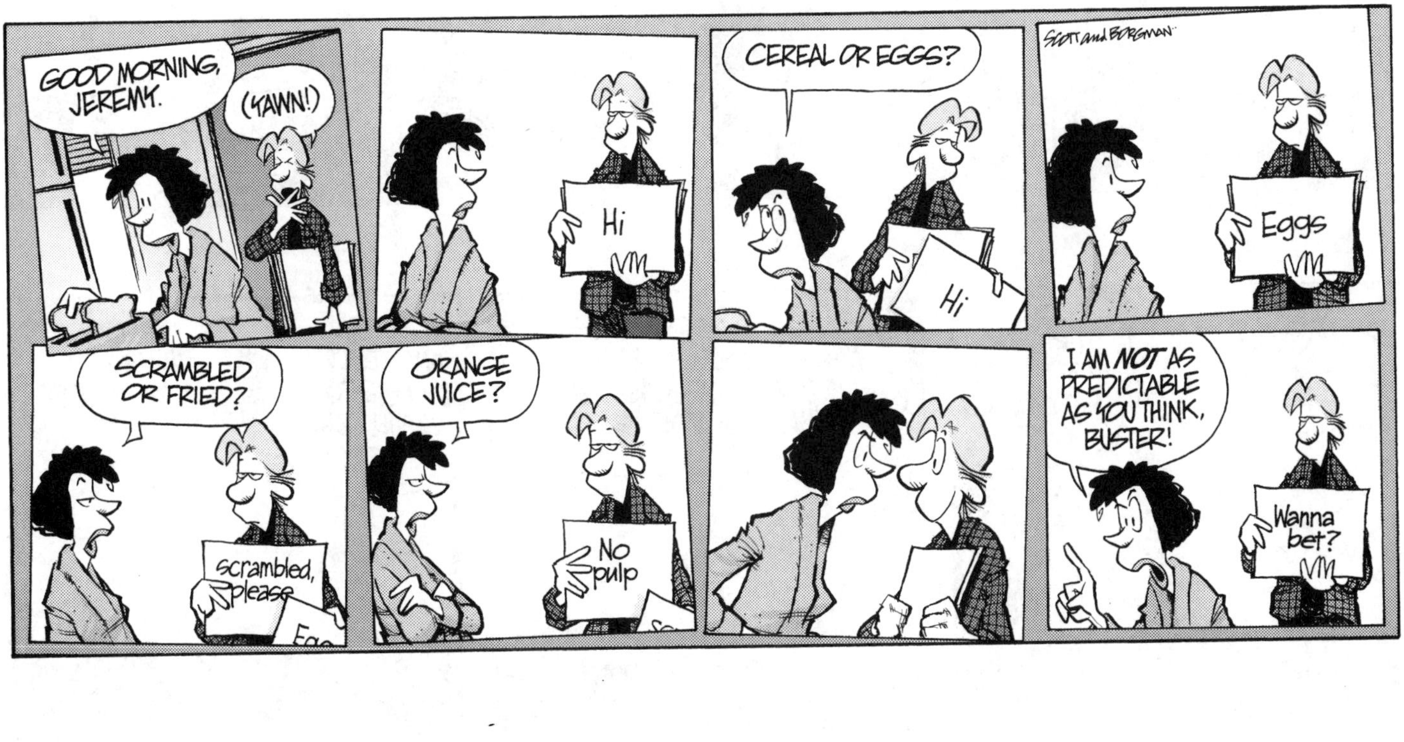
GOOD MORNING, JEREMY.
(YAWN!)
Hi
CEREAL OR EGGS?
Hi
SCOTT and BORGMAN
Eggs
SCRAMBLED OR FRIED?
scrambled, please
ORANGE JUICE?
No pulp
I AM ***NOT*** AS PREDICTABLE AS YOU THINK, BUSTER!
Wanna bet?

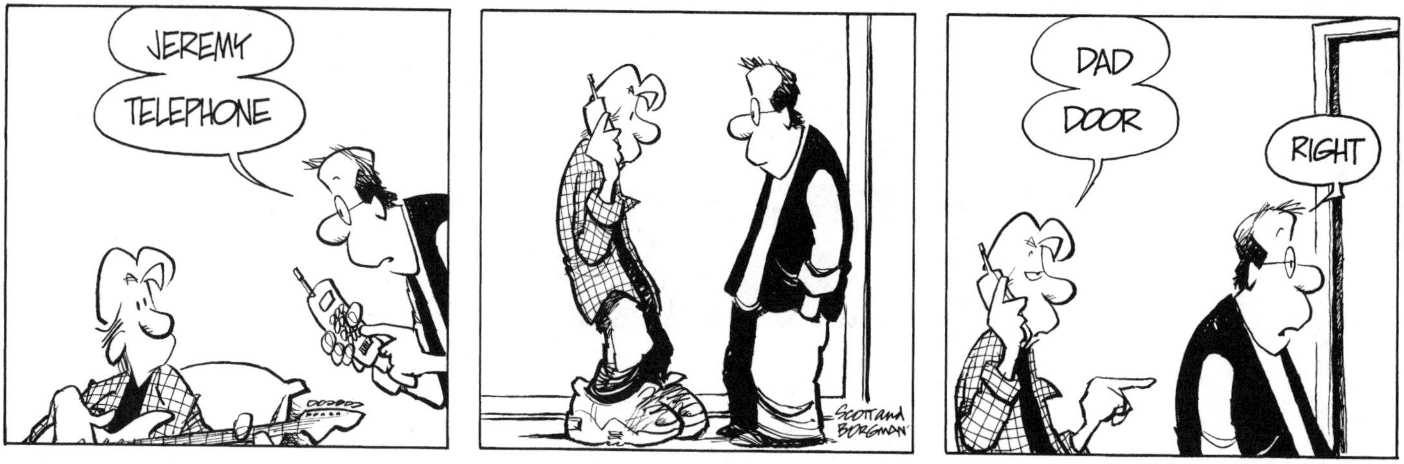
JEREMY
TELEPHONE
DAD
DOOR
RIGHT
SCOTT AND BORGMAN

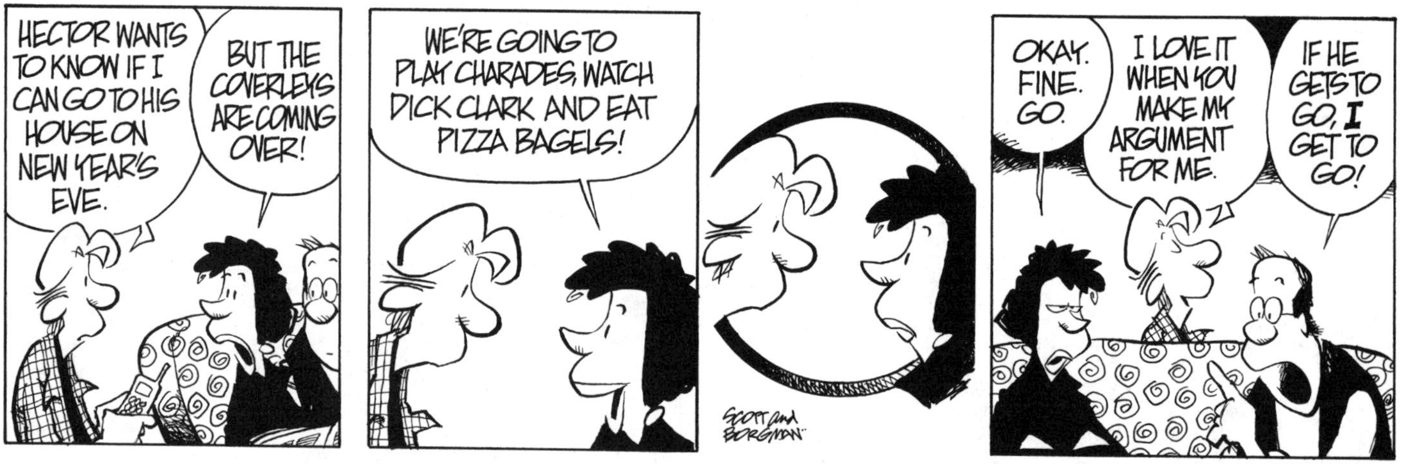
HECTOR WANTS TO KNOW IF I CAN GO TO HIS HOUSE ON NEW YEAR'S EVE.
BUT THE COVERLEYS ARE COMING OVER!
WE'RE GOING TO PLAY CHARADES, WATCH DICK CLARK AND EAT PIZZA BAGELS!
SCOTT AND BORGMAN
OKAY. FINE. GO.
I LOVE IT WHEN YOU MAKE MY ARGUMENT FOR ME.
IF HE GETS TO GO, I GET TO GO!

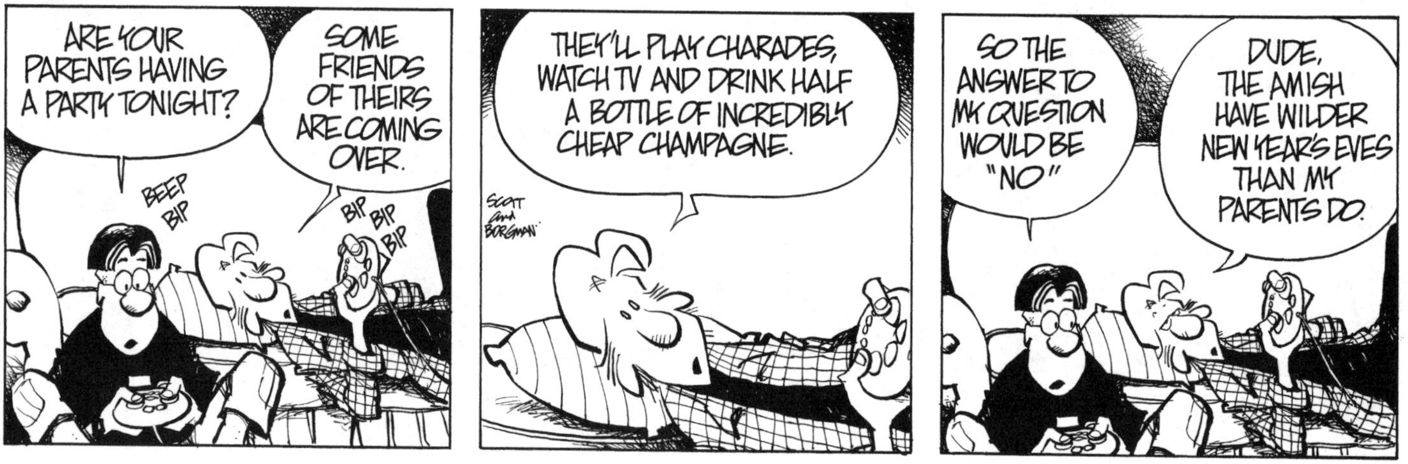
ARE YOUR PARENTS HAVING A PARTY TONIGHT?
BEEP BIP
SOME FRIENDS OF THEIRS ARE COMING OVER.
BIP BIP BIP
THEY'LL PLAY CHARADES, WATCH TV AND DRINK HALF A BOTTLE OF INCREDIBLY CHEAP CHAMPAGNE.
SCOTT AND BORGMAN
SO THE ANSWER TO MY QUESTION WOULD BE "NO"
DUDE, THE AMISH HAVE WILDER NEW YEAR'S EVES THAN MY PARENTS DO.

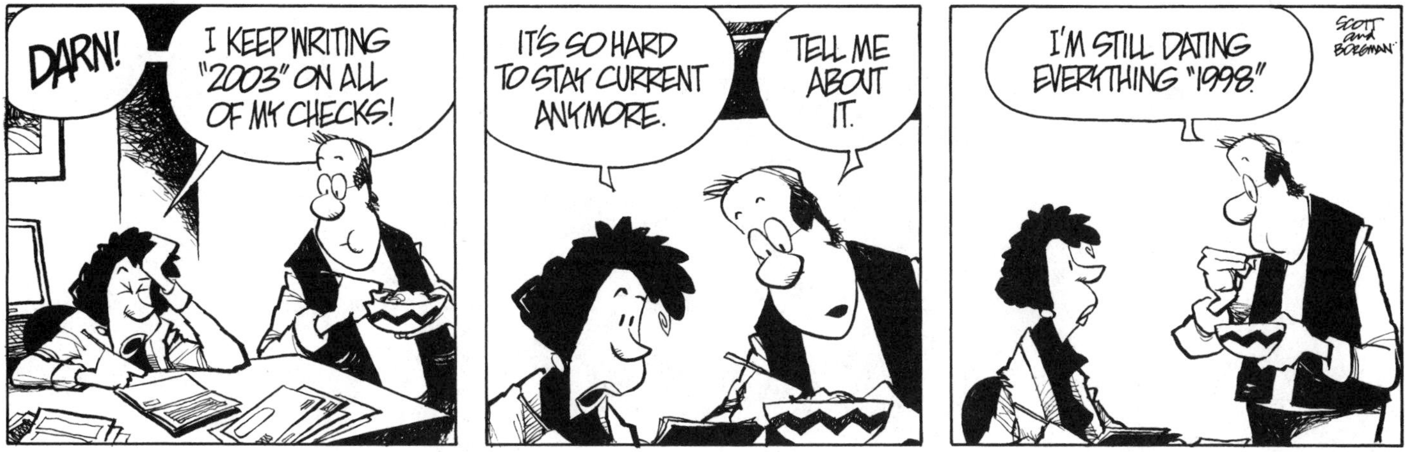
DARN!
I KEEP WRITING "2003" ON ALL OF MY CHECKS!
IT'S SO HARD TO STAY CURRENT ANYMORE.
TELL ME ABOUT IT.
I'M STILL DATING EVERYTHING "1998."
SCOTT and BORGMAN

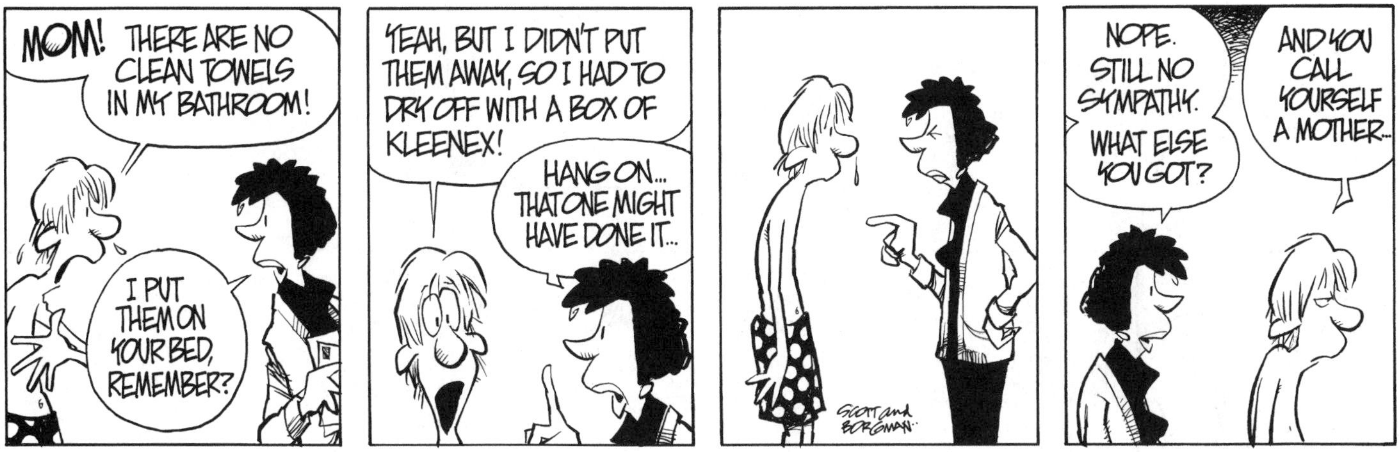
MOM! THERE ARE NO CLEAN TOWELS IN MY BATHROOM!
I PUT THEM ON YOUR BED, REMEMBER?
YEAH, BUT I DIDN'T PUT THEM AWAY, SO I HAD TO DRY OFF WITH A BOX OF KLEENEX!
HANG ON... THAT ONE MIGHT HAVE DONE IT...
SCOTT and BORGMAN
NOPE. STILL NO SYMPATHY.
WHAT ELSE YOU GOT?
AND YOU CALL YOURSELF A MOTHER...

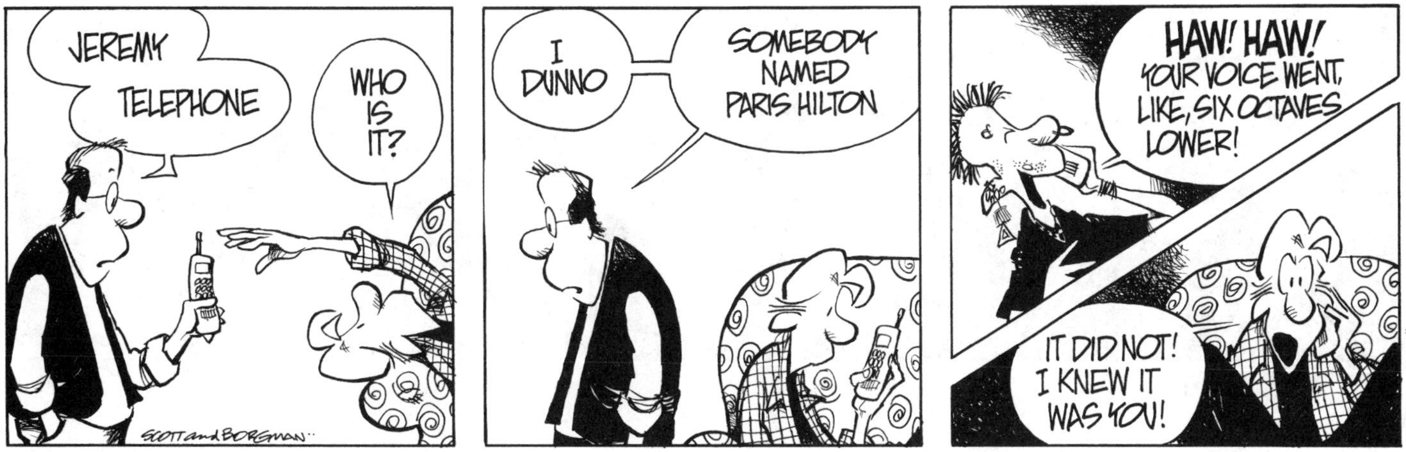
JEREMY
TELEPHONE
WHO IS IT?
SCOTT and BORGMAN
I DUNNO
SOMEBODY NAMED PARIS HILTON
HAW! HAW! YOUR VOICE WENT, LIKE, SIX OCTAVES LOWER!
IT DID NOT! I KNEW IT WAS YOU!

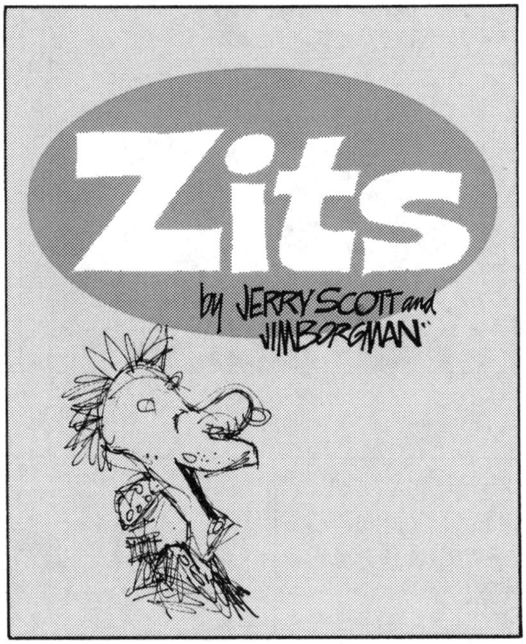
Zits
by JERRY SCOTT and JIM BORGMAN

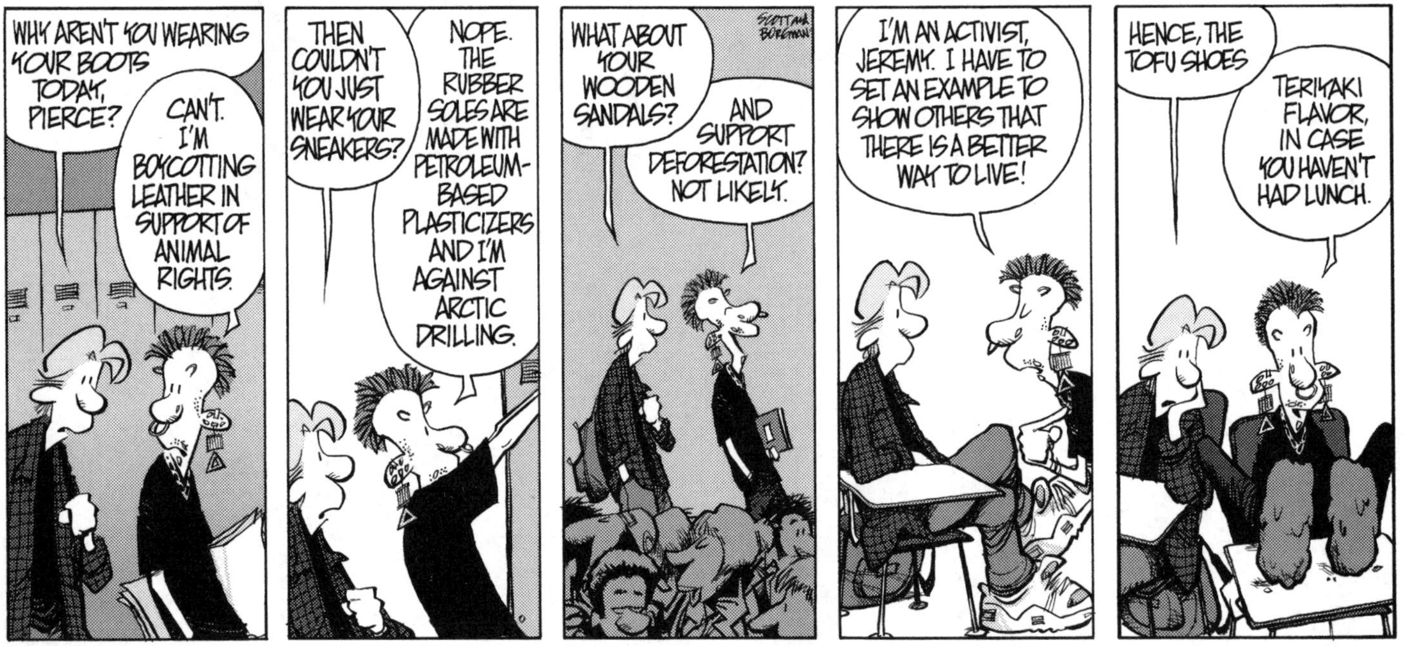
WHY AREN'T YOU WEARING YOUR BOOTS TODAY, PIERCE?
CAN'T. I'M BOYCOTTING LEATHER IN SUPPORT OF ANIMAL RIGHTS.
THEN COULDN'T YOU JUST WEAR YOUR SNEAKERS?
NOPE. THE RUBBER SOLES ARE MADE WITH PETROLEUM-BASED PLASTICIZERS AND I'M AGAINST ARCTIC DRILLING.
SCOTT and BORGMAN
WHAT ABOUT YOUR WOODEN SANDALS?
AND SUPPORT DEFORESTATION? NOT LIKELY.
I'M AN ACTIVIST, JEREMY. I HAVE TO SET AN EXAMPLE TO SHOW OTHERS THAT THERE IS A BETTER WAY TO LIVE!
HENCE, THE TOFU SHOES
TERIYAKI FLAVOR, IN CASE YOU HAVEN'T HAD LUNCH.

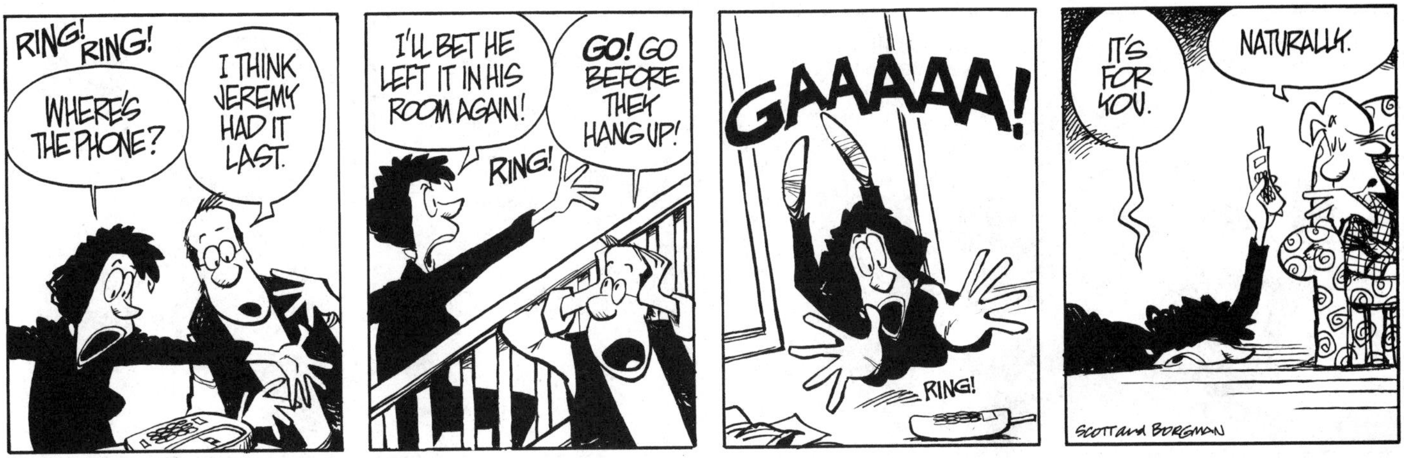
RING! RING!
WHERE'S THE PHONE?
I THINK JEREMY HAD IT LAST.
I'LL BET HE LEFT IT IN HIS ROOM AGAIN!
RING!
GO! GO BEFORE THEY HANG UP!
GAAAAA!
RING!
IT'S FOR YOU.
NATURALLY.
SCOTT and BORGMAN

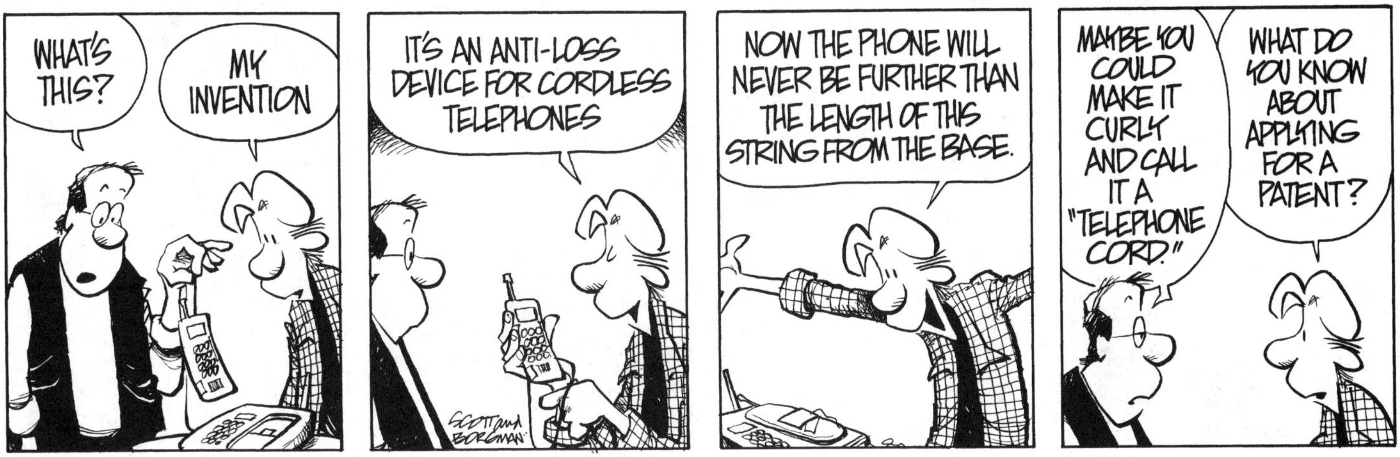
WHAT'S THIS?
MY INVENTION
IT'S AN ANTI-LOSS DEVICE FOR CORDLESS TELEPHONES
SCOTT and BORGMAN
NOW THE PHONE WILL NEVER BE FURTHER THAN THE LENGTH OF THIS STRING FROM THE BASE.
MAYBE YOU COULD MAKE IT CURLY AND CALL IT A "TELEPHONE CORD."
WHAT DO YOU KNOW ABOUT APPLYING FOR A PATENT?

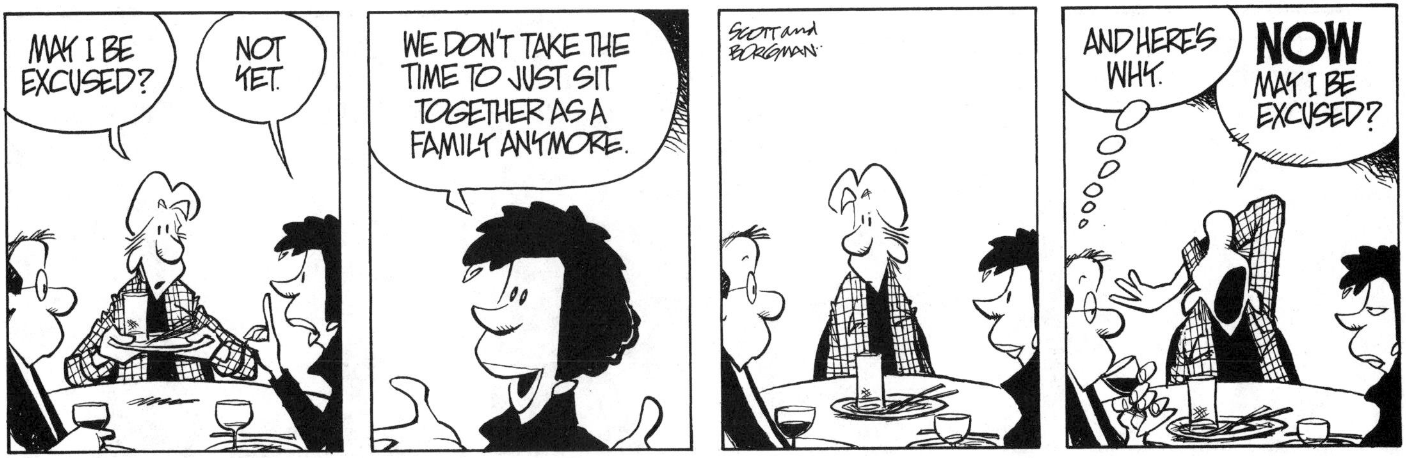
MAY I BE EXCUSED?
NOT YET.
WE DON'T TAKE THE TIME TO JUST SIT TOGETHER AS A FAMILY ANYMORE.
SCOTT and BORGMAN
AND HERE'S WHY.
NOW MAY I BE EXCUSED?

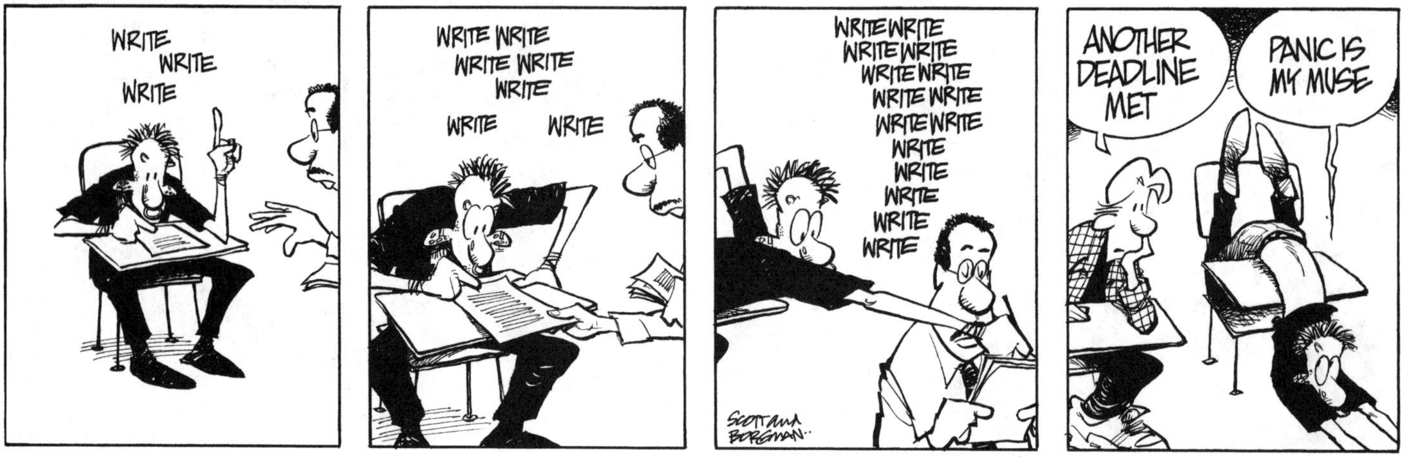
WRITE
WRITE
WRITE
WRITE WRITE
WRITE WRITE
WRITE
WRITE
WRITE
WRITE WRITE
WRITE WRITE
WRITE WRITE
WRITE WRITE
WRITE WRITE
WRITE
WRITE
WRITE
WRITE
WRITE
SCOTT AND BORGMAN
ANOTHER DEADLINE MET
PANIC IS MY MUSE

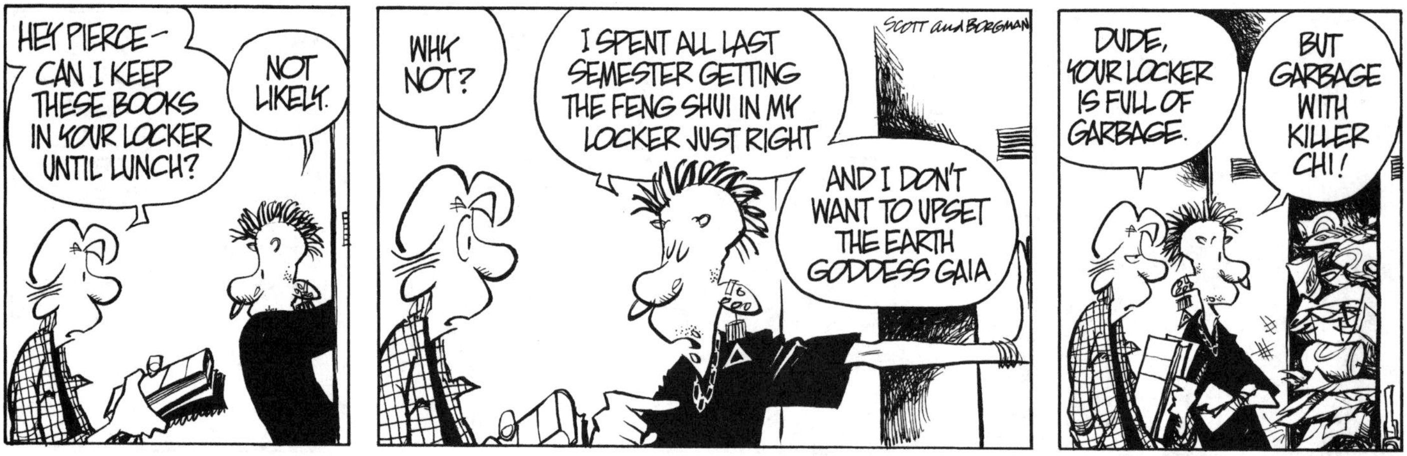
HEY PIERCE- CAN I KEEP THESE BOOKS IN YOUR LOCKER UNTIL LUNCH?
NOT LIKELY.
WHY NOT?
I SPENT ALL LAST SEMESTER GETTING THE FENG SHUI IN MY LOCKER JUST RIGHT
AND I DON'T WANT TO UPSET THE EARTH GODDESS GAIA
SCOTT AND BORGMAN
DUDE, YOUR LOCKER IS FULL OF GARBAGE.
BUT GARBAGE WITH KILLER CHI!

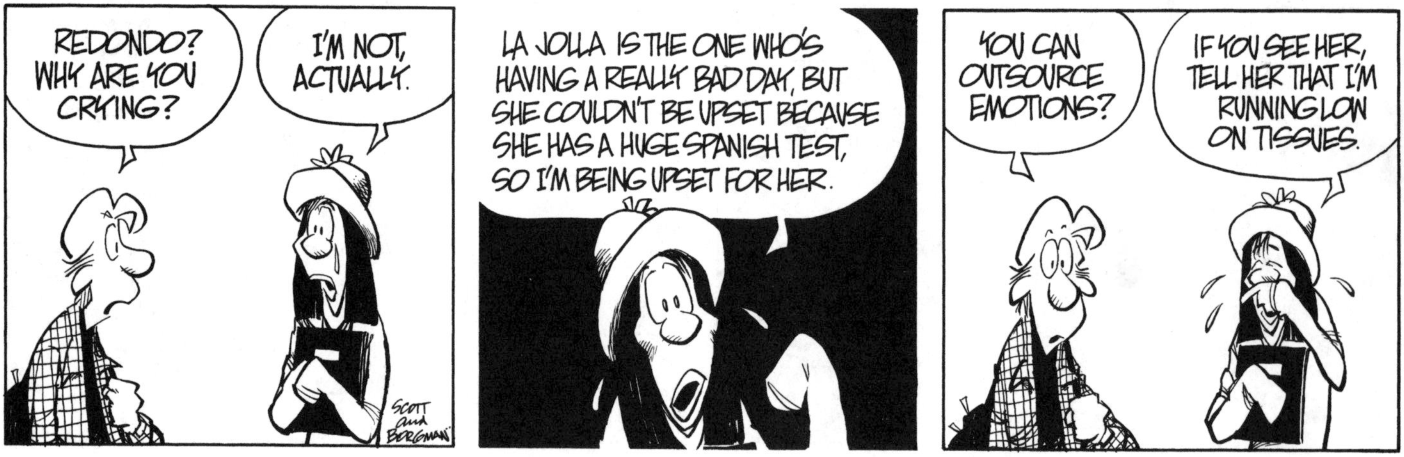
REDONDO? WHY ARE YOU CRYING?
I'M NOT, ACTUALLY.
SCOTT AND BORGMAN
LA JOLLA IS THE ONE WHO'S HAVING A REALLY BAD DAY, BUT SHE COULDN'T BE UPSET BECAUSE SHE HAS A HUGE SPANISH TEST, SO I'M BEING UPSET FOR HER.
YOU CAN OUTSOURCE EMOTIONS?
IF YOU SEE HER, TELL HER THAT I'M RUNNING LOW ON TISSUES.

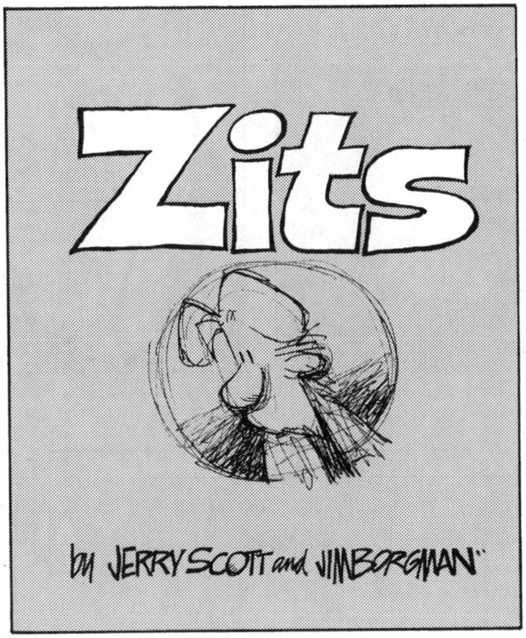
Zits
by JERRY SCOTT and JIM BORGMAN

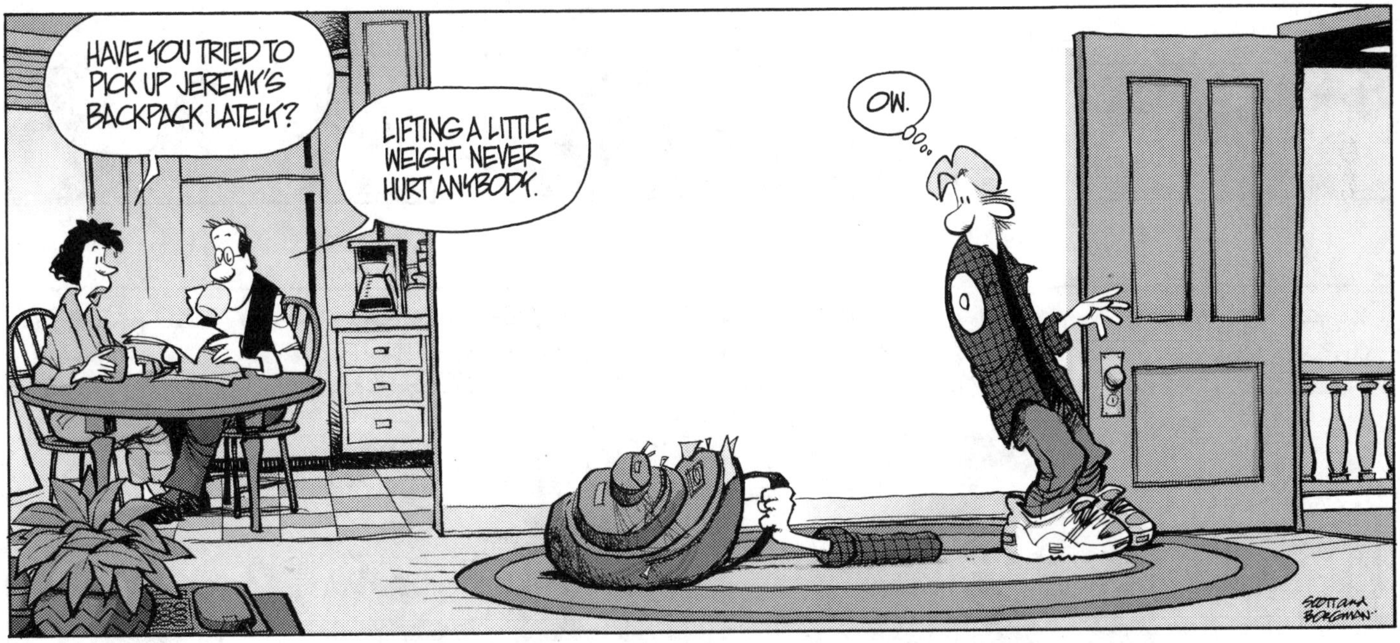
HAVE YOU TRIED TO PICK UP JEREMY'S BACKPACK LATELY?
LIFTING A LITTLE WEIGHT NEVER HURT ANYBODY.
OW.
SCOTT and BORGMAN

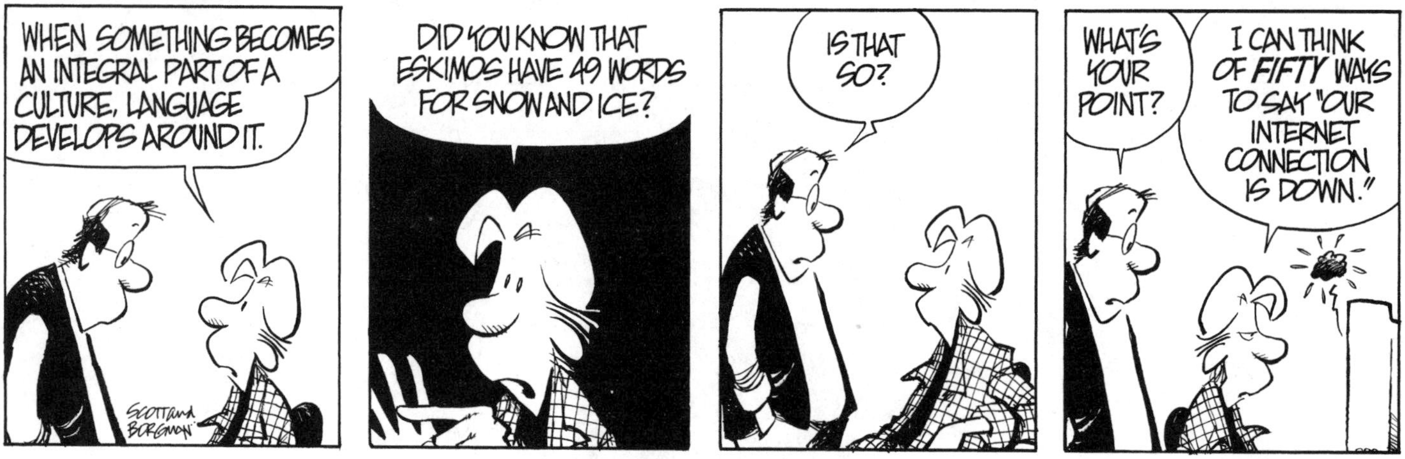
WHEN SOMETHING BECOMES AN INTEGRAL PART OF A CULTURE, LANGUAGE DEVELOPS AROUND IT.
DID YOU KNOW THAT ESKIMOS HAVE 49 WORDS FOR SNOW AND ICE?
IS THAT SO?
WHAT'S YOUR POINT?
I CAN THINK OF **FIFTY** WAYS TO SAY "OUR INTERNET CONNECTION IS DOWN."

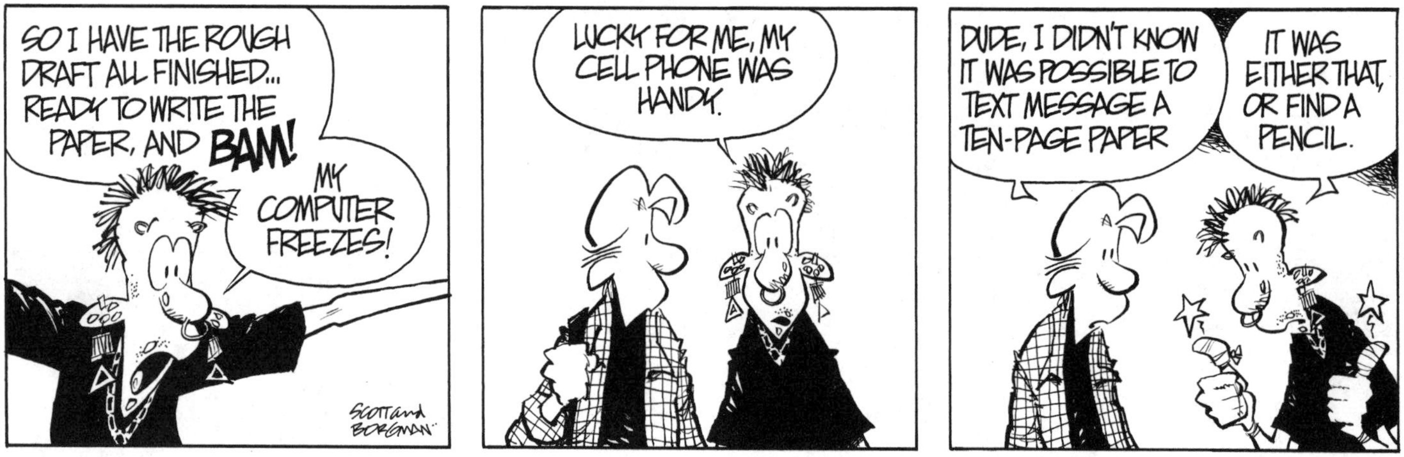
SO I HAVE THE ROUGH DRAFT ALL FINISHED... READY TO WRITE THE PAPER, AND **BAM!**
MY COMPUTER FREEZES!
LUCKY FOR ME, MY CELL PHONE WAS HANDY.
DUDE, I DIDN'T KNOW IT WAS POSSIBLE TO TEXT MESSAGE A TEN-PAGE PAPER
IT WAS EITHER THAT, OR FIND A PENCIL.

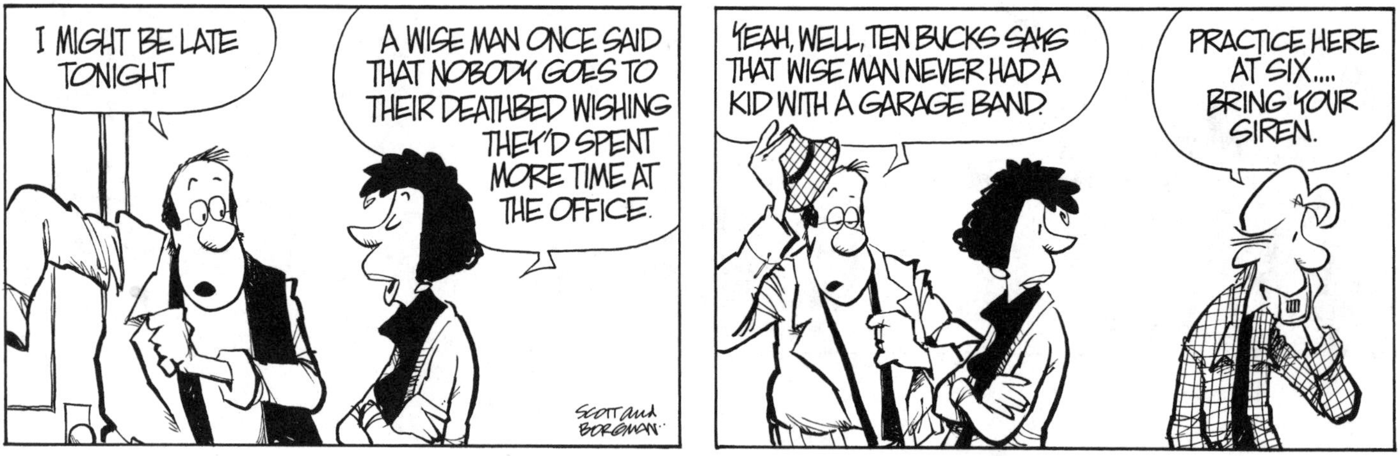
I MIGHT BE LATE TONIGHT
A WISE MAN ONCE SAID THAT NOBODY GOES TO THEIR DEATHBED WISHING THEY'D SPENT MORE TIME AT THE OFFICE.
YEAH, WELL, TEN BUCKS SAYS THAT WISE MAN NEVER HAD A KID WITH A GARAGE BAND.
PRACTICE HERE AT SIX.... BRING YOUR SIREN.

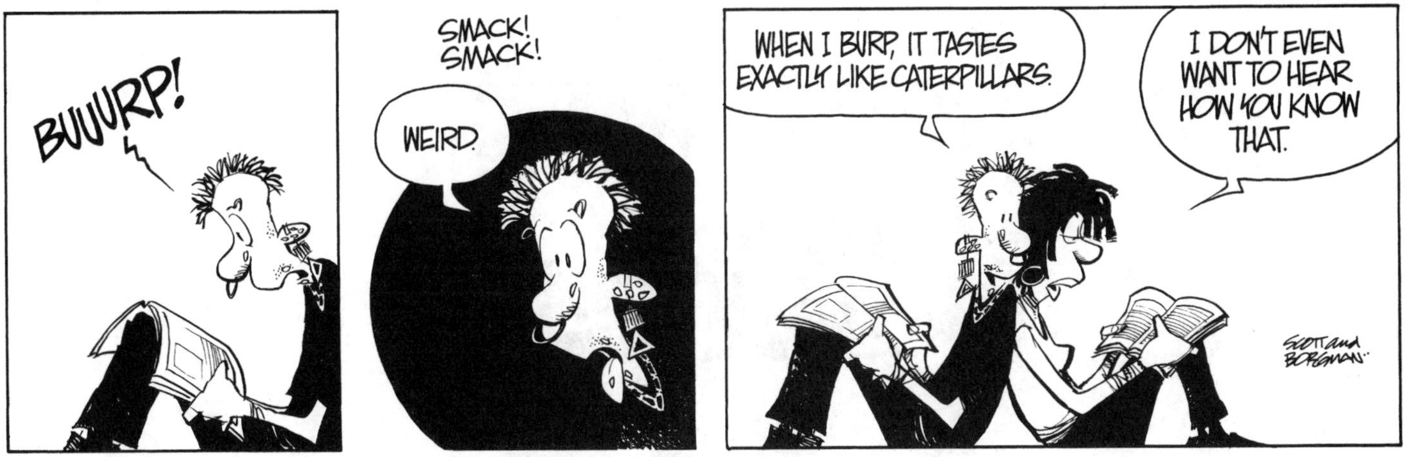
BUUURP!
SMACK! SMACK!
WEIRD.
WHEN I BURP, IT TASTES EXACTLY LIKE CATERPILLARS.
I DON'T EVEN WANT TO HEAR HOW YOU KNOW THAT.
SCOTT and BORGMAN

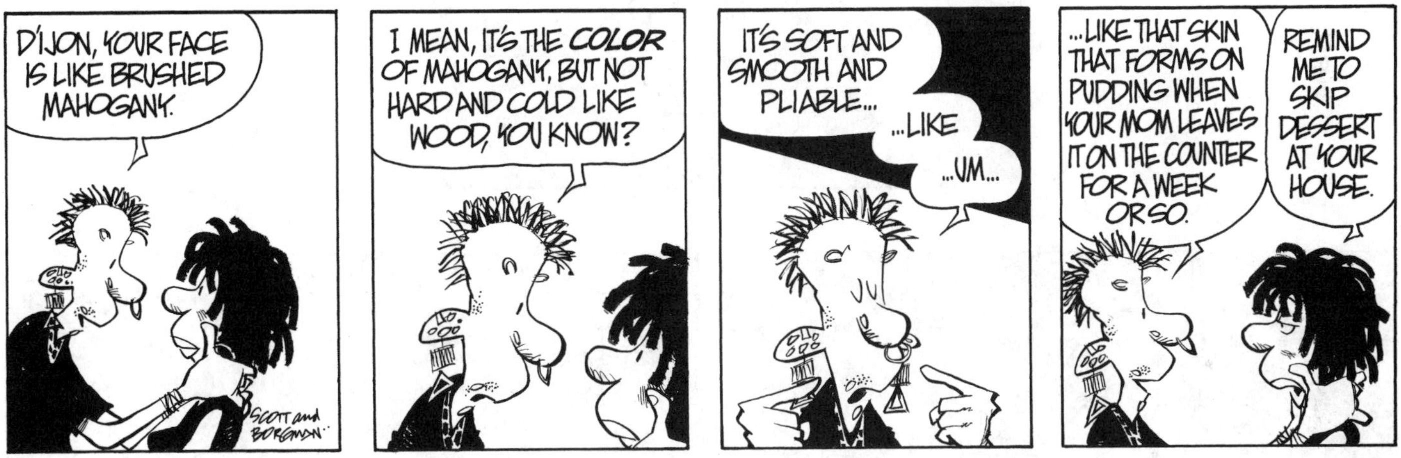
D'JON, YOUR FACE IS LIKE BRUSHED MAHOGANY.
SCOTT and BORGMAN
I MEAN, IT'S THE COLOR OF MAHOGANY, BUT NOT HARD AND COLD LIKE WOOD, YOU KNOW?
IT'S SOFT AND SMOOTH AND PLIABLE...
...LIKE
...UM...
...LIKE THAT SKIN THAT FORMS ON PUDDING WHEN YOUR MOM LEAVES IT ON THE COUNTER FOR A WEEK OR SO.
REMIND ME TO SKIP DESSERT AT YOUR HOUSE.

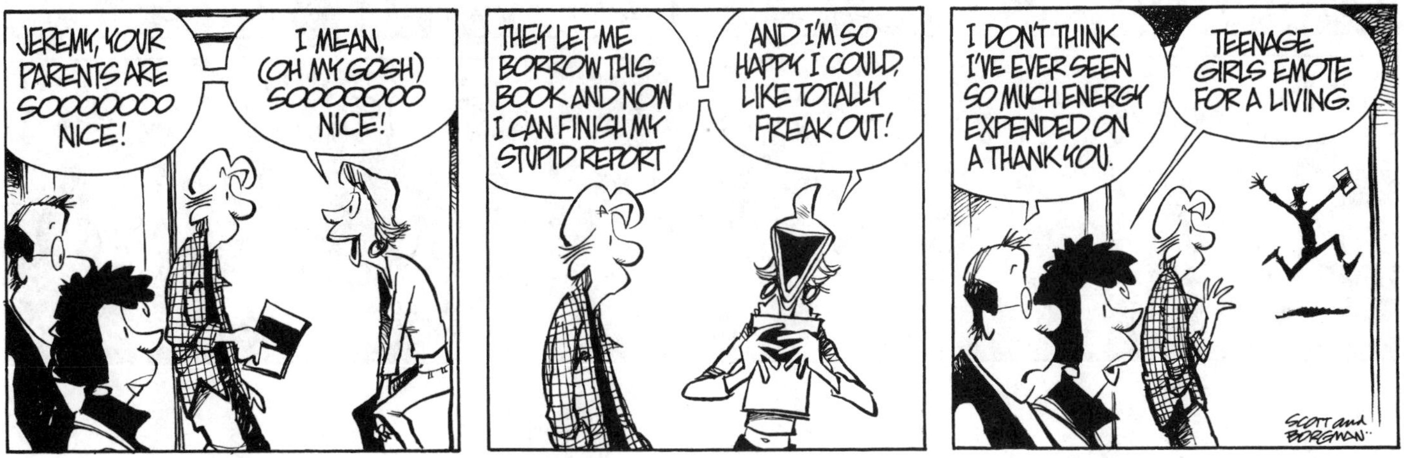
JEREMY, YOUR PARENTS ARE SOOOOOOO NICE!
I MEAN, (OH MY GOSH) SOOOOOOO NICE!
THEY LET ME BORROW THIS BOOK AND NOW I CAN FINISH MY STUPID REPORT
AND I'M SO HAPPY I COULD, LIKE TOTALLY FREAK OUT!
I DON'T THINK I'VE EVER SEEN SO MUCH ENERGY EXPENDED ON A THANK YOU.
TEENAGE GIRLS EMOTE FOR A LIVING.
SCOTT and BORGMAN

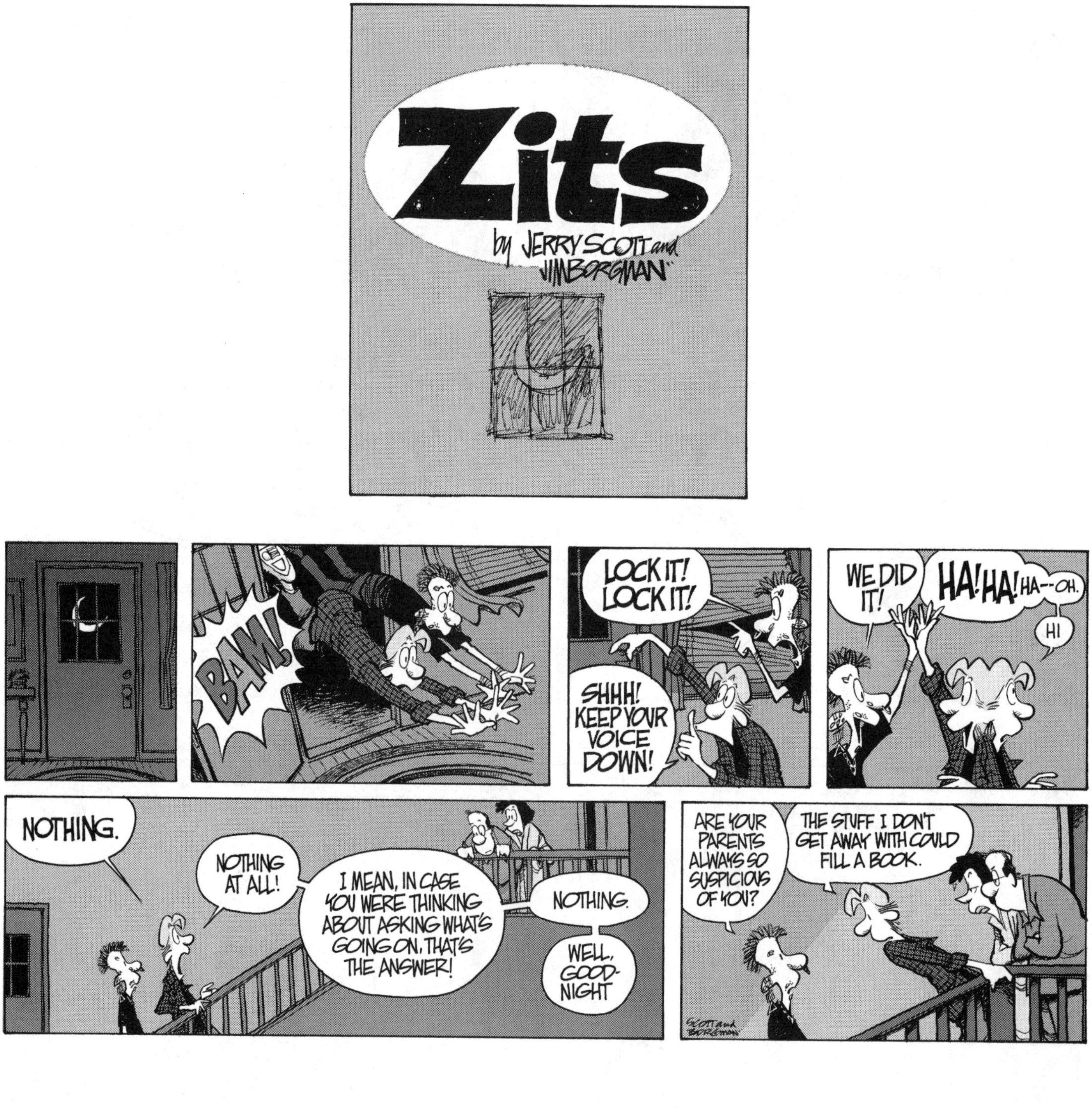
Zits
by JERRY SCOTT and JIM BORGMAN
BAM!
LOCK IT! LOCK IT!
SHHH! KEEP YOUR VOICE DOWN!
WE DID IT!
HA! HA! HA--OH.
HI
NOTHING.
NOTHING AT ALL!
I MEAN, IN CASE YOU WERE THINKING ABOUT ASKING WHAT'S GOING ON, THAT'S THE ANSWER!
NOTHING.
WELL, GOOD-NIGHT
ARE YOUR PARENTS ALWAYS SO SUSPICIOUS OF YOU?
THE STUFF I DON'T GET AWAY WITH COULD FILL A BOOK.

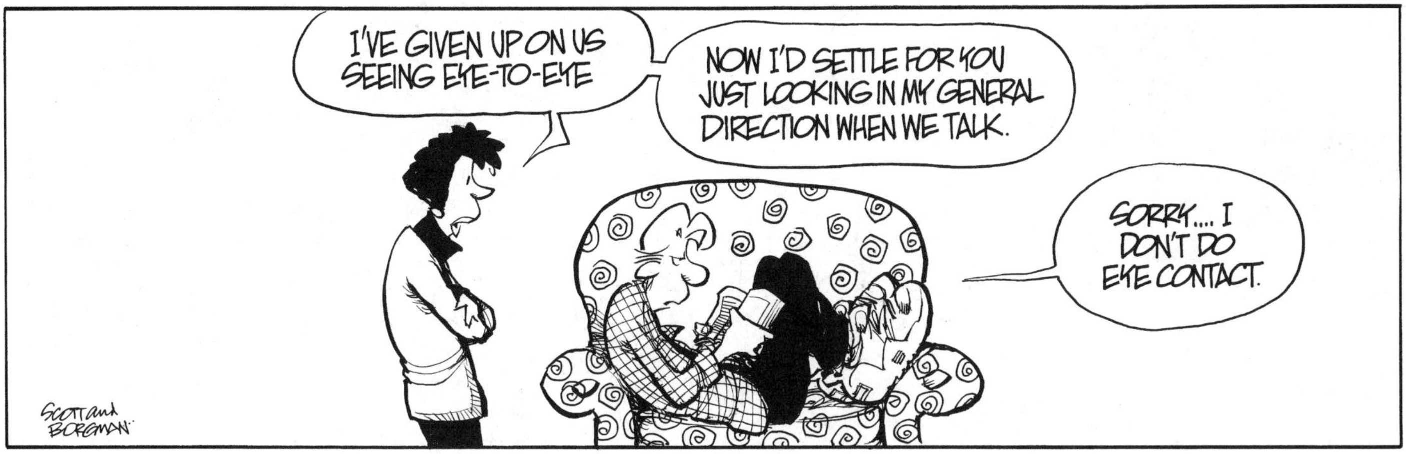
I'VE GIVEN UP ON US SEEING EYE-TO-EYE
NOW I'D SETTLE FOR YOU JUST LOOKING IN MY GENERAL DIRECTION WHEN WE TALK.
SORRY.... I DON'T DO EYE CONTACT.
SCOTT and BORGMAN

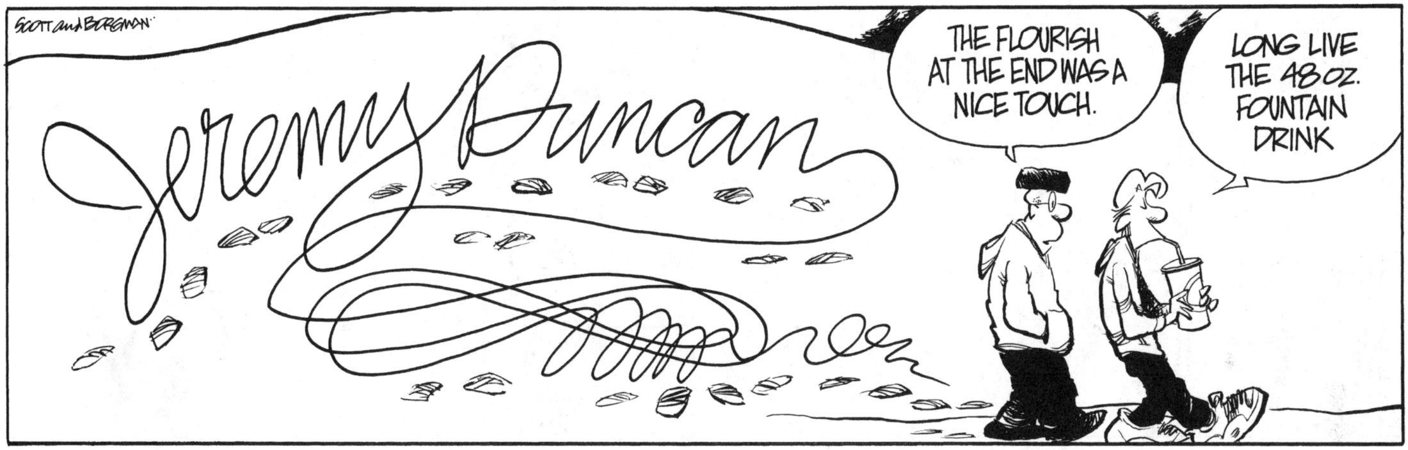
SCOTT and BORGMAN
Jeremy Duncan
THE FLOURISH AT THE END WAS A NICE TOUCH.
LONG LIVE THE 48 OZ. FOUNTAIN DRINK

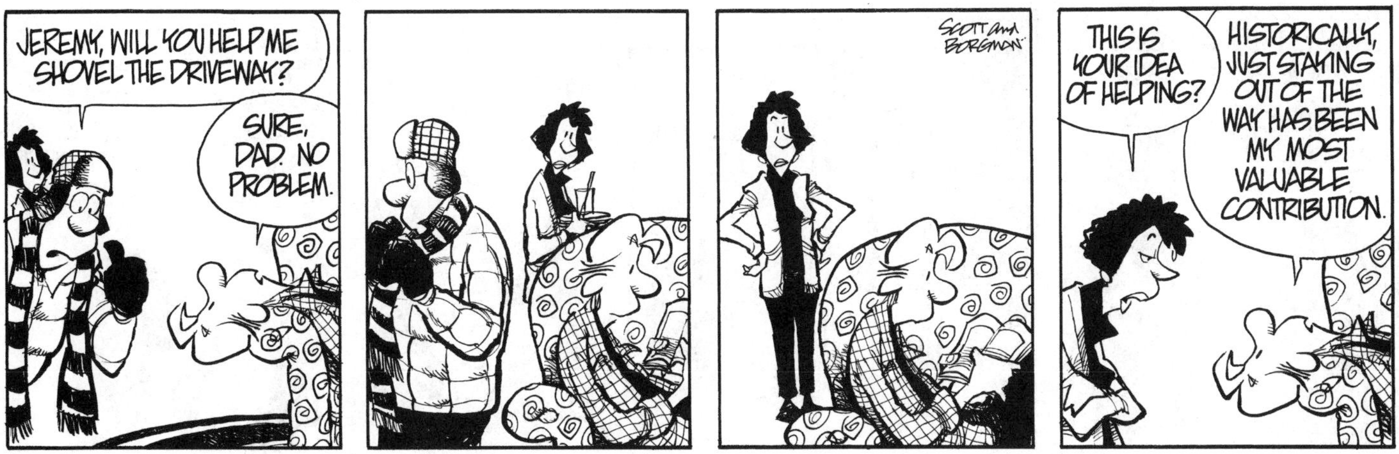
JEREMY, WILL YOU HELP ME SHOVEL THE DRIVEWAY?
SURE, DAD. NO PROBLEM.
SCOTT and BORGMAN
THIS IS YOUR IDEA OF HELPING?
HISTORICALLY, JUST STAYING OUT OF THE WAY HAS BEEN MY MOST VALUABLE CONTRIBUTION.

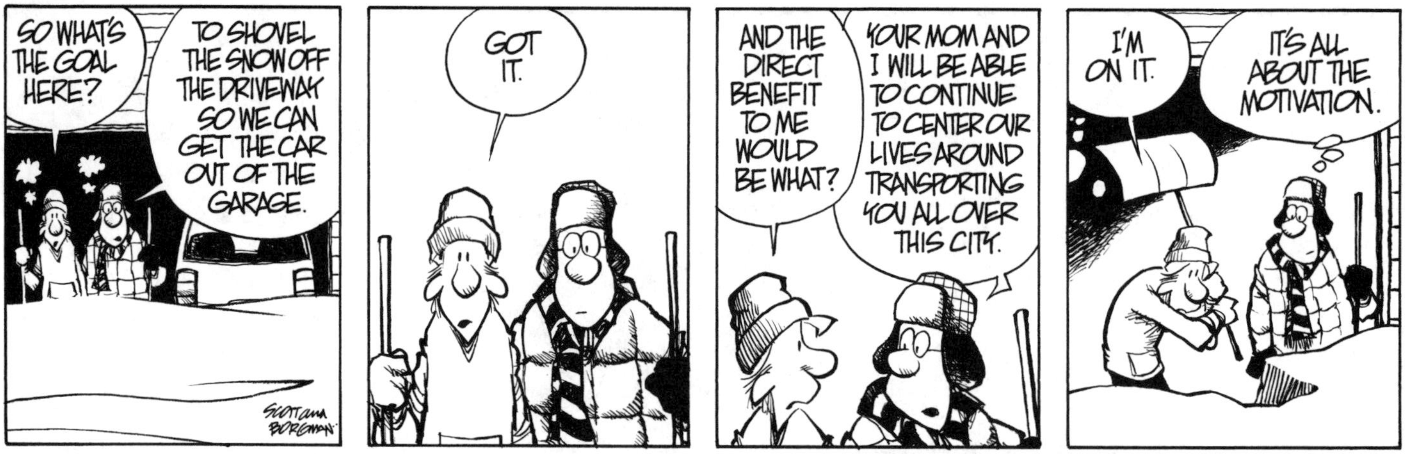
SO WHAT'S THE GOAL HERE?
TO SHOVEL THE SNOW OFF THE DRIVEWAY SO WE CAN GET THE CAR OUT OF THE GARAGE.
SCOTT and BORGMAN
GOT IT.
AND THE DIRECT BENEFIT TO ME WOULD BE WHAT?
YOUR MOM AND I WILL BE ABLE TO CONTINUE TO CENTER OUR LIVES AROUND TRANSPORTING YOU ALL OVER THIS CITY.
I'M ON IT.
IT'S ALL ABOUT THE MOTIVATION.

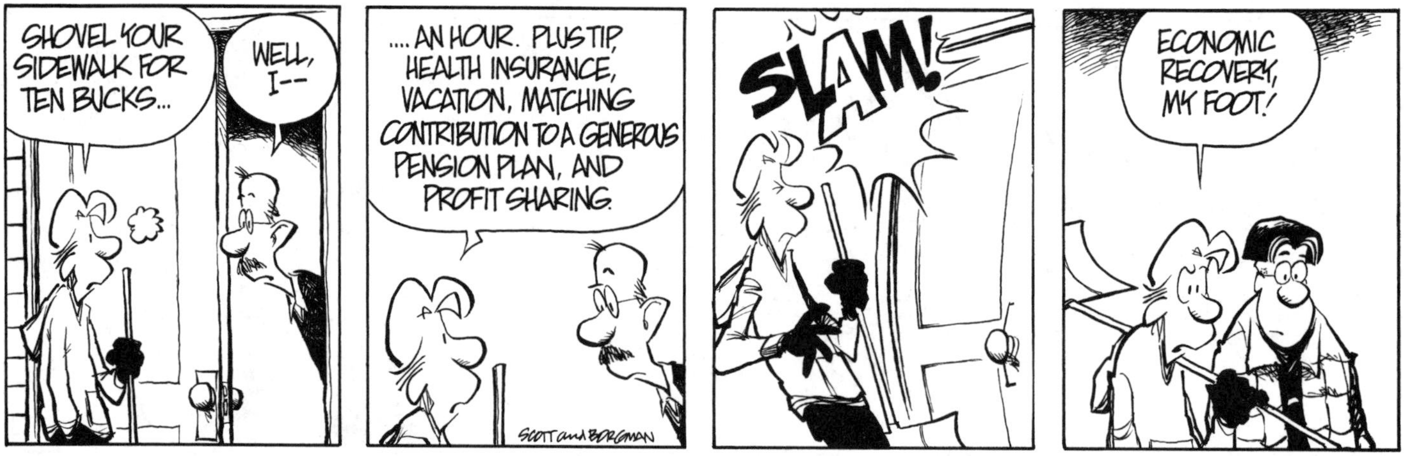
SHOVEL YOUR SIDEWALK FOR TEN BUCKS...
WELL, I--
....AN HOUR. PLUS TIP, HEALTH INSURANCE, VACATION, MATCHING CONTRIBUTION TO A GENEROUS PENSION PLAN, AND PROFIT SHARING.
SCOTT and BORGMAN
SLAM!
ECONOMIC RECOVERY, MY FOOT!

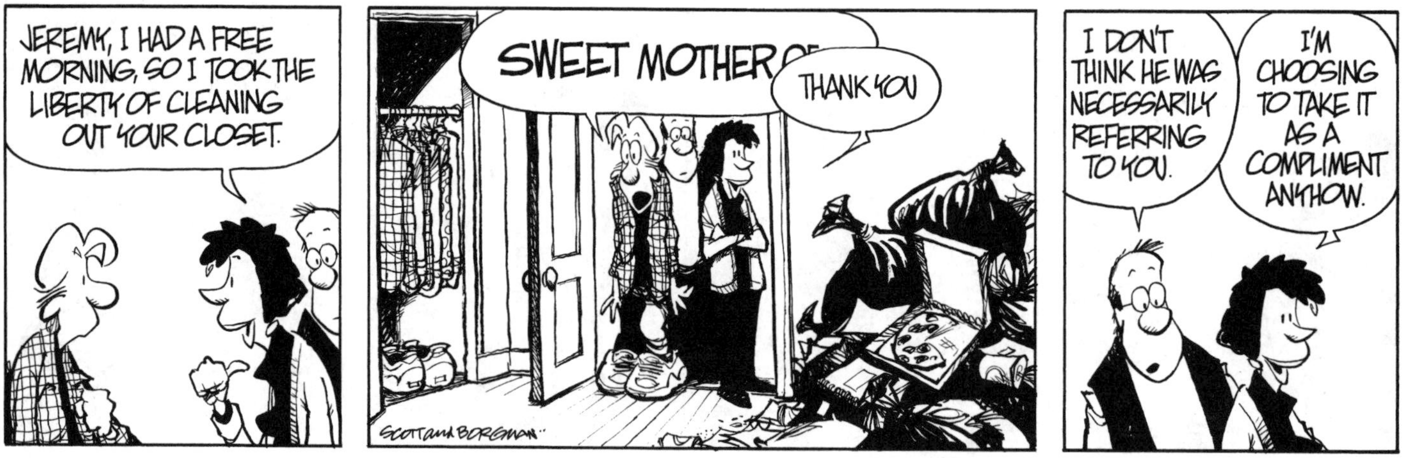
JEREMY, I HAD A FREE MORNING, SO I TOOK THE LIBERTY OF CLEANING OUT YOUR CLOSET.
SWEET MOTHER
THANK YOU
SCOTT and BORGMAN
I DON'T THINK HE WAS NECESSARILY REFERRING TO YOU.
I'M CHOOSING TO TAKE IT AS A COMPLIMENT ANYHOW.

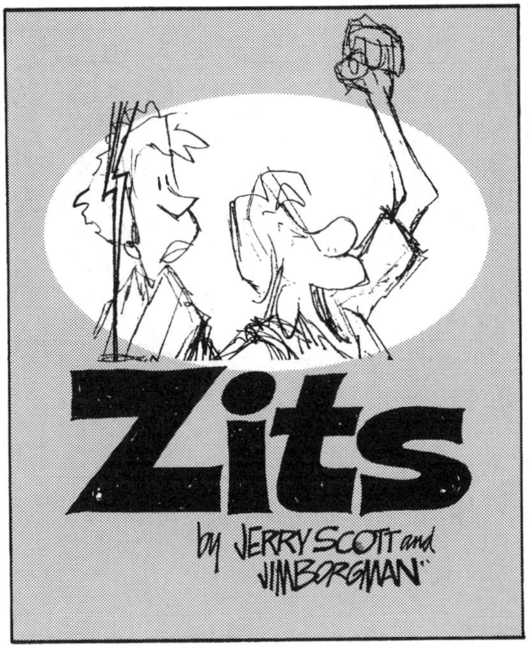
Zits
by JERRY SCOTT and JIM BORGMAN

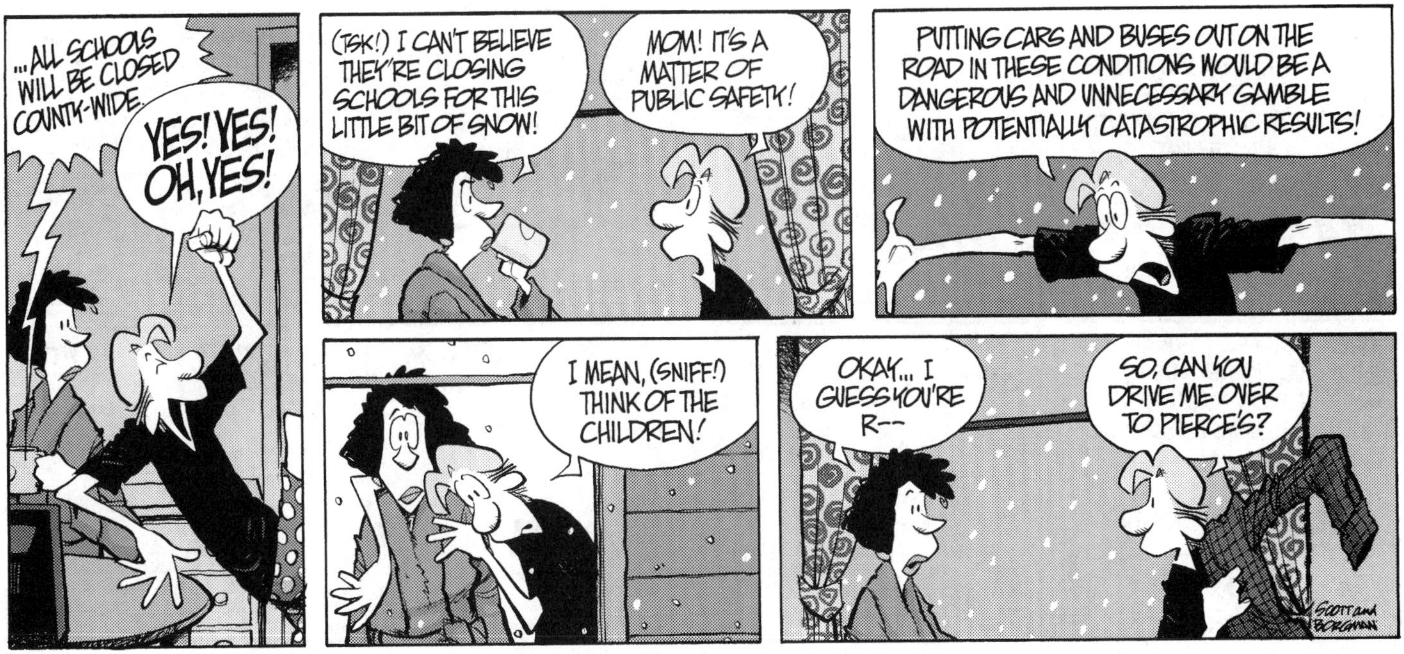
...ALL SCHOOLS WILL BE CLOSED COUNTY-WIDE.
YES! YES! OH, YES!
(TSK!) I CAN'T BELIEVE THEY'RE CLOSING SCHOOLS FOR THIS LITTLE BIT OF SNOW!
MOM! IT'S A MATTER OF PUBLIC SAFETY!
PUTTING CARS AND BUSES OUT ON THE ROAD IN THESE CONDITIONS WOULD BE A DANGEROUS AND UNNECESSARY GAMBLE WITH POTENTIALLY CATASTROPHIC RESULTS!
I MEAN, (SNIFF!) THINK OF THE CHILDREN!
OKAY... I GUESS YOU'RE R--
SO, CAN YOU DRIVE ME OVER TO PIERCE'S?
SCOTT and BORGMAN

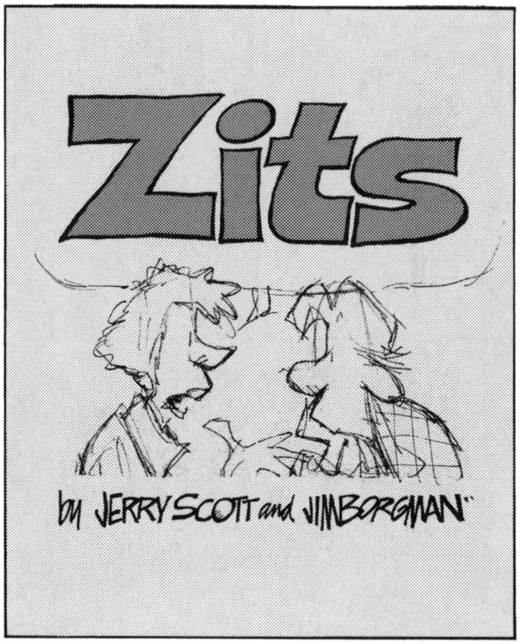
Zits
by JERRY SCOTT and JIM BORGMAN

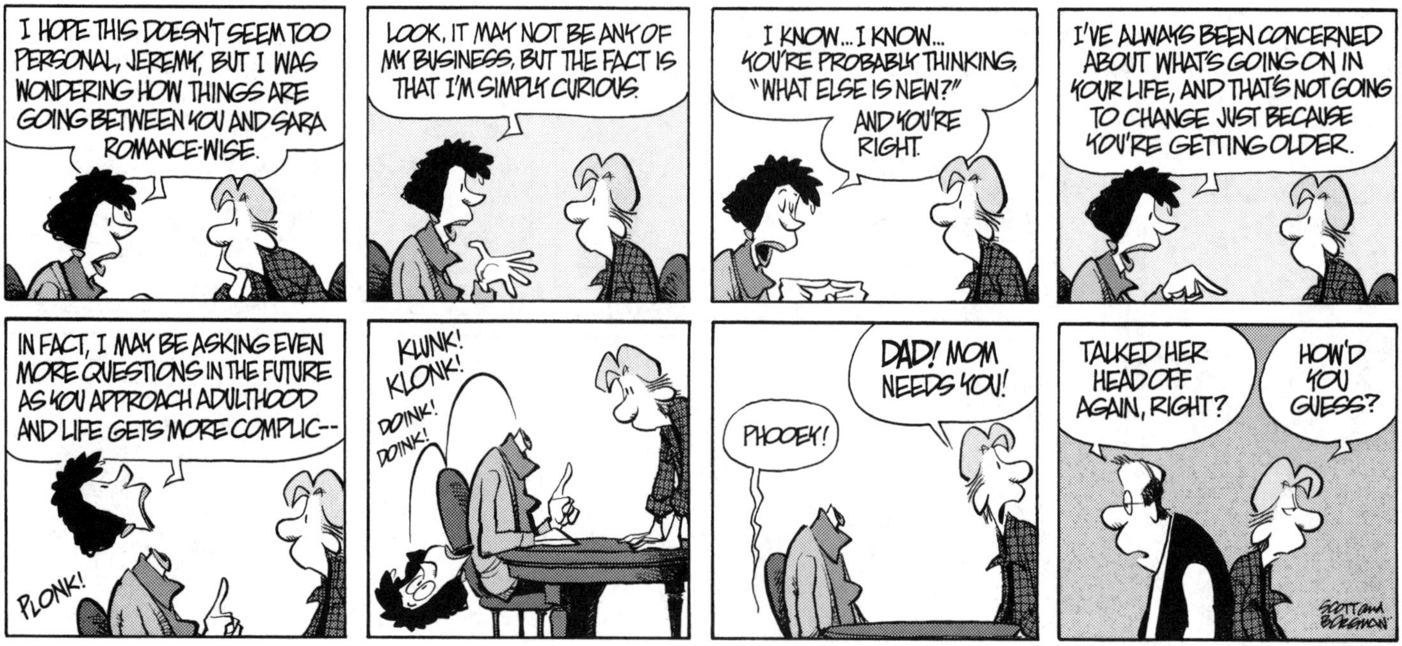
I HOPE THIS DOESN'T SEEM TOO PERSONAL, JEREMY, BUT I WAS WONDERING HOW THINGS ARE GOING BETWEEN YOU AND SARA ROMANCE-WISE.
LOOK, IT MAY NOT BE ANY OF MY BUSINESS, BUT THE FACT IS THAT I'M SIMPLY CURIOUS.
I KNOW... I KNOW... YOU'RE PROBABLY THINKING, "WHAT ELSE IS NEW?"
AND YOU'RE RIGHT.
I'VE ALWAYS BEEN CONCERNED ABOUT WHAT'S GOING ON IN YOUR LIFE, AND THAT'S NOT GOING TO CHANGE JUST BECAUSE YOU'RE GETTING OLDER.
IN FACT, I MAY BE ASKING EVEN MORE QUESTIONS IN THE FUTURE AS YOU APPROACH ADULTHOOD AND LIFE GETS MORE COMPLIC--
PLONK!
KLUNK! KLONK!
DOINK! DOINK!
DAD! MOM NEEDS YOU!
PHOOEY!
TALKED HER HEAD OFF AGAIN, RIGHT?
HOW'D YOU GUESS?
SCOTT and BORGMAN

WHAT'S WITH ALL OF THE INDEX CARDS, JEREMY?

WE HAVE TO DO A GROUP PROJECT FOR GOVERNMENT CLASS, AND I'M DECIDING WHO I WANT TO WORK WITH.

THE MOST IMPORTANT THING IS TO BE SURE THAT THERE'S AT LEAST ONE GIRL ON THE TEAM.

SO THE GROUP IS DIVERSE AND BALANCED?

SO SOME OF THE WORK GETS DONE ON TIME.

SCOTT and BORGMAN

SCOTT and BORGMAN

YOUR LOCKER IS, LIKE, WHOA!

FLATTERER

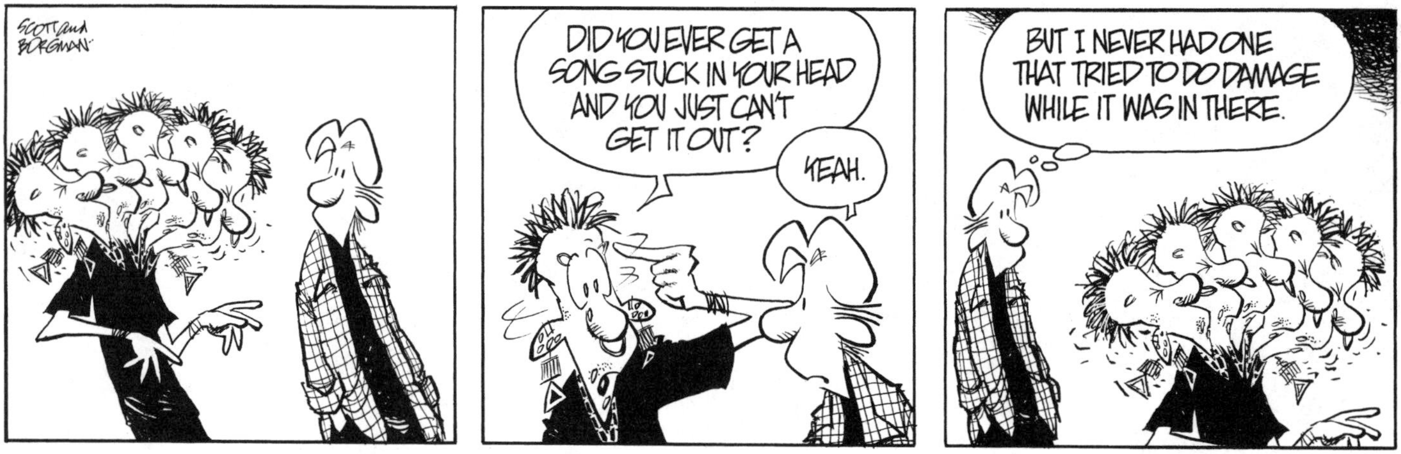
SCOTT and BORGMAN
DID YOU EVER GET A SONG STUCK IN YOUR HEAD AND YOU JUST CAN'T GET IT OUT?
YEAH.
BUT I NEVER HAD ONE THAT TRIED TO DO DAMAGE WHILE IT WAS IN THERE.

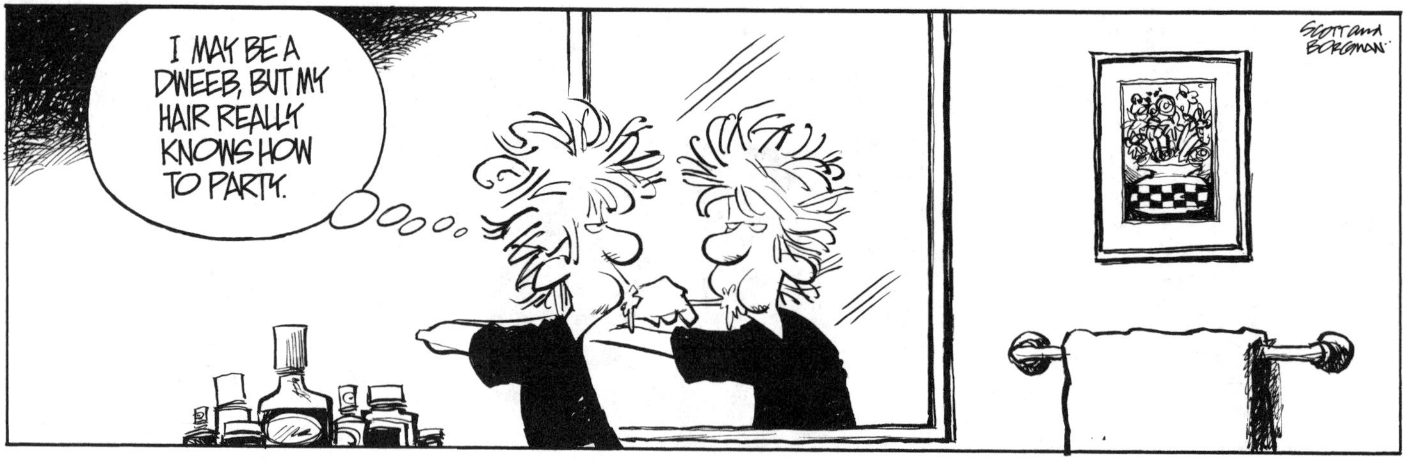
I MAY BE A DWEEB, BUT MY HAIR REALLY KNOWS HOW TO PARTY.
SCOTT and BORGMAN

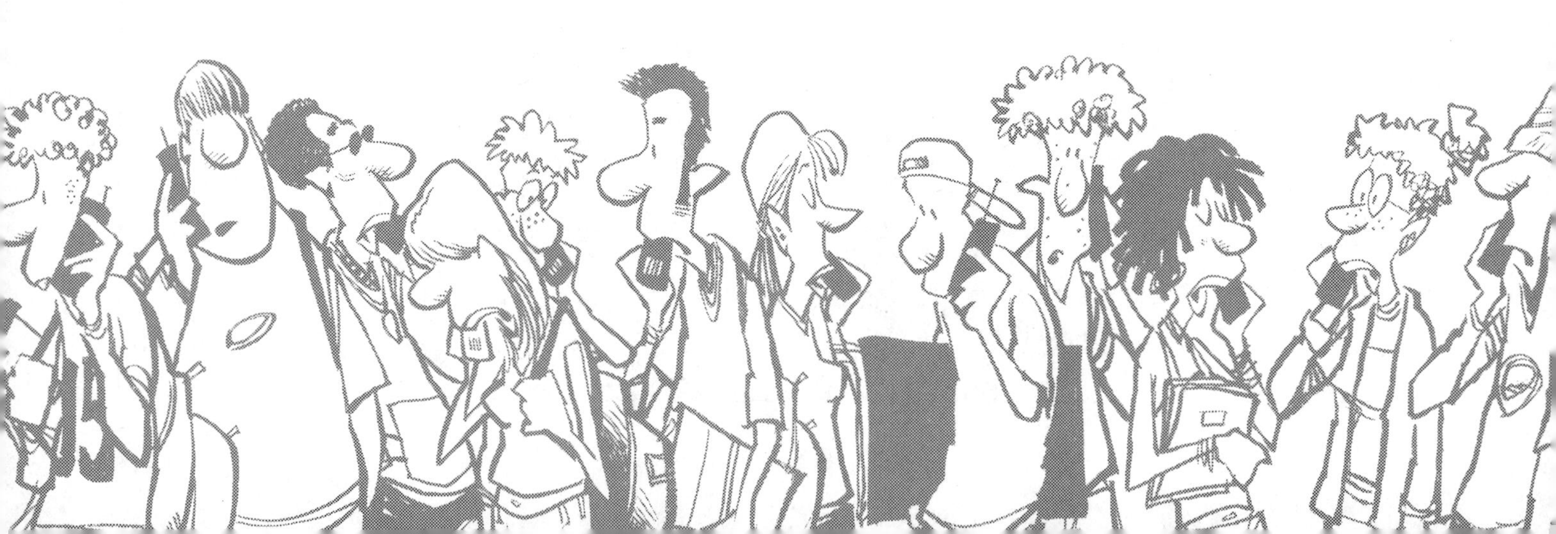

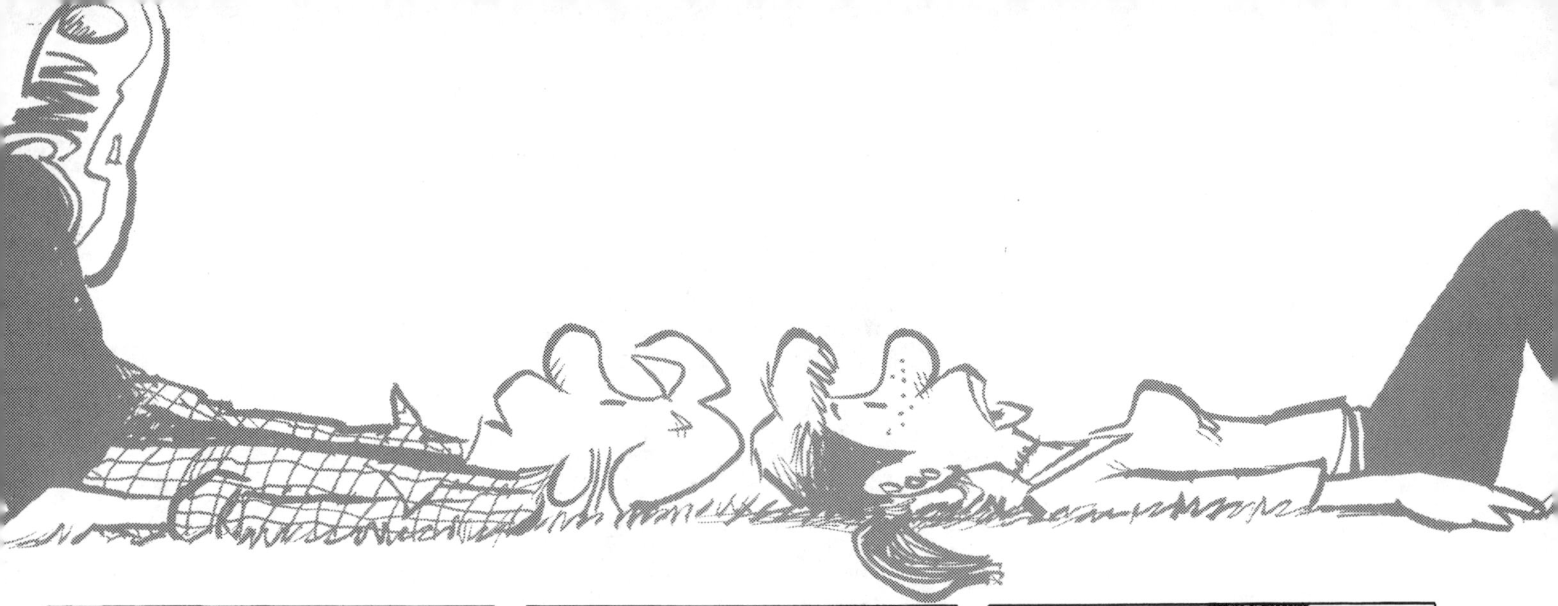

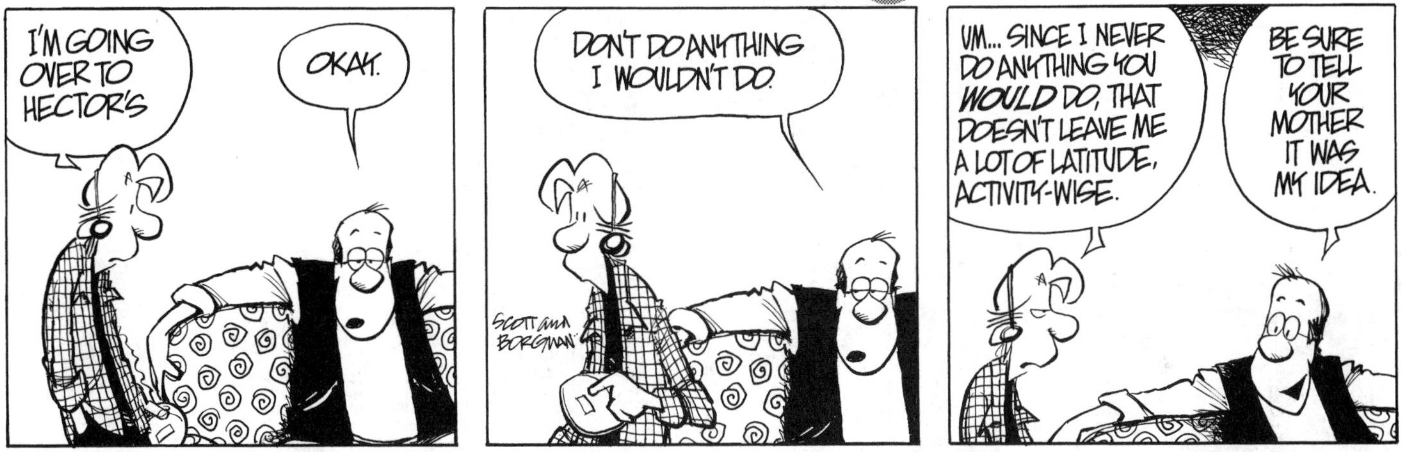
I'M GOING OVER TO HECTOR'S
OKAY.
DON'T DO ANYTHING I WOULDN'T DO.
SCOTT and BORGMAN
UM... SINCE I NEVER DO ANYTHING YOU **WOULD** DO, THAT DOESN'T LEAVE ME A LOT OF LATITUDE, ACTIVITY-WISE.
BE SURE TO TELL YOUR MOTHER IT WAS MY IDEA.

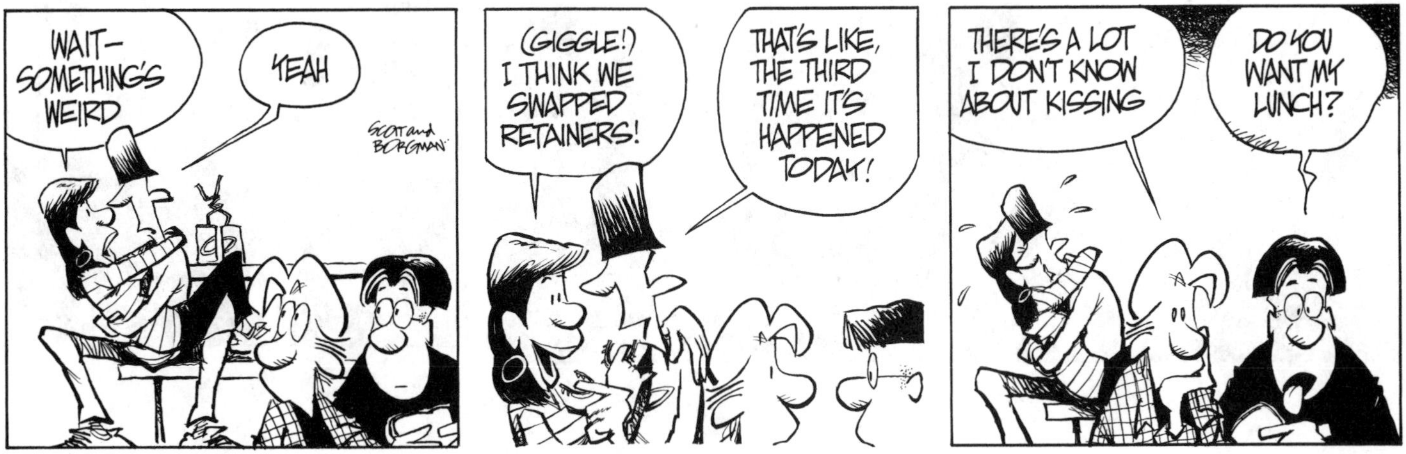
WAIT- SOMETHING'S WEIRD
YEAH
SCOTT and BORGMAN
(GIGGLE!) I THINK WE SWAPPED RETAINERS!
THAT'S LIKE, THE THIRD TIME IT'S HAPPENED TODAY!
THERE'S A LOT I DON'T KNOW ABOUT KISSING
DO YOU WANT MY LUNCH?

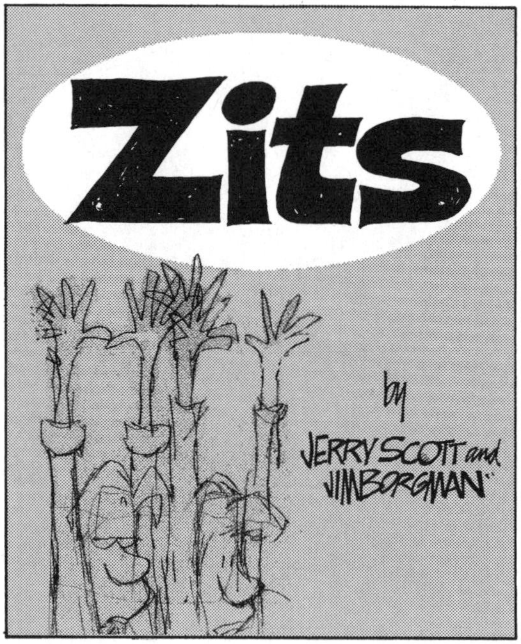
Zits
by
JERRY SCOTT and
JIM BORGMAN

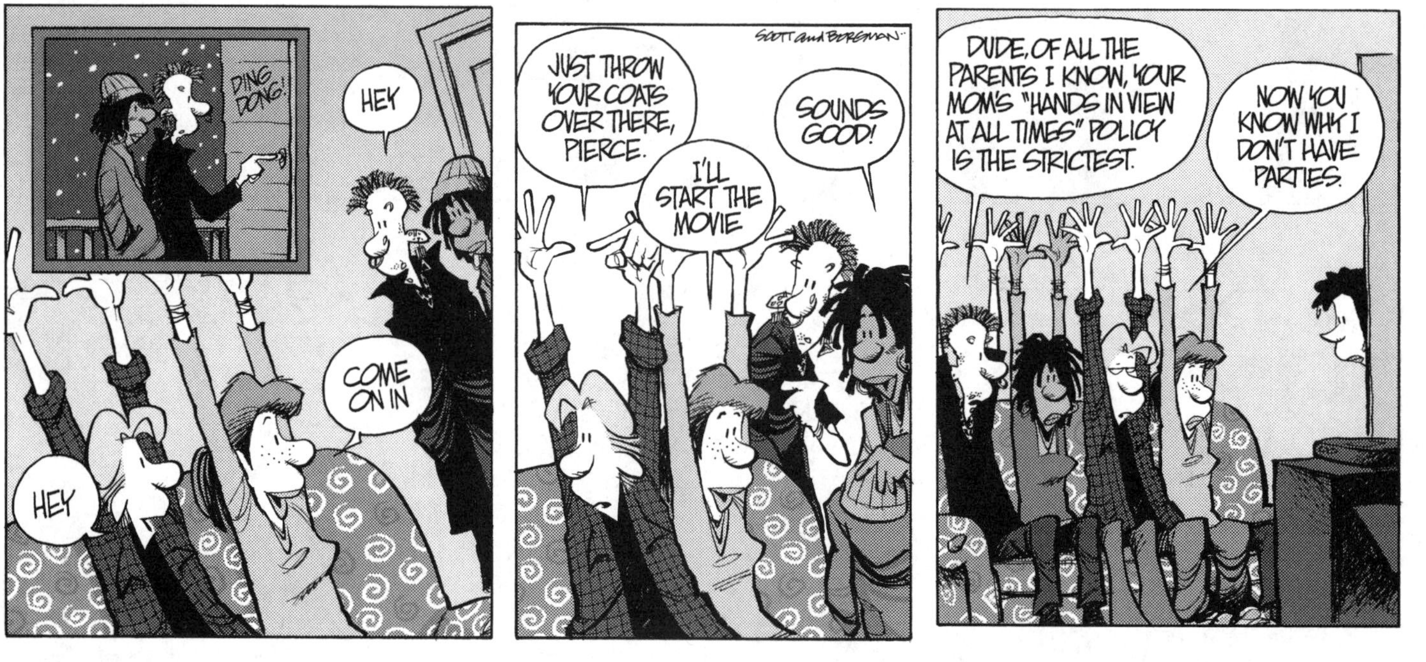
DING DONG!
HEY
COME ON IN
HEY
SCOTT and BORGMAN
JUST THROW YOUR COATS OVER THERE, PIERCE.
I'LL START THE MOVIE
SOUNDS GOOD!
DUDE, OF ALL THE PARENTS I KNOW, YOUR MOM'S "HANDS IN VIEW AT ALL TIMES" POLICY IS THE STRICTEST.
NOW YOU KNOW WHY I DON'T HAVE PARTIES.

Zits
by JERRY SCOTT and JIM BORGMAN

CLOTHES
BOOKS
STUFF
AND LAST, BUT NOT LEAST....
ATTITUDE
JEREMY! YOU'RE AWAKE!
ACUTE OBSERVATION, MOM.
SCOTT and BORGMAN

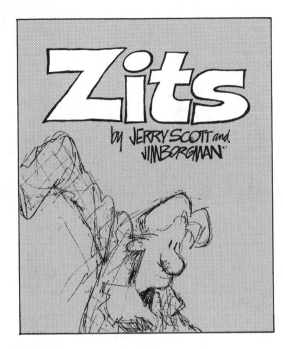

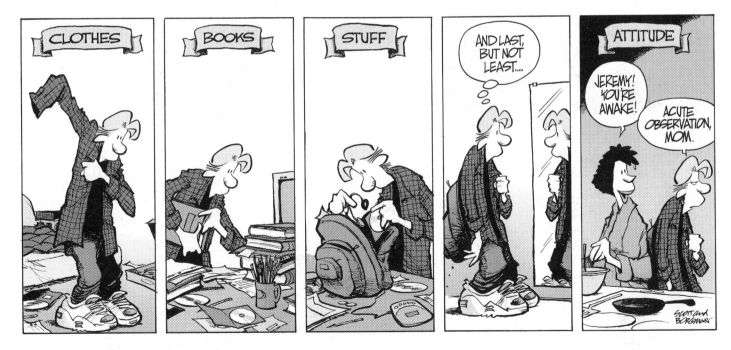

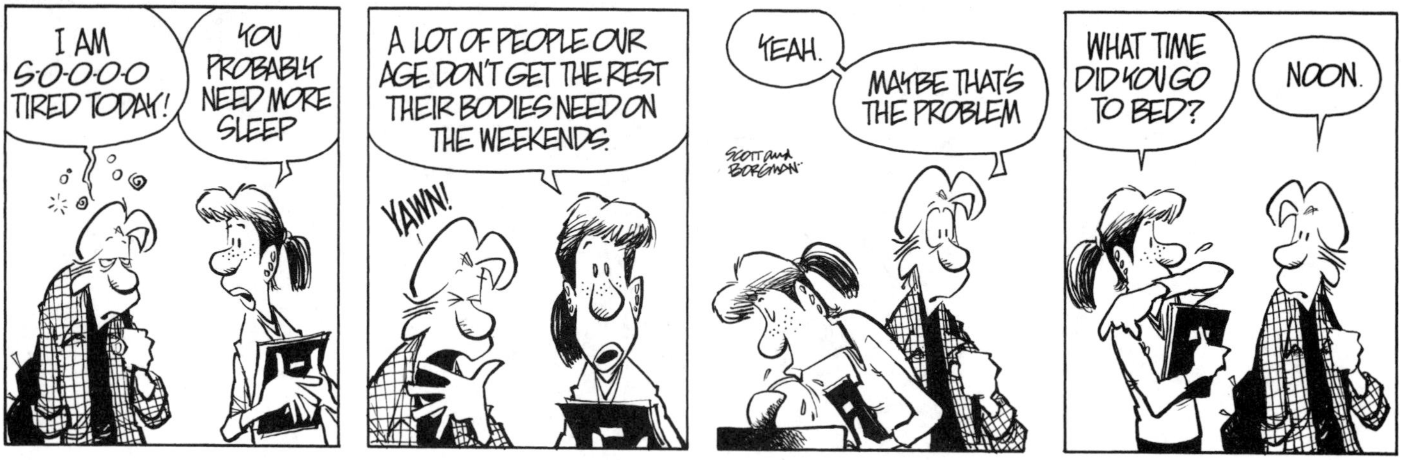
I AM S-O-O-O-O TIRED TODAY!
YOU PROBABLY NEED MORE SLEEP
A LOT OF PEOPLE OUR AGE DON'T GET THE REST THEIR BODIES NEED ON THE WEEKENDS.
YAWN!
YEAH.
MAYBE THAT'S THE PROBLEM
WHAT TIME DID YOU GO TO BED?
NOON.

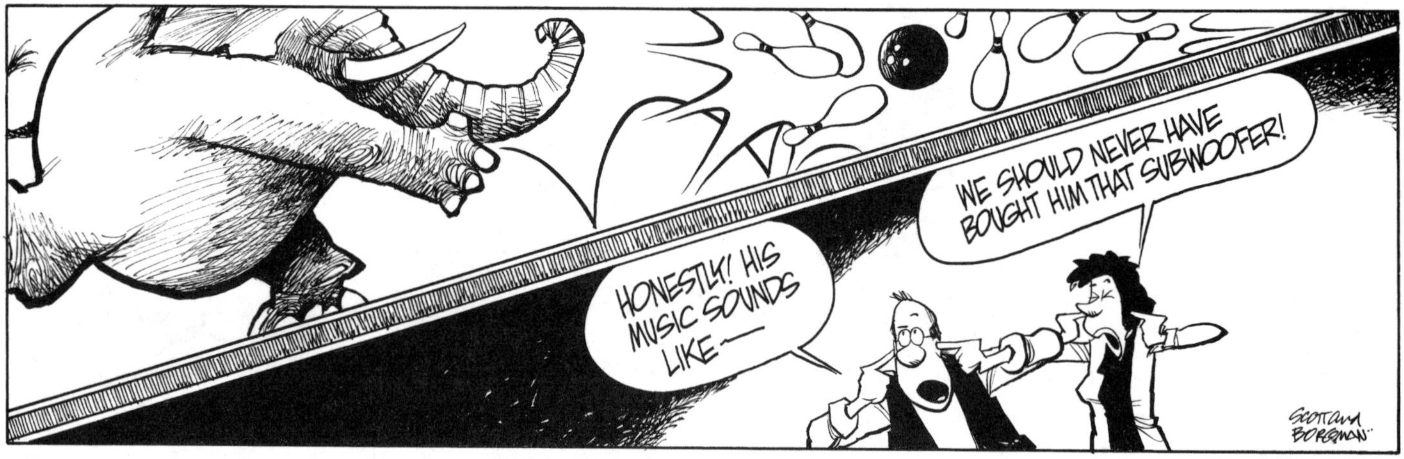
WE SHOULD NEVER HAVE BOUGHT HIM THAT SUBWOOFER!
HONESTLY! HIS MUSIC SOUNDS LIKE—

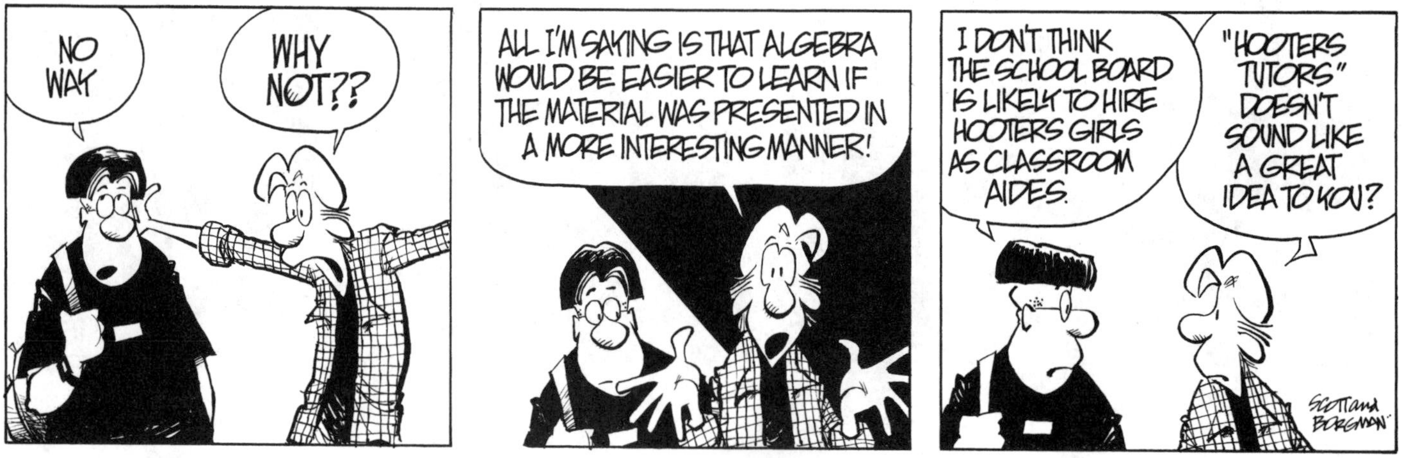
NO WAY
WHY NOT??
ALL I'M SAYING IS THAT ALGEBRA WOULD BE EASIER TO LEARN IF THE MATERIAL WAS PRESENTED IN A MORE INTERESTING MANNER!
I DON'T THINK THE SCHOOL BOARD IS LIKELY TO HIRE HOOTERS GIRLS AS CLASSROOM AIDES.
"HOOTERS TUTORS" DOESN'T SOUND LIKE A GREAT IDEA TO YOU?

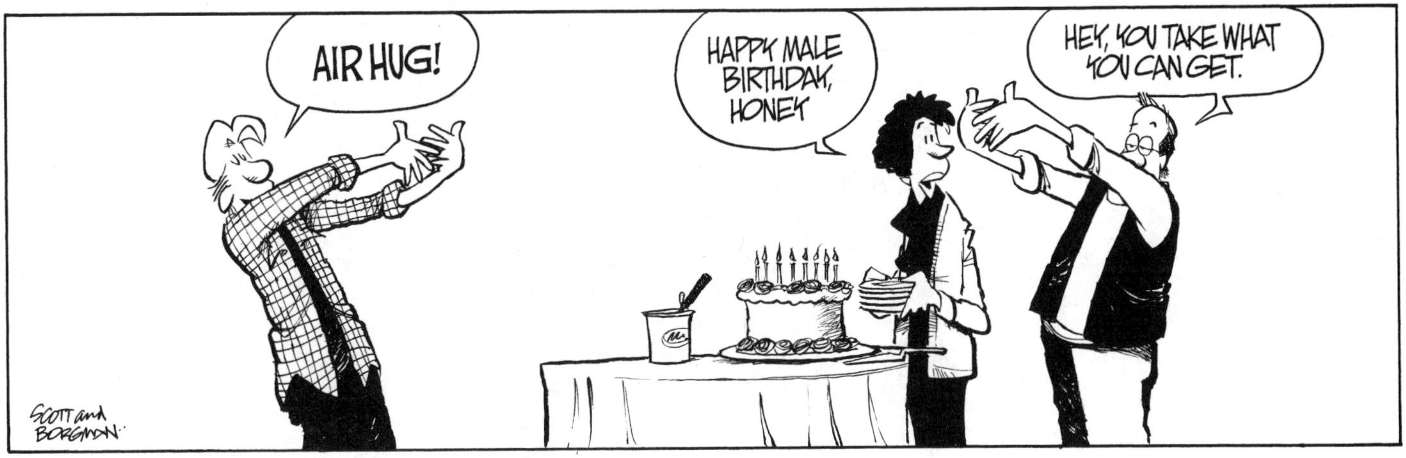
AIR HUG!
HAPPY MALE BIRTHDAY, HONEY
HEY, YOU TAKE WHAT YOU CAN GET.
SCOTT and BORGMAN

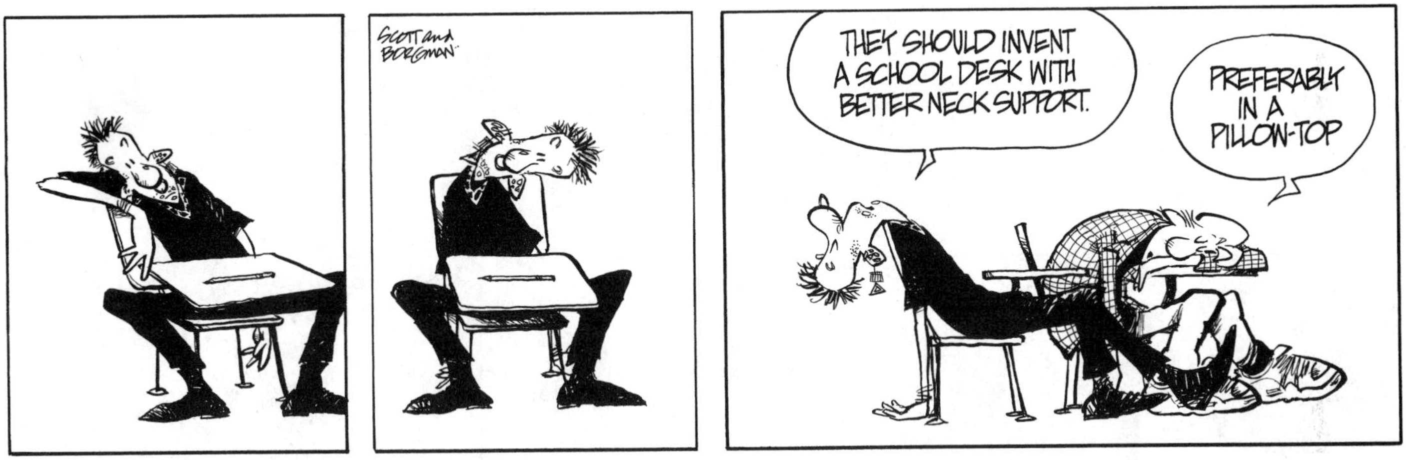
SCOTT and BORGMAN
THEY SHOULD INVENT A SCHOOL DESK WITH BETTER NECK SUPPORT.
PREFERABLY IN A PILLOW-TOP

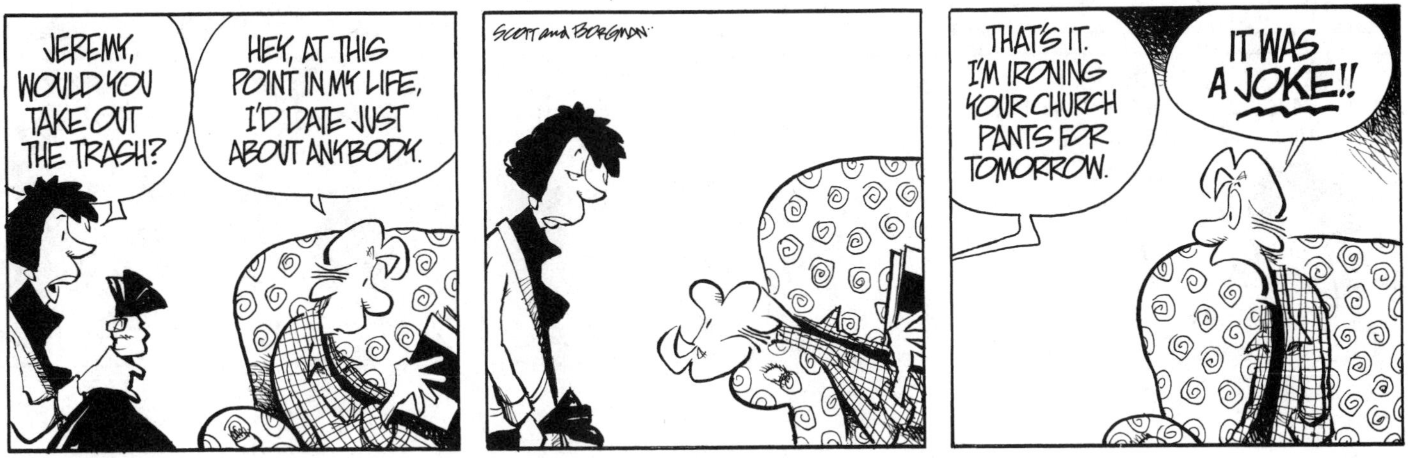
JEREMY, WOULD YOU TAKE OUT THE TRASH?
HEY, AT THIS POINT IN MY LIFE, I'D DATE JUST ABOUT ANYBODY.
SCOTT and BORGMAN
THAT'S IT. I'M IRONING YOUR CHURCH PANTS FOR TOMORROW.
IT WAS A JOKE!!

Zits
by JERRY SCOTT and
JIM BORGMAN

JEREMY?
IT'S GETTING PRETTY LATE, SWEETIE.
UM-HMM
YOU'VE BEEN AT IT QUITE AWHILE THIS EVENING, HAVEN'T YOU?
UM-HMMMM
SO WHAT'S THIS BIG REPORT ABOUT?
I HAVE NO IDEA.
I'M STILL DOWNLOADING THE PERFECT MIX OF SONGS TO PLAY WHILE WRITING A TWELVE-PAGE PAPER.
SCOTT AND BORGMAN
WITH A LITTLE LUCK, I SHOULD BE ABLE TO GET STARTED BY DAYBREAK.
PASS THE ANTACIDS
"REGULAR," "EXTRA-STRENGTH," OR "PARENT OF A TEENAGER"?

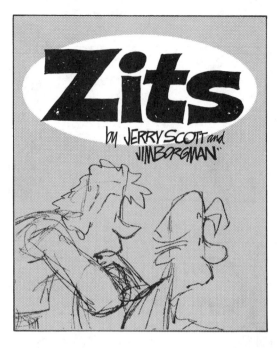

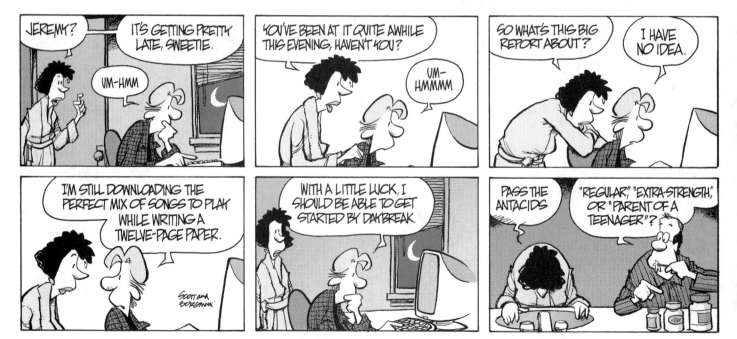

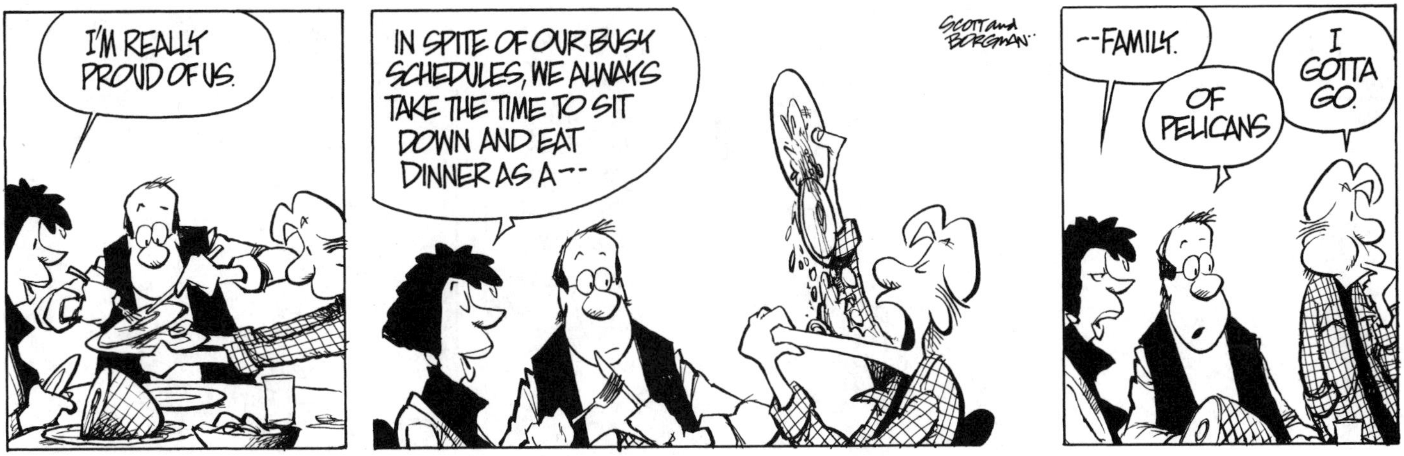
I'M REALLY PROUD OF US.
IN SPITE OF OUR BUSY SCHEDULES, WE ALWAYS TAKE THE TIME TO SIT DOWN AND EAT DINNER AS A--
SCOTT and BORGMAN
--FAMILY.
OF PELICANS
I GOTTA GO.

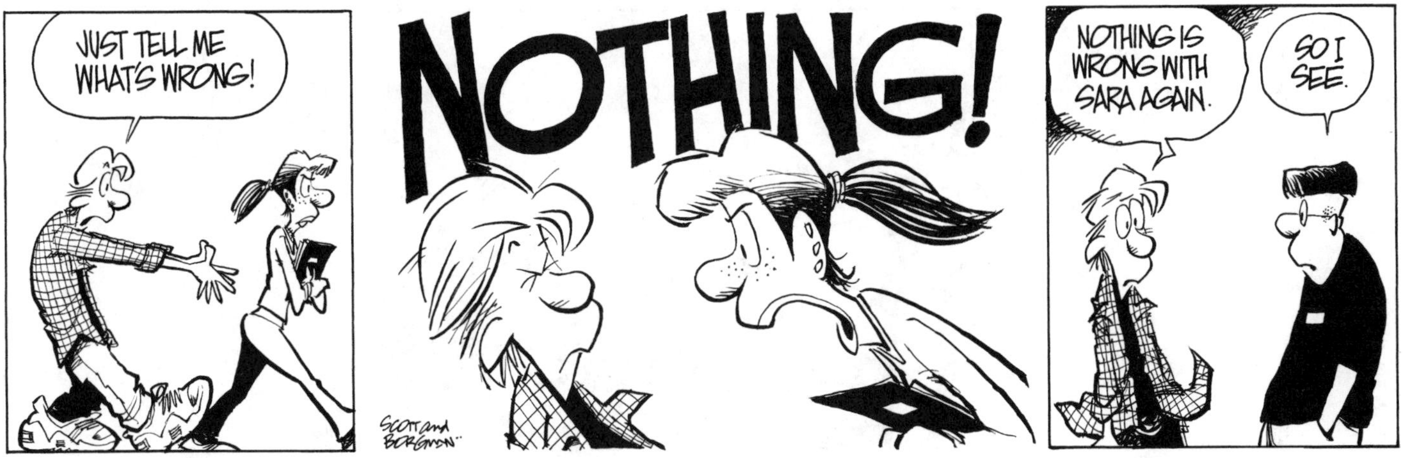
JUST TELL ME WHAT'S WRONG!
NOTHING!
SCOTT and BORGMAN
NOTHING IS WRONG WITH SARA AGAIN.
SO I SEE.

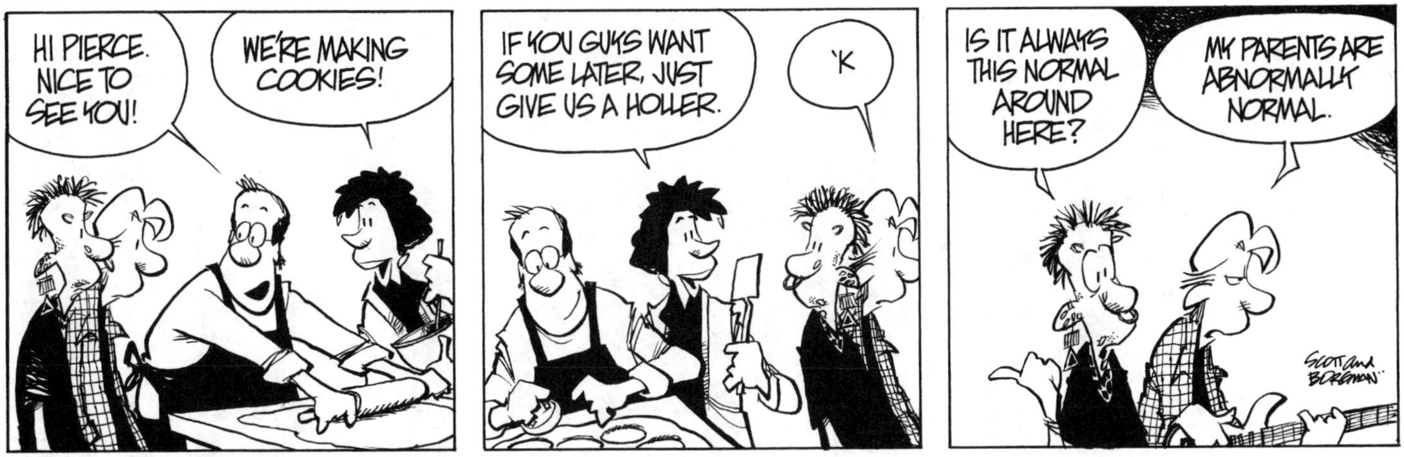
HI PIERCE. NICE TO SEE YOU!
WE'RE MAKING COOKIES!
IF YOU GUYS WANT SOME LATER, JUST GIVE US A HOLLER.
'K
IS IT ALWAYS THIS NORMAL AROUND HERE?
MY PARENTS ARE ABNORMALLY NORMAL.
SCOTT and BORGMAN

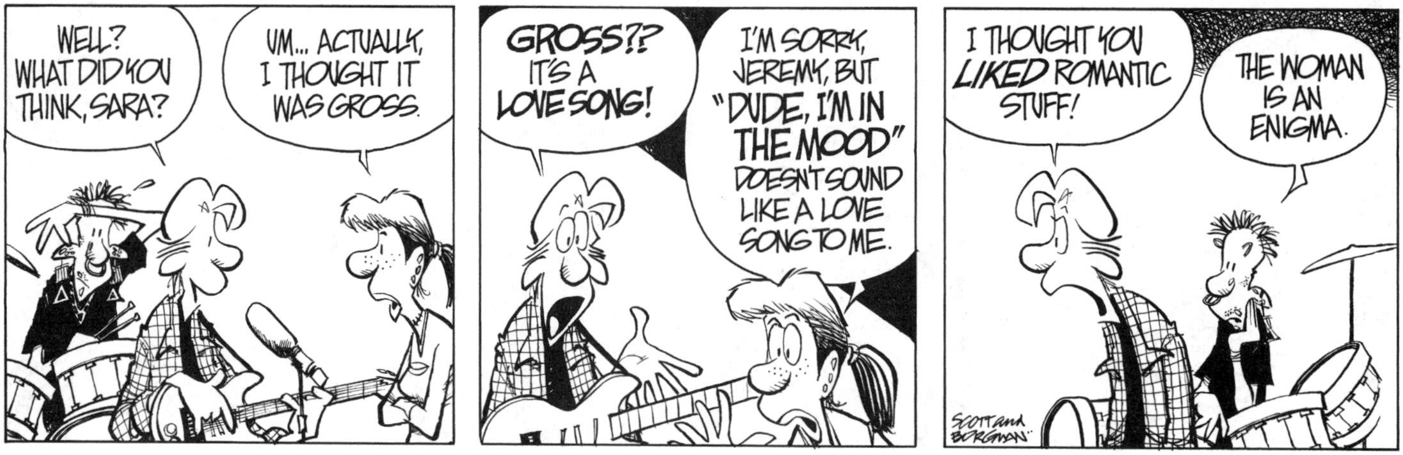
WELL? WHAT DID YOU THINK, SARA?
UM... ACTUALLY, I THOUGHT IT WAS GROSS.
GROSS?? IT'S A LOVE SONG!
I'M SORRY, JEREMY, BUT "DUDE, I'M IN THE MOOD" DOESN'T SOUND LIKE A LOVE SONG TO ME.
I THOUGHT YOU LIKED ROMANTIC STUFF!
THE WOMAN IS AN ENIGMA.
SCOTT and BORGMAN

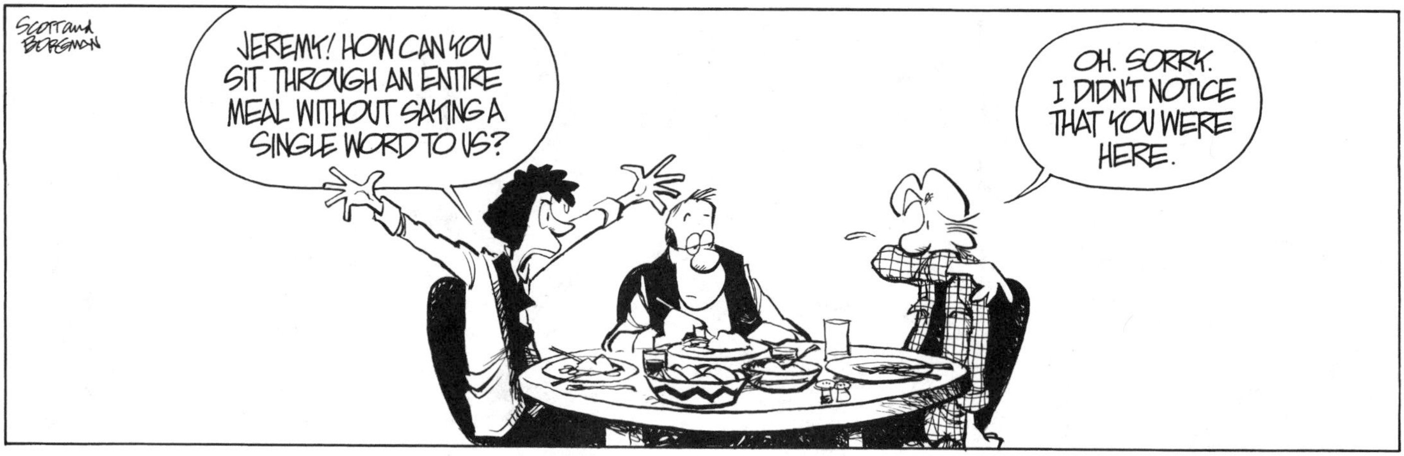
SCOTT and BORGMAN
JEREMY! HOW CAN YOU SIT THROUGH AN ENTIRE MEAL WITHOUT SAYING A SINGLE WORD TO US?
OH. SORRY. I DIDN'T NOTICE THAT YOU WERE HERE.

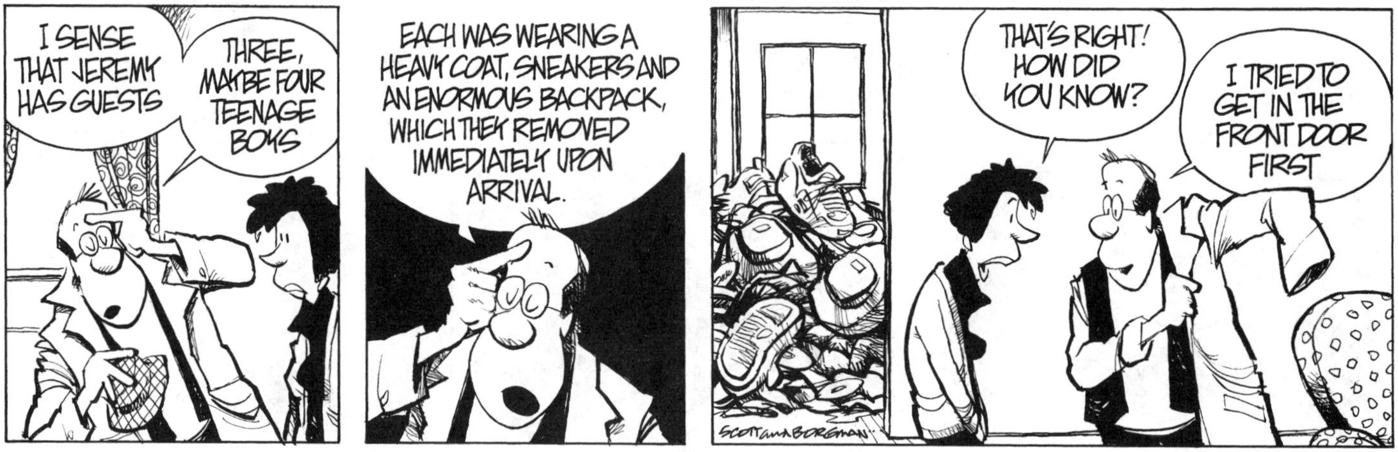
I SENSE THAT JEREMY HAS GUESTS
THREE, MAYBE FOUR TEENAGE BOYS
EACH WAS WEARING A HEAVY COAT, SNEAKERS AND AN ENORMOUS BACKPACK, WHICH THEY REMOVED IMMEDIATELY UPON ARRIVAL.
THAT'S RIGHT! HOW DID YOU KNOW?
I TRIED TO GET IN THE FRONT DOOR FIRST
SCOTT and BORGMAN

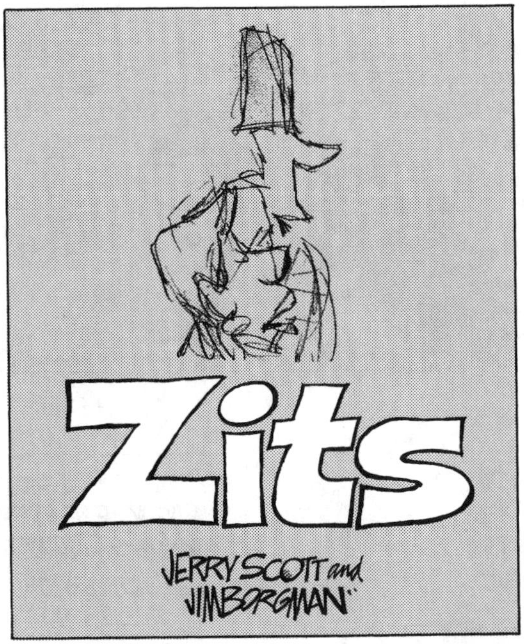
Zits
JERRY SCOTT and
JIM BORGMAN

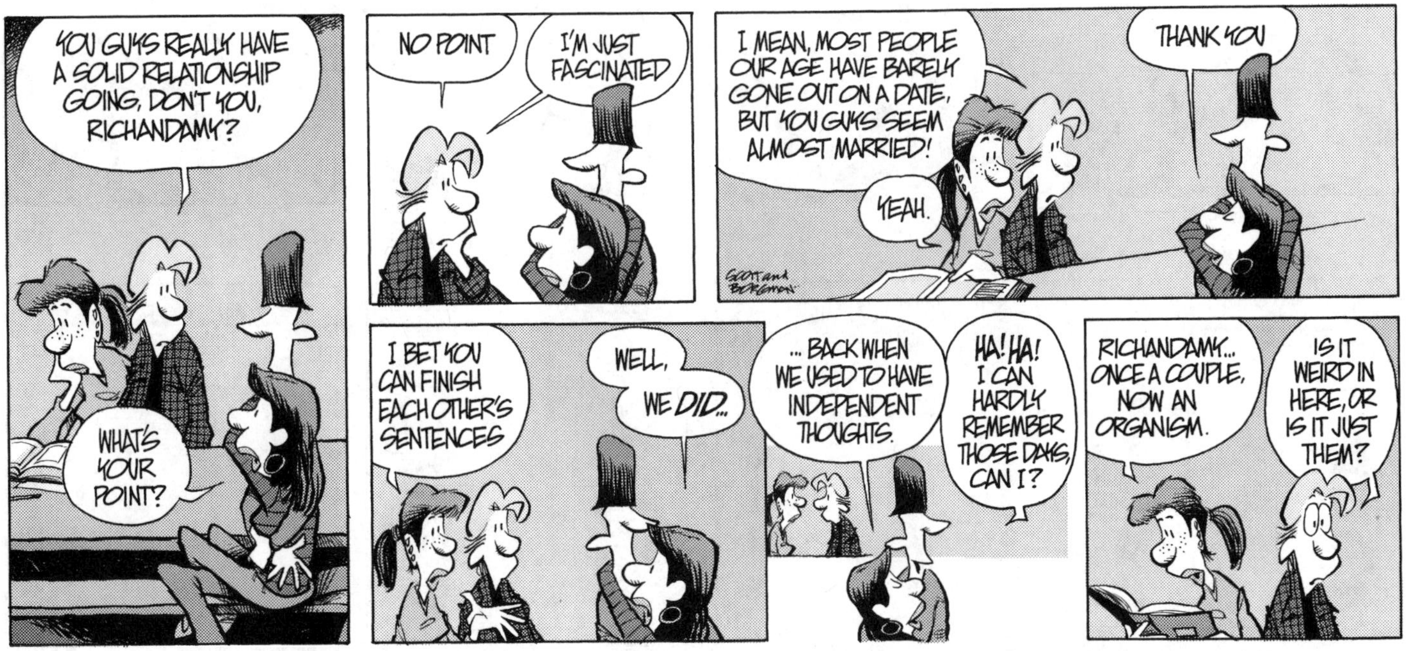
YOU GUYS REALLY HAVE A SOLID RELATIONSHIP GOING, DON'T YOU, RICHANDAMY?
WHAT'S YOUR POINT?
NO POINT
I'M JUST FASCINATED
I MEAN, MOST PEOPLE OUR AGE HAVE BARELY GONE OUT ON A DATE, BUT YOU GUYS SEEM ALMOST MARRIED!
YEAH.
THANK YOU
SCOTT and BORGMAN
I BET YOU CAN FINISH EACH OTHER'S SENTENCES
WELL,
WE DID...
... BACK WHEN WE USED TO HAVE INDEPENDENT THOUGHTS.
HA! HA! I CAN HARDLY REMEMBER THOSE DAYS, CAN I?
RICHANDAMY... ONCE A COUPLE, NOW AN ORGANISM.
IS IT WEIRD IN HERE, OR IS IT JUST THEM?

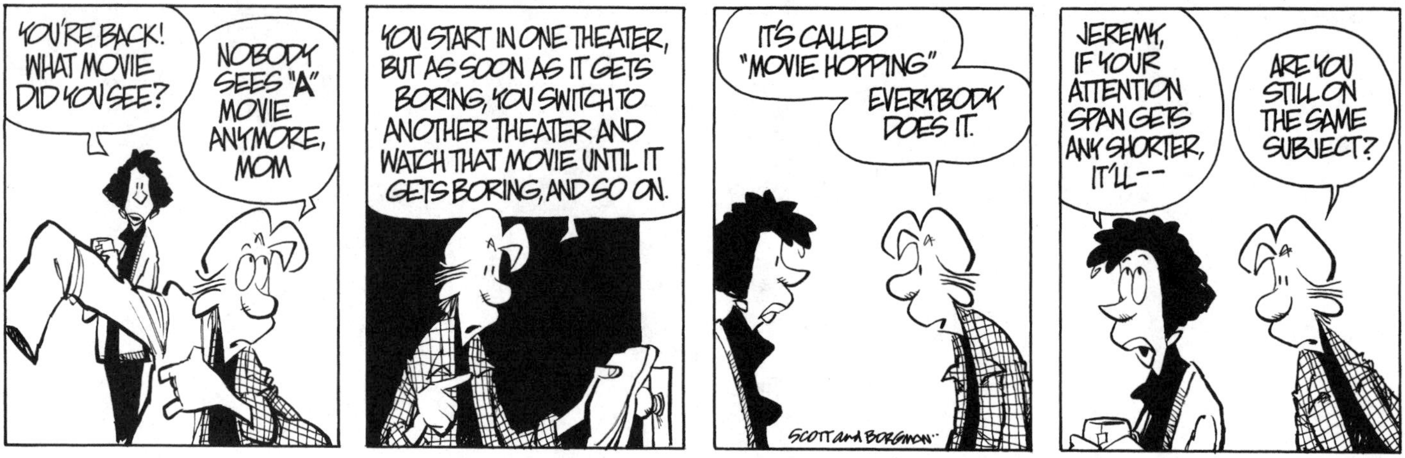
YOU'RE BACK! WHAT MOVIE DID YOU SEE?
NOBODY SEES "A" MOVIE ANYMORE, MOM
YOU START IN ONE THEATER, BUT AS SOON AS IT GETS BORING, YOU SWITCH TO ANOTHER THEATER AND WATCH THAT MOVIE UNTIL IT GETS BORING, AND SO ON.
IT'S CALLED "MOVIE HOPPING"
EVERYBODY DOES IT.
SCOTT and BORGMAN
JEREMY, IF YOUR ATTENTION SPAN GETS ANY SHORTER, IT'LL--
ARE YOU STILL ON THE SAME SUBJECT?

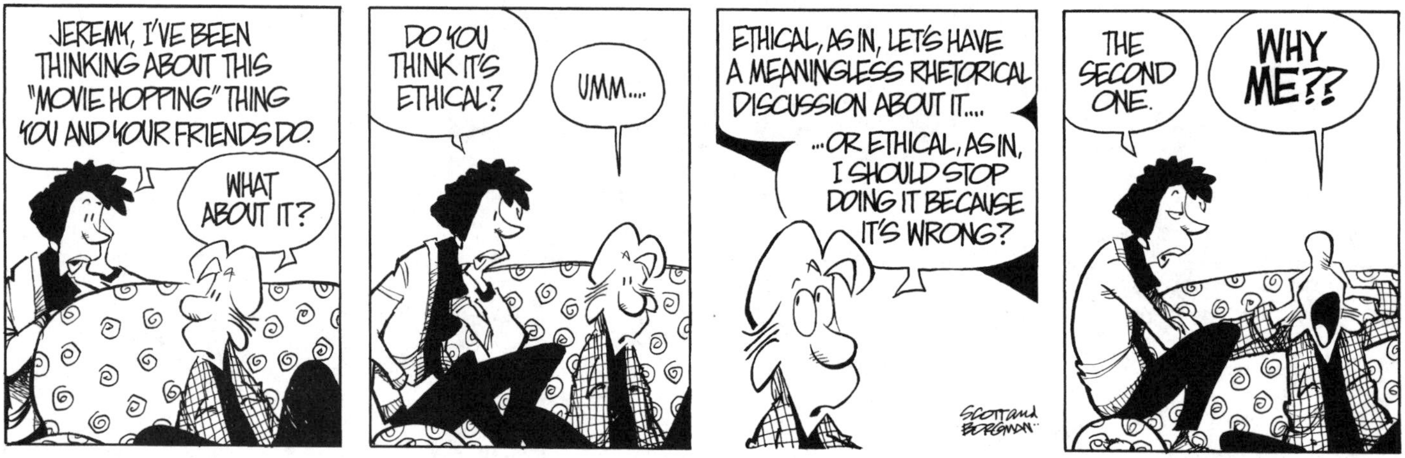
JEREMY, I'VE BEEN THINKING ABOUT THIS "MOVIE HOPPING" THING YOU AND YOUR FRIENDS DO.
WHAT ABOUT IT?
DO YOU THINK IT'S ETHICAL?
UMM....
ETHICAL, AS IN, LET'S HAVE A MEANINGLESS RHETORICAL DISCUSSION ABOUT IT....
...OR ETHICAL, AS IN, I SHOULD STOP DOING IT BECAUSE IT'S WRONG?
SCOTT and BORGMAN
THE SECOND ONE.
WHY ME??

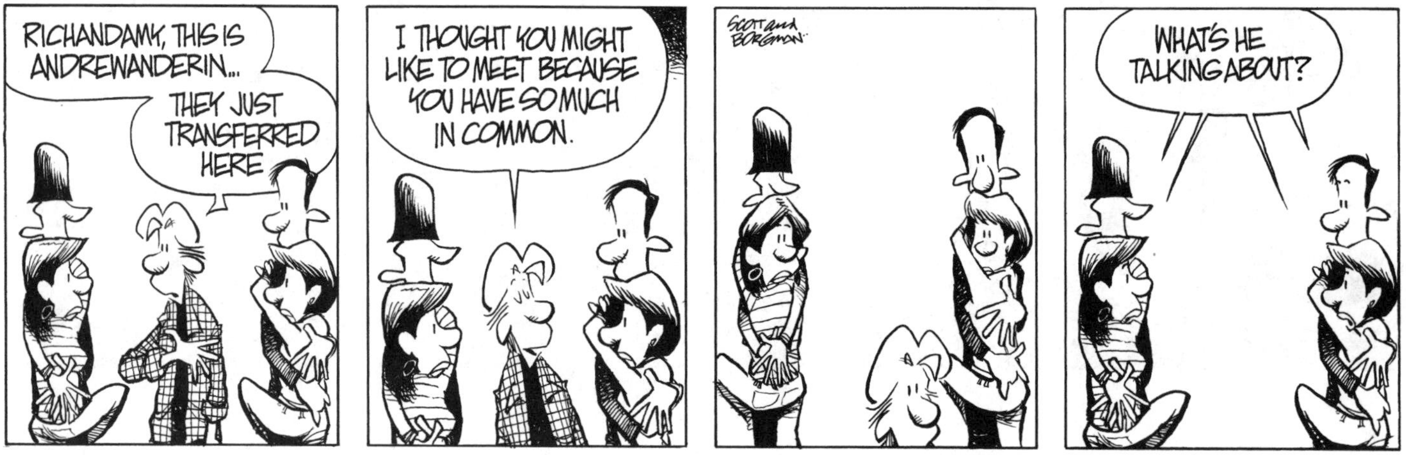
RICHANDAMY, THIS IS ANDREWANDERIN...
THEY JUST TRANSFERRED HERE
I THOUGHT YOU MIGHT LIKE TO MEET BECAUSE YOU HAVE SO MUCH IN COMMON.
SCOTT and BORGMAN
WHAT'S HE TALKING ABOUT?

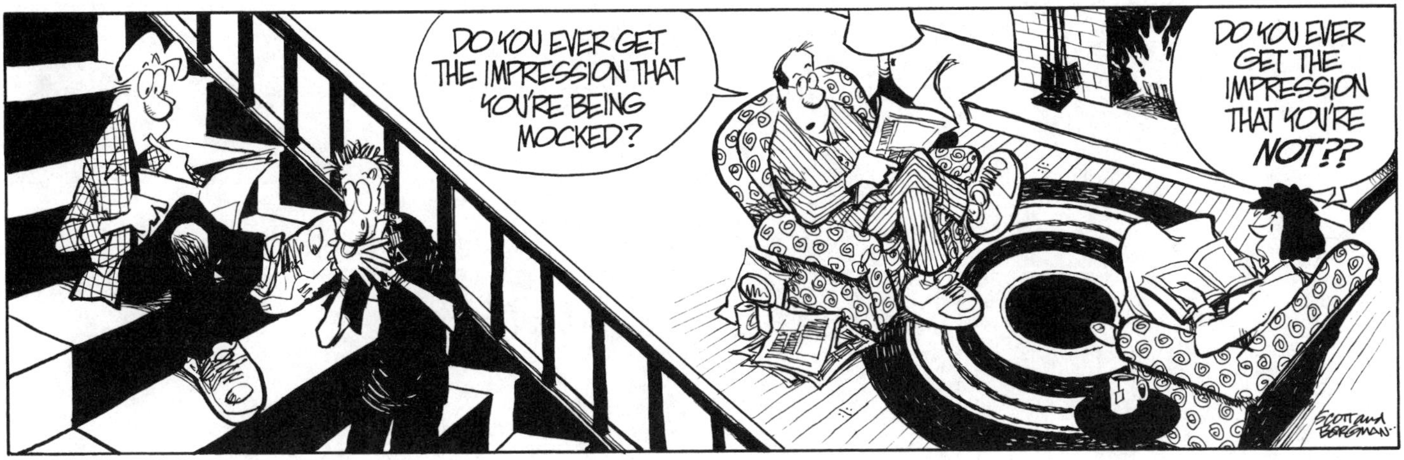
DO YOU EVER GET THE IMPRESSION THAT YOU'RE BEING MOCKED?
DO YOU EVER GET THE IMPRESSION THAT YOU'RE NOT??
SCOTT and BORGMAN

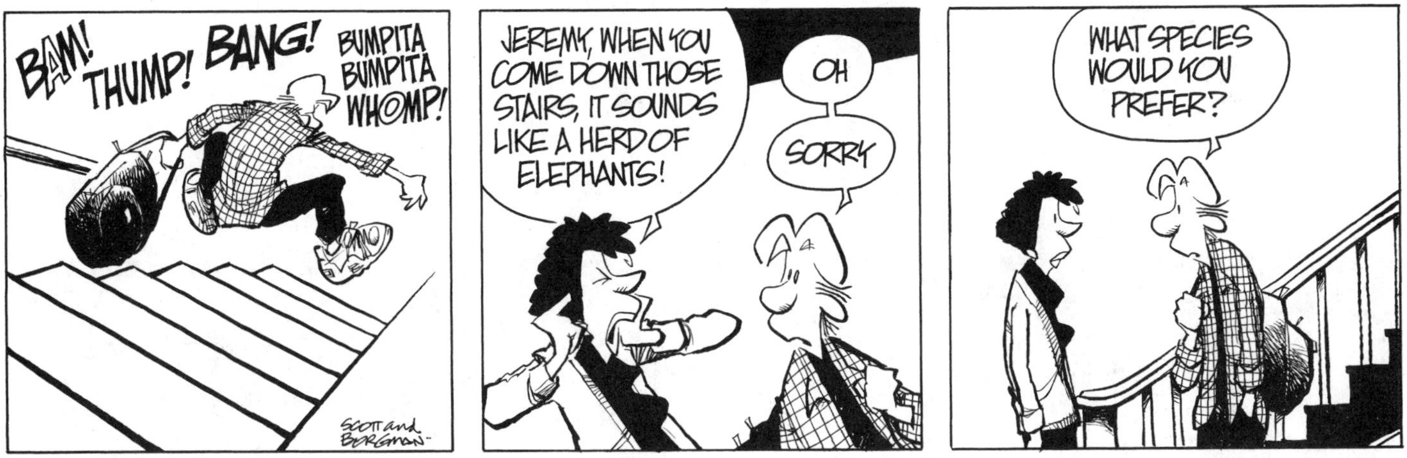
BAM! THUMP! BANG! BUMPITA BUMPITA WHOMP!
SCOTT and BORGMAN
JEREMY, WHEN YOU COME DOWN THOSE STAIRS, IT SOUNDS LIKE A HERD OF ELEPHANTS!
OH
SORRY
WHAT SPECIES WOULD YOU PREFER?

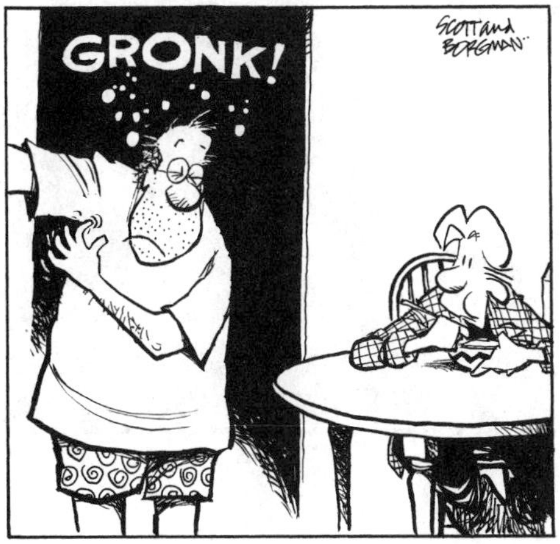
GRONK!
SCOTT and BORGMAN

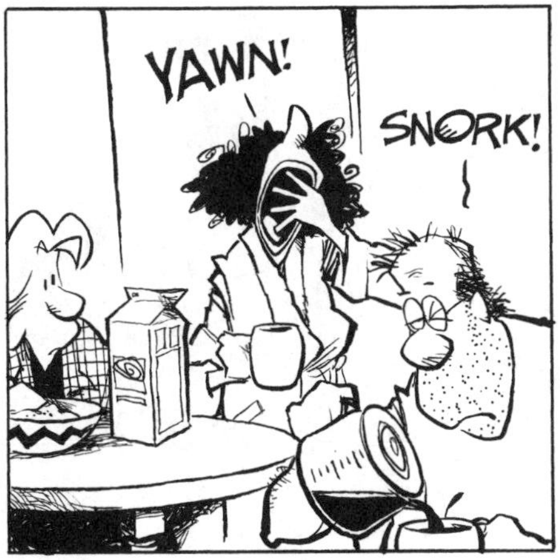
YAWN!
SNORK!

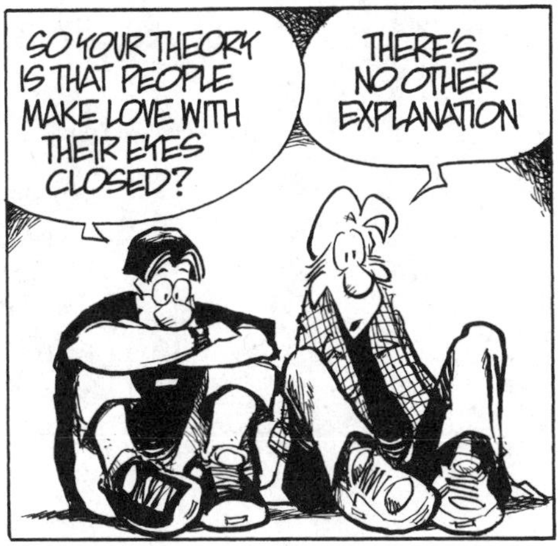
SO YOUR THEORY IS THAT PEOPLE MAKE LOVE WITH THEIR EYES CLOSED?
THERE'S NO OTHER EXPLANATION

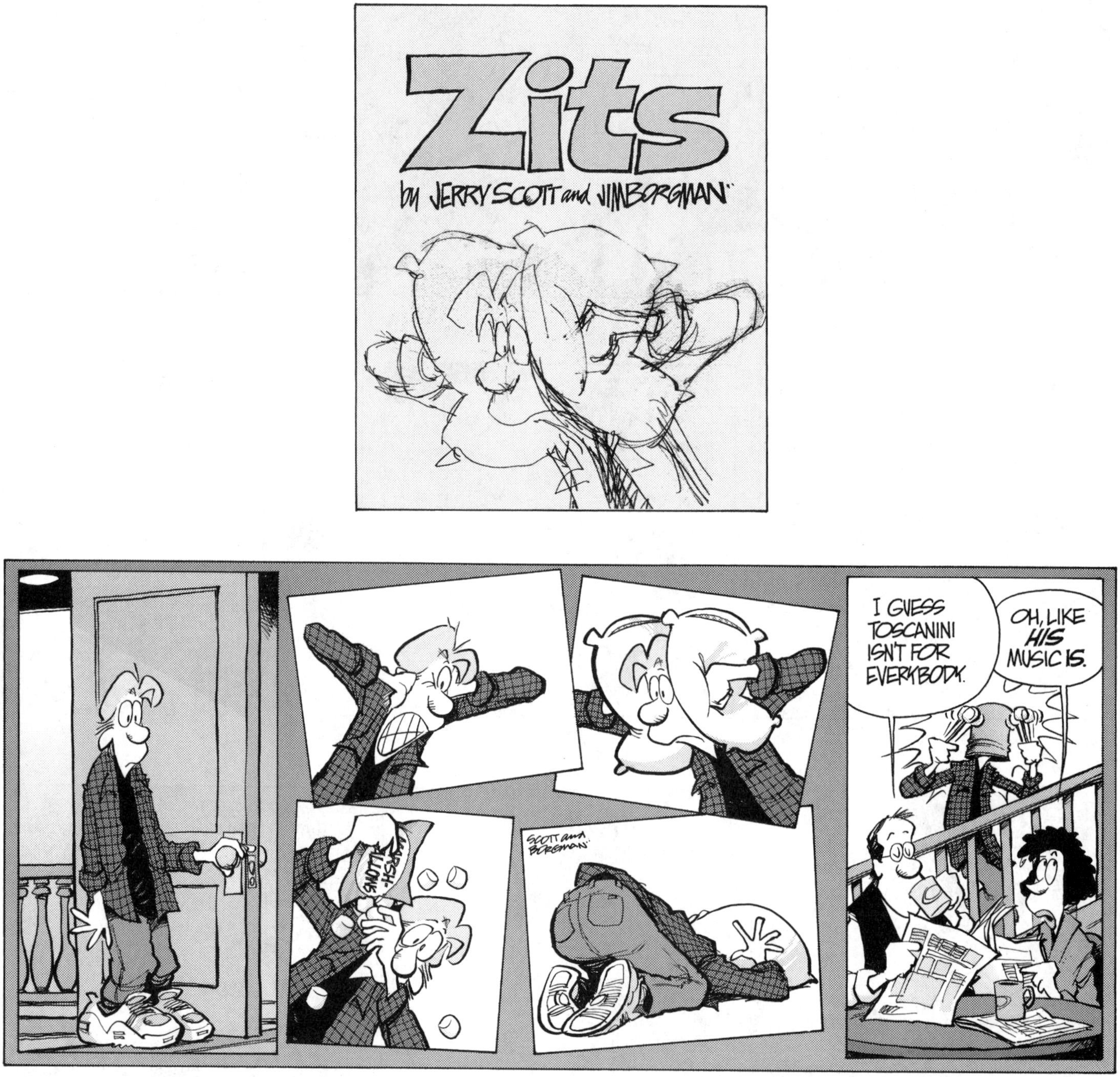
Zits
by JERRY SCOTT and JIM BORGMAN
MARSH-MALLOWS
SCOTT and BORGMAN
I GUESS TOSCANINI ISN'T FOR EVERYBODY.
OH, LIKE *HIS* MUSIC IS.

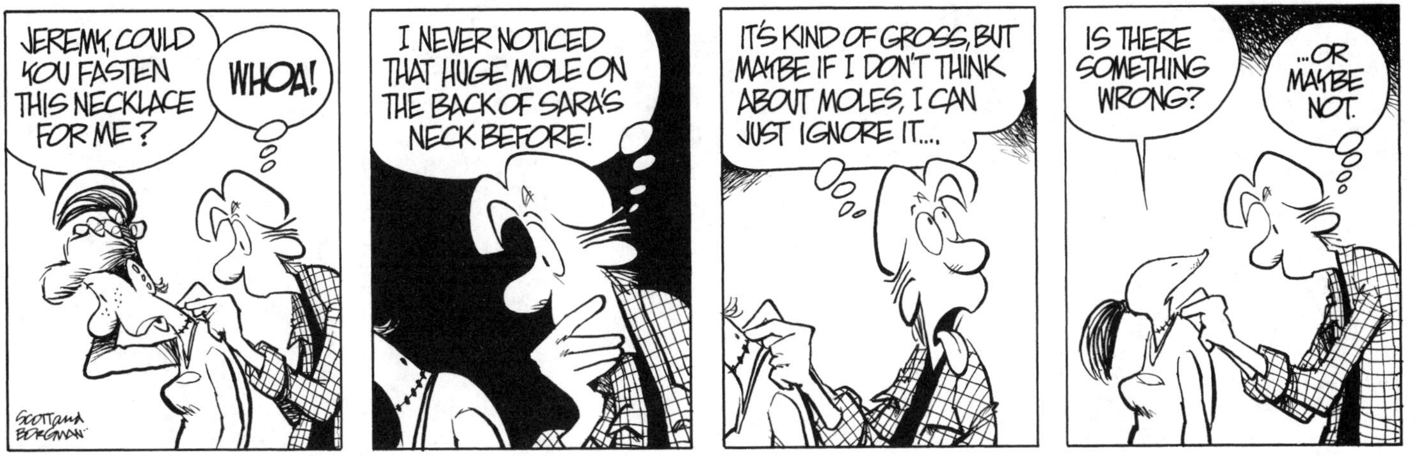
JEREMY, COULD YOU FASTEN THIS NECKLACE FOR ME?
WHOA!
I NEVER NOTICED THAT HUGE MOLE ON THE BACK OF SARA'S NECK BEFORE!
IT'S KIND OF GROSS, BUT MAYBE IF I DON'T THINK ABOUT MOLES, I CAN JUST IGNORE IT....
IS THERE SOMETHING WRONG?
...OR MAYBE NOT.

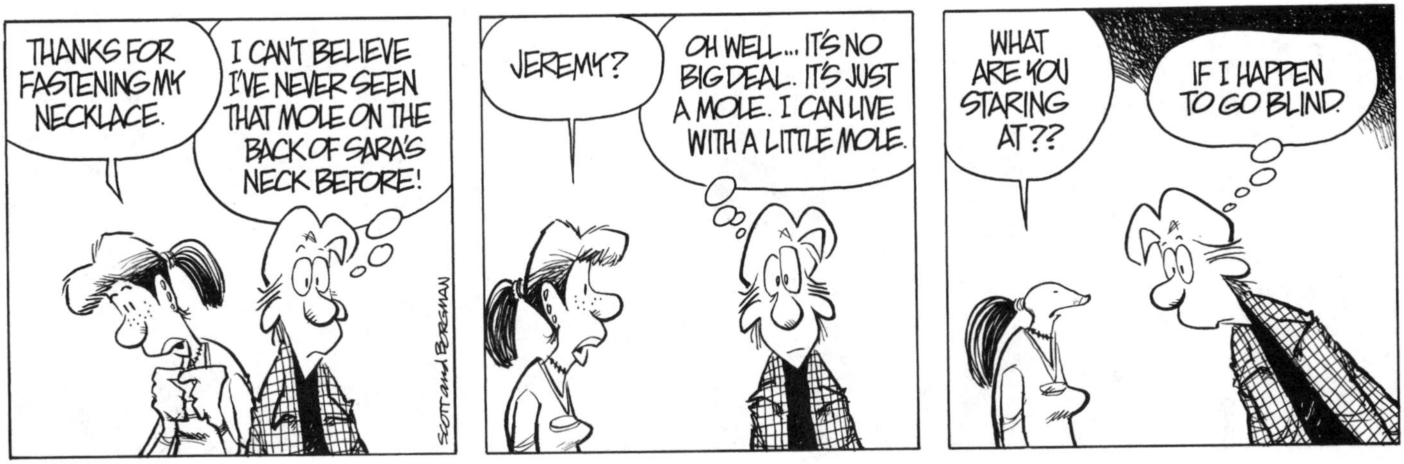
THANKS FOR FASTENING MY NECKLACE.
I CAN'T BELIEVE I'VE NEVER SEEN THAT MOLE ON THE BACK OF SARA'S NECK BEFORE!
SCOTT and BORGMAN
JEREMY?
OH WELL... IT'S NO BIG DEAL. IT'S JUST A MOLE. I CAN LIVE WITH A LITTLE MOLE.
WHAT ARE YOU STARING AT??
IF I HAPPEN TO GO BLIND.

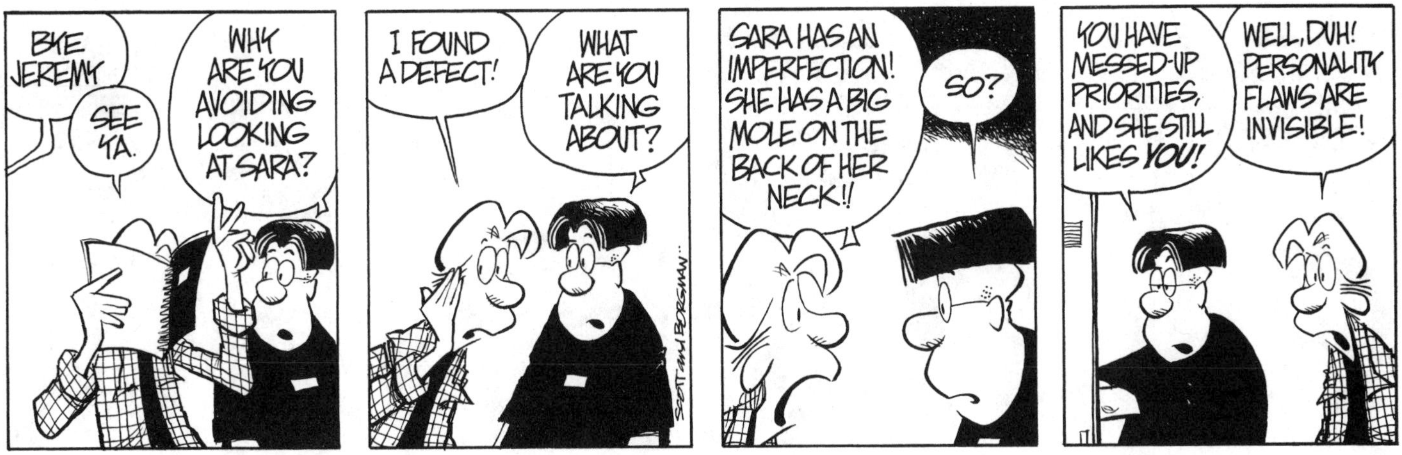
BYE JEREMY
SEE YA.
WHY ARE YOU AVOIDING LOOKING AT SARA?
I FOUND A DEFECT!
WHAT ARE YOU TALKING ABOUT?
SARA HAS AN IMPERFECTION! SHE HAS A BIG MOLE ON THE BACK OF HER NECK!!
SO?
YOU HAVE MESSED-UP PRIORITIES, AND SHE STILL LIKES YOU!
WELL, DUH! PERSONALITY FLAWS ARE INVISIBLE!

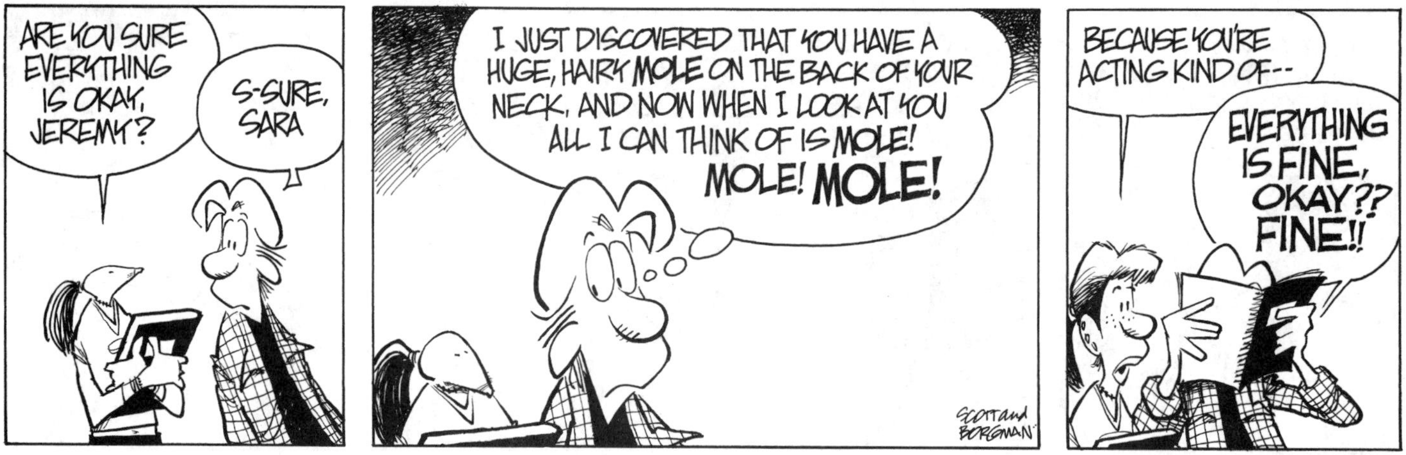
ARE YOU SURE EVERYTHING IS OKAY, JEREMY?
S-SURE, SARA
I JUST DISCOVERED THAT YOU HAVE A HUGE, HAIRY MOLE ON THE BACK OF YOUR NECK, AND NOW WHEN I LOOK AT YOU ALL I CAN THINK OF IS MOLE! MOLE! MOLE!
SCOTT and BORGMAN
BECAUSE YOU'RE ACTING KIND OF--
EVERYTHING IS FINE, OKAY?? FINE!!

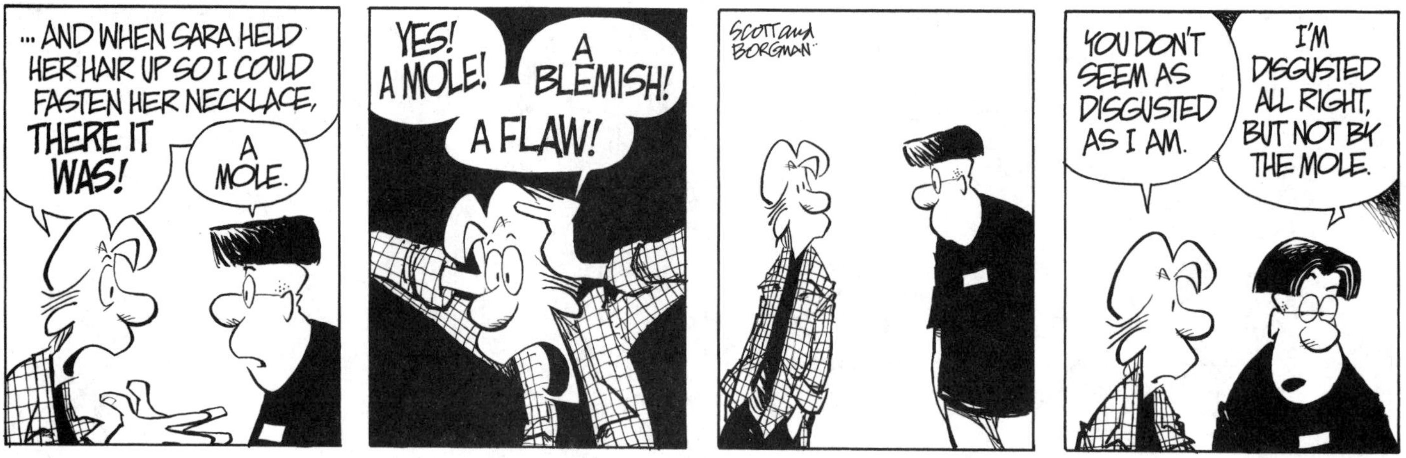
... AND WHEN SARA HELD HER HAIR UP SO I COULD FASTEN HER NECKLACE, THERE IT WAS!
A MOLE.
YES! A MOLE!
A BLEMISH!
A FLAW!
SCOTT and BORGMAN
YOU DON'T SEEM AS DISGUSTED AS I AM.
I'M DISGUSTED ALL RIGHT, BUT NOT BY THE MOLE.

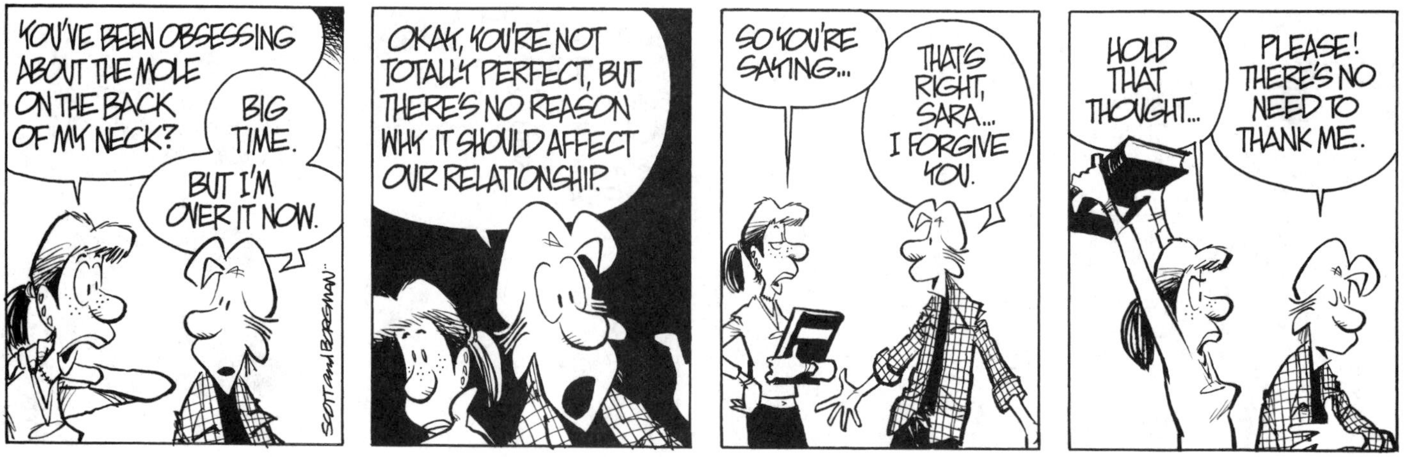
YOU'VE BEEN OBSESSING ABOUT THE MOLE ON THE BACK OF MY NECK?
BIG TIME.
BUT I'M OVER IT NOW.
SCOTT and BORGMAN
OKAY, YOU'RE NOT TOTALLY PERFECT, BUT THERE'S NO REASON WHY IT SHOULD AFFECT OUR RELATIONSHIP.
SO YOU'RE SAYING...
THAT'S RIGHT, SARA... I FORGIVE YOU.
HOLD THAT THOUGHT...
PLEASE! THERE'S NO NEED TO THANK ME.

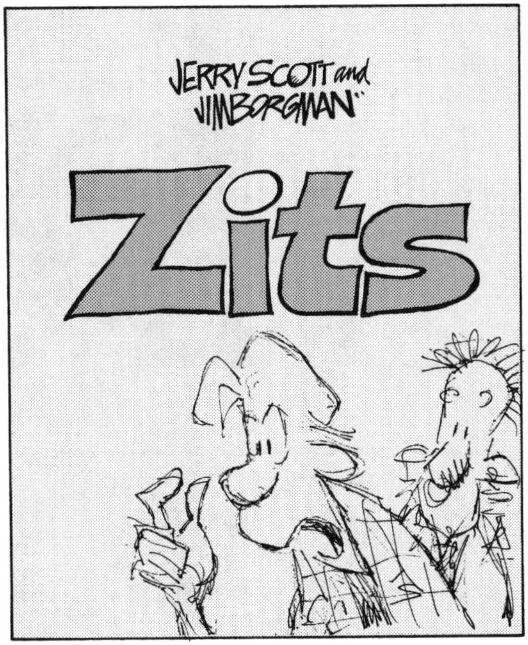
JERRY SCOTT and JIM BORGMAN
Zits

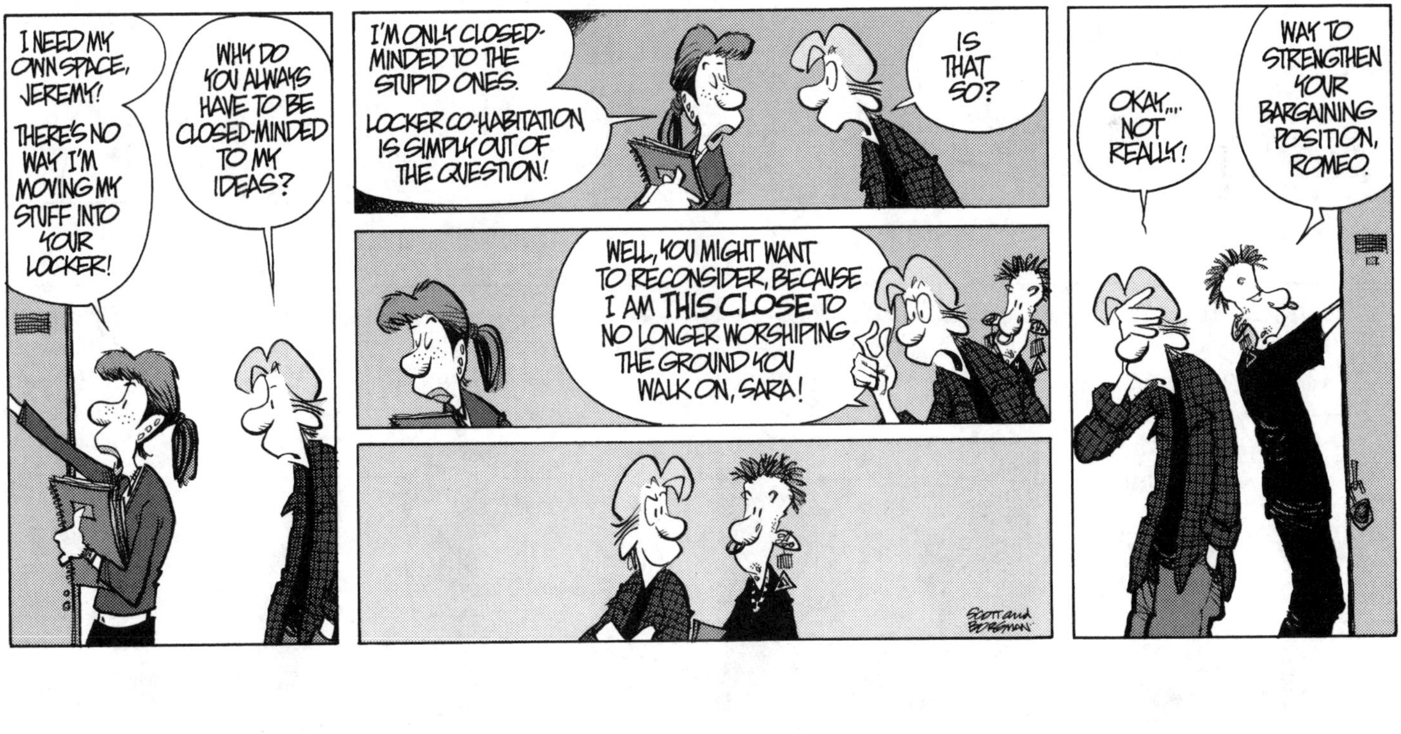
I NEED MY OWN SPACE, JEREMY!
THERE'S NO WAY I'M MOVING MY STUFF INTO YOUR LOCKER!
WHY DO YOU ALWAYS HAVE TO BE CLOSED-MINDED TO MY IDEAS?
I'M ONLY CLOSED-MINDED TO THE STUPID ONES.
LOCKER CO-HABITATION IS SIMPLY OUT OF THE QUESTION!
IS THAT SO?
WELL, YOU MIGHT WANT TO RECONSIDER, BECAUSE I AM THIS CLOSE TO NO LONGER WORSHIPING THE GROUND YOU WALK ON, SARA!
SCOTT and BORGMAN
OKAY.... NOT REALLY!
WAY TO STRENGTHEN YOUR BARGAINING POSITION, ROMEO.

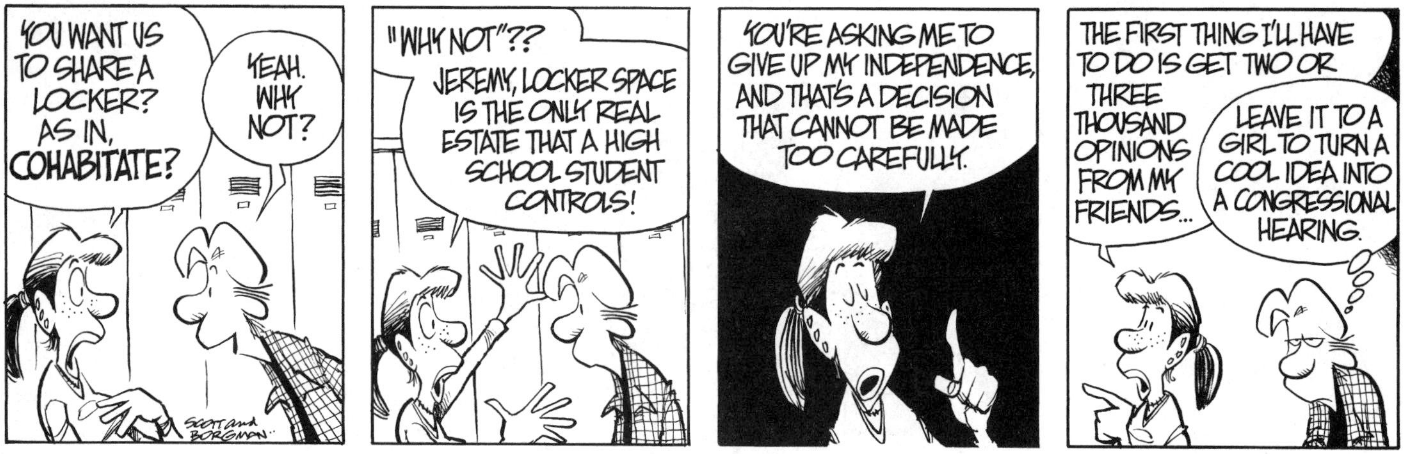
YOU WANT US TO SHARE A LOCKER? AS IN, COHABITATE?
YEAH. WHY NOT?
SCOTT and BORGMAN
"WHY NOT"??
JEREMY, LOCKER SPACE IS THE ONLY REAL ESTATE THAT A HIGH SCHOOL STUDENT CONTROLS!
YOU'RE ASKING ME TO GIVE UP MY INDEPENDENCE, AND THAT'S A DECISION THAT CANNOT BE MADE TOO CAREFULLY.
THE FIRST THING I'LL HAVE TO DO IS GET TWO OR THREE THOUSAND OPINIONS FROM MY FRIENDS...
LEAVE IT TO A GIRL TO TURN A COOL IDEA INTO A CONGRESSIONAL HEARING.

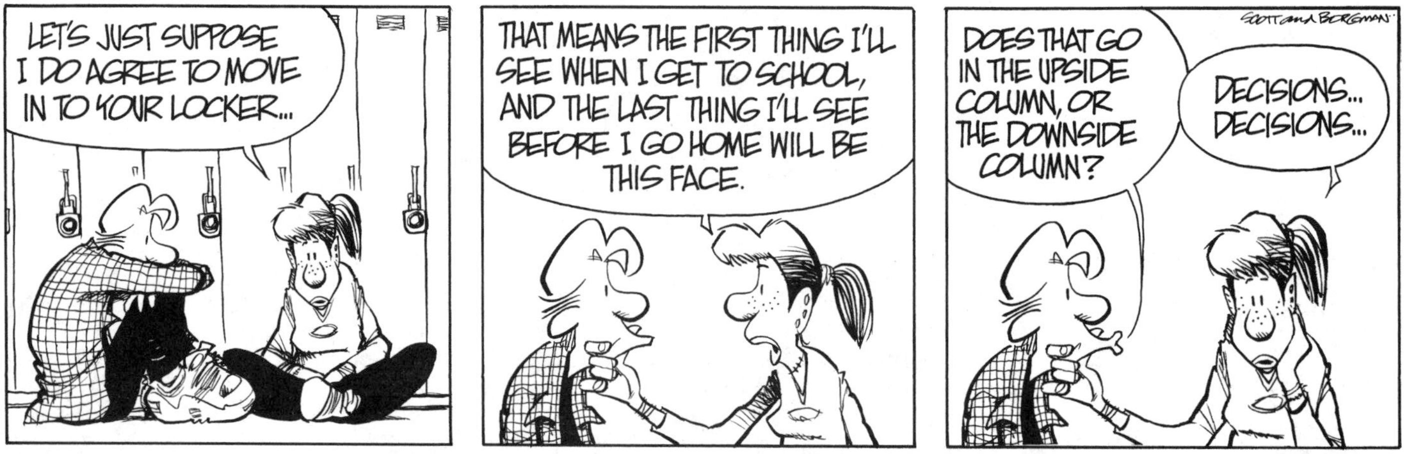
LET'S JUST SUPPOSE I DO AGREE TO MOVE IN TO YOUR LOCKER...
THAT MEANS THE FIRST THING I'LL SEE WHEN I GET TO SCHOOL, AND THE LAST THING I'LL SEE BEFORE I GO HOME WILL BE THIS FACE.
SCOTT and BORGMAN
DOES THAT GO IN THE UPSIDE COLUMN, OR THE DOWNSIDE COLUMN?
DECISIONS... DECISIONS...

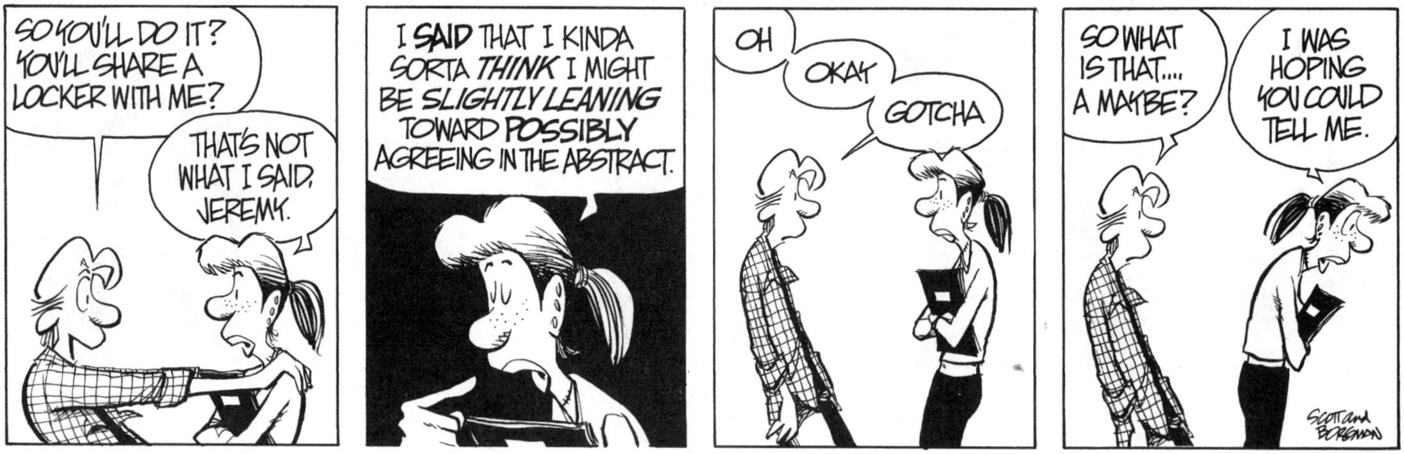
SO YOU'LL DO IT? YOU'LL SHARE A LOCKER WITH ME?
THAT'S NOT WHAT I SAID, JEREMY.
I SAID THAT I KINDA SORTA THINK I MIGHT BE SLIGHTLY LEANING TOWARD POSSIBLY AGREEING IN THE ABSTRACT.
OH
OKAY
GOTCHA
SO WHAT IS THAT.... A MAYBE?
I WAS HOPING YOU COULD TELL ME.
SCOTT and BORGMAN

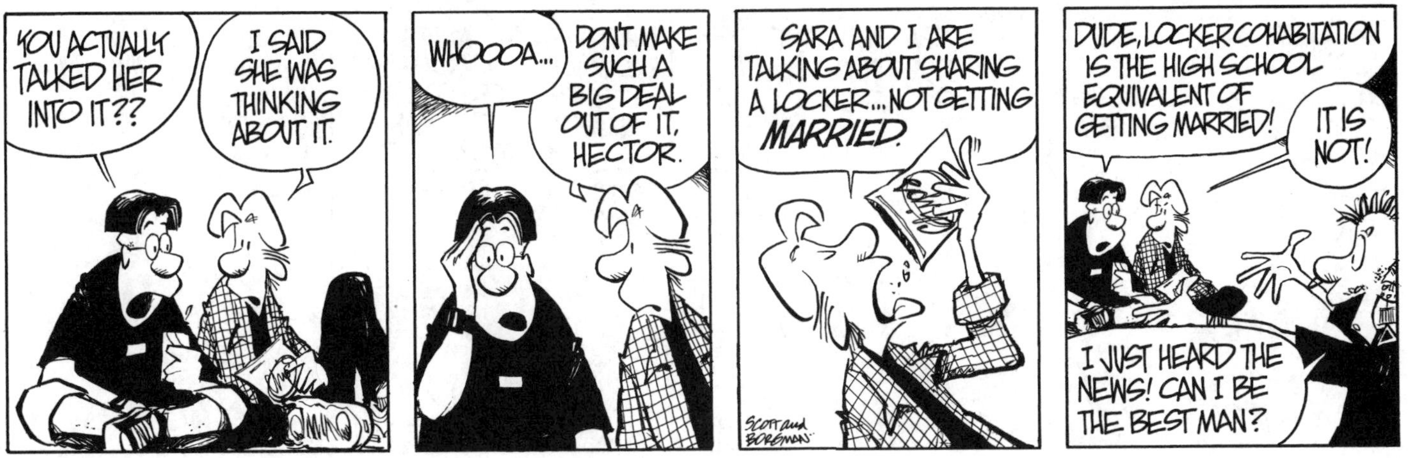
YOU ACTUALLY TALKED HER INTO IT??
I SAID SHE WAS THINKING ABOUT IT.
WHOOOOA...
DON'T MAKE SUCH A BIG DEAL OUT OF IT, HECTOR.
SARA AND I ARE TALKING ABOUT SHARING A LOCKER... NOT GETTING MARRIED.
DUDE, LOCKER COHABITATION IS THE HIGH SCHOOL EQUIVALENT OF GETTING MARRIED!
IT IS NOT!
I JUST HEARD THE NEWS! CAN I BE THE BEST MAN?

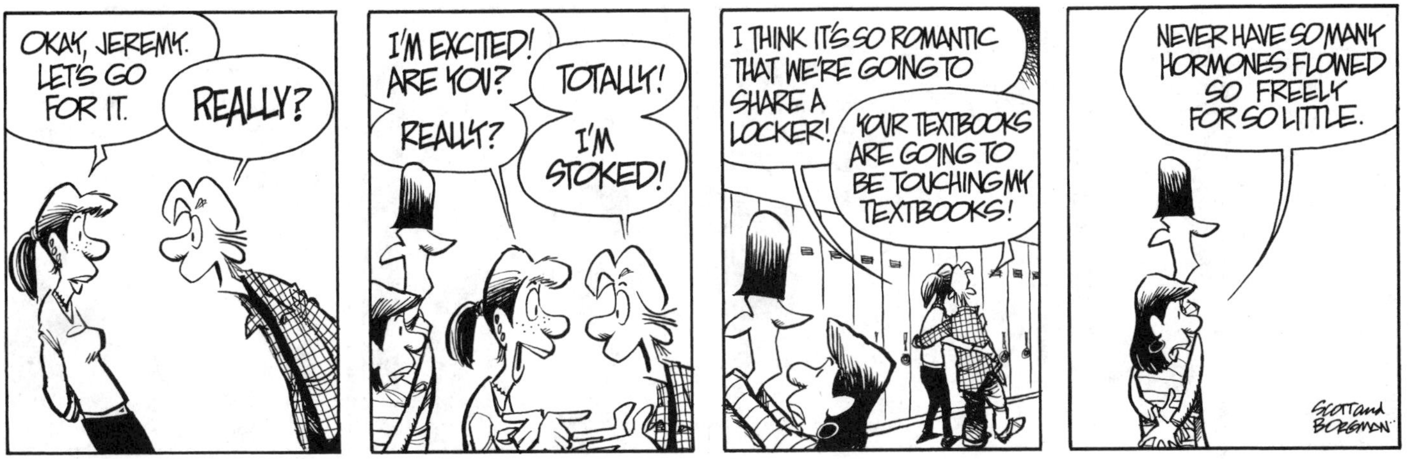
OKAY, JEREMY. LET'S GO FOR IT.
REALLY?
I'M EXCITED! ARE YOU?
TOTALLY!
REALLY?
I'M STOKED!
I THINK IT'S SO ROMANTIC THAT WE'RE GOING TO SHARE A LOCKER!
YOUR TEXTBOOKS ARE GOING TO BE TOUCHING MY TEXTBOOKS!
NEVER HAVE SO MANY HORMONES FLOWED SO FREELY FOR SO LITTLE.

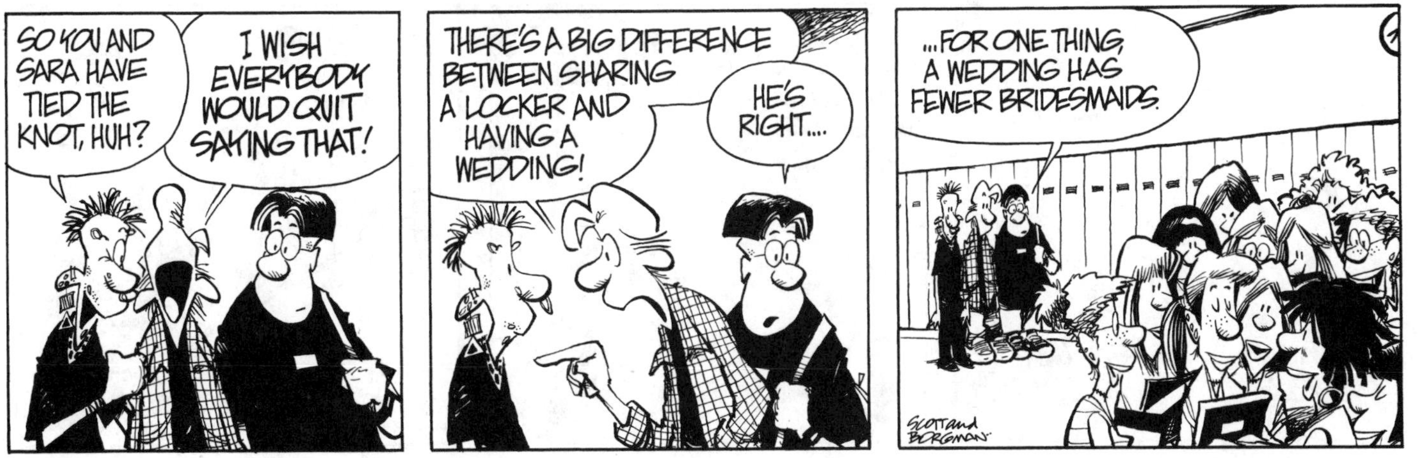
SO YOU AND SARA HAVE TIED THE KNOT, HUH?
I WISH EVERYBODY WOULD QUIT SAYING THAT!
THERE'S A BIG DIFFERENCE BETWEEN SHARING A LOCKER AND HAVING A WEDDING!
HE'S RIGHT....
...FOR ONE THING, A WEDDING HAS FEWER BRIDESMAIDS.

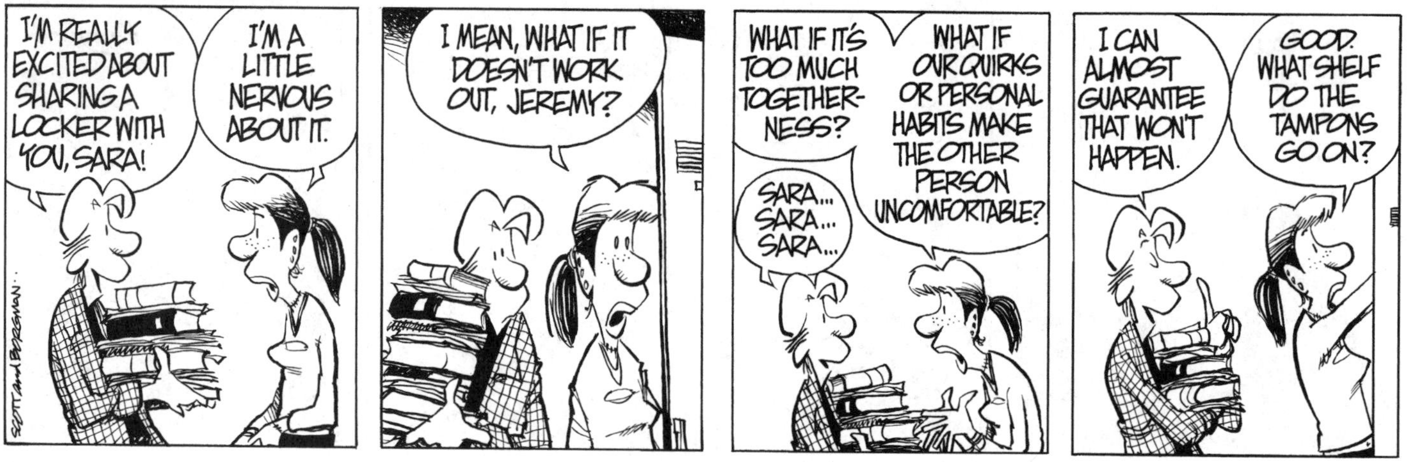
I'M REALLY EXCITED ABOUT SHARING A LOCKER WITH YOU, SARA!
I'M A LITTLE NERVOUS ABOUT IT.
SCOTT and BORGMAN
I MEAN, WHAT IF IT DOESN'T WORK OUT, JEREMY?
WHAT IF IT'S TOO MUCH TOGETHER-NESS?
WHAT IF OUR QUIRKS OR PERSONAL HABITS MAKE THE OTHER PERSON UNCOMFORTABLE?
SARA... SARA... SARA...
I CAN ALMOST GUARANTEE THAT WON'T HAPPEN.
GOOD. WHAT SHELF DO THE TAMPONS GO ON?

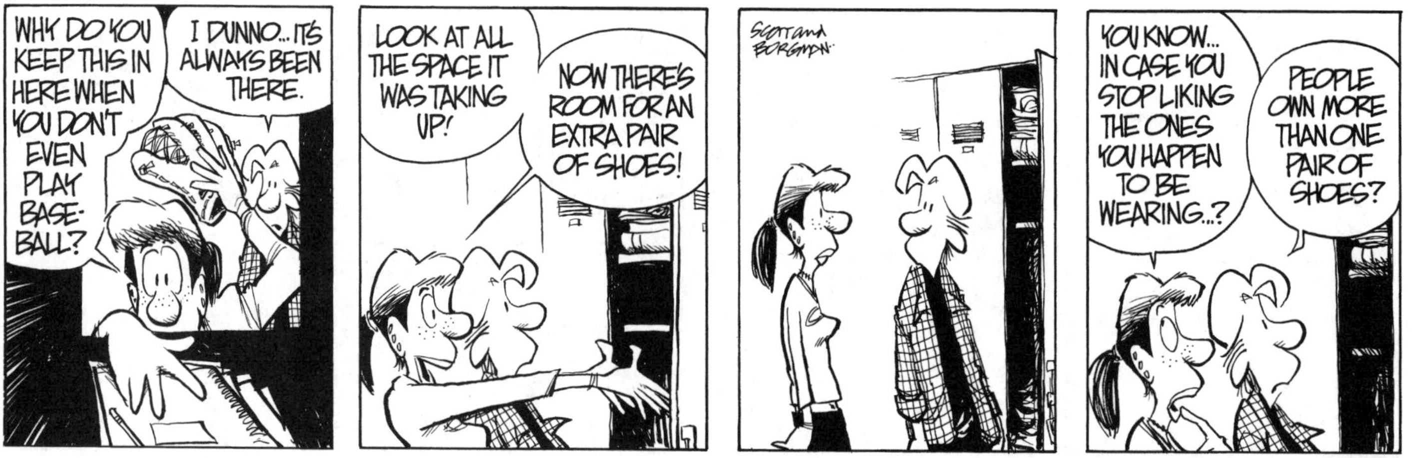
WHY DO YOU KEEP THIS IN HERE WHEN YOU DON'T EVEN PLAY BASE-BALL?
I DUNNO... IT'S ALWAYS BEEN THERE.
LOOK AT ALL THE SPACE IT WAS TAKING UP!
NOW THERE'S ROOM FOR AN EXTRA PAIR OF SHOES!
SCOTT and BORGMAN
YOU KNOW... IN CASE YOU STOP LIKING THE ONES YOU HAPPEN TO BE WEARING...?
PEOPLE OWN MORE THAN ONE PAIR OF SHOES?

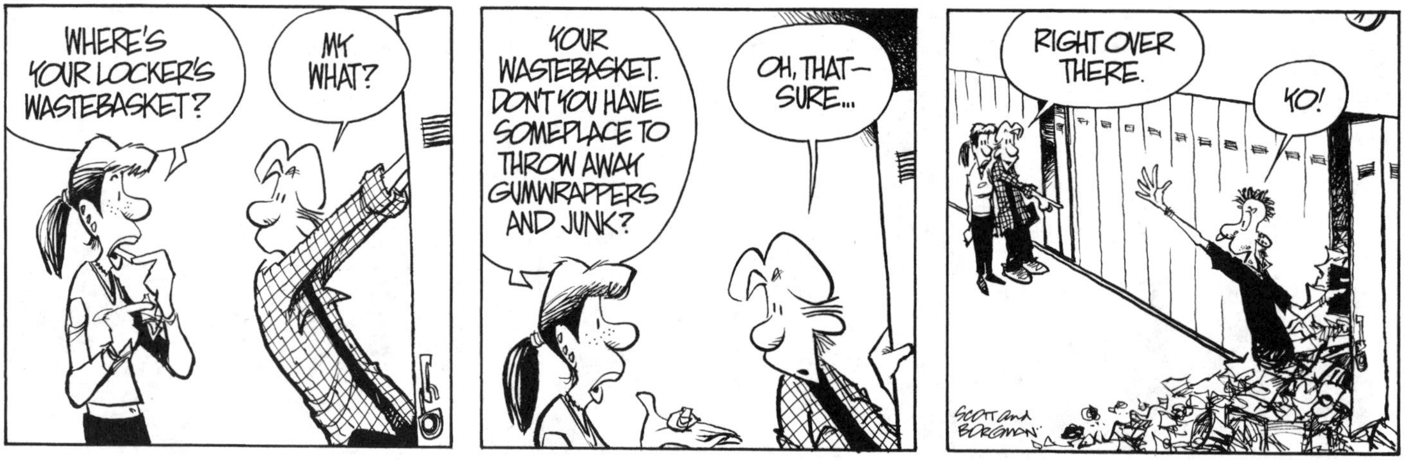
WHERE'S YOUR LOCKER'S WASTEBASKET?
MY WHAT?
YOUR WASTEBASKET. DON'T YOU HAVE SOMEPLACE TO THROW AWAY GUMWRAPPERS AND JUNK?
OH, THAT-SURE...
RIGHT OVER THERE.
YO!
SCOTT and BORGMAN

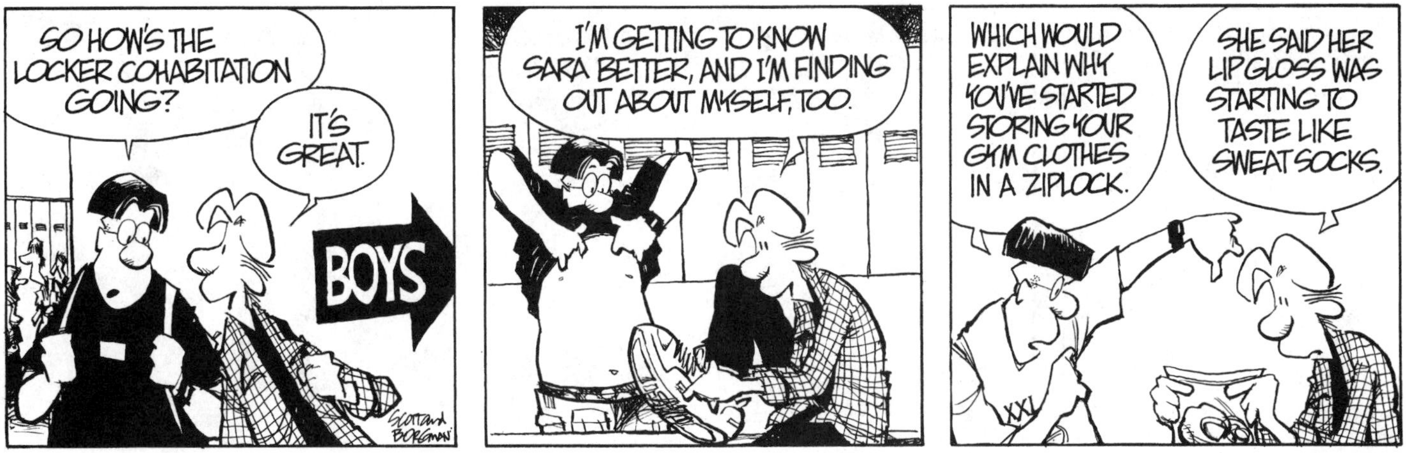
SO HOW'S THE LOCKER COHABITATION GOING?
IT'S GREAT.
BOYS
SCOTT and BORGMAN
I'M GETTING TO KNOW SARA BETTER, AND I'M FINDING OUT ABOUT MYSELF, TOO.
WHICH WOULD EXPLAIN WHY YOU'VE STARTED STORING YOUR GYM CLOTHES IN A ZIPLOCK.
SHE SAID HER LIP GLOSS WAS STARTING TO TASTE LIKE SWEAT SOCKS.
XXL

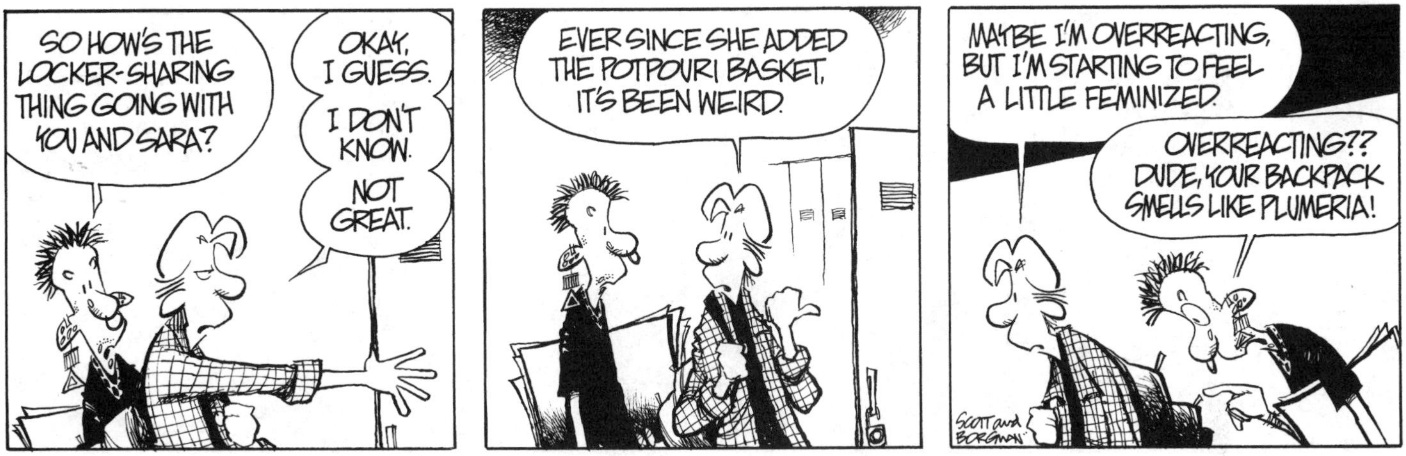
SO HOW'S THE LOCKER-SHARING THING GOING WITH YOU AND SARA?
OKAY, I GUESS.
I DON'T KNOW.
NOT GREAT.
EVER SINCE SHE ADDED THE POTPOURI BASKET, IT'S BEEN WEIRD.
MAYBE I'M OVERREACTING, BUT I'M STARTING TO FEEL A LITTLE FEMINIZED.
OVERREACTING?? DUDE, YOUR BACKPACK SMELLS LIKE PLUMERIA!
SCOTT and BORGMAN

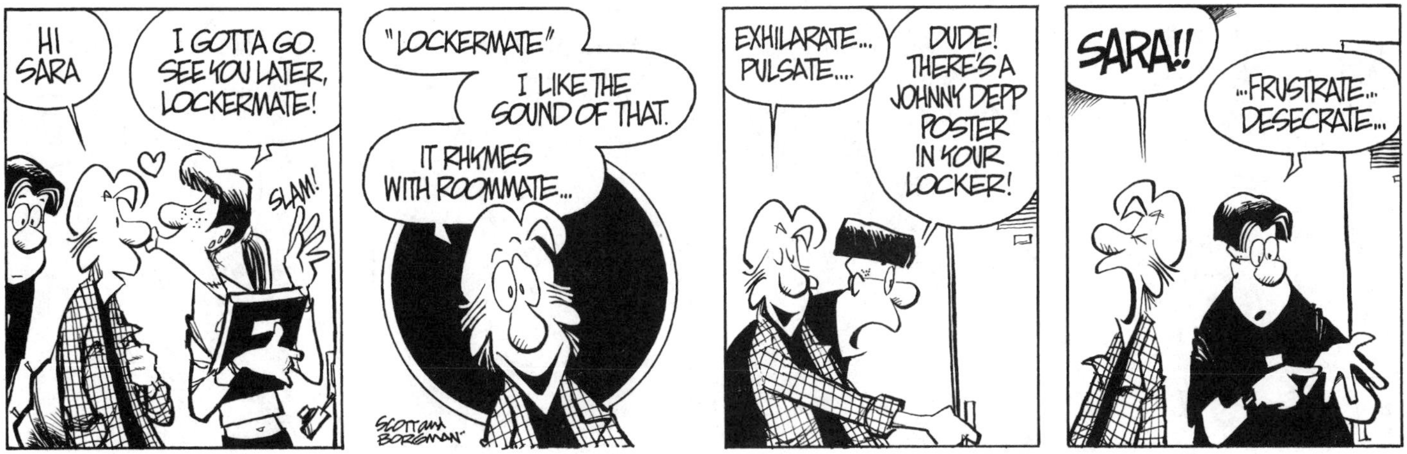
HI SARA
I GOTTA GO. SEE YOU LATER, LOCKERMATE!
SLAM!
"LOCKERMATE"
I LIKE THE SOUND OF THAT.
IT RHYMES WITH ROOMMATE...
SCOTT and BORGMAN
EXHILARATE... PULSATE....
DUDE! THERE'S A JOHNNY DEPP POSTER IN YOUR LOCKER!
SARA!!
...FRUSTRATE... DESECRATE...

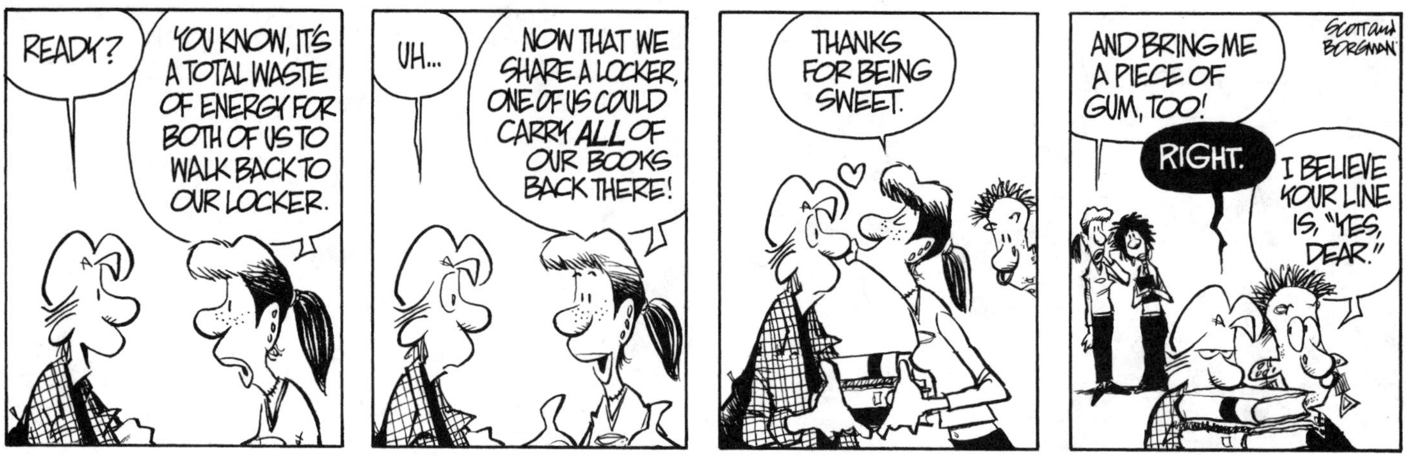
READY?
YOU KNOW, IT'S A TOTAL WASTE OF ENERGY FOR BOTH OF US TO WALK BACK TO OUR LOCKER.
UH...
NOW THAT WE SHARE A LOCKER, ONE OF US COULD CARRY ALL OF OUR BOOKS BACK THERE!
THANKS FOR BEING SWEET.
AND BRING ME A PIECE OF GUM, TOO!
RIGHT.
I BELIEVE YOUR LINE IS, "YES, DEAR."
SCOTT AND BORGMAN

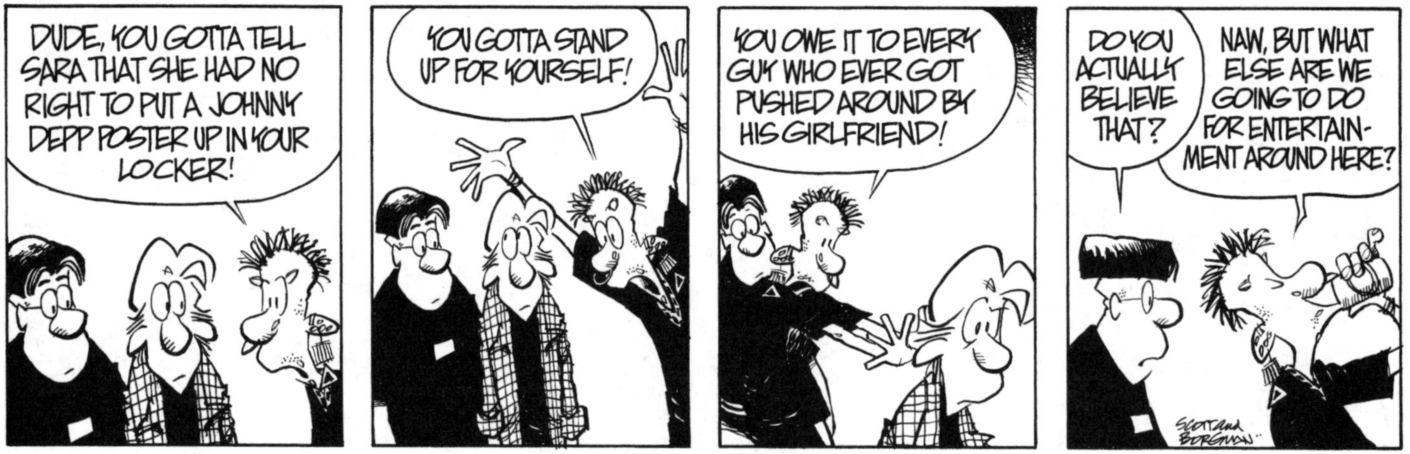
DUDE, YOU GOTTA TELL SARA THAT SHE HAD NO RIGHT TO PUT A JOHNNY DEPP POSTER UP IN YOUR LOCKER!
YOU GOTTA STAND UP FOR YOURSELF!
YOU OWE IT TO EVERY GUY WHO EVER GOT PUSHED AROUND BY HIS GIRLFRIEND!
DO YOU ACTUALLY BELIEVE THAT?
NAW, BUT WHAT ELSE ARE WE GOING TO DO FOR ENTERTAIN-MENT AROUND HERE?
SCOTT AND BORGMAN

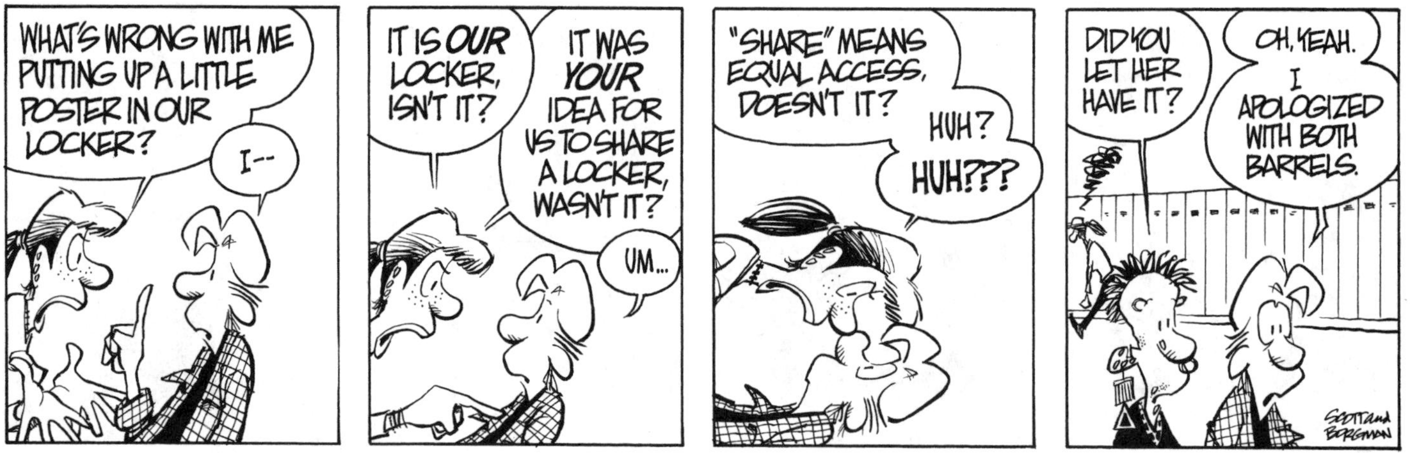
WHAT'S WRONG WITH ME PUTTING UP A LITTLE POSTER IN OUR LOCKER?
I--
IT IS OUR LOCKER, ISN'T IT?
IT WAS YOUR IDEA FOR US TO SHARE A LOCKER, WASN'T IT?
UM...
"SHARE" MEANS EQUAL ACCESS, DOESN'T IT?
HUH?
HUH???
DID YOU LET HER HAVE IT?
OH, YEAH.
I APOLOGIZED WITH BOTH BARRELS.
SCOTT AND BORGMAN

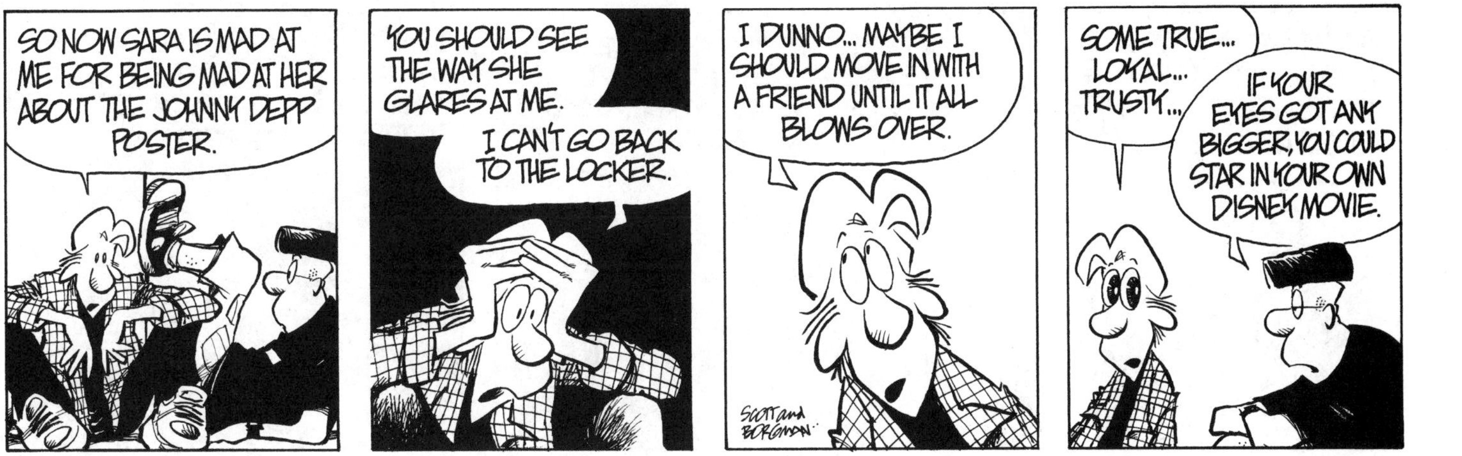
SO NOW SARA IS MAD AT ME FOR BEING MAD AT HER ABOUT THE JOHNNY DEPP POSTER.
YOU SHOULD SEE THE WAY SHE GLARES AT ME.
I CAN'T GO BACK TO THE LOCKER.
I DUNNO... MAYBE I SHOULD MOVE IN WITH A FRIEND UNTIL IT ALL BLOWS OVER.
SCOTT and BORGMAN
SOME TRUE... LOYAL... TRUSTY...
IF YOUR EYES GOT ANY BIGGER, YOU COULD STAR IN YOUR OWN DISNEY MOVIE.

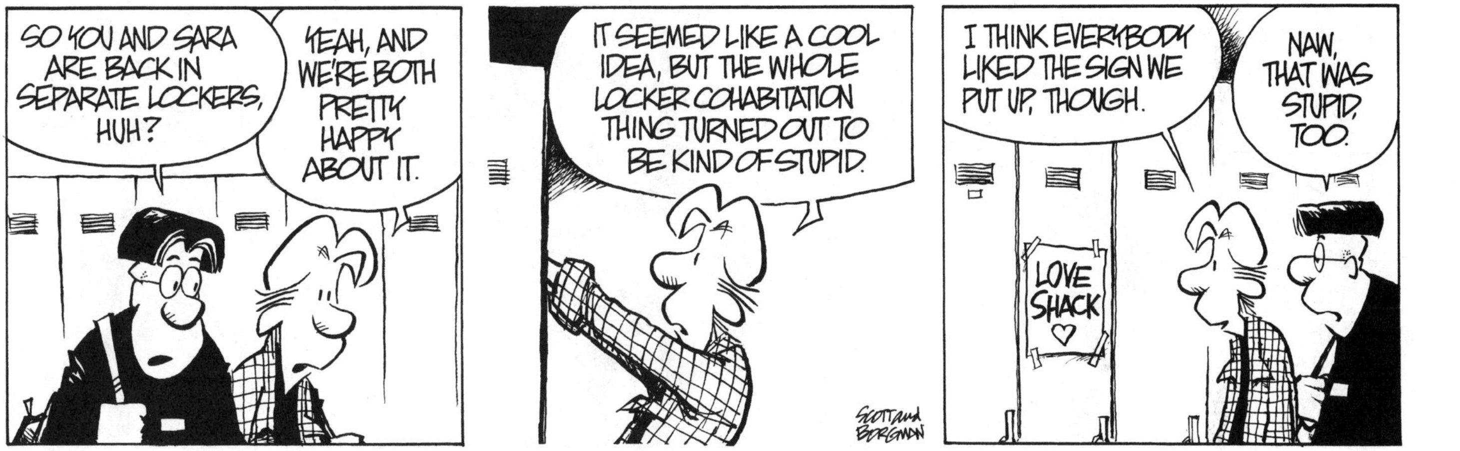
SO YOU AND SARA ARE BACK IN SEPARATE LOCKERS, HUH?
YEAH, AND WE'RE BOTH PRETTY HAPPY ABOUT IT.
IT SEEMED LIKE A COOL IDEA, BUT THE WHOLE LOCKER COHABITATION THING TURNED OUT TO BE KIND OF STUPID.
SCOTT and BORGMAN
I THINK EVERYBODY LIKED THE SIGN WE PUT UP, THOUGH.
NAW, THAT WAS STUPID, TOO.
LOVE SHACK

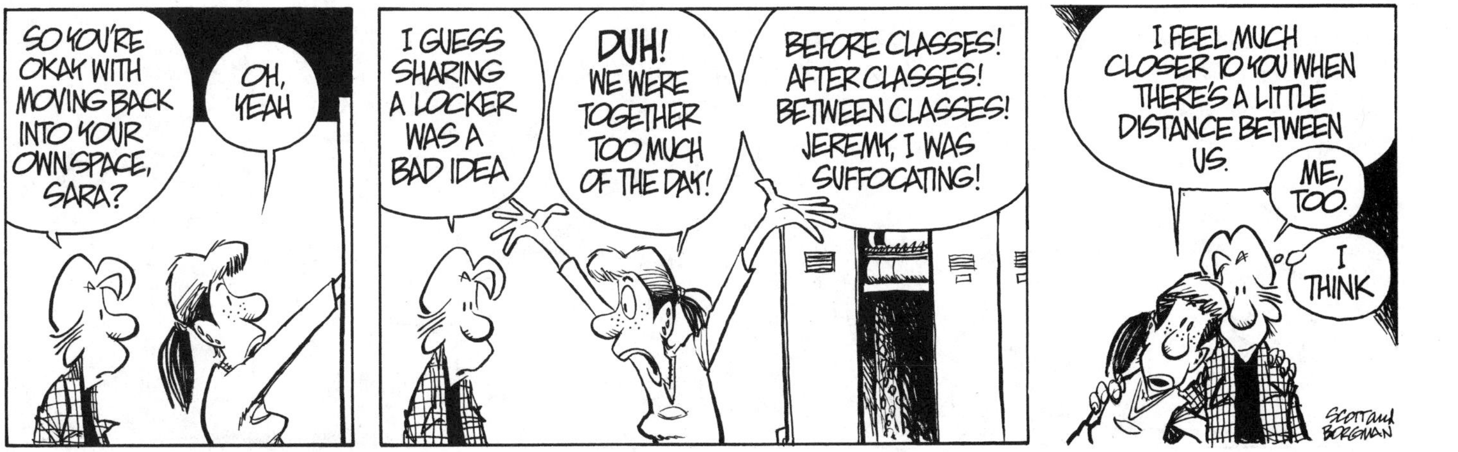
SO YOU'RE OKAY WITH MOVING BACK INTO YOUR OWN SPACE, SARA?
OH, YEAH
I GUESS SHARING A LOCKER WAS A BAD IDEA
DUH! WE WERE TOGETHER TOO MUCH OF THE DAY!
BEFORE CLASSES! AFTER CLASSES! BETWEEN CLASSES! JEREMY, I WAS SUFFOCATING!
I FEEL MUCH CLOSER TO YOU WHEN THERE'S A LITTLE DISTANCE BETWEEN US.
ME, TOO.
I THINK
SCOTT and BORGMAN

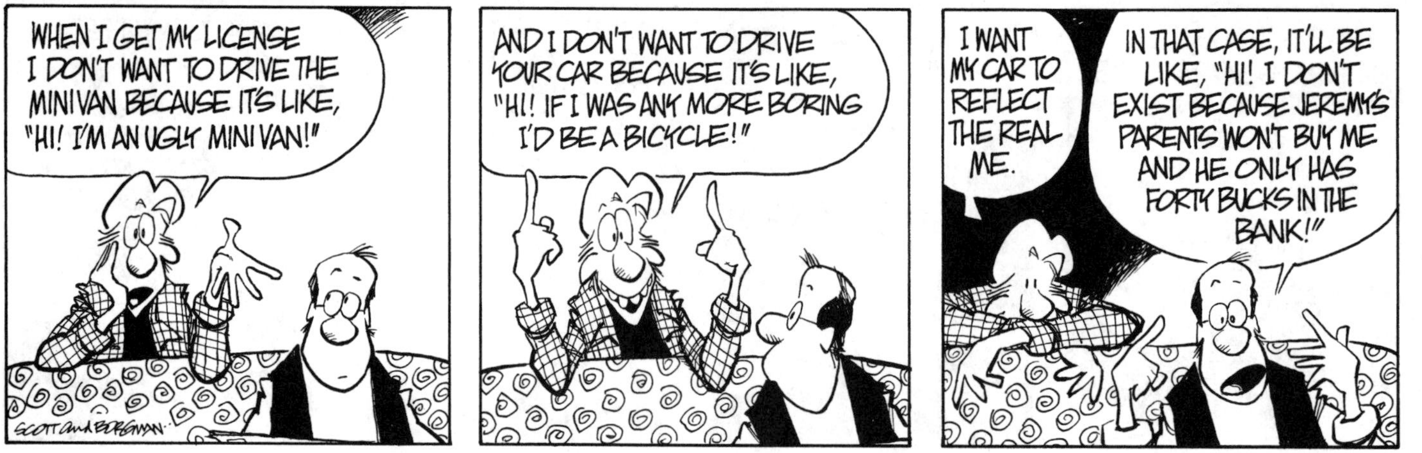
WHEN I GET MY LICENSE I DON'T WANT TO DRIVE THE MINIVAN BECAUSE IT'S LIKE, "HI! I'M AN UGLY MINIVAN!"
SCOTT and BORGMAN
AND I DON'T WANT TO DRIVE YOUR CAR BECAUSE IT'S LIKE, "HI! IF I WAS ANY MORE BORING I'D BE A BICYCLE!"
I WANT MY CAR TO REFLECT THE REAL ME.
IN THAT CASE, IT'LL BE LIKE, "HI! I DON'T EXIST BECAUSE JEREMY'S PARENTS WON'T BUY ME AND HE ONLY HAS FORTY BUCKS IN THE BANK!"

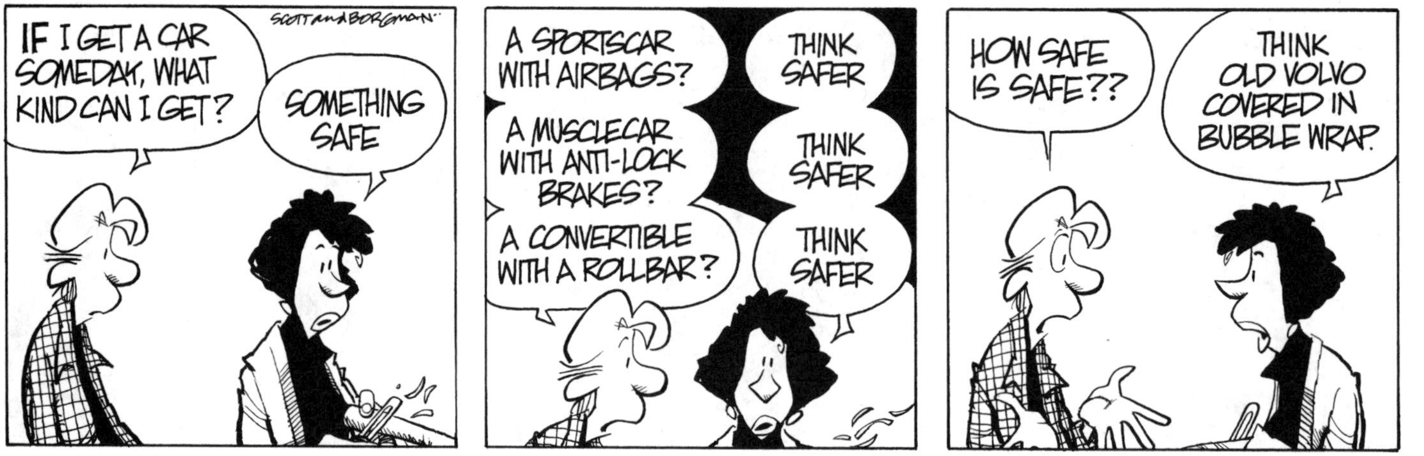
SCOTT and BORGMAN
IF I GET A CAR SOMEDAY, WHAT KIND CAN I GET?
SOMETHING SAFE
A SPORTSCAR WITH AIRBAGS?
THINK SAFER
A MUSCLECAR WITH ANTI-LOCK BRAKES?
THINK SAFER
A CONVERTIBLE WITH A ROLLBAR?
THINK SAFER
HOW SAFE IS SAFE??
THINK OLD VOLVO COVERED IN BUBBLE WRAP.

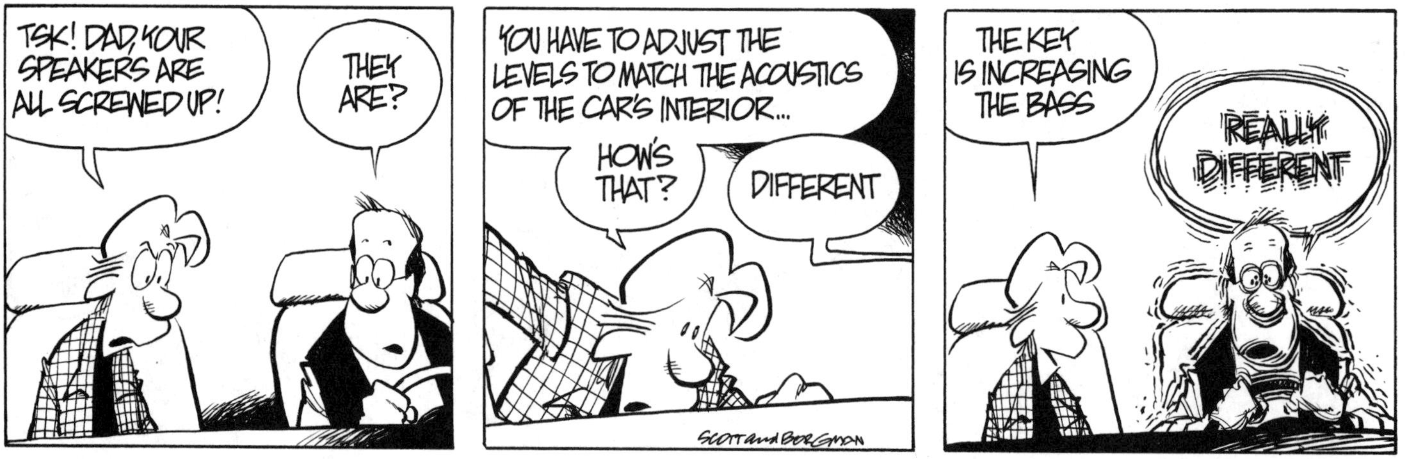
TSK! DAD, YOUR SPEAKERS ARE ALL SCREWED UP!
THEY ARE?
YOU HAVE TO ADJUST THE LEVELS TO MATCH THE ACOUSTICS OF THE CAR'S INTERIOR...
HOW'S THAT?
DIFFERENT
SCOTT and BORGMAN
THE KEY IS INCREASING THE BASS
REALLY DIFFERENT

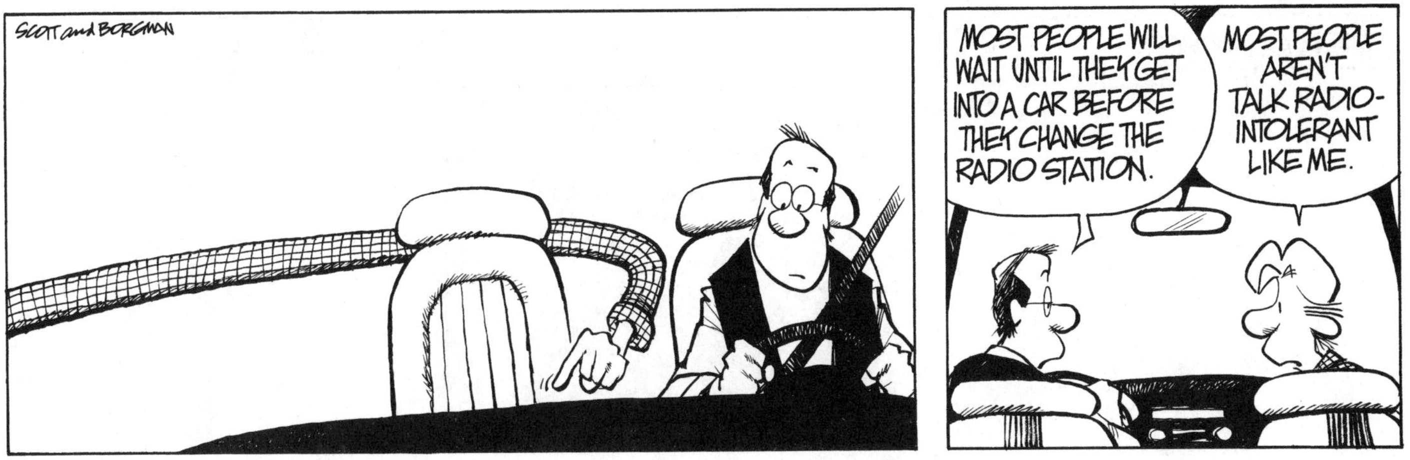
SCOTT and BORGMAN
MOST PEOPLE WILL WAIT UNTIL THEY GET INTO A CAR BEFORE THEY CHANGE THE RADIO STATION.
MOST PEOPLE AREN'T TALK RADIO-INTOLERANT LIKE ME.

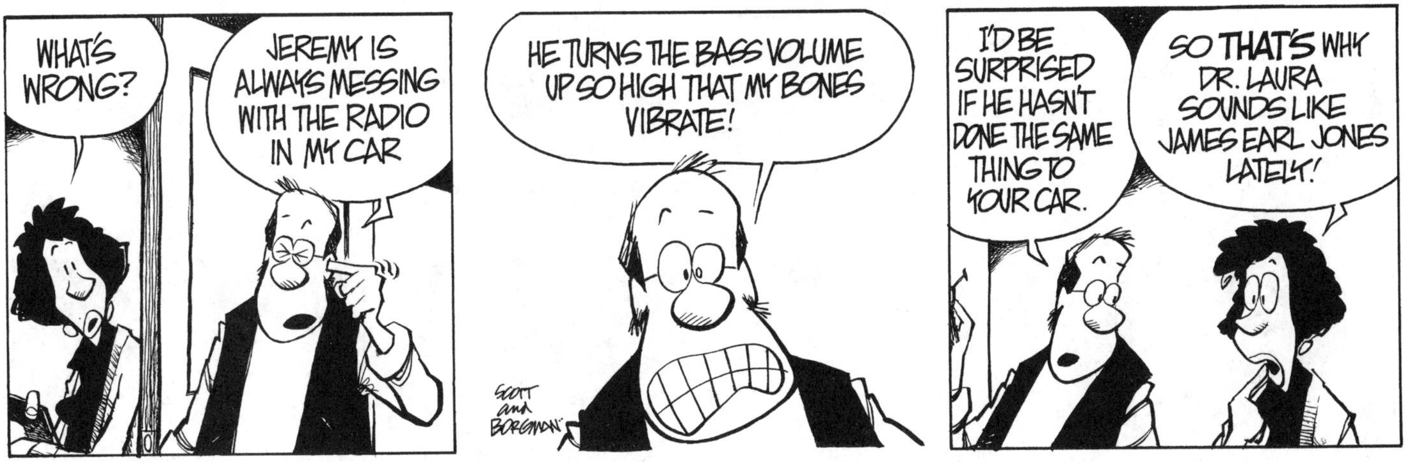
WHAT'S WRONG?
JEREMY IS ALWAYS MESSING WITH THE RADIO IN MY CAR
HE TURNS THE BASS VOLUME UP SO HIGH THAT MY BONES VIBRATE!
SCOTT and BORGMAN
I'D BE SURPRISED IF HE HASN'T DONE THE SAME THING TO YOUR CAR.
SO THAT'S WHY DR. LAURA SOUNDS LIKE JAMES EARL JONES LATELY!

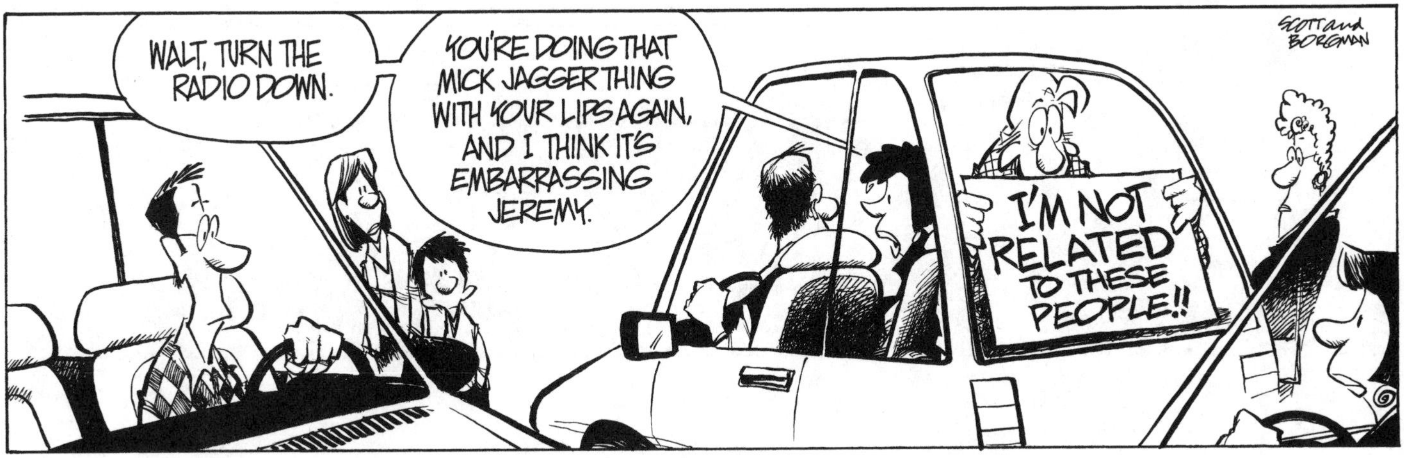
WALT, TURN THE RADIO DOWN.
YOU'RE DOING THAT MICK JAGGER THING WITH YOUR LIPS AGAIN, AND I THINK IT'S EMBARRASSING JEREMY.
I'M NOT RELATED TO THESE PEOPLE!!
SCOTT and BORGMAN

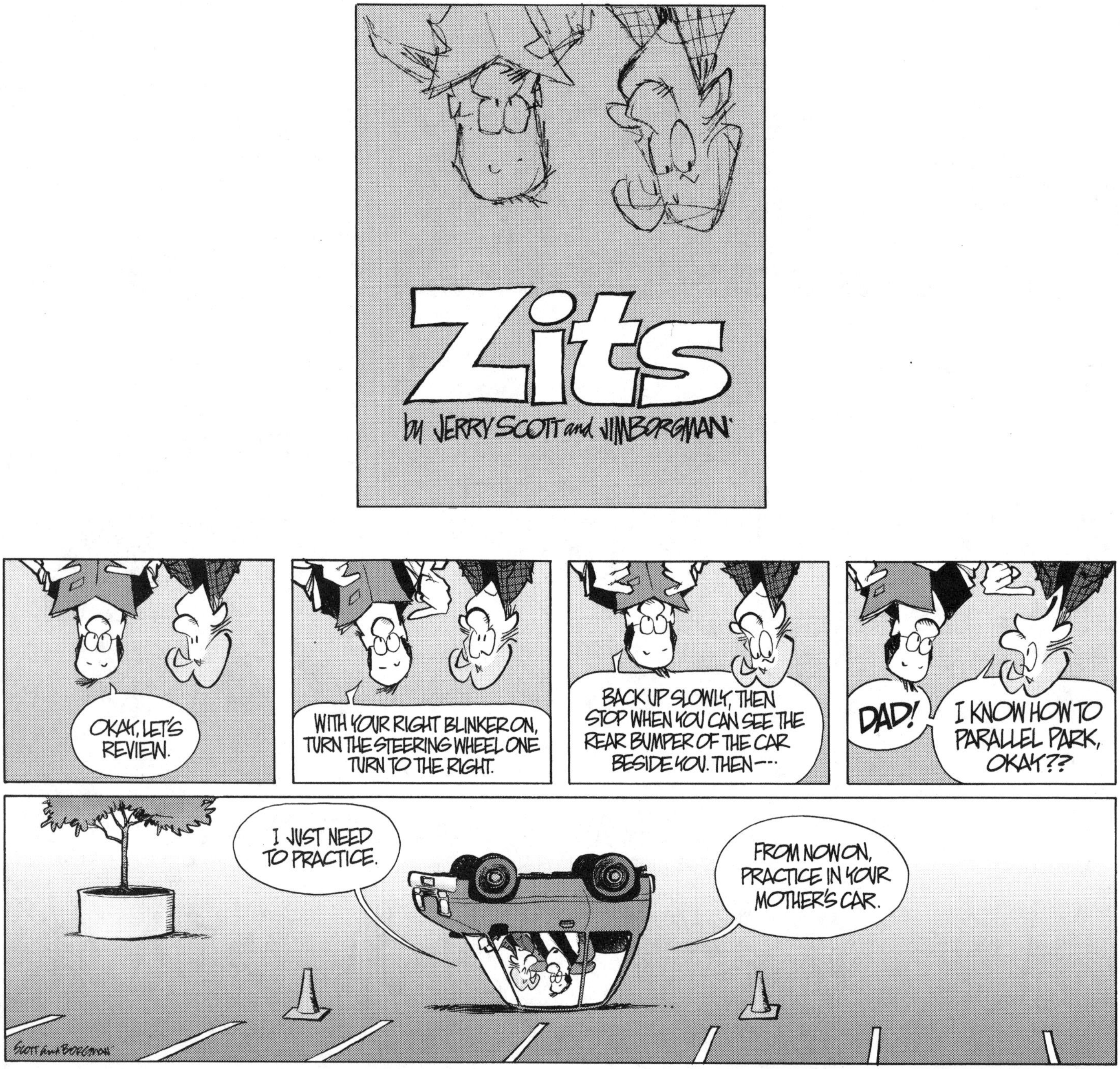

Zits
by JERRY SCOTT and JIM BORGMAN
OKAY, LET'S REVIEW.
WITH YOUR RIGHT BLINKER ON, TURN THE STEERING WHEEL ONE TURN TO THE RIGHT.
BACK UP SLOWLY, THEN STOP WHEN YOU CAN SEE THE REAR BUMPER OF THE CAR BESIDE YOU. THEN---
DAD!
I KNOW HOW TO PARALLEL PARK, OKAY??
I JUST NEED TO PRACTICE.
FROM NOW ON, PRACTICE IN YOUR MOTHER'S CAR.
SCOTT and BORGMAN

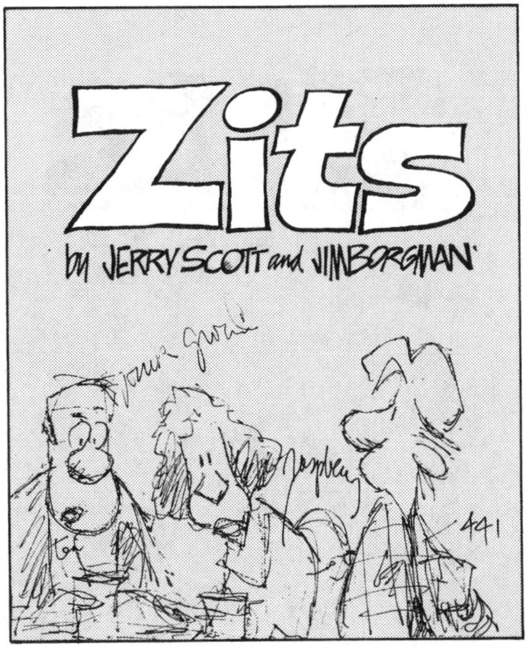
Zits
by JERRY SCOTT and JIM BORGMAN

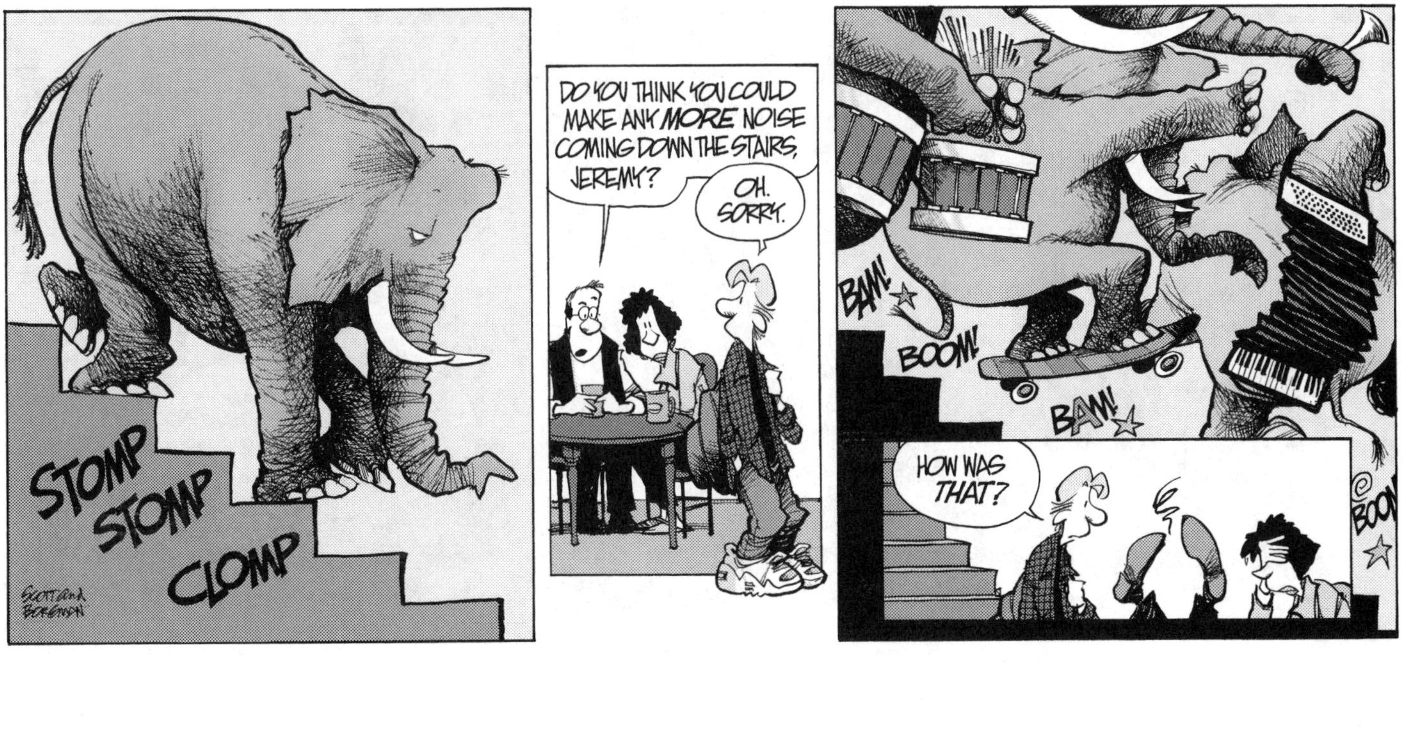
STOMP
STOMP
CLOMP
DO YOU THINK YOU COULD MAKE ANY MORE NOISE COMING DOWN THE STAIRS, JEREMY?
OH. SORRY.
BAM!
BOOM!
BAM!
BOOM
HOW WAS THAT?

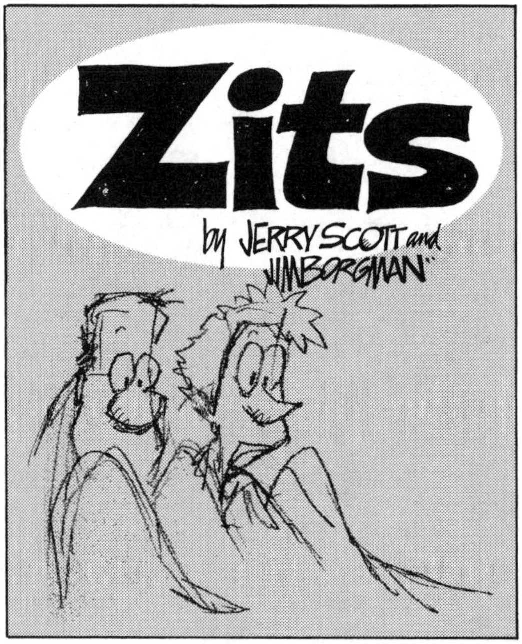
Zits
by JERRY SCOTT and JIM BORGMAN

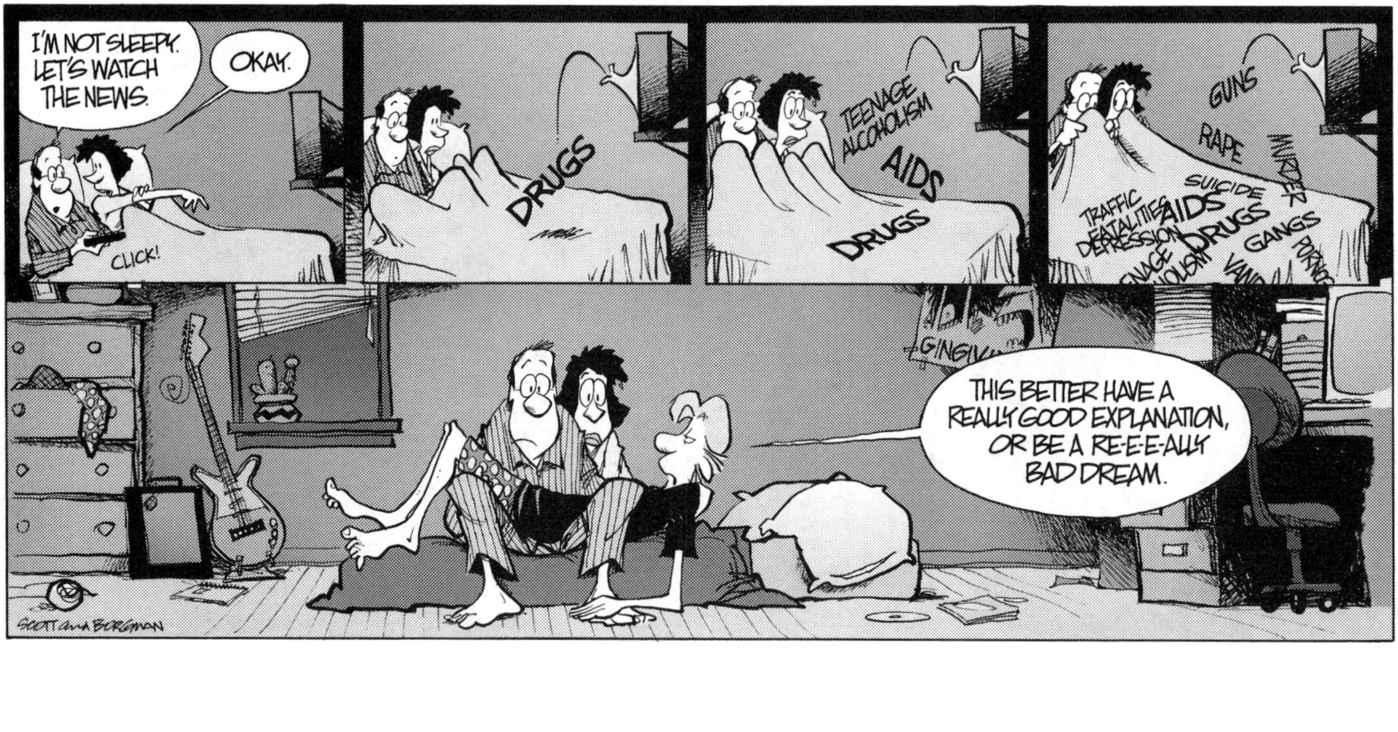
I'M NOT SLEEPY. LET'S WATCH THE NEWS.
OKAY.
CLICK!
DRUGS
TEENAGE ALCOHOLISM
AIDS
DRUGS
GUNS
RAPE
MURDER
SUICIDE
TRAFFIC FATALITIES
AIDS
DEPRESSION
DRUGS
GANGS
THIS BETTER HAVE A REALLY GOOD EXPLANATION, OR BE A RE-E-E-ALLY BAD DREAM.
SCOTT and BORGMAN

Zits
STUDENT DRIVER
by
JERRY SCOTT and JIM BORGMAN

HEY! THERE GOES SARA!
STUDENT DRIVER
YO! SARA!
FWEEEEEE
HEY, BABY!
AROOOOOO!
SCREEEEE
ECH
★@#! IDIOTS!
IT PROBABLY WASN'T A GOOD IDEA TO DO THAT WHILE SHE WAS MERGING INTO TRAFFIC.
YEAH. THAT DEFINITELY WASN'T A AAA-APPROVED HAND SIGNAL WE JUST GOT FROM HER DRIVING INSTRUCTOR.

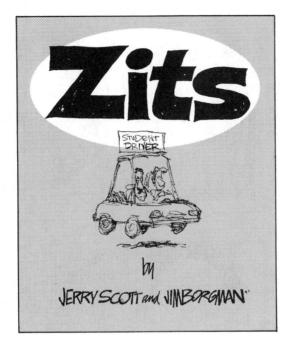

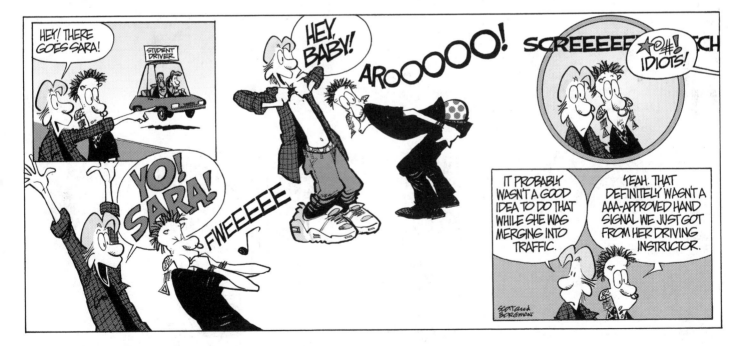

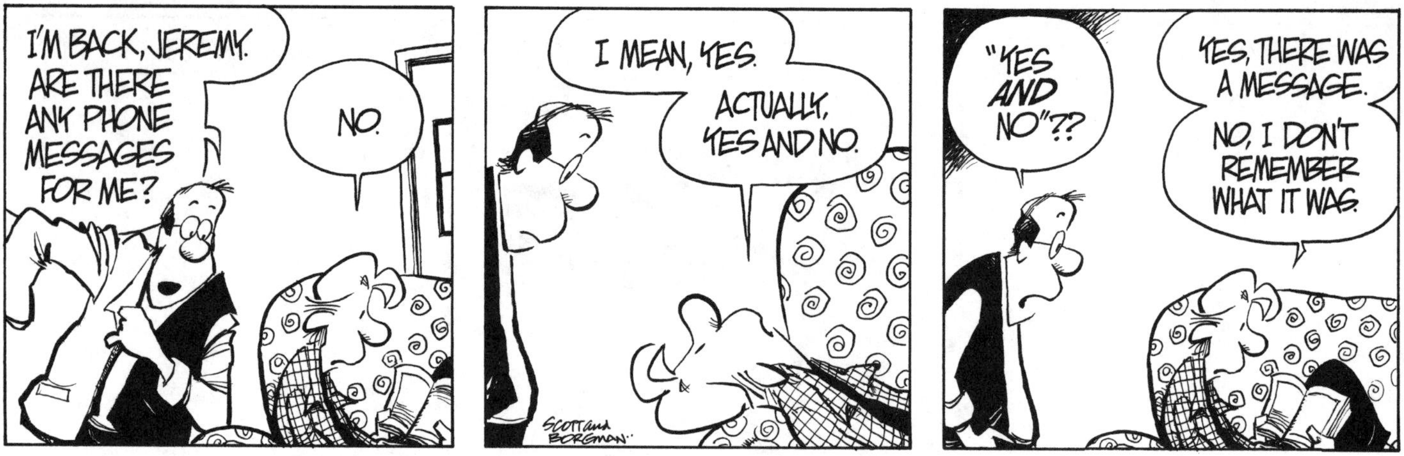
I'M BACK, JEREMY. ARE THERE ANY PHONE MESSAGES FOR ME?
NO.
I MEAN, YES.
ACTUALLY, YES AND NO.
SCOTT and BORGMAN
"YES AND NO"??
YES, THERE WAS A MESSAGE.
NO, I DON'T REMEMBER WHAT IT WAS.

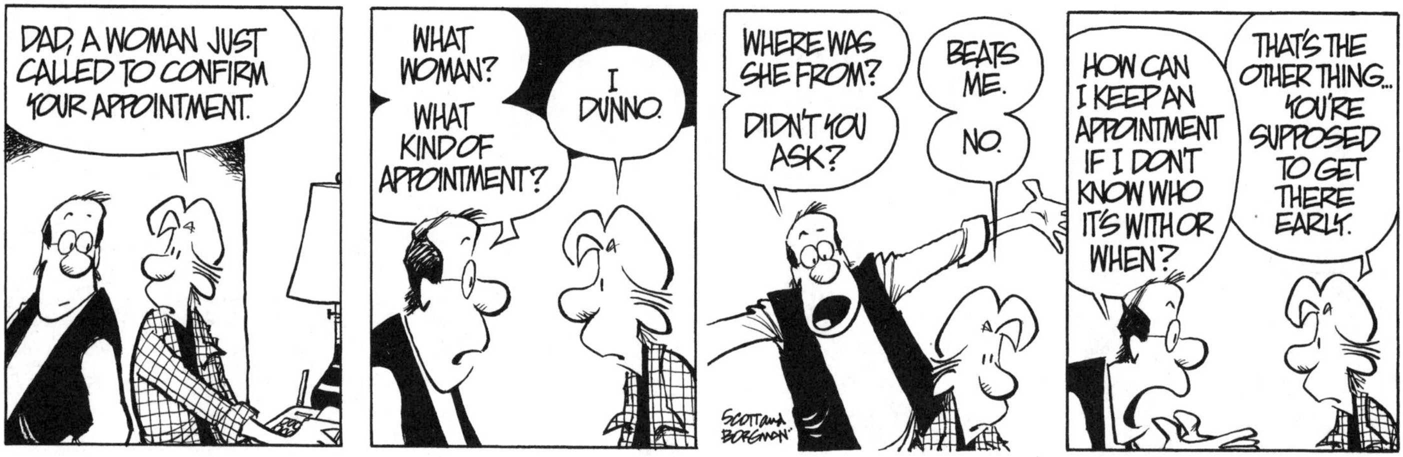
DAD, A WOMAN JUST CALLED TO CONFIRM YOUR APPOINTMENT.
WHAT WOMAN?
WHAT KIND OF APPOINTMENT?
I DUNNO.
WHERE WAS SHE FROM?
DIDN'T YOU ASK?
BEATS ME.
NO.
SCOTT and BORGMAN
HOW CAN I KEEP AN APPOINTMENT IF I DON'T KNOW WHO IT'S WITH OR WHEN?
THAT'S THE OTHER THING... YOU'RE SUPPOSED TO GET THERE EARLY.

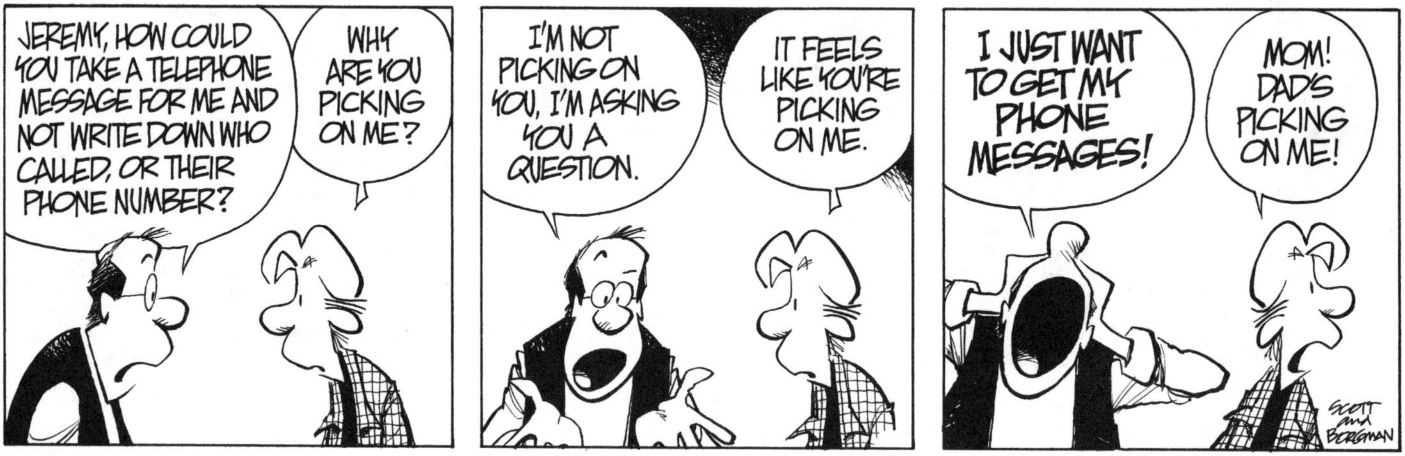
JEREMY, HOW COULD YOU TAKE A TELEPHONE MESSAGE FOR ME AND NOT WRITE DOWN WHO CALLED, OR THEIR PHONE NUMBER?
WHY ARE YOU PICKING ON ME?
I'M NOT PICKING ON YOU, I'M ASKING YOU A QUESTION.
IT FEELS LIKE YOU'RE PICKING ON ME.
I JUST WANT TO GET MY PHONE MESSAGES!
MOM! DAD'S PICKING ON ME!
SCOTT and BORGMAN

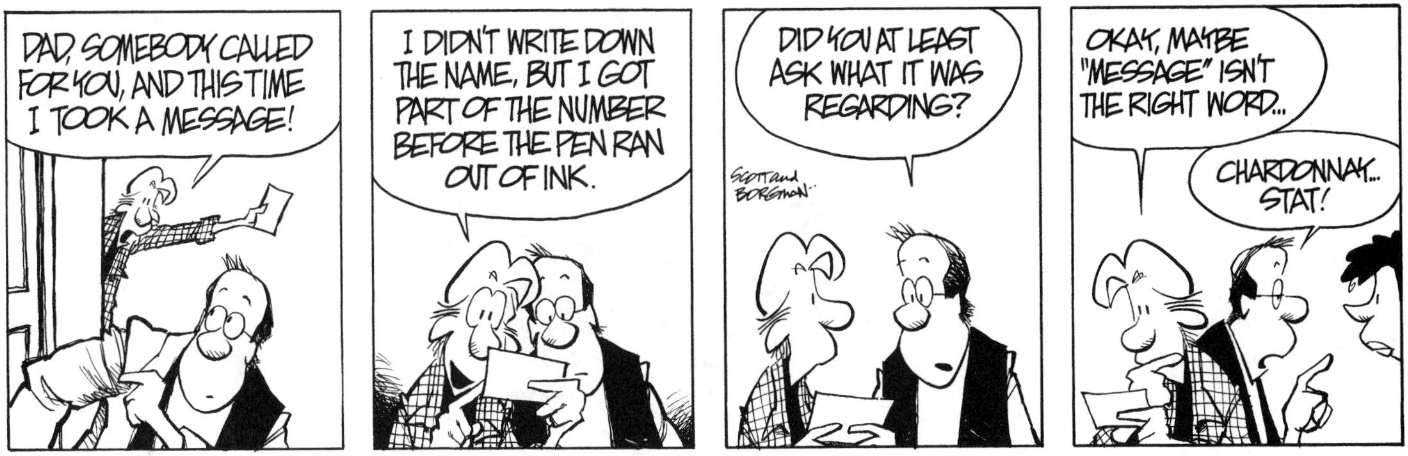
DAD, SOMEBODY CALLED FOR YOU, AND THIS TIME I TOOK A MESSAGE!
I DIDN'T WRITE DOWN THE NAME, BUT I GOT PART OF THE NUMBER BEFORE THE PEN RAN OUT OF INK.
SCOTT and BORGMAN
DID YOU AT LEAST ASK WHAT IT WAS REGARDING?
OKAY, MAYBE "MESSAGE" ISN'T THE RIGHT WORD...
CHARDONNAY... STAT!

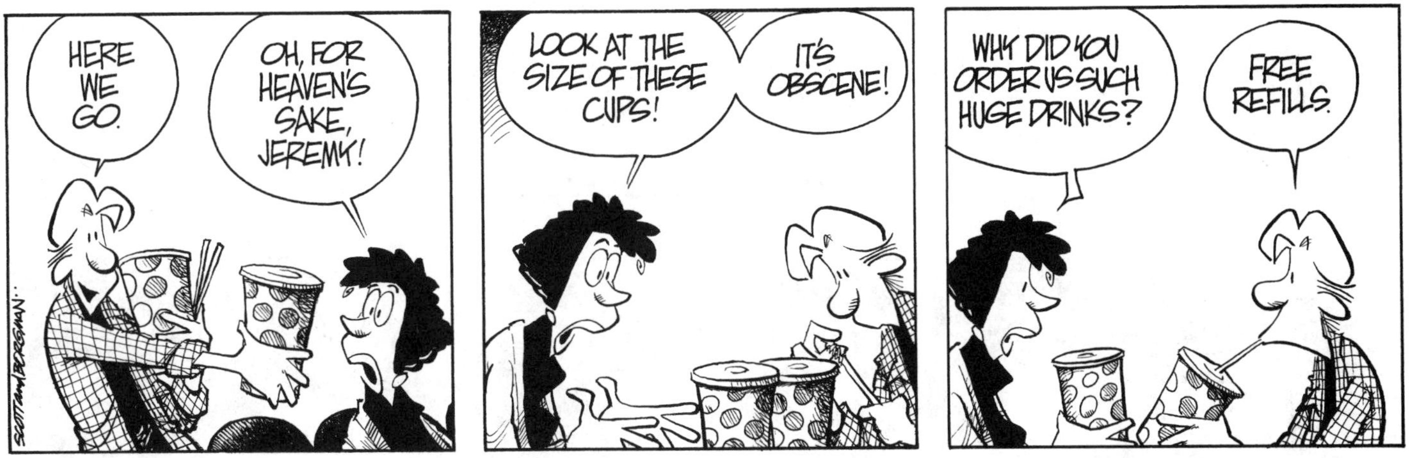
HERE WE GO.
OH, FOR HEAVEN'S SAKE, JEREMY!
SCOTT and BORGMAN
LOOK AT THE SIZE OF THESE CUPS!
IT'S OBSCENE!
WHY DID YOU ORDER US SUCH HUGE DRINKS?
FREE REFILLS.

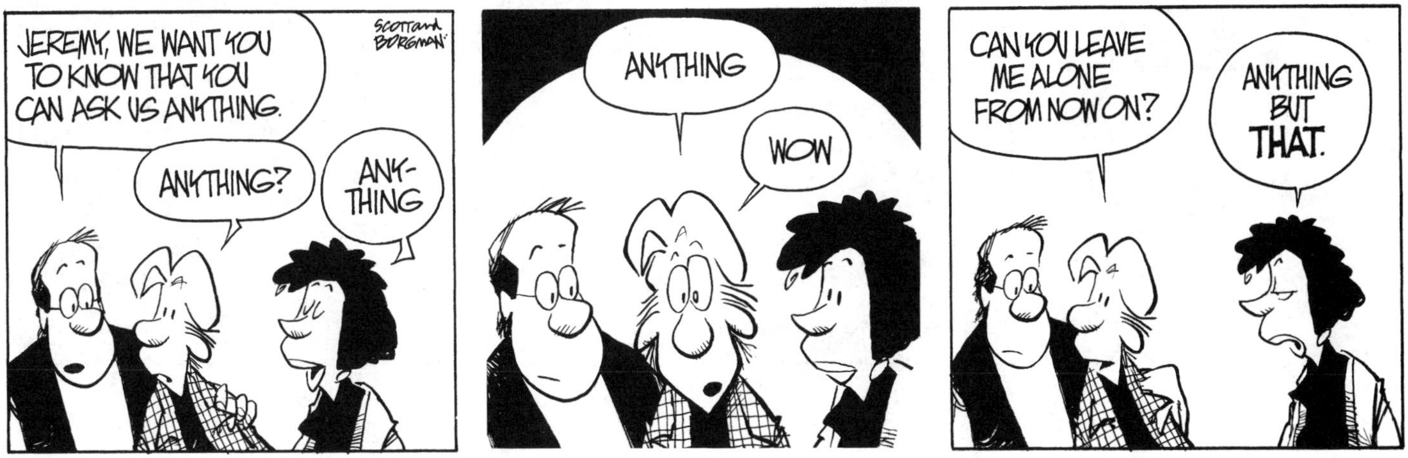
JEREMY, WE WANT YOU TO KNOW THAT YOU CAN ASK US ANYTHING.
SCOTT and BORGMAN
ANYTHING?
ANY-THING
ANYTHING
WOW
CAN YOU LEAVE ME ALONE FROM NOW ON?
ANYTHING BUT THAT.

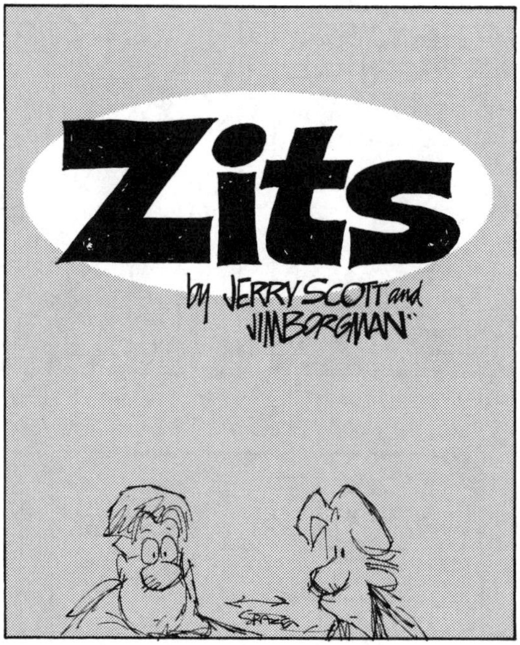
Zits
by JERRY SCOTT and JIM BORGMAN

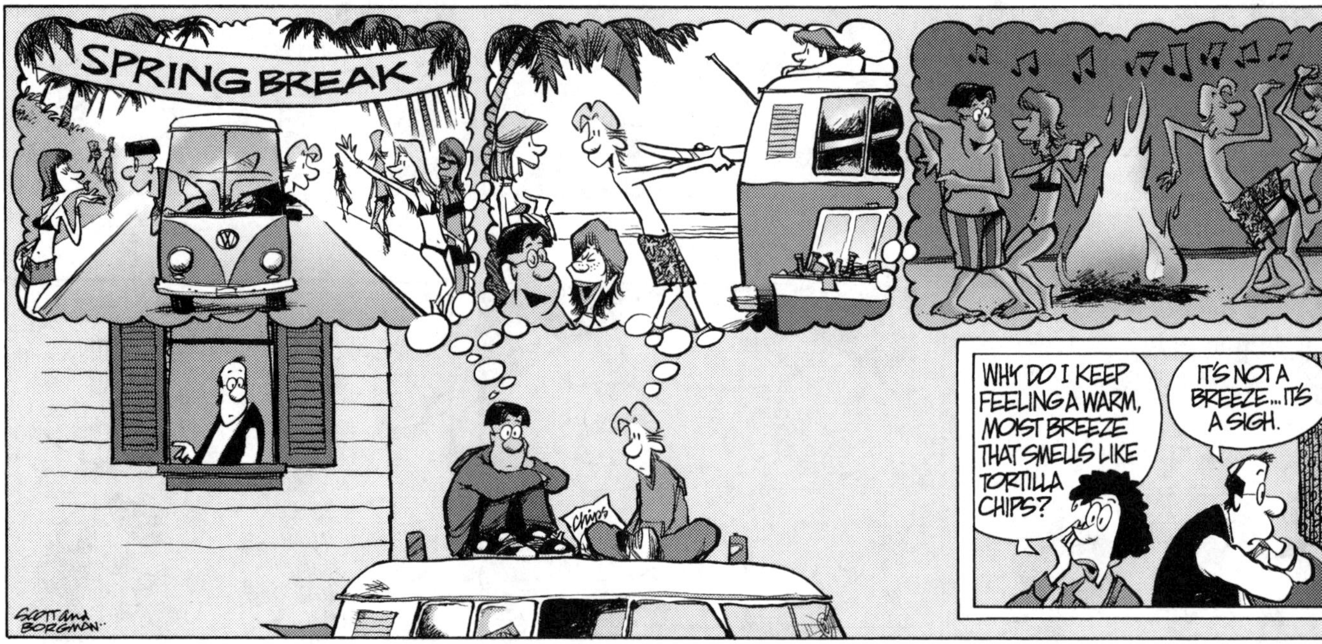
SPRING BREAK
CHIPS
WHY DO I KEEP FEELING A WARM, MOIST BREEZE THAT SMELLS LIKE TORTILLA CHIPS?
IT'S NOT A BREEZE... IT'S A SIGH.
SCOTT AND BORGMAN

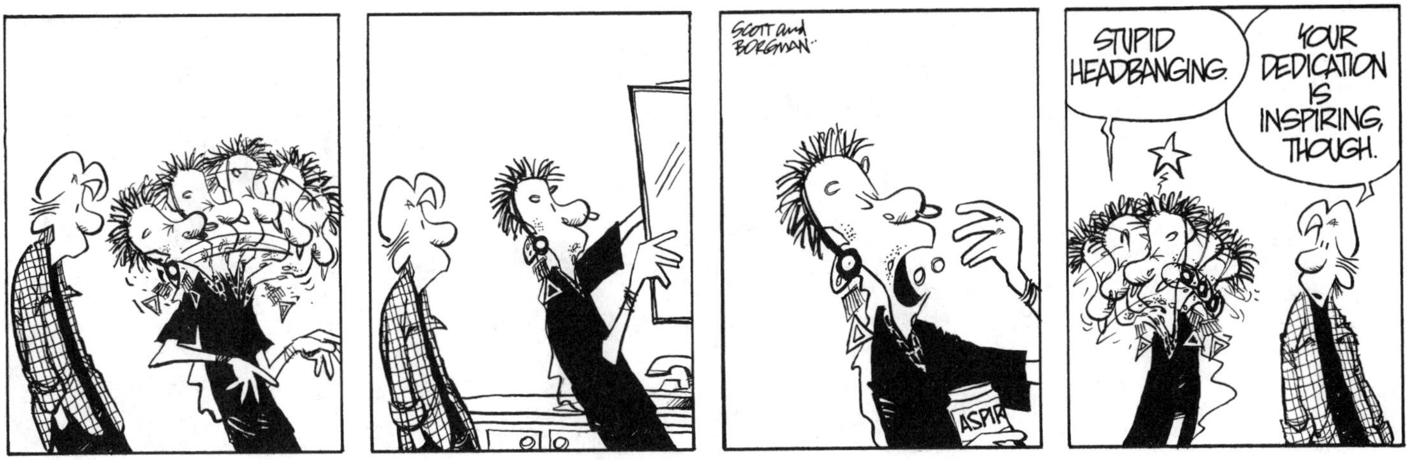
SCOTT and BORGMAN
ASPIR
STUPID HEADBANGING.
YOUR DEDICATION IS INSPIRING, THOUGH.

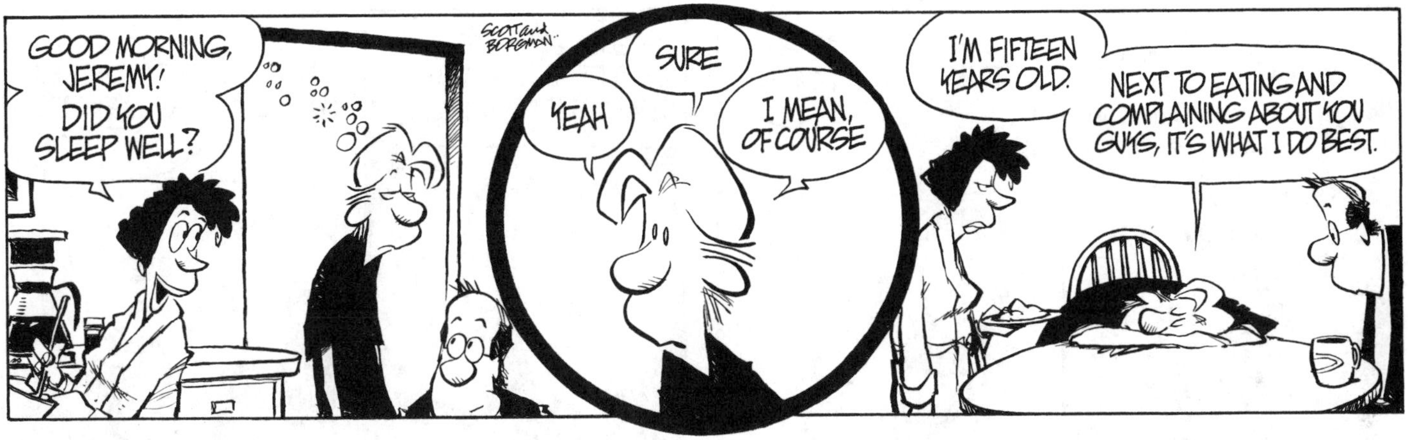
GOOD MORNING, JEREMY!
DID YOU SLEEP WELL?
SCOTT and BORGMAN
YEAH
SURE
I MEAN, OF COURSE
I'M FIFTEEN YEARS OLD.
NEXT TO EATING AND COMPLAINING ABOUT YOU GUYS, IT'S WHAT I DO BEST.

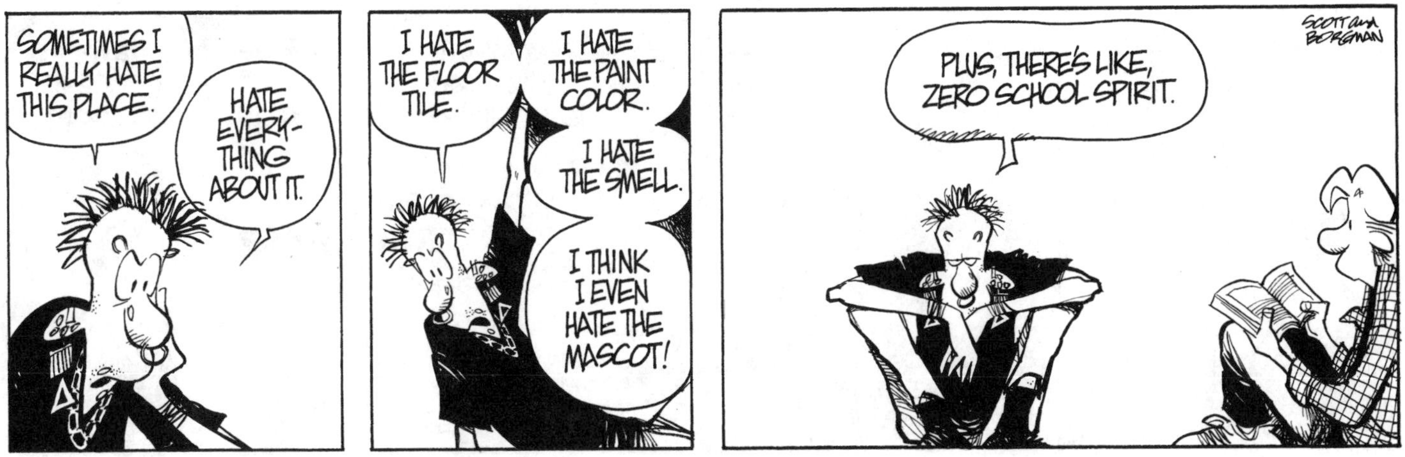
SOMETIMES I REALLY HATE THIS PLACE.
HATE EVERYTHING ABOUT IT.
I HATE THE FLOOR TILE.
I HATE THE PAINT COLOR.
I HATE THE SMELL.
I THINK I EVEN HATE THE MASCOT!
SCOTT and BORGMAN
PLUS, THERE'S LIKE, ZERO SCHOOL SPIRIT.

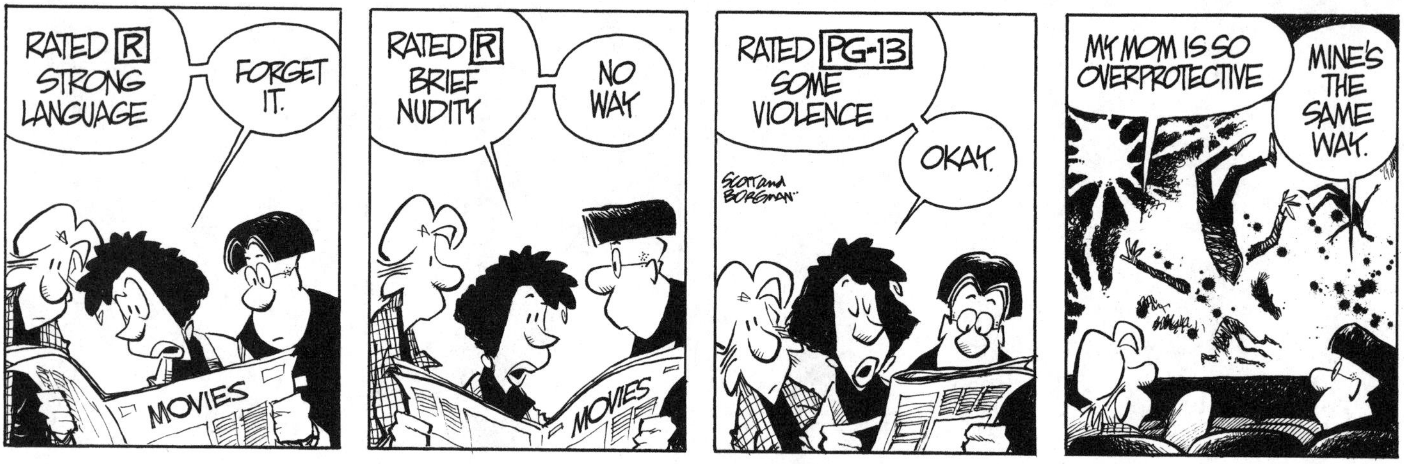
RATED R STRONG LANGUAGE
FORGET IT.
RATED R BRIEF NUDITY
NO WAY
MOVIES
RATED PG-13 SOME VIOLENCE
OKAY.
SCOTT and BORGMAN
MY MOM IS SO OVERPROTECTIVE
MINE'S THE SAME WAY.

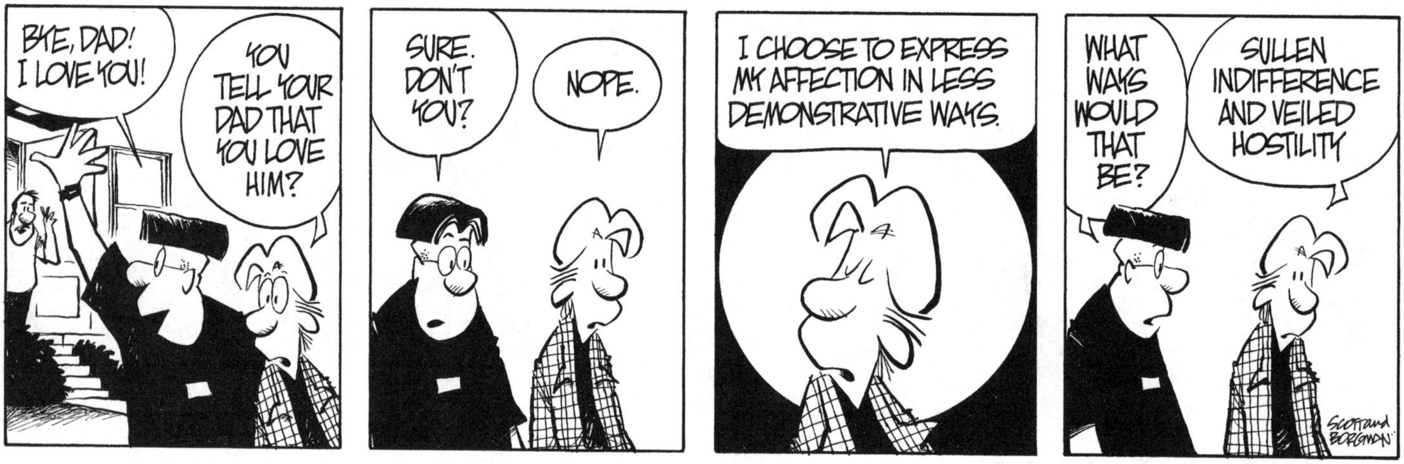
BYE, DAD! I LOVE YOU!
YOU TELL YOUR DAD THAT YOU LOVE HIM?
SURE. DON'T YOU?
NOPE.
I CHOOSE TO EXPRESS MY AFFECTION IN LESS DEMONSTRATIVE WAYS.
WHAT WAYS WOULD THAT BE?
SULLEN INDIFFERENCE AND VEILED HOSTILITY
SCOTT and BORGMAN

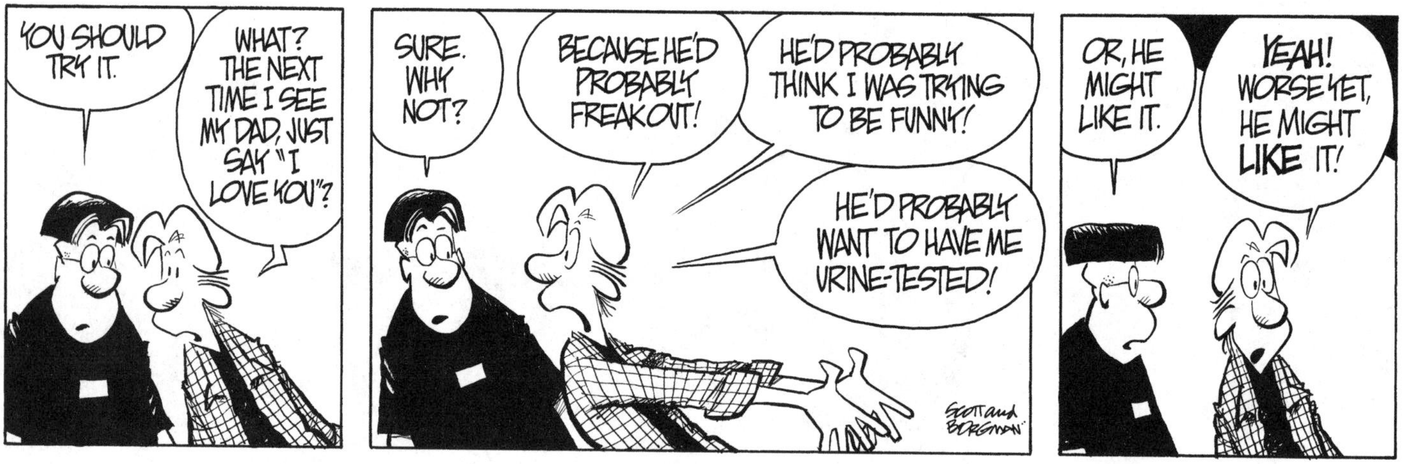
YOU SHOULD TRY IT.
WHAT? THE NEXT TIME I SEE MY DAD, JUST SAY "I LOVE YOU"?
SURE. WHY NOT?
BECAUSE HE'D PROBABLY FREAK OUT!
HE'D PROBABLY THINK I WAS TRYING TO BE FUNNY!
HE'D PROBABLY WANT TO HAVE ME URINE-TESTED!
SCOTT and BORGMAN
OR, HE MIGHT LIKE IT.
YEAH! WORSE YET, HE MIGHT LIKE IT!

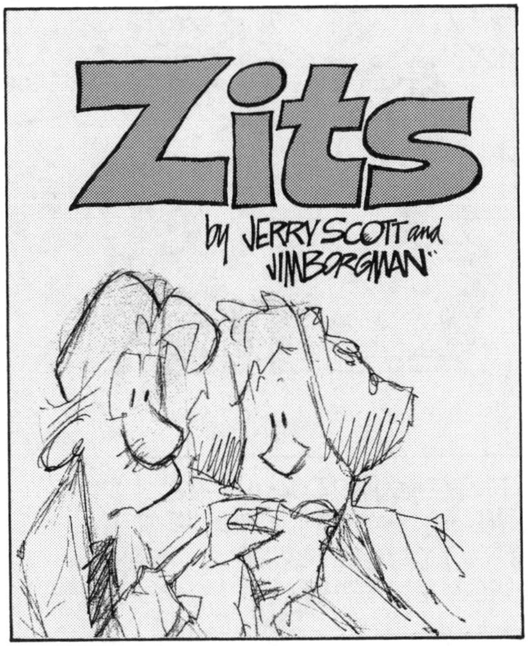
Zits
by JERRY SCOTT and JIM BORGMAN

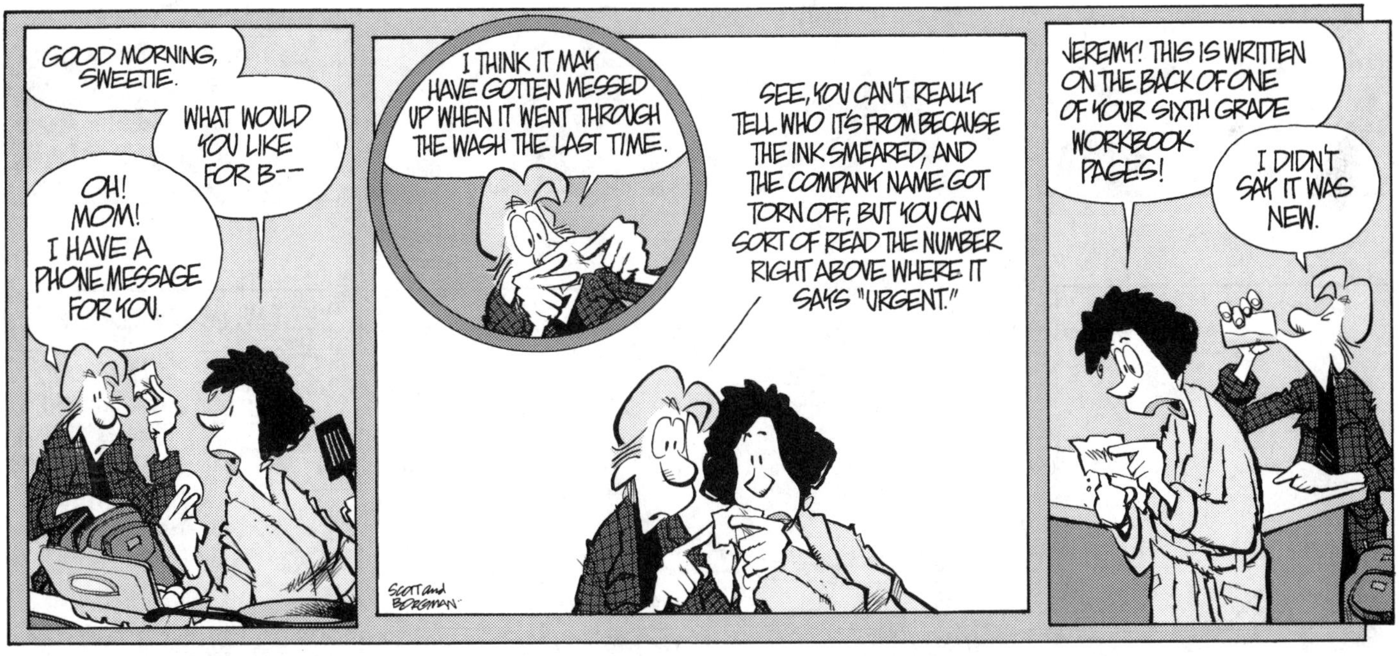
GOOD MORNING, SWEETIE.
WHAT WOULD YOU LIKE FOR B--
OH! MOM! I HAVE A PHONE MESSAGE FOR YOU.
I THINK IT MAY HAVE GOTTEN MESSED UP WHEN IT WENT THROUGH THE WASH THE LAST TIME.
SEE, YOU CAN'T REALLY TELL WHO IT'S FROM BECAUSE THE INK SMEARED, AND THE COMPANY NAME GOT TORN OFF, BUT YOU CAN SORT OF READ THE NUMBER RIGHT ABOVE WHERE IT SAYS "URGENT."
SCOTT and BORGMAN
JEREMY! THIS IS WRITTEN ON THE BACK OF ONE OF YOUR SIXTH GRADE WORKBOOK PAGES!
I DIDN'T SAY IT WAS NEW.

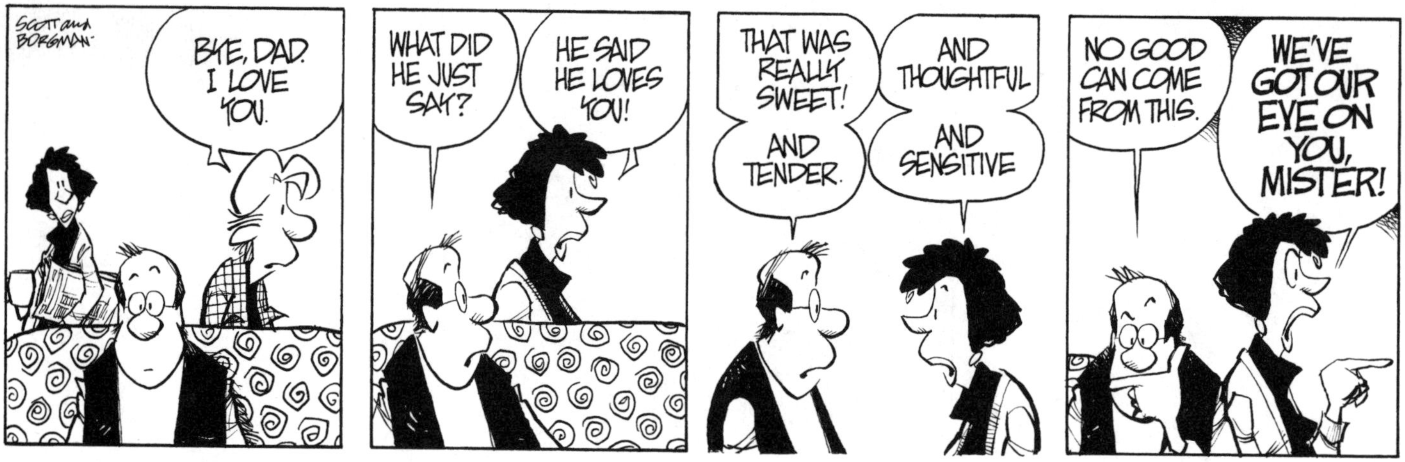
SCOTT and BORGMAN
BYE, DAD. I LOVE YOU.
WHAT DID HE JUST SAY?
HE SAID HE LOVES YOU!
THAT WAS REALLY SWEET!
AND TENDER.
AND THOUGHTFUL
AND SENSITIVE
NO GOOD CAN COME FROM THIS.
WE'VE GOT OUR EYE ON YOU, MISTER!

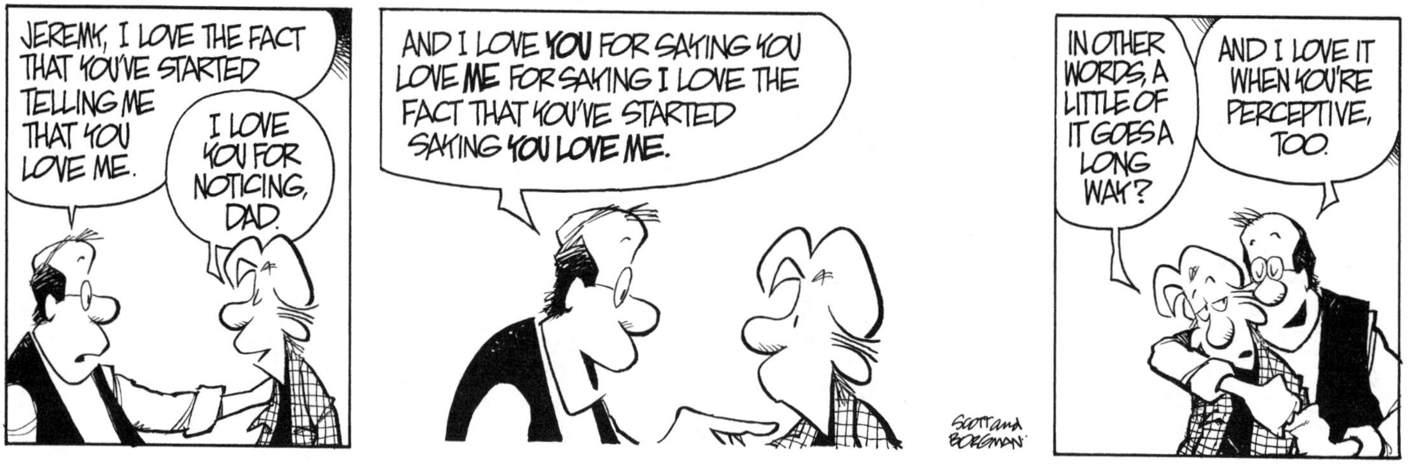
JEREMY, I LOVE THE FACT THAT YOU'VE STARTED TELLING ME THAT YOU LOVE ME.
I LOVE YOU FOR NOTICING, DAD.
AND I LOVE YOU FOR SAYING YOU LOVE ME FOR SAYING I LOVE THE FACT THAT YOU'VE STARTED SAYING YOU LOVE ME.
SCOTT and BORGMAN
IN OTHER WORDS, A LITTLE OF IT GOES A LONG WAY?
AND I LOVE IT WHEN YOU'RE PERCEPTIVE, TOO.

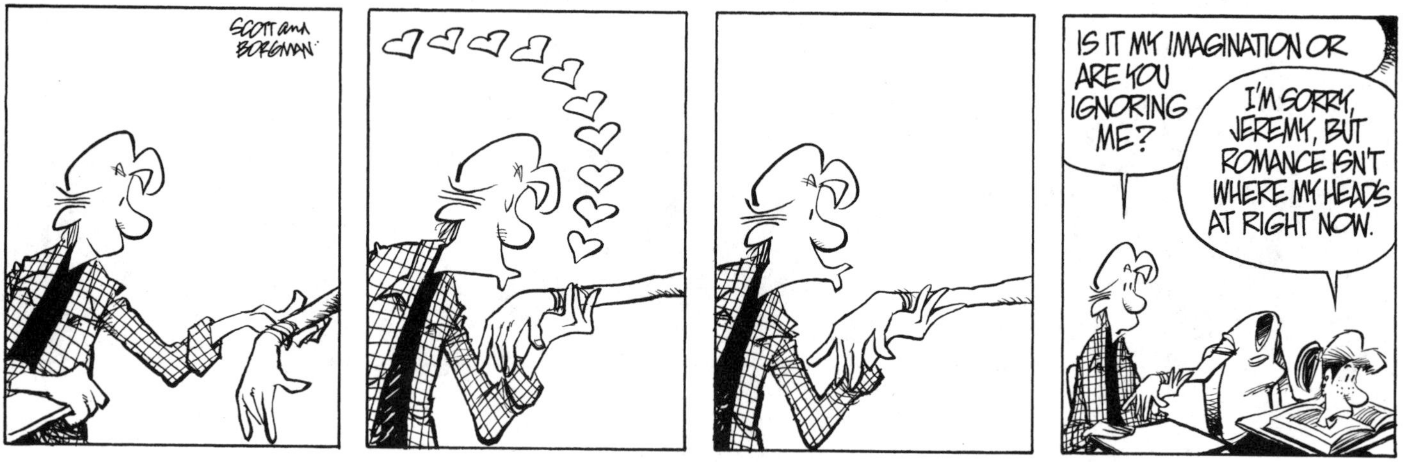
SCOTT and BORGMAN
IS IT MY IMAGINATION OR ARE YOU IGNORING ME?
I'M SORRY, JEREMY, BUT ROMANCE ISN'T WHERE MY HEAD'S AT RIGHT NOW.

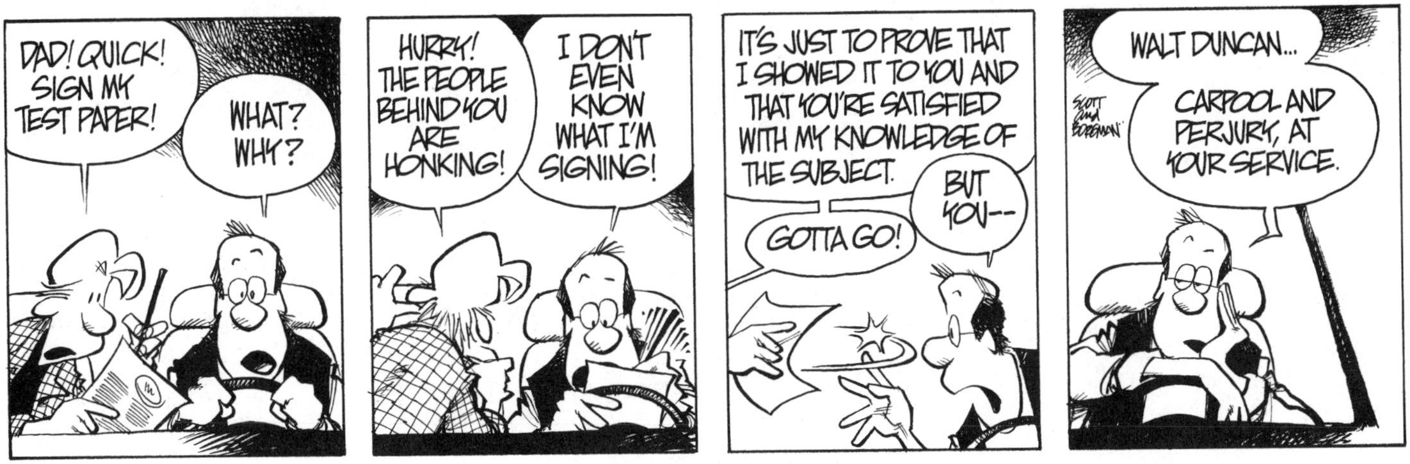
DAD! QUICK! SIGN MY TEST PAPER!
WHAT? WHY?
HURRY! THE PEOPLE BEHIND YOU ARE HONKING!
I DON'T EVEN KNOW WHAT I'M SIGNING!
IT'S JUST TO PROVE THAT I SHOWED IT TO YOU AND THAT YOU'RE SATISFIED WITH MY KNOWLEDGE OF THE SUBJECT.
GOTTA GO!
BUT YOU--
WALT DUNCAN...
CARPOOL AND PERJURY, AT YOUR SERVICE.

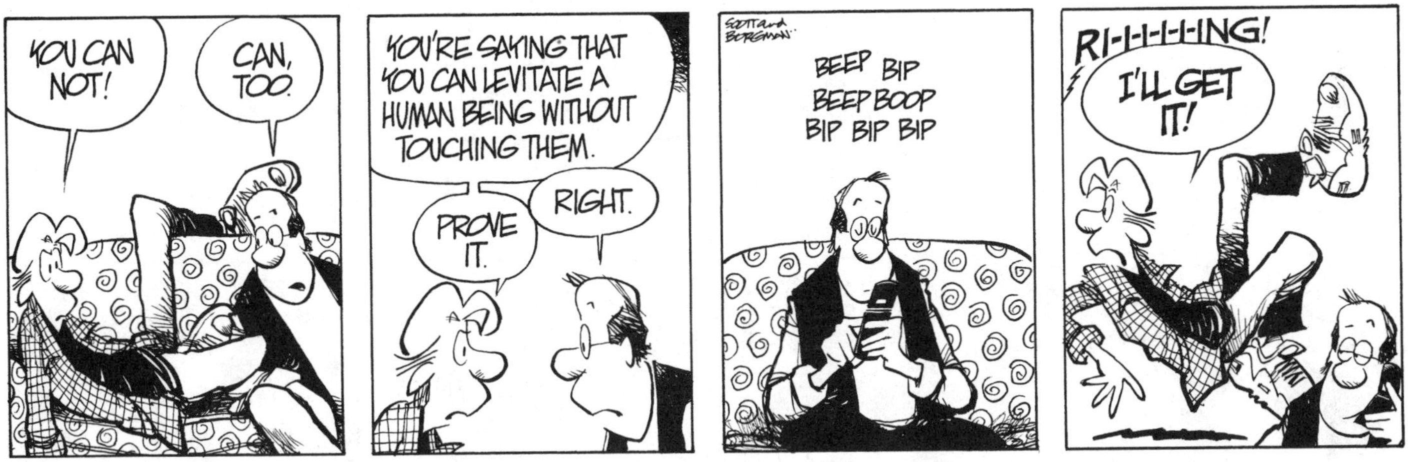
YOU CAN NOT!
CAN, TOO.
YOU'RE SAYING THAT YOU CAN LEVITATE A HUMAN BEING WITHOUT TOUCHING THEM.
PROVE IT.
RIGHT.
BEEP BIP
BEEP BOOP
BIP BIP BIP
RI-I-I-I-I-ING!
I'LL GET IT!

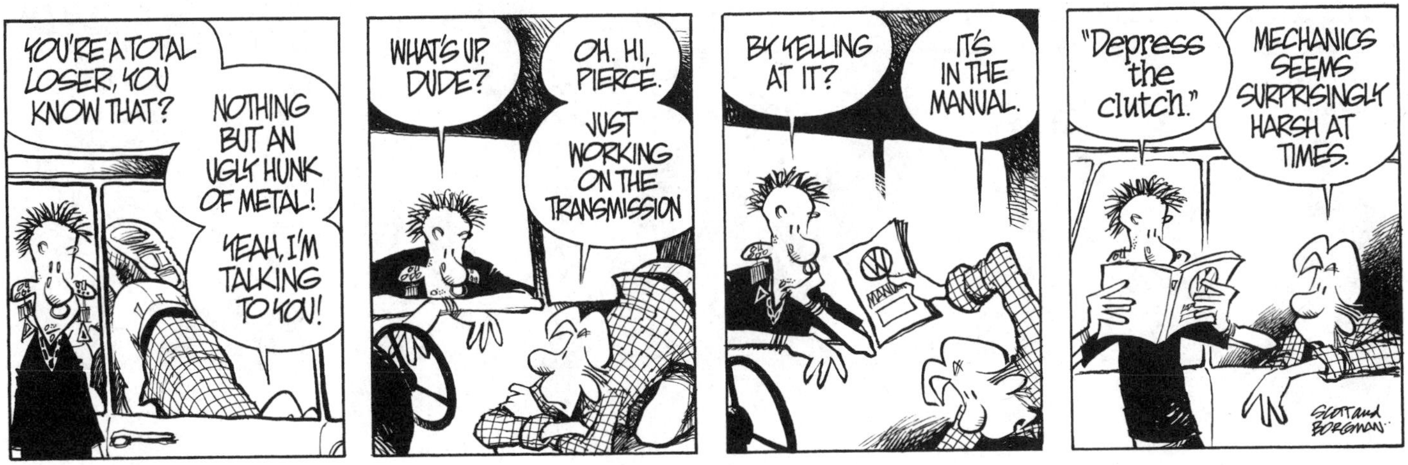
YOU'RE A TOTAL LOSER, YOU KNOW THAT?
NOTHING BUT AN UGLY HUNK OF METAL!
YEAH, I'M TALKING TO YOU!
WHAT'S UP, DUDE?
OH. HI, PIERCE.
JUST WORKING ON THE TRANSMISSION
BY YELLING AT IT?
IT'S IN THE MANUAL.
"Depress the clutch."
MECHANICS SEEMS SURPRISINGLY HARSH AT TIMES.

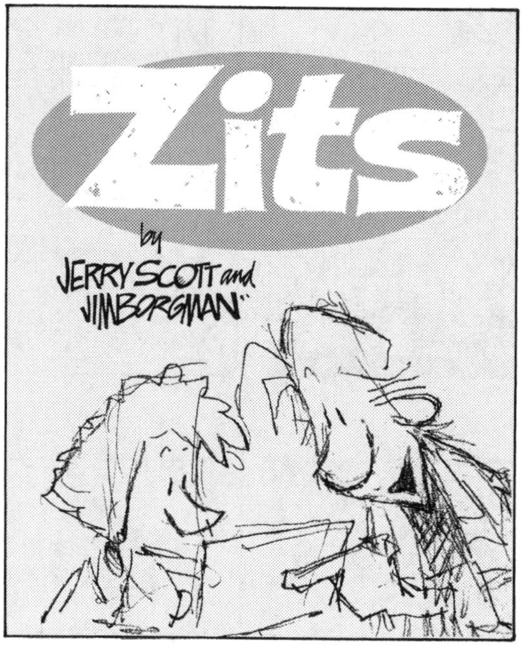
Zits
by
JERRY SCOTT and
JIM BORGMAN

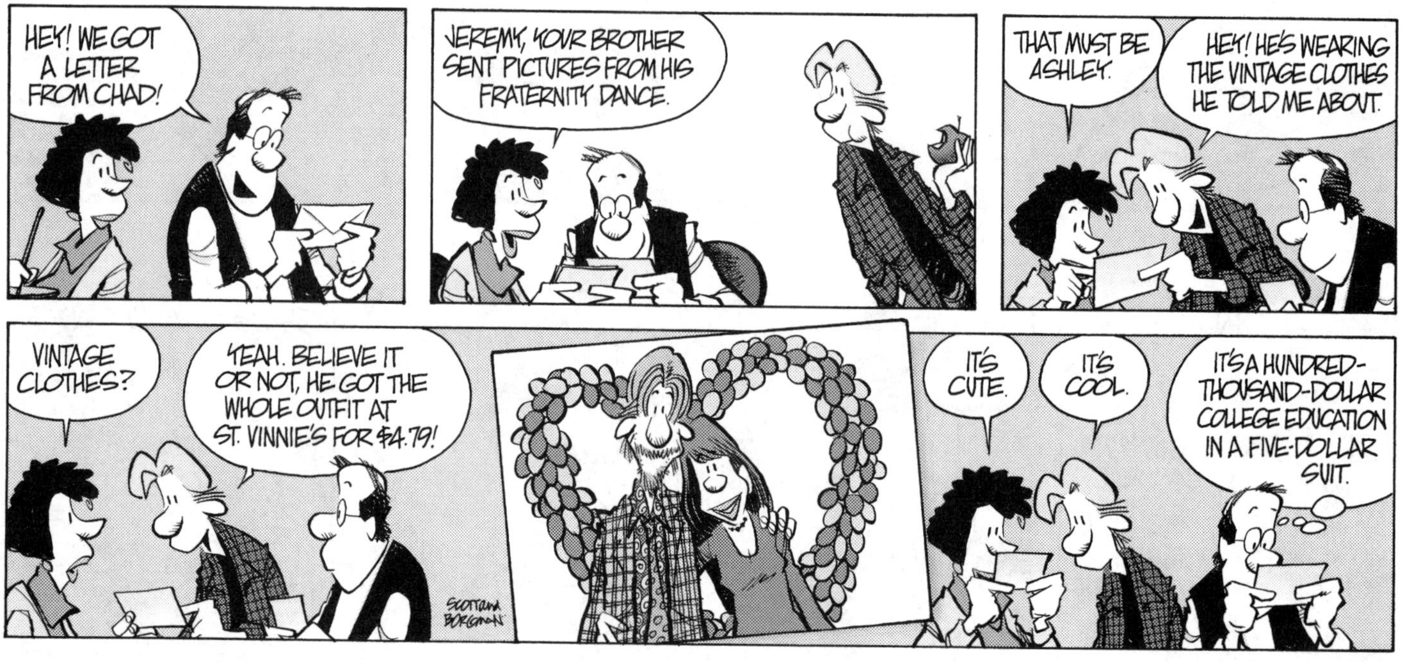
HEY! WE GOT A LETTER FROM CHAD!
JEREMY, YOUR BROTHER SENT PICTURES FROM HIS FRATERNITY DANCE.
THAT MUST BE ASHLEY.
HEY! HE'S WEARING THE VINTAGE CLOTHES HE TOLD ME ABOUT.
VINTAGE CLOTHES?
YEAH. BELIEVE IT OR NOT, HE GOT THE WHOLE OUTFIT AT ST. VINNIE'S FOR $4.79!
IT'S CUTE.
IT'S COOL.
IT'S A HUNDRED-THOUSAND-DOLLAR COLLEGE EDUCATION IN A FIVE-DOLLAR SUIT.

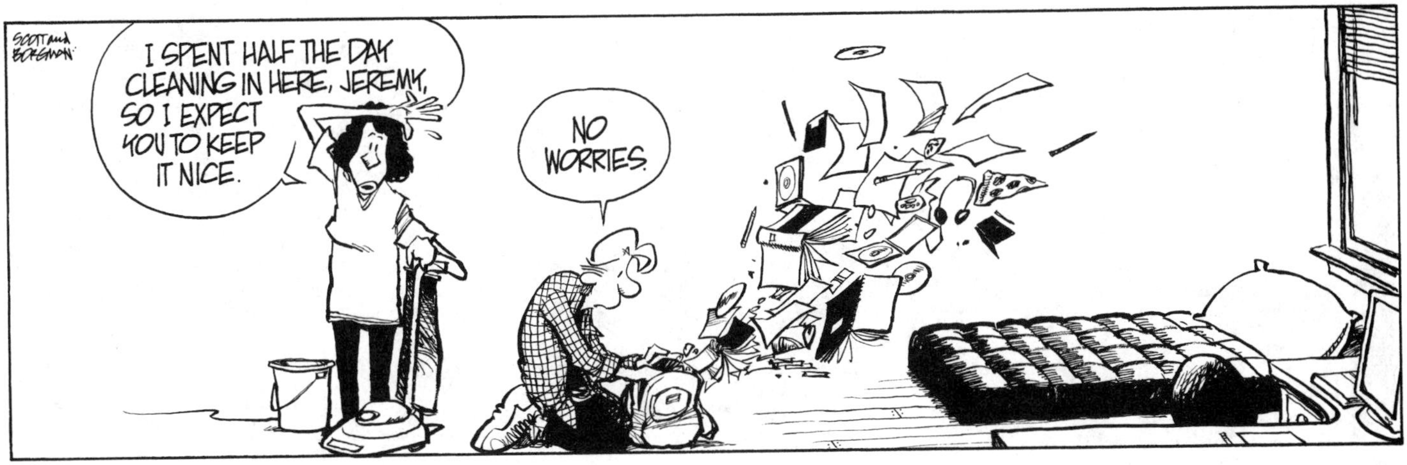
I SPENT HALF THE DAY CLEANING IN HERE, JEREMY, SO I EXPECT YOU TO KEEP IT NICE.
NO WORRIES.

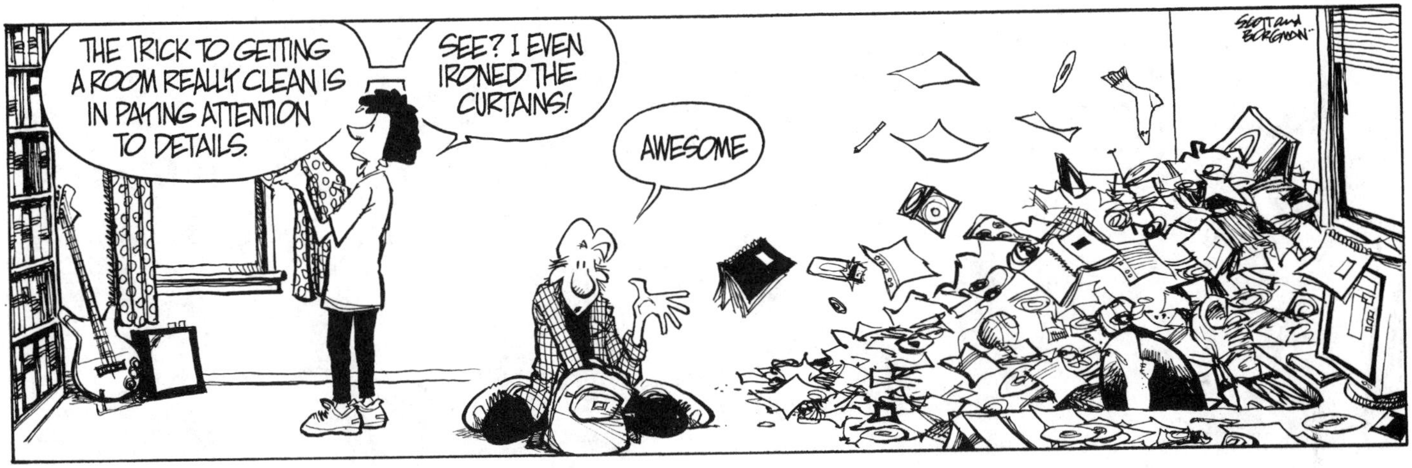
THE TRICK TO GETTING A ROOM REALLY CLEAN IS IN PAYING ATTENTION TO DETAILS.
SEE? I EVEN IRONED THE CURTAINS!
AWESOME

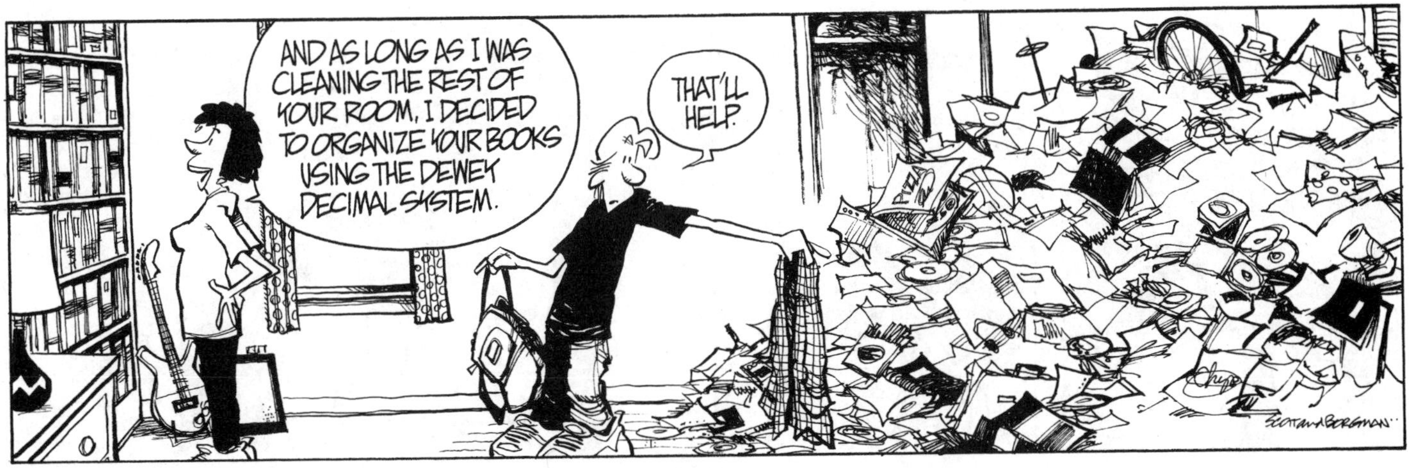
AND AS LONG AS I WAS CLEANING THE REST OF YOUR ROOM, I DECIDED TO ORGANIZE YOUR BOOKS USING THE DEWEY DECIMAL SYSTEM.
THAT'LL HELP.

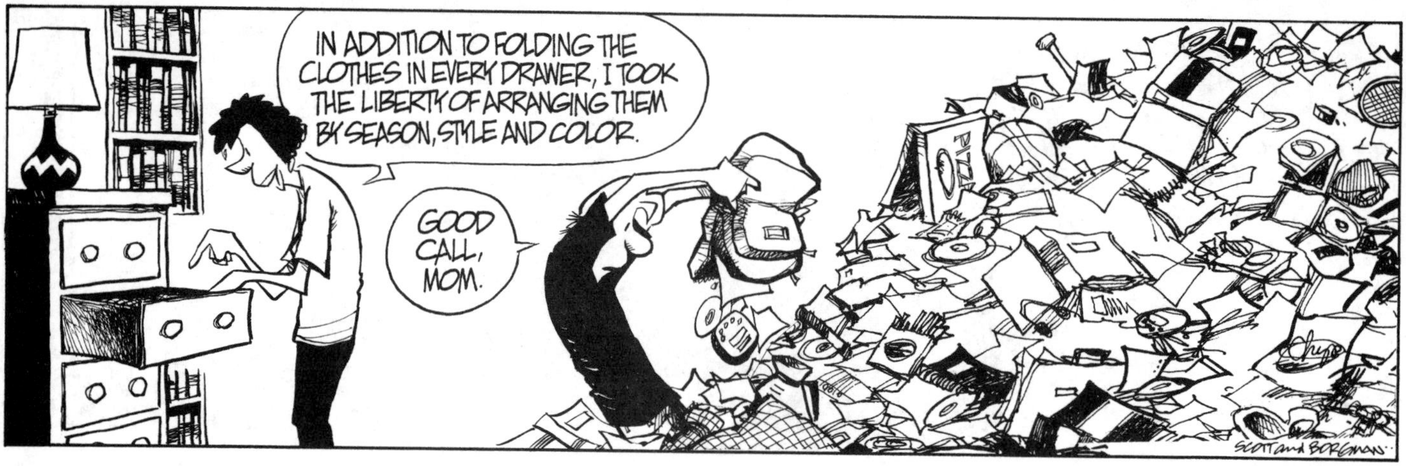
IN ADDITION TO FOLDING THE CLOTHES IN EVERY DRAWER, I TOOK THE LIBERTY OF ARRANGING THEM BY SEASON, STYLE AND COLOR.
GOOD CALL, MOM.

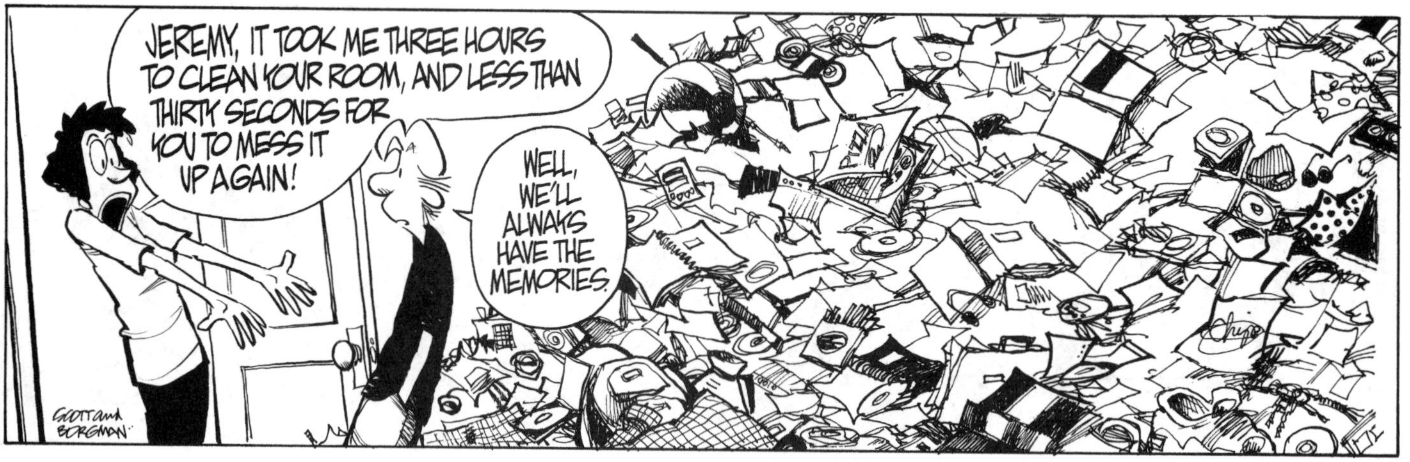
JEREMY, IT TOOK ME THREE HOURS TO CLEAN YOUR ROOM, AND LESS THAN THIRTY SECONDS FOR YOU TO MESS IT UP AGAIN!
WELL, WE'LL ALWAYS HAVE THE MEMORIES.

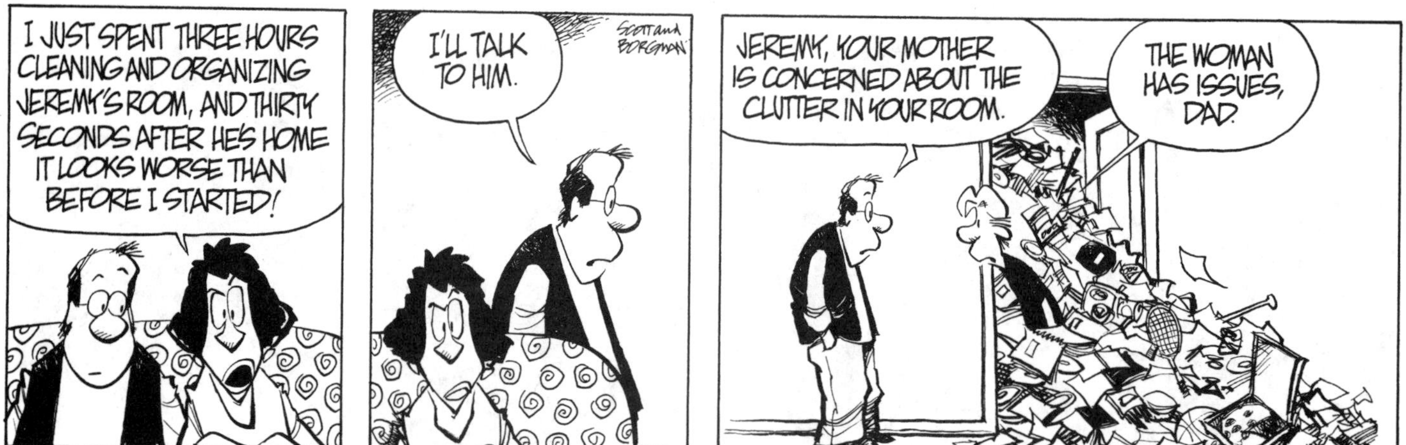
I JUST SPENT THREE HOURS CLEANING AND ORGANIZING JEREMY'S ROOM, AND THIRTY SECONDS AFTER HE'S HOME IT LOOKS WORSE THAN BEFORE I STARTED!
I'LL TALK TO HIM.
JEREMY, YOUR MOTHER IS CONCERNED ABOUT THE CLUTTER IN YOUR ROOM.
THE WOMAN HAS ISSUES, DAD.

Zits
JERRY SCOTT and
JIM BORGMAN

HAPPY MOTHER-OF-A-TEENAGER'S DAY.
HERE'S YOUR MEDAL
CAN I GO NOW?

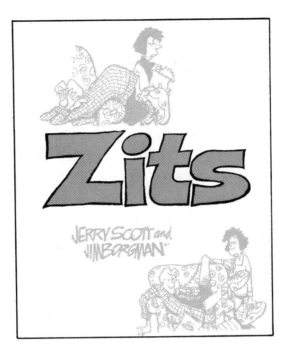

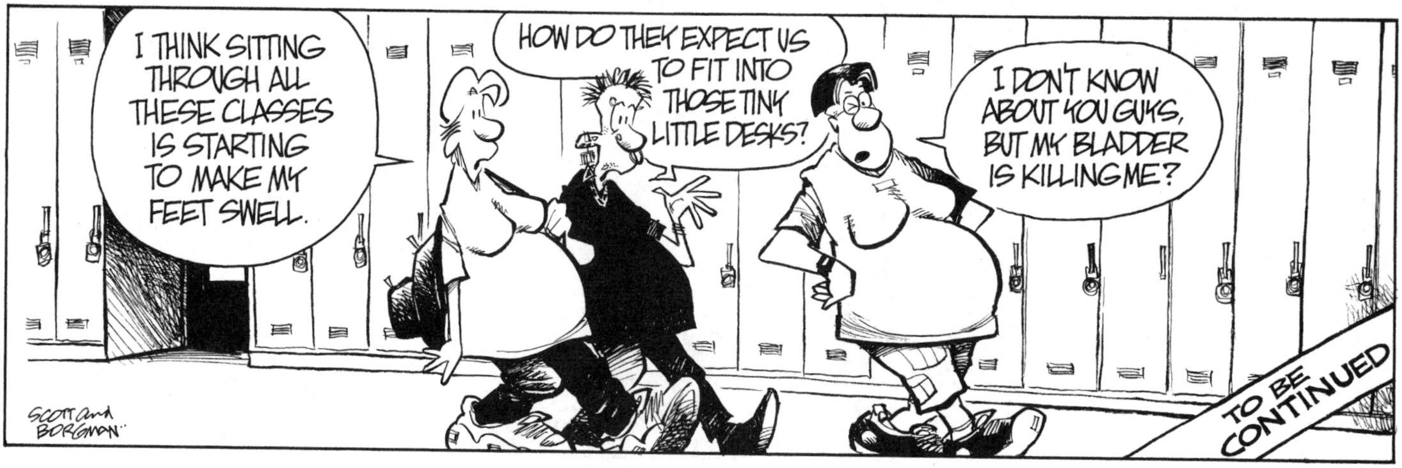
I THINK SITTING THROUGH ALL THESE CLASSES IS STARTING TO MAKE MY FEET SWELL.
HOW DO THEY EXPECT US TO FIT INTO THOSE TINY LITTLE DESKS?
I DON'T KNOW ABOUT YOU GUYS, BUT MY BLADDER IS KILLING ME?
TO BE CONTINUED
SCOTT and BORGMAN

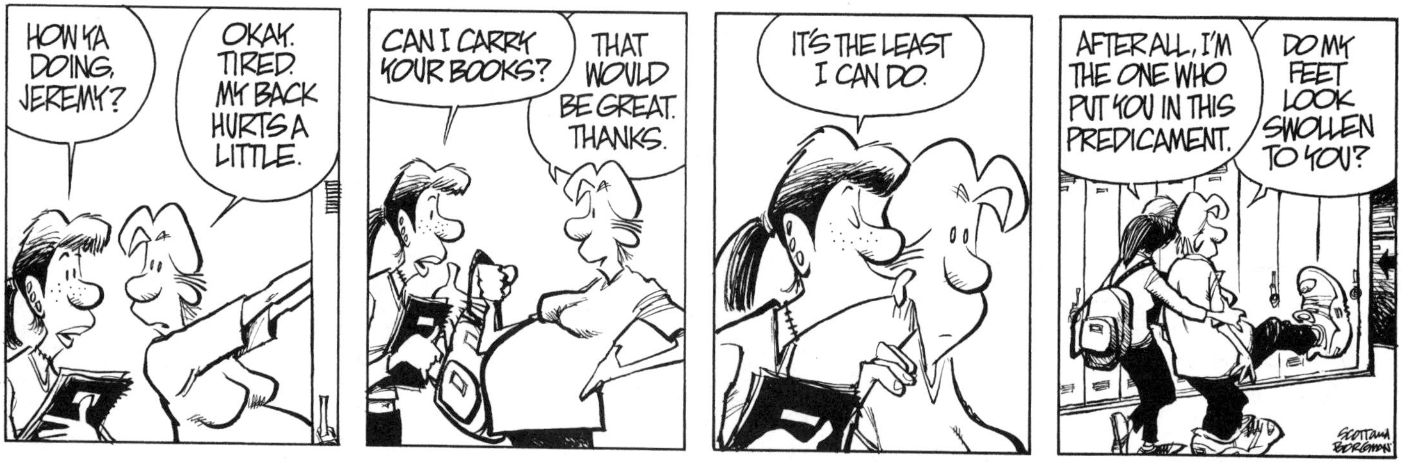
HOW YA DOING, JEREMY?
OKAY. TIRED. MY BACK HURTS A LITTLE.
CAN I CARRY YOUR BOOKS?
THAT WOULD BE GREAT. THANKS.
IT'S THE LEAST I CAN DO.
AFTER ALL, I'M THE ONE WHO PUT YOU IN THIS PREDICAMENT.
DO MY FEET LOOK SWOLLEN TO YOU?
SCOTT and BORGMAN

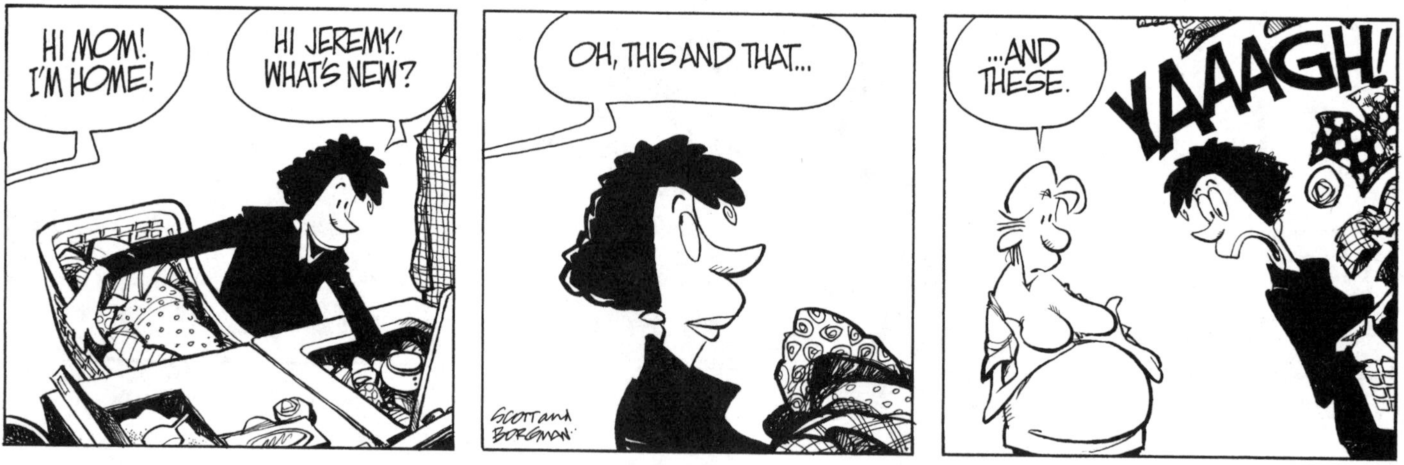
HI MOM! I'M HOME!
HI JEREMY! WHAT'S NEW?
OH, THIS AND THAT...
...AND THESE.
YAAAGH!
SCOTT and BORGMAN

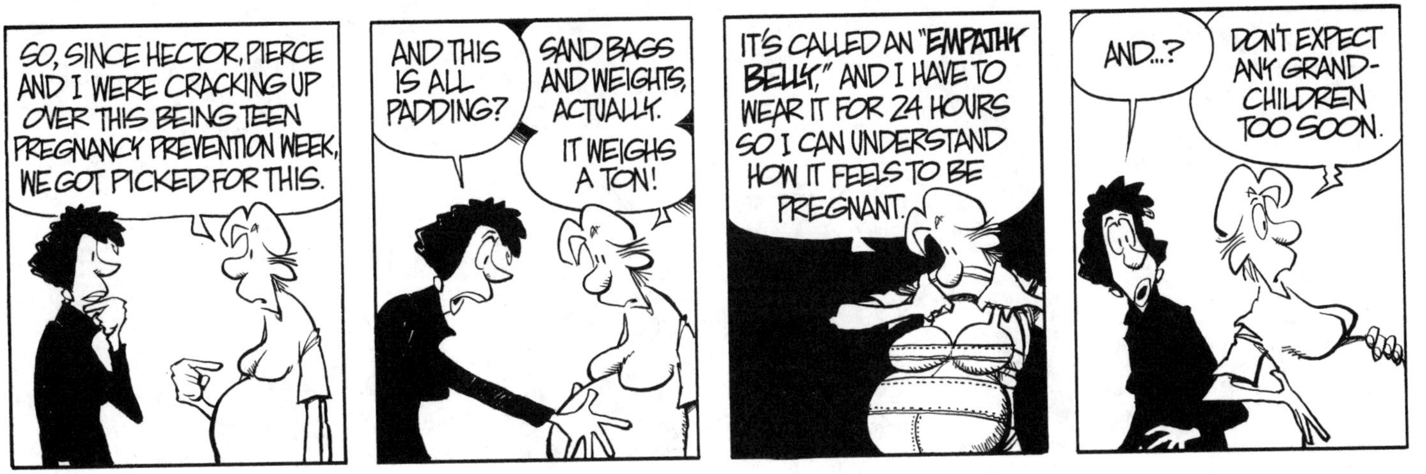
SO, SINCE HECTOR, PIERCE AND I WERE CRACKING UP OVER THIS BEING TEEN PREGNANCY PREVENTION WEEK, WE GOT PICKED FOR THIS.
AND THIS IS ALL PADDING?
SAND BAGS AND WEIGHTS, ACTUALLY.
IT WEIGHS A TON!
IT'S CALLED AN "EMPATHY BELLY," AND I HAVE TO WEAR IT FOR 24 HOURS SO I CAN UNDERSTAND HOW IT FEELS TO BE PREGNANT.
AND...?
DON'T EXPECT ANY GRAND-CHILDREN TOO SOON.

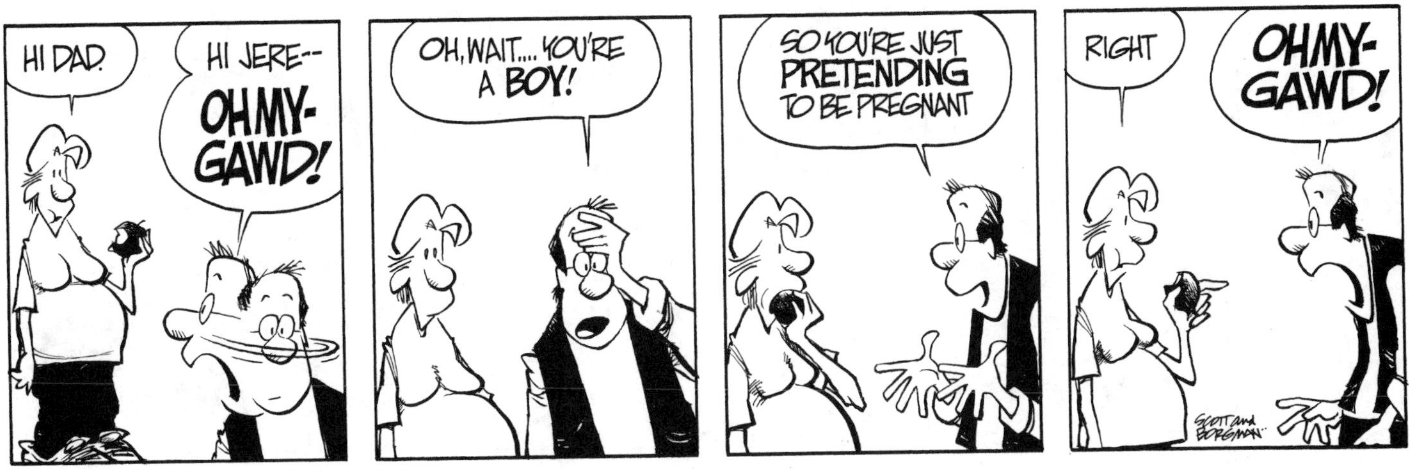
HI DAD.
HI JERE--
OHMY-GAWD!
OH, WAIT.... YOU'RE A BOY!
SO YOU'RE JUST PRETENDING TO BE PREGNANT
RIGHT
OHMY-GAWD!
SCOTT and BORGMAN

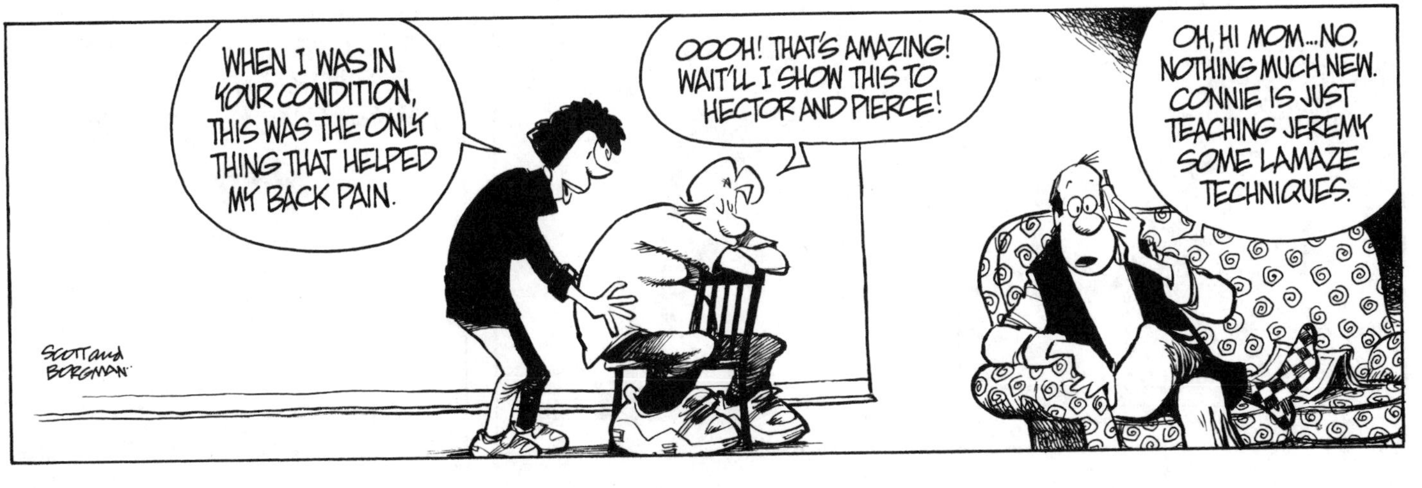
WHEN I WAS IN YOUR CONDITION, THIS WAS THE ONLY THING THAT HELPED MY BACK PAIN.
OOOH! THAT'S AMAZING! WAIT'LL I SHOW THIS TO HECTOR AND PIERCE!
OH, HI MOM...NO, NOTHING MUCH NEW. CONNIE IS JUST TEACHING JEREMY SOME LAMAZE TECHNIQUES.
SCOTT and BORGMAN

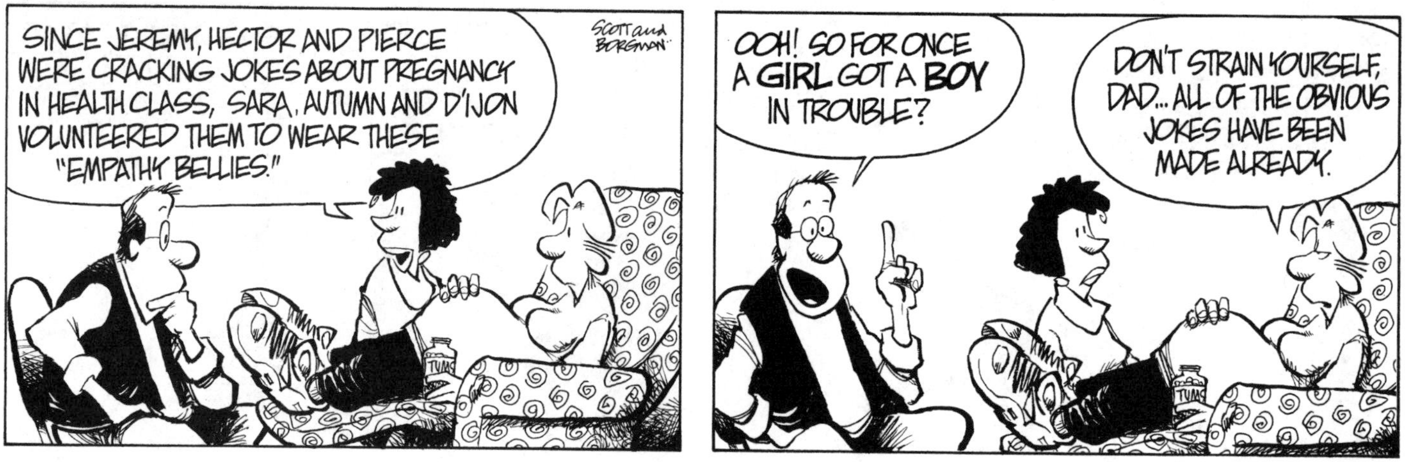
SINCE JEREMY, HECTOR AND PIERCE WERE CRACKING JOKES ABOUT PREGNANCY IN HEALTH CLASS, SARA, AUTUMN AND D'IJON VOLUNTEERED THEM TO WEAR THESE "EMPATHY BELLIES."
OOH! SO FOR ONCE A GIRL GOT A BOY IN TROUBLE?
DON'T STRAIN YOURSELF, DAD... ALL OF THE OBVIOUS JOKES HAVE BEEN MADE ALREADY.

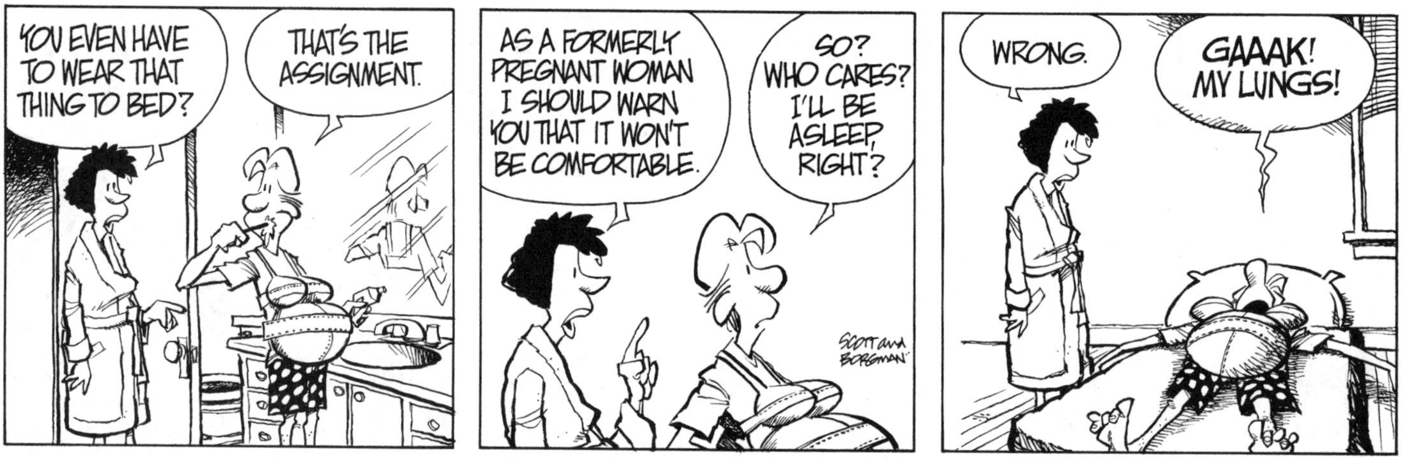
YOU EVEN HAVE TO WEAR THAT THING TO BED?
THAT'S THE ASSIGNMENT.
AS A FORMERLY PREGNANT WOMAN I SHOULD WARN YOU THAT IT WON'T BE COMFORTABLE.
SO? WHO CARES? I'LL BE ASLEEP, RIGHT?
WRONG.
GAAAK! MY LUNGS!

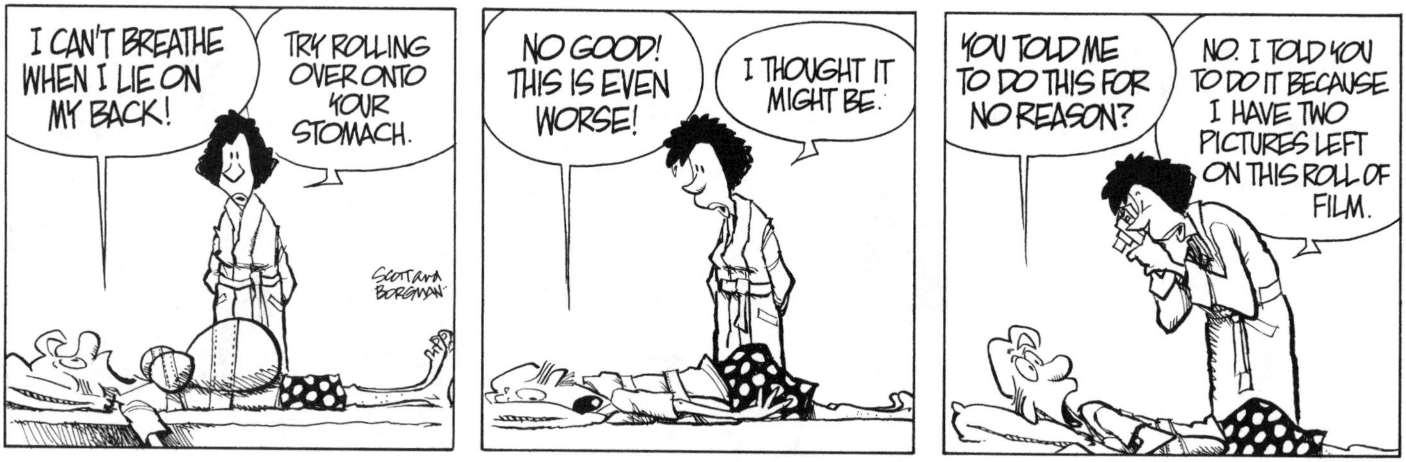
I CAN'T BREATHE WHEN I LIE ON MY BACK!
TRY ROLLING OVER ONTO YOUR STOMACH.
NO GOOD! THIS IS EVEN WORSE!
I THOUGHT IT MIGHT BE.
YOU TOLD ME TO DO THIS FOR NO REASON?
NO. I TOLD YOU TO DO IT BECAUSE I HAVE TWO PICTURES LEFT ON THIS ROLL OF FILM.

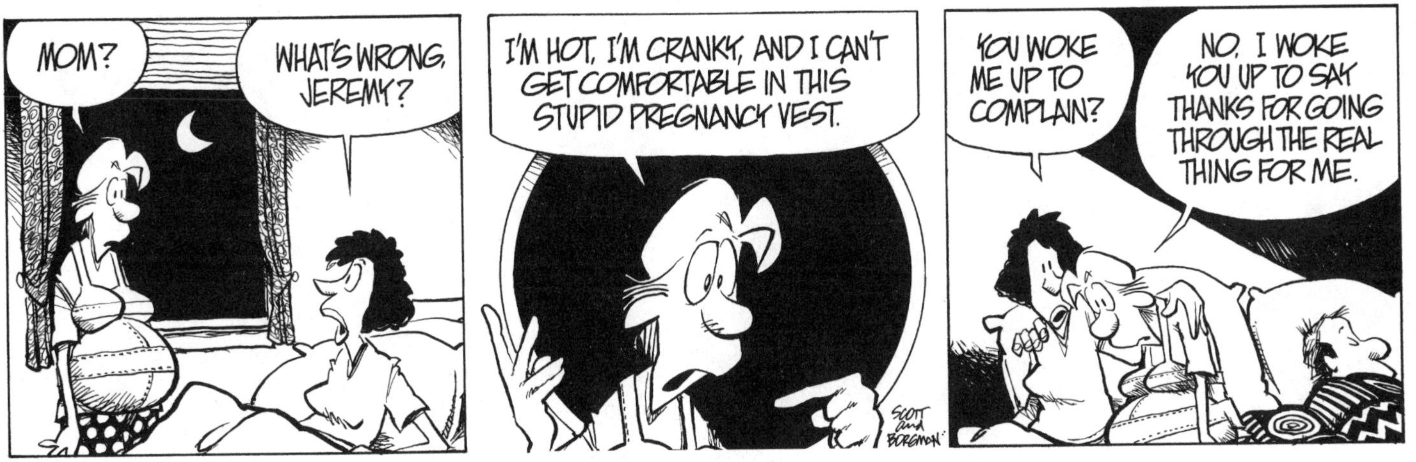
MOM?
WHAT'S WRONG, JEREMY?
I'M HOT, I'M CRANKY, AND I CAN'T GET COMFORTABLE IN THIS STUPID PREGNANCY VEST.
YOU WOKE ME UP TO COMPLAIN?
NO, I WOKE YOU UP TO SAY THANKS FOR GOING THROUGH THE REAL THING FOR ME.

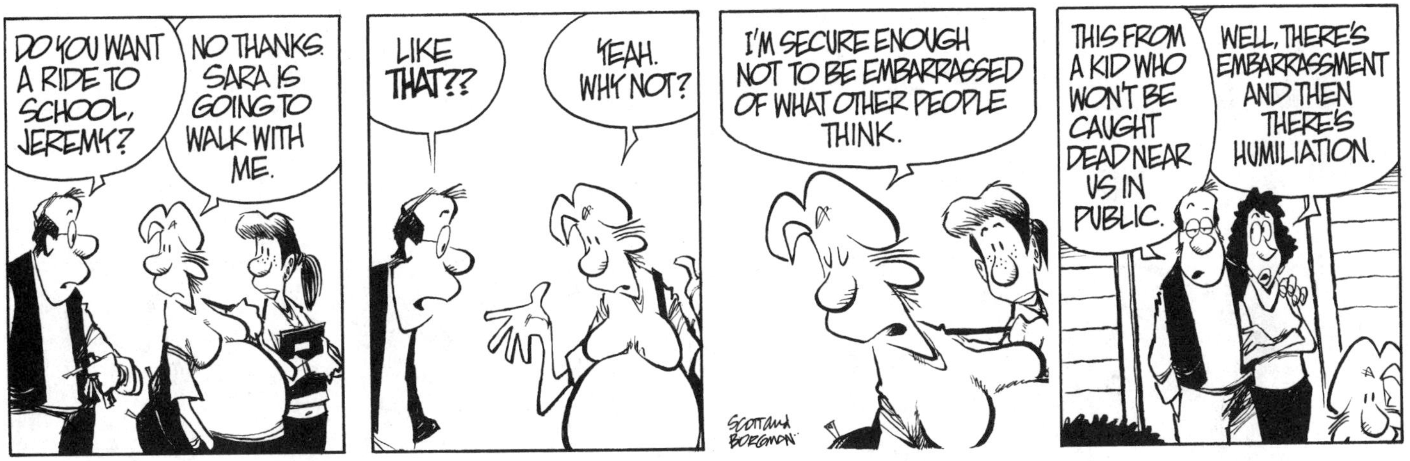
DO YOU WANT A RIDE TO SCHOOL, JEREMY?
NO THANKS. SARA IS GOING TO WALK WITH ME.
LIKE **THAT**??
YEAH. WHY NOT?
I'M SECURE ENOUGH NOT TO BE EMBARRASSED OF WHAT OTHER PEOPLE THINK.
THIS FROM A KID WHO WON'T BE CAUGHT DEAD NEAR US IN PUBLIC.
WELL, THERE'S EMBARRASSMENT AND THEN THERE'S HUMILIATION.

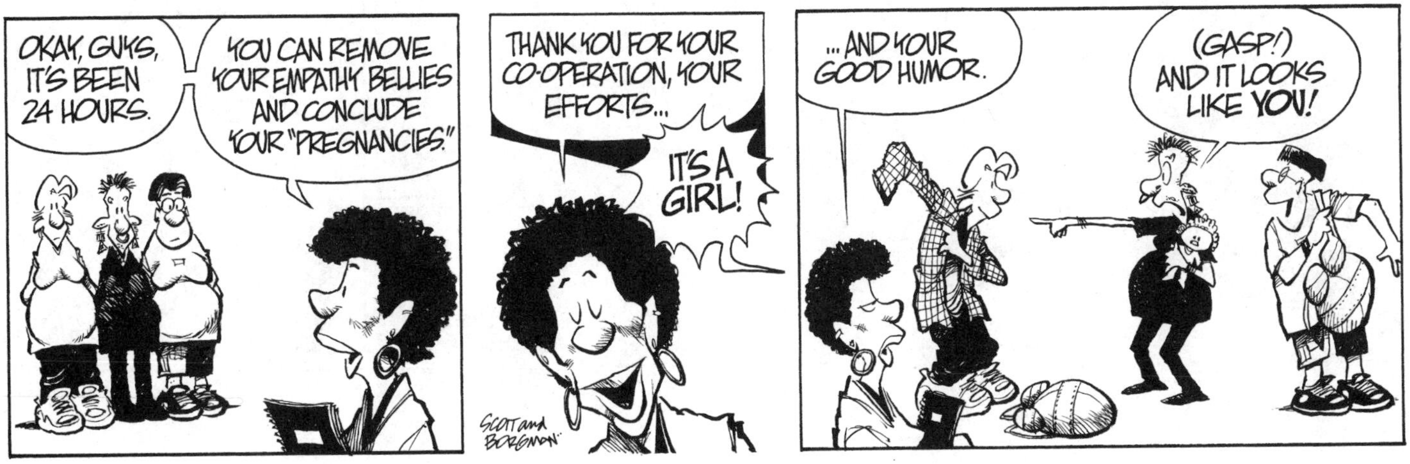
OKAY, GUYS, IT'S BEEN 24 HOURS.
YOU CAN REMOVE YOUR EMPATHY BELLIES AND CONCLUDE YOUR "PREGNANCIES."
THANK YOU FOR YOUR CO-OPERATION, YOUR EFFORTS...
IT'S A GIRL!
...AND YOUR GOOD HUMOR.
(GASP!) AND IT LOOKS LIKE **YOU**!

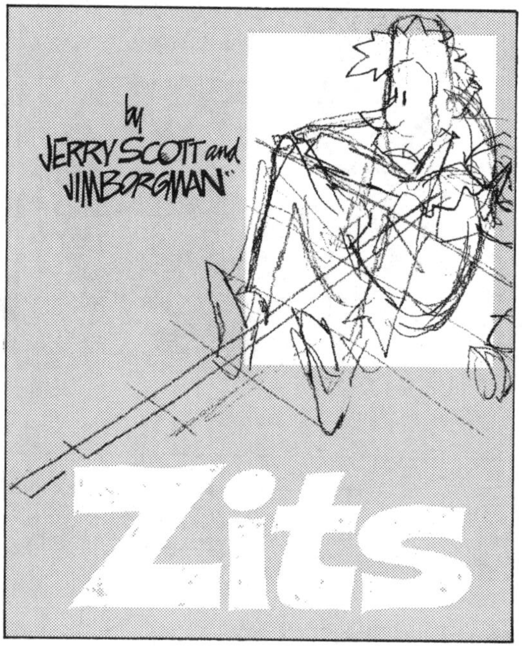
by
JERRY SCOTT and
JIM BORGMAN
Zits

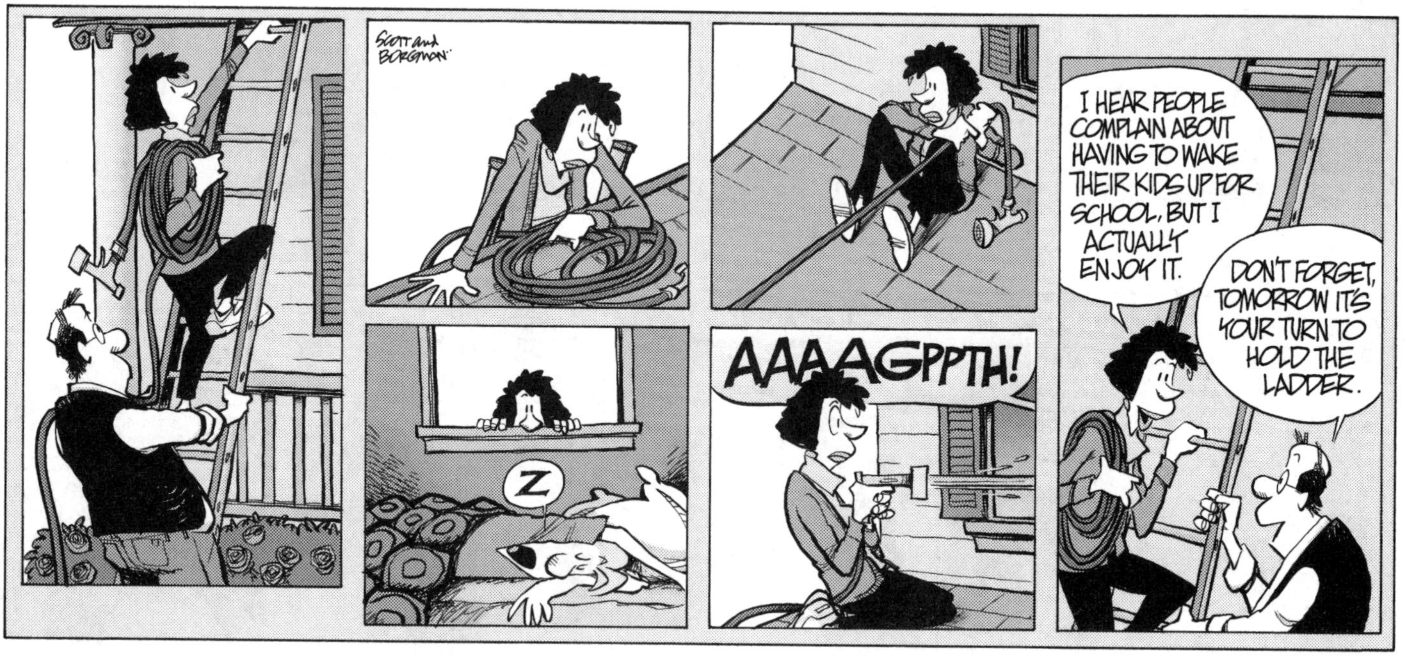
SCOTT and BORGMAN
AAAAGPPTH!
I HEAR PEOPLE COMPLAIN ABOUT HAVING TO WAKE THEIR KIDS UP FOR SCHOOL, BUT I ACTUALLY ENJOY IT.
DON'T FORGET, TOMORROW IT'S YOUR TURN TO HOLD THE LADDER.

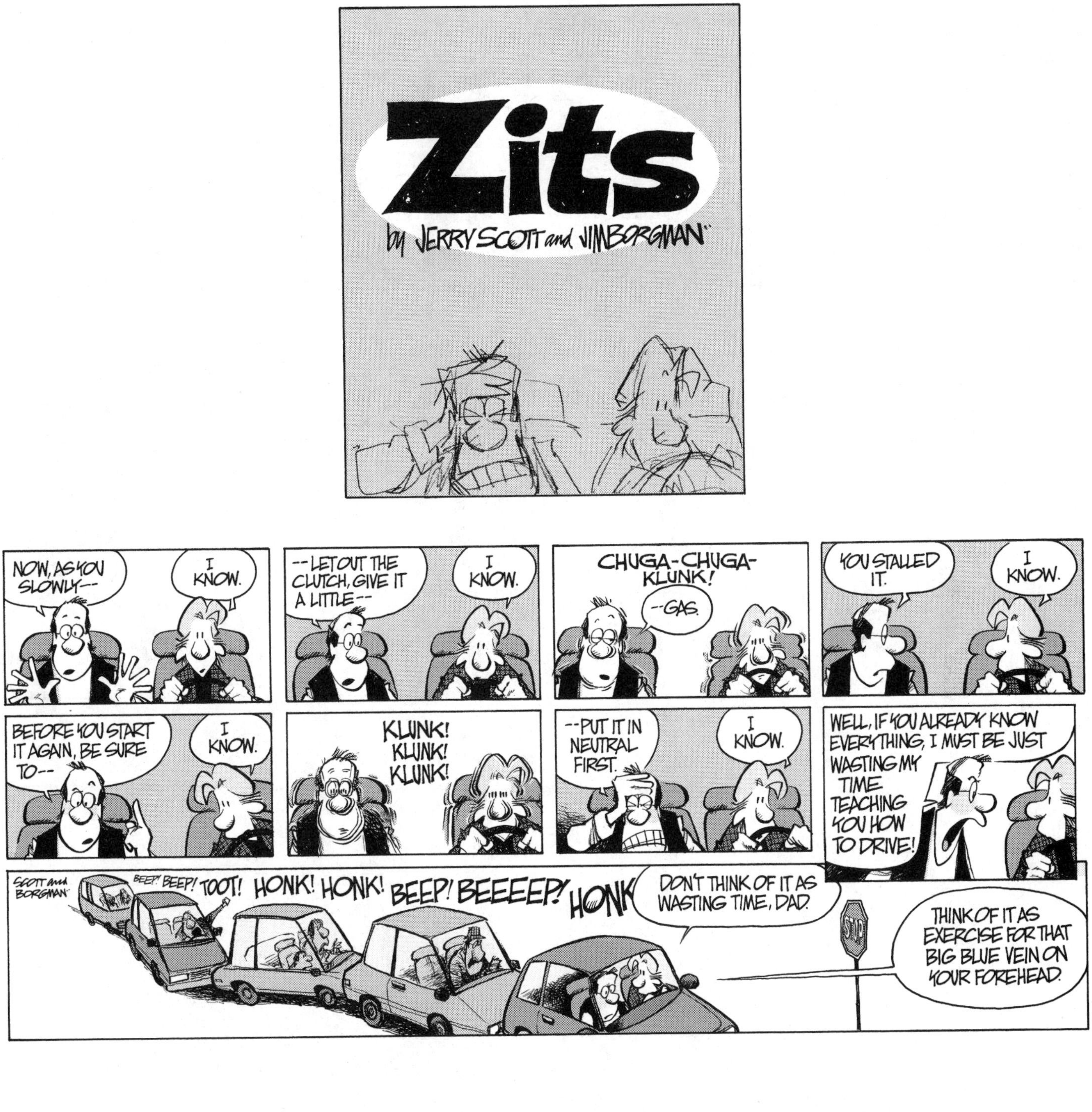
Zits
by JERRY SCOTT and JIM BORGMAN
NOW, AS YOU SLOWLY--
I KNOW.
--LET OUT THE CLUTCH, GIVE IT A LITTLE--
I KNOW.
CHUGA-CHUGA-KLUNK!
--GAS.
YOU STALLED IT.
I KNOW.
BEFORE YOU START IT AGAIN, BE SURE TO--
I KNOW.
KLUNK! KLUNK! KLUNK!
--PUT IT IN NEUTRAL FIRST.
I KNOW.
WELL, IF YOU ALREADY KNOW EVERYTHING, I MUST BE JUST WASTING MY TIME TEACHING YOU HOW TO DRIVE!
SCOTT and BORGMAN
BEEP! BEEP! TOOT! HONK! HONK! BEEP! BEEEEP! HONK
DON'T THINK OF IT AS WASTING TIME, DAD.
STOP
THINK OF IT AS EXERCISE FOR THAT BIG BLUE VEIN ON YOUR FOREHEAD.

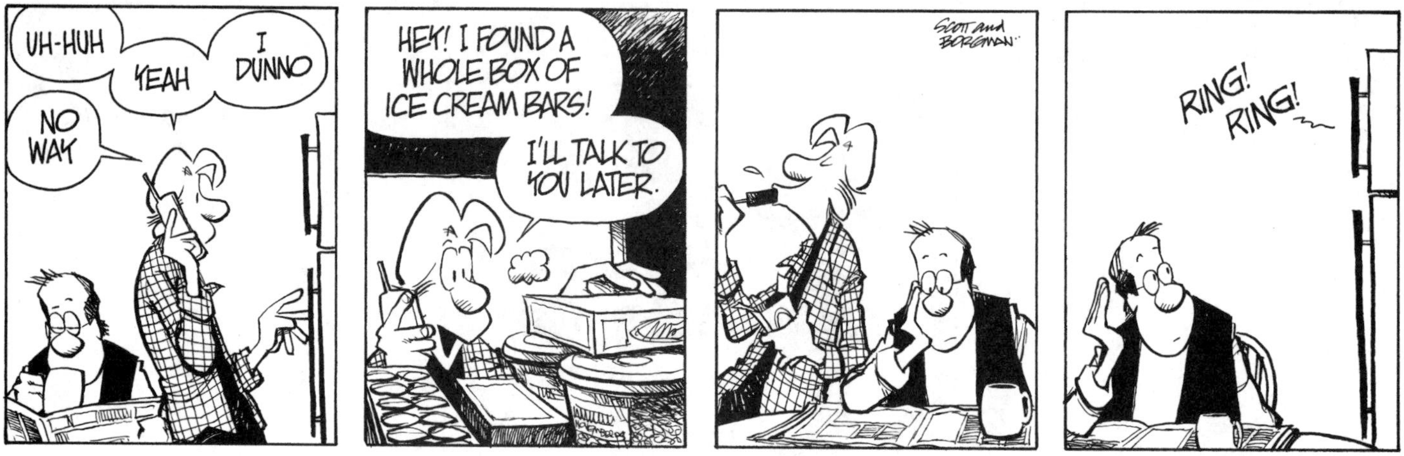
UH-HUH
YEAH
I DUNNO
NO WAY
HEY! I FOUND A WHOLE BOX OF ICE CREAM BARS!
I'LL TALK TO YOU LATER.
SCOTT and BORGMAN
RING! RING!

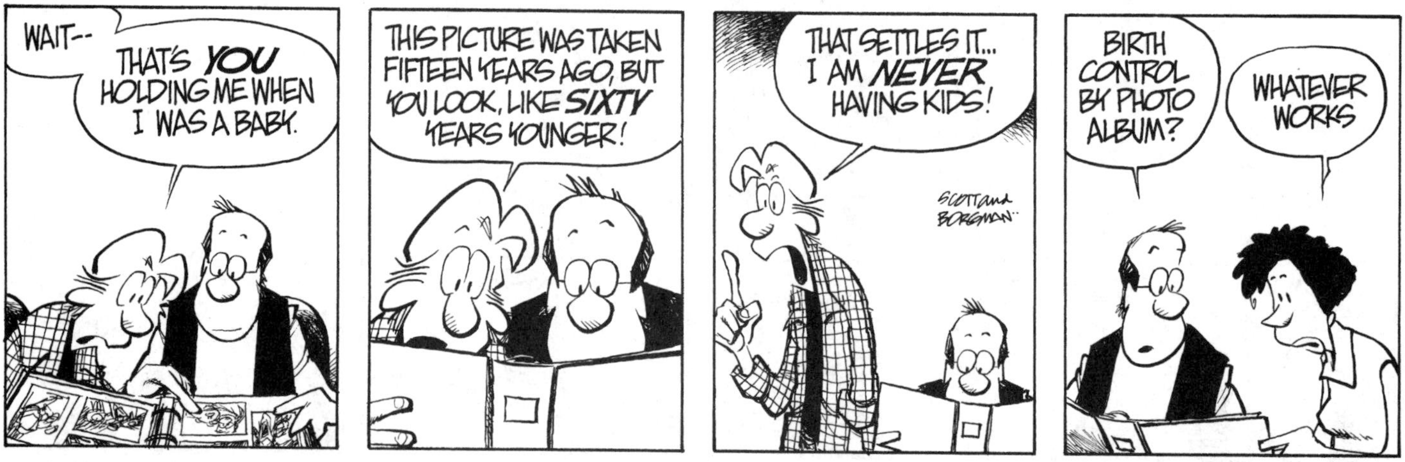
WAIT--
THAT'S ***YOU*** HOLDING ME WHEN I WAS A BABY.
THIS PICTURE WAS TAKEN FIFTEEN YEARS AGO, BUT YOU LOOK, LIKE ***SIXTY*** YEARS YOUNGER!
THAT SETTLES IT... I AM ***NEVER*** HAVING KIDS!
SCOTT and BORGMAN
BIRTH CONTROL BY PHOTO ALBUM?
WHATEVER WORKS

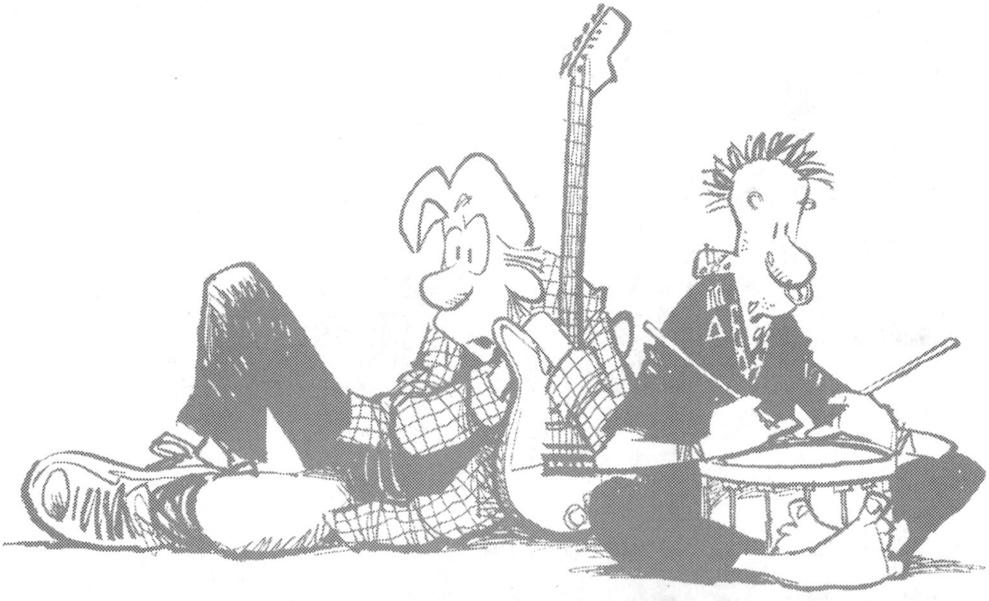

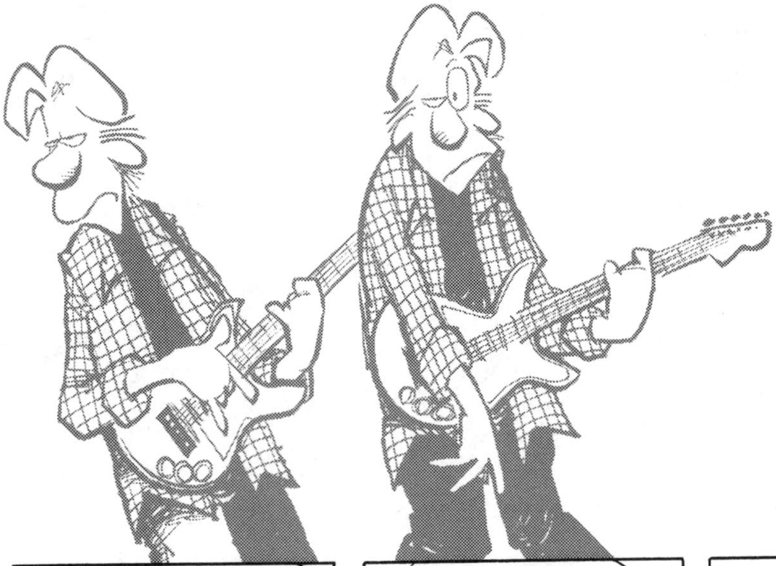

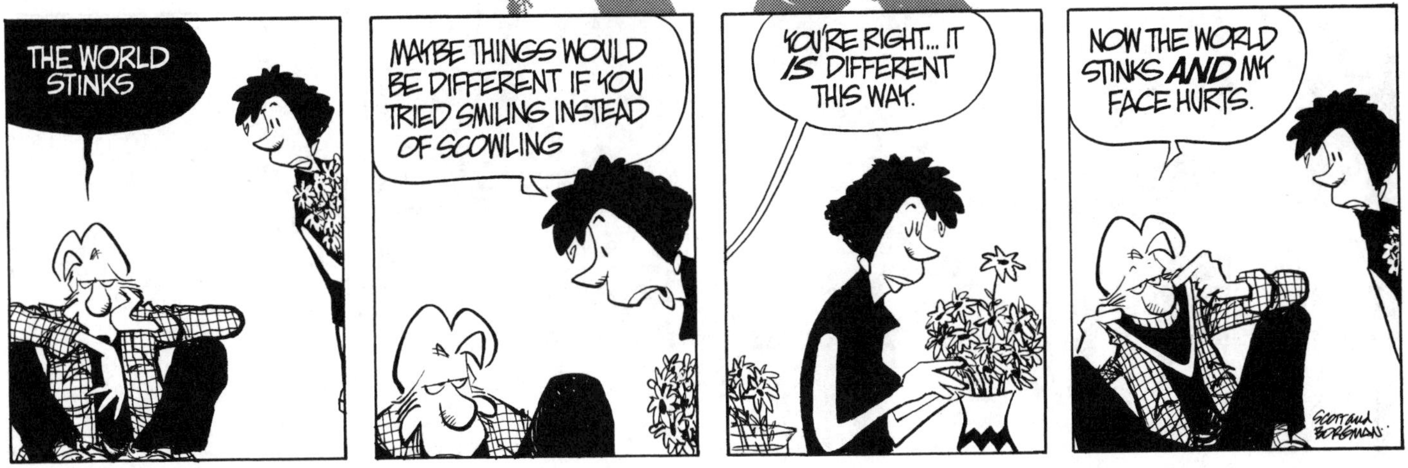
THE WORLD STINKS
MAYBE THINGS WOULD BE DIFFERENT IF YOU TRIED SMILING INSTEAD OF SCOWLING
YOU'RE RIGHT... IT *IS* DIFFERENT THIS WAY.
NOW THE WORLD STINKS ***AND*** MY FACE HURTS.
SCOTT and BORGMAN

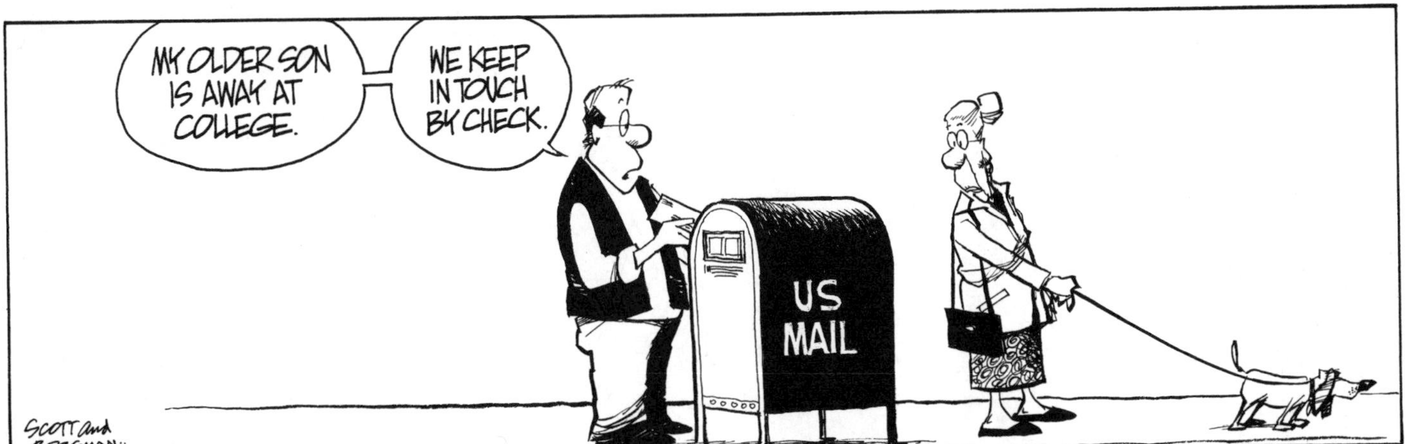
MY OLDER SON IS AWAY AT COLLEGE.
WE KEEP IN TOUCH BY CHECK.
US MAIL
SCOTT and BORGMAN

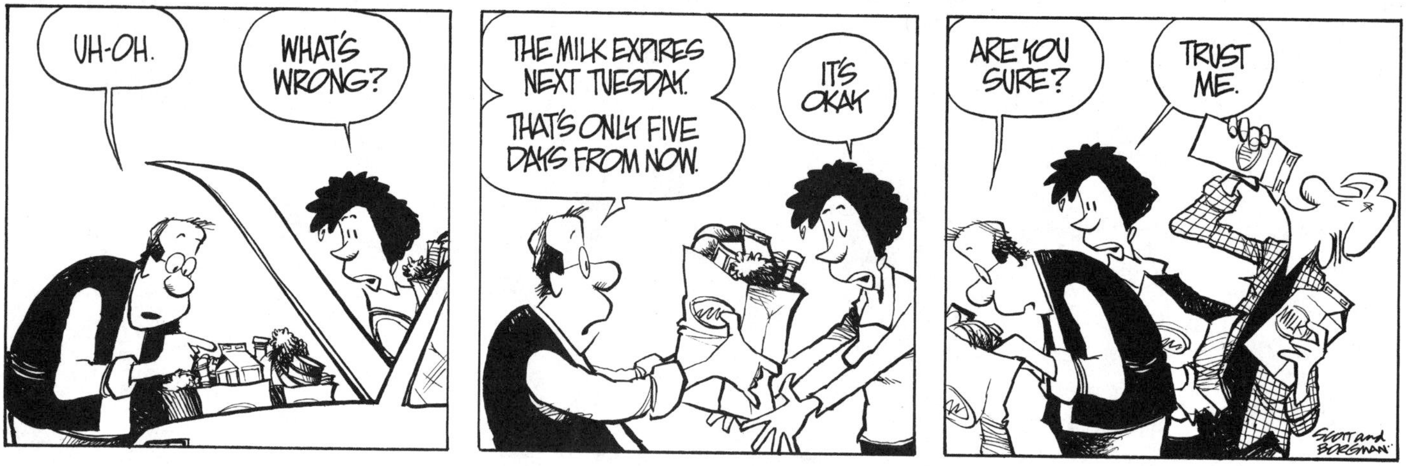
UH-OH.
WHAT'S WRONG?
THE MILK EXPIRES NEXT TUESDAY.
THAT'S ONLY FIVE DAYS FROM NOW.
IT'S OKAY
ARE YOU SURE?
TRUST ME.
SCOTT and BORGMAN

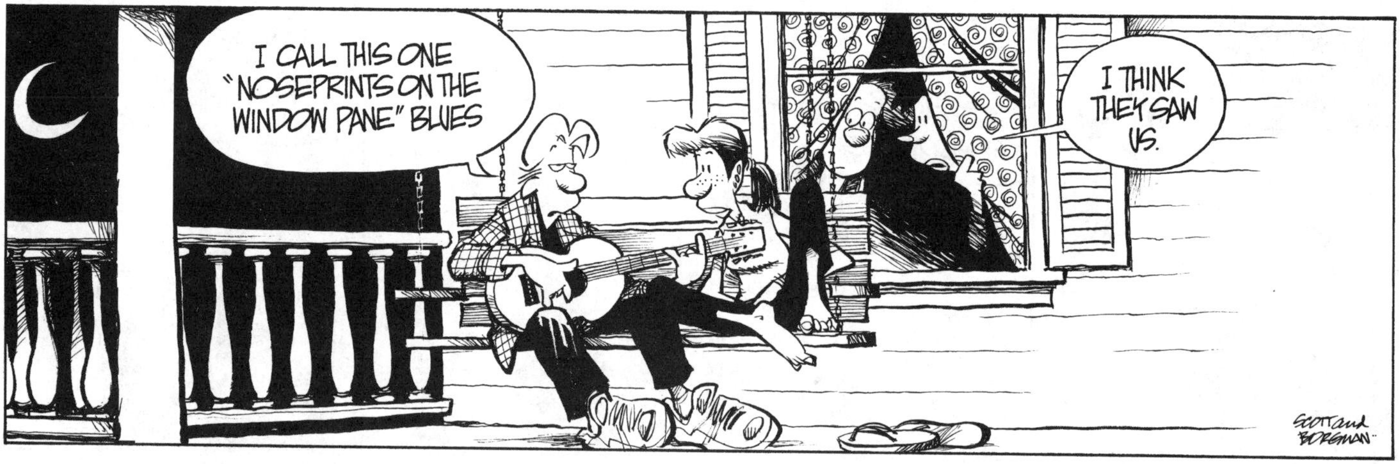
I CALL THIS ONE "NOSEPRINTS ON THE WINDOW PANE" BLUES
I THINK THEY SAW US.
SCOTT and BORGMAN

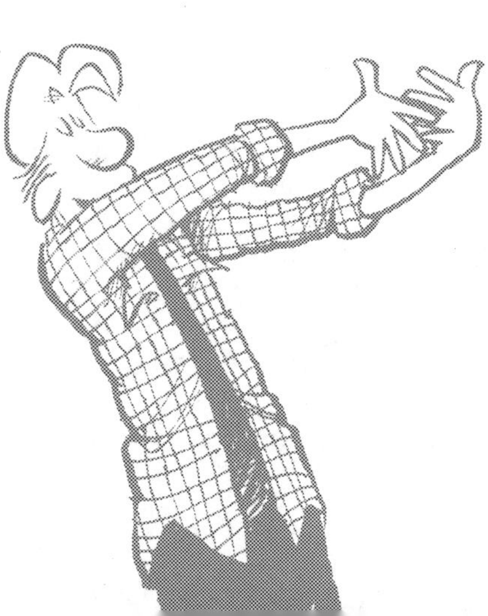

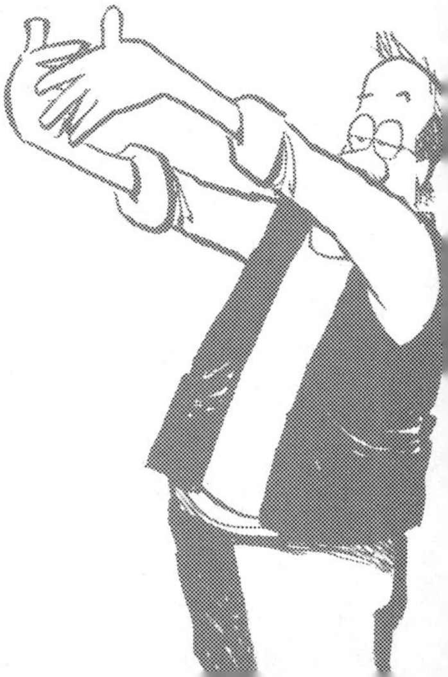

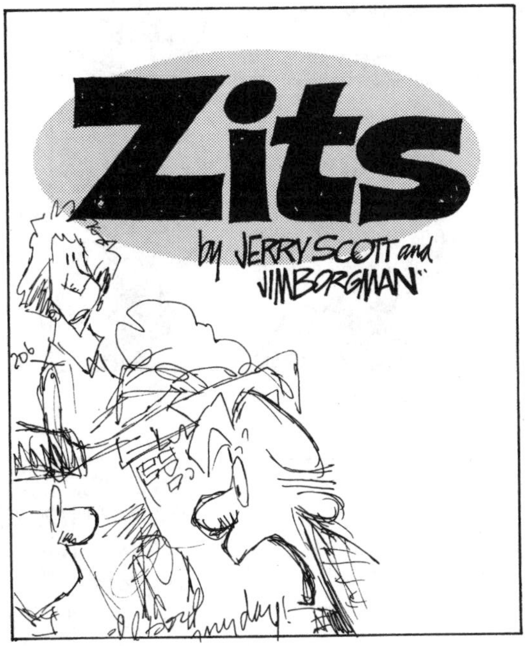
Zits
by JERRY SCOTT and JIM BORGMAN

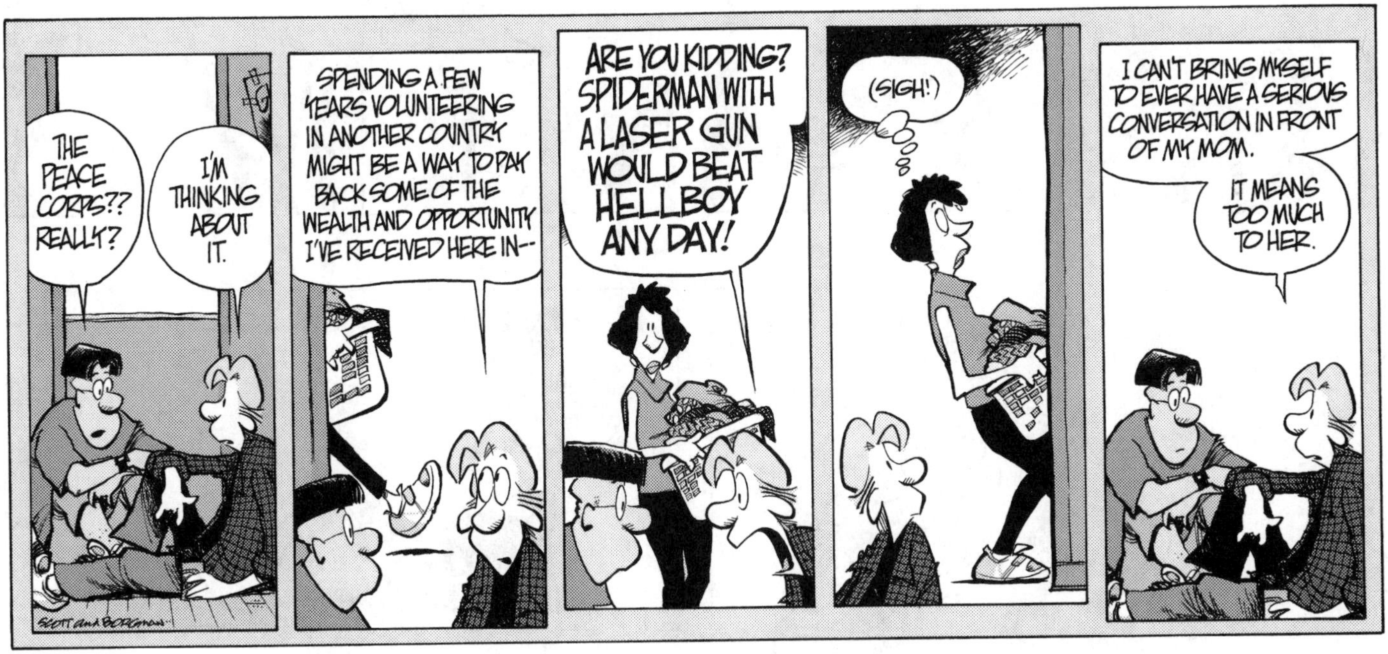
THE PEACE CORPS?? REALLY?
I'M THINKING ABOUT IT.
SPENDING A FEW YEARS VOLUNTEERING IN ANOTHER COUNTRY MIGHT BE A WAY TO PAY BACK SOME OF THE WEALTH AND OPPORTUNITY I'VE RECEIVED HERE IN--
ARE YOU KIDDING? SPIDERMAN WITH A LASER GUN WOULD BEAT HELLBOY ANY DAY!
(SIGH!)
I CAN'T BRING MYSELF TO EVER HAVE A SERIOUS CONVERSATION IN FRONT OF MY MOM.
IT MEANS TOO MUCH TO HER.
SCOTT and BORGMAN

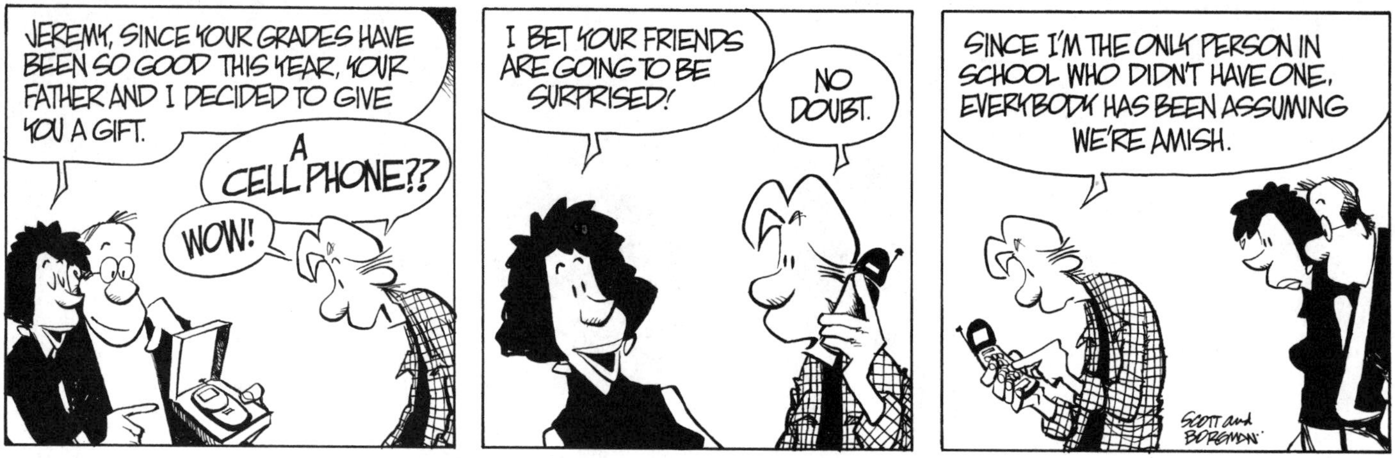
JEREMY, SINCE YOUR GRADES HAVE BEEN SO GOOD THIS YEAR, YOUR FATHER AND I DECIDED TO GIVE YOU A GIFT.
WOW!
A CELL PHONE??
I BET YOUR FRIENDS ARE GOING TO BE SURPRISED!
NO DOUBT.
SINCE I'M THE ONLY PERSON IN SCHOOL WHO DIDN'T HAVE ONE, EVERYBODY HAS BEEN ASSUMING WE'RE AMISH.
SCOTT and BORGMAN

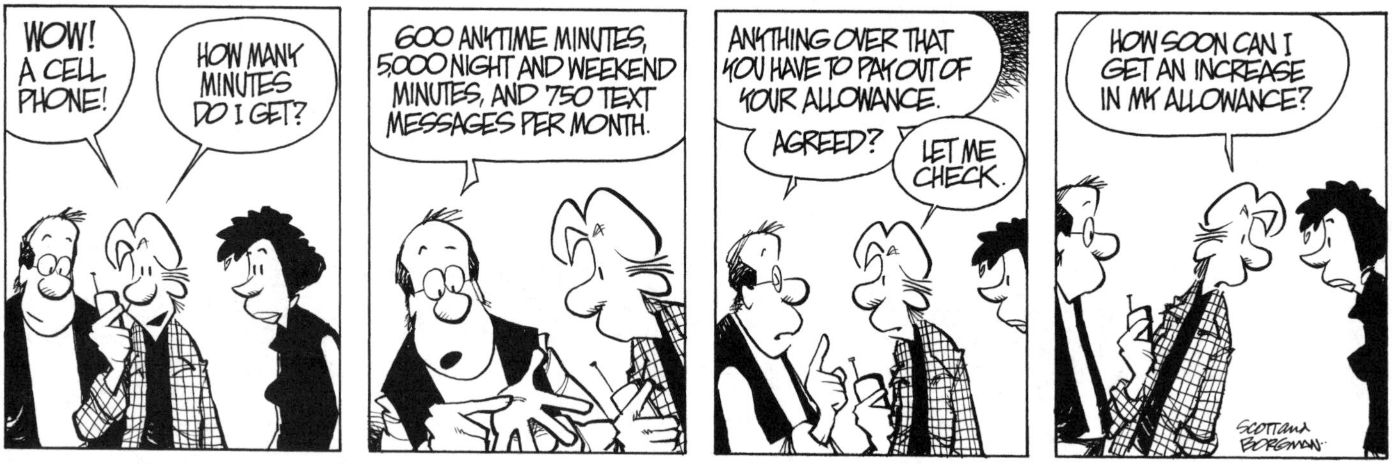
WOW! A CELL PHONE!
HOW MANY MINUTES DO I GET?
600 ANYTIME MINUTES, 5,000 NIGHT AND WEEKEND MINUTES, AND 750 TEXT MESSAGES PER MONTH.
ANYTHING OVER THAT YOU HAVE TO PAY OUT OF YOUR ALLOWANCE.
AGREED?
LET ME CHECK.
HOW SOON CAN I GET AN INCREASE IN MY ALLOWANCE?
SCOTT and BORGMAN

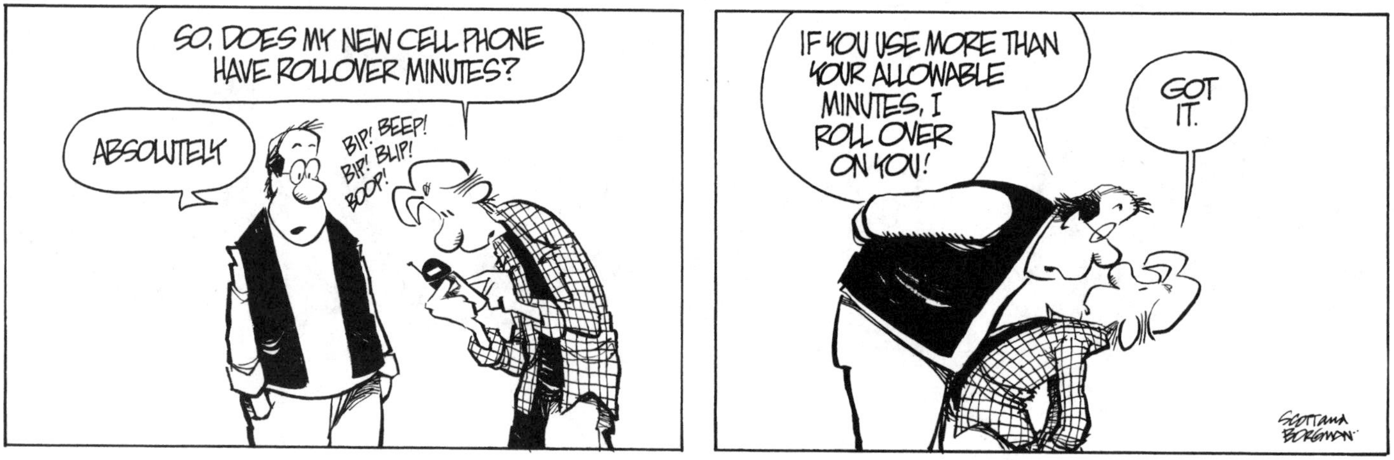
SO, DOES MY NEW CELL PHONE HAVE ROLLOVER MINUTES?
ABSOLUTELY.
BIP! BEEP! BIP! BLIP! BOOP!
IF YOU USE MORE THAN YOUR ALLOWABLE MINUTES, I ROLL OVER ON YOU!
GOT IT.
SCOTT and BORGMAN

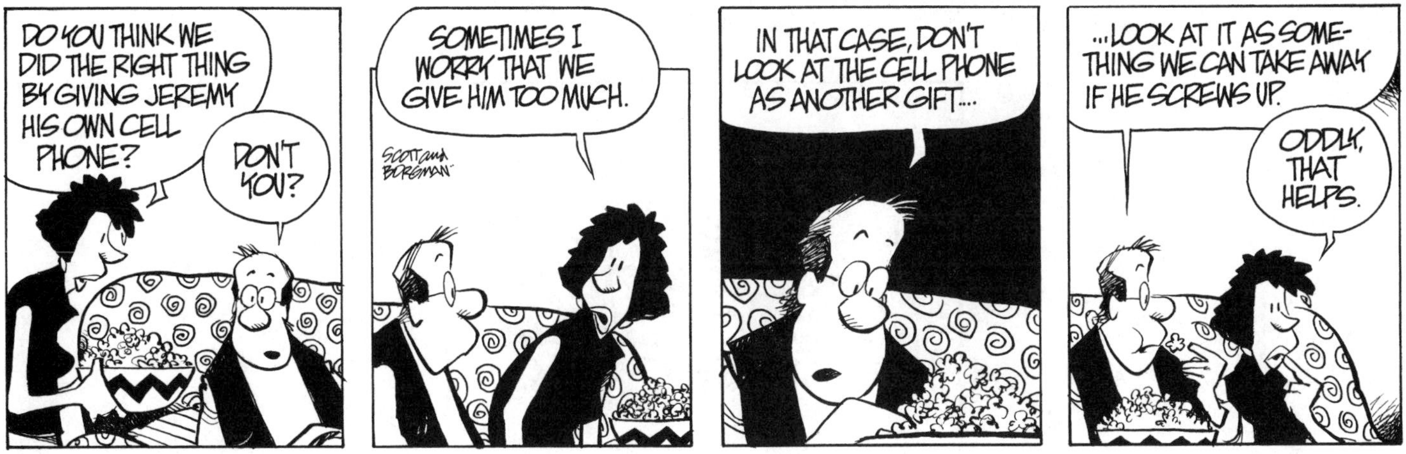
DO YOU THINK WE DID THE RIGHT THING BY GIVING JEREMY HIS OWN CELL PHONE?
DON'T YOU?
SOMETIMES I WORRY THAT WE GIVE HIM TOO MUCH.
IN THAT CASE, DON'T LOOK AT THE CELL PHONE AS ANOTHER GIFT....
...LOOK AT IT AS SOMETHING WE CAN TAKE AWAY IF HE SCREWS UP.
ODDLY, THAT HELPS.

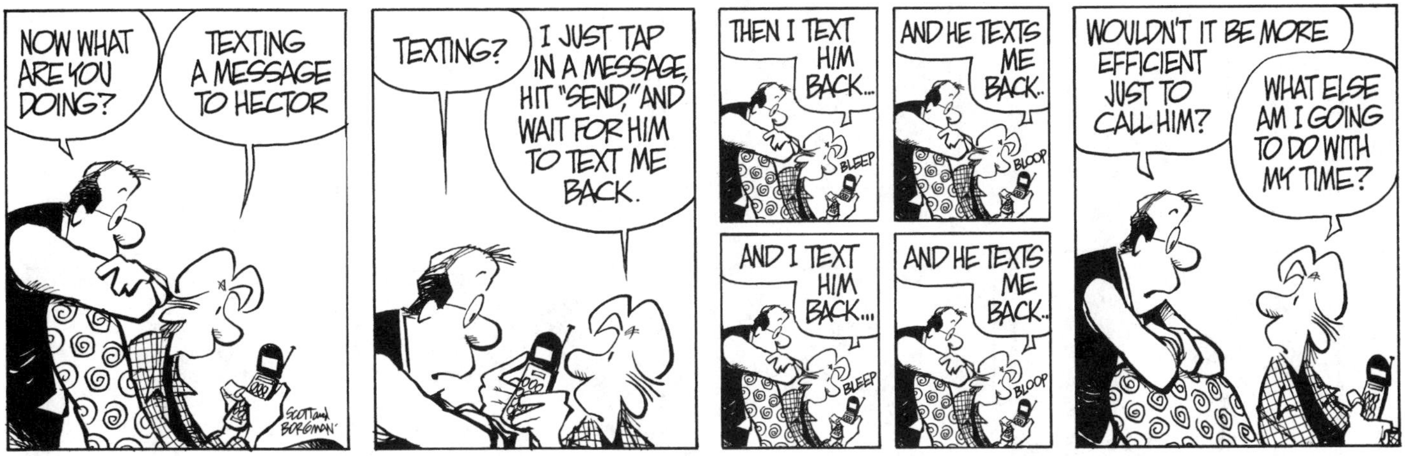
NOW WHAT ARE YOU DOING?
TEXTING A MESSAGE TO HECTOR
TEXTING?
I JUST TAP IN A MESSAGE, HIT "SEND," AND WAIT FOR HIM TO TEXT ME BACK.
THEN I TEXT HIM BACK...
BLEEP
AND HE TEXTS ME BACK...
BLOOP
AND I TEXT HIM BACK...
BLEEP
AND HE TEXTS ME BACK...
BLOOP
WOULDN'T IT BE MORE EFFICIENT JUST TO CALL HIM?
WHAT ELSE AM I GOING TO DO WITH MY TIME?

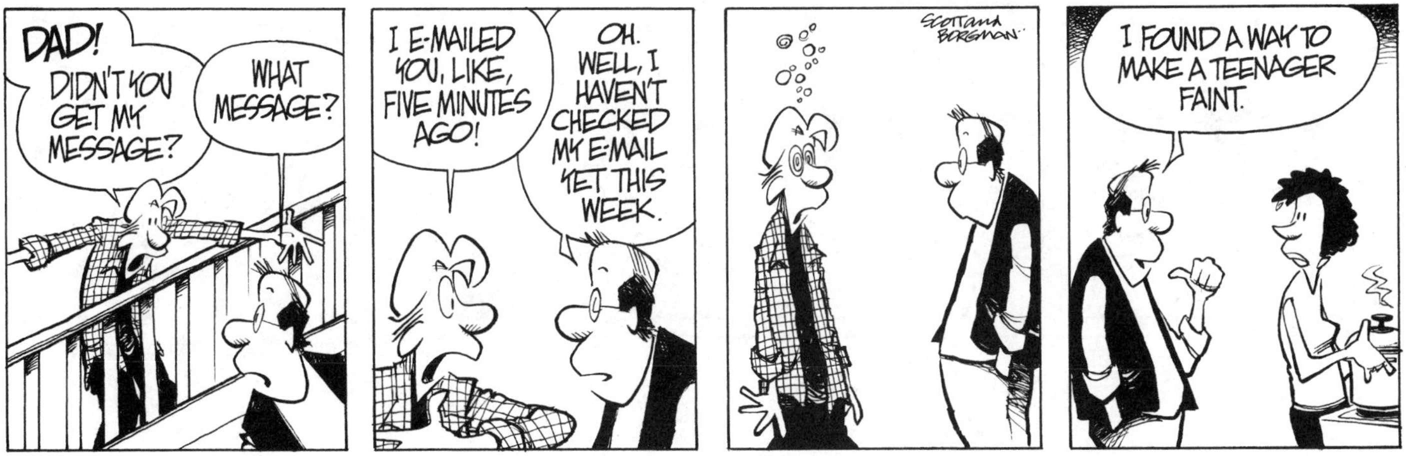
DAD! DIDN'T YOU GET MY MESSAGE?
WHAT MESSAGE?
I E-MAILED YOU, LIKE, FIVE MINUTES AGO!
OH. WELL, I HAVEN'T CHECKED MY E-MAIL YET THIS WEEK.
I FOUND A WAY TO MAKE A TEENAGER FAINT.

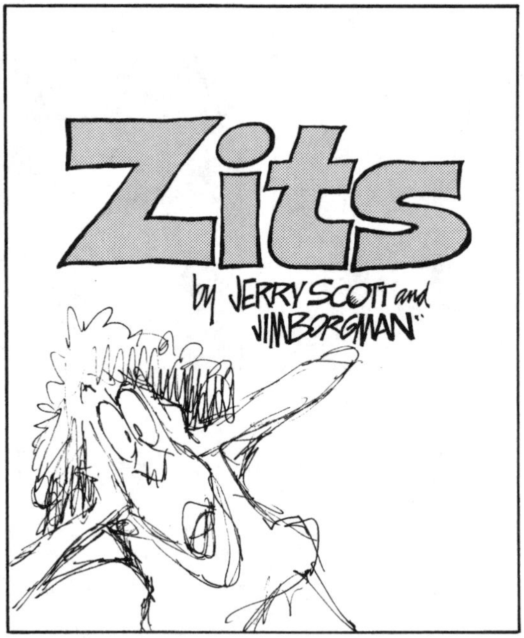
Zits
by JERRY SCOTT and JIMBORGMAN

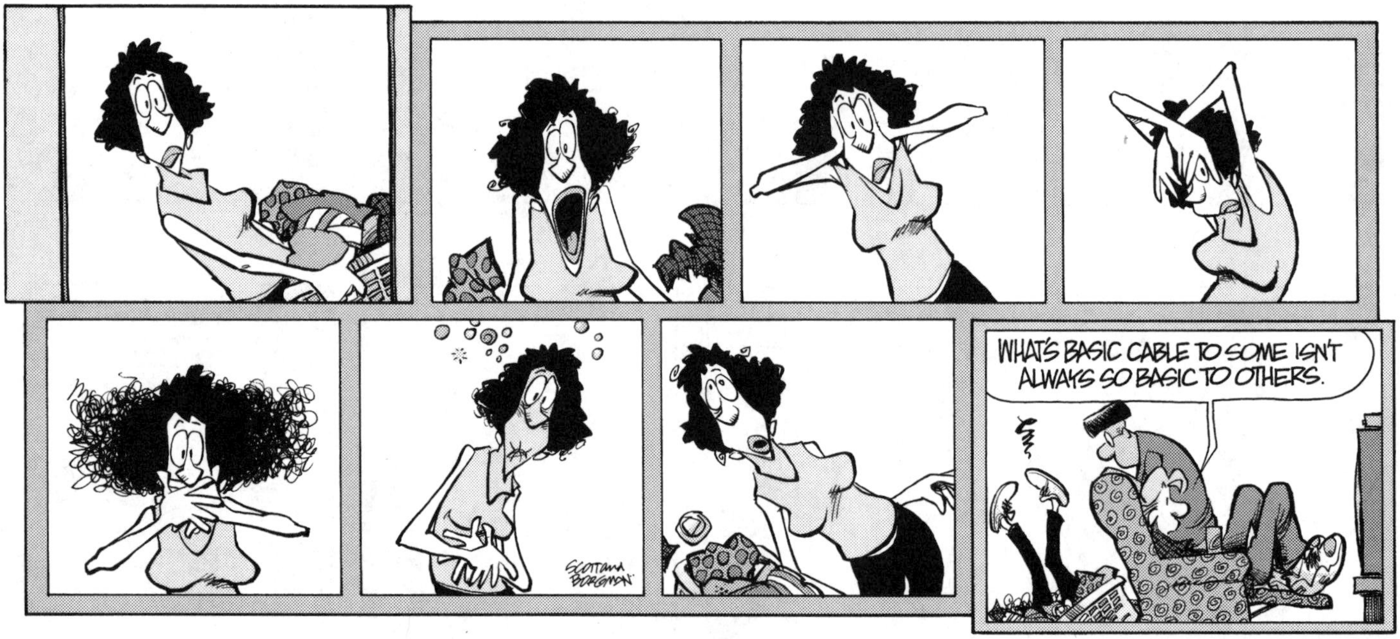
SCOTT AND BORGMAN
WHAT'S BASIC CABLE TO SOME ISN'T ALWAYS SO BASIC TO OTHERS.

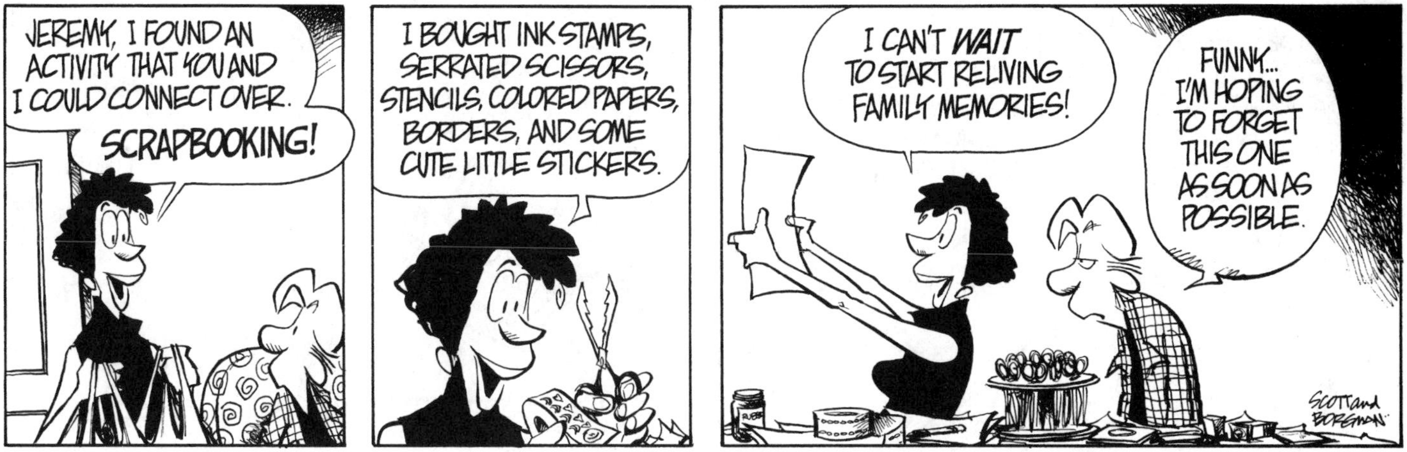
JEREMY, I FOUND AN ACTIVITY THAT YOU AND I COULD CONNECT OVER.
SCRAPBOOKING!
I BOUGHT INK STAMPS, SERRATED SCISSORS, STENCILS, COLORED PAPERS, BORDERS, AND SOME CUTE LITTLE STICKERS.
I CAN'T **WAIT** TO START RELIVING FAMILY MEMORIES!
FUNNY... I'M HOPING TO FORGET THIS ONE AS SOON AS POSSIBLE.
SCOTT and BORGMAN

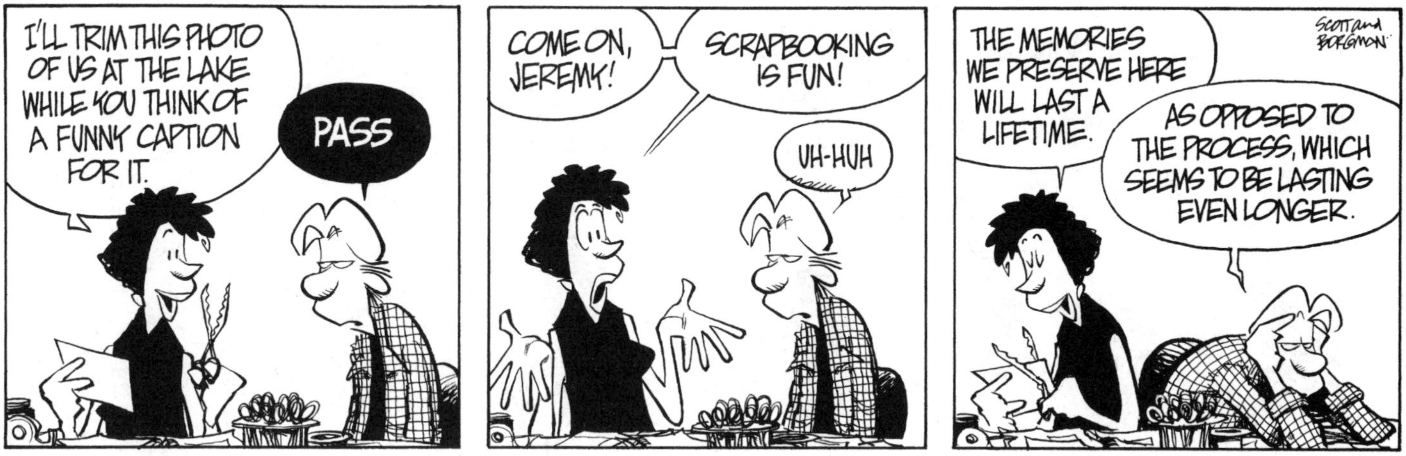
I'LL TRIM THIS PHOTO OF US AT THE LAKE WHILE YOU THINK OF A FUNNY CAPTION FOR IT.
PASS
COME ON, JEREMY!
SCRAPBOOKING IS FUN!
UH-HUH
THE MEMORIES WE PRESERVE HERE WILL LAST A LIFETIME.
AS OPPOSED TO THE PROCESS, WHICH SEEMS TO BE LASTING EVEN LONGER.
SCOTT and BORGMAN

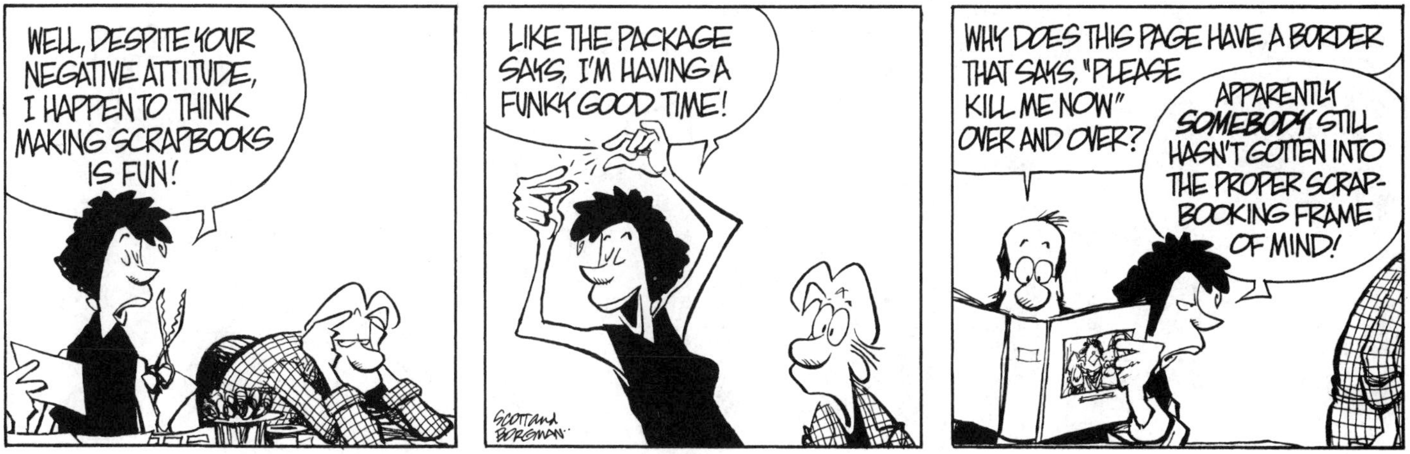
WELL, DESPITE YOUR NEGATIVE ATTITUDE, I HAPPEN TO THINK MAKING SCRAPBOOKS IS FUN!
LIKE THE PACKAGE SAYS, I'M HAVING A FUNKY GOOD TIME!
SCOTT and BORGMAN
WHY DOES THIS PAGE HAVE A BORDER THAT SAYS, "PLEASE KILL ME NOW" OVER AND OVER?
APPARENTLY ***SOMEBODY*** STILL HASN'T GOTTEN INTO THE PROPER SCRAP-BOOKING FRAME OF MIND!

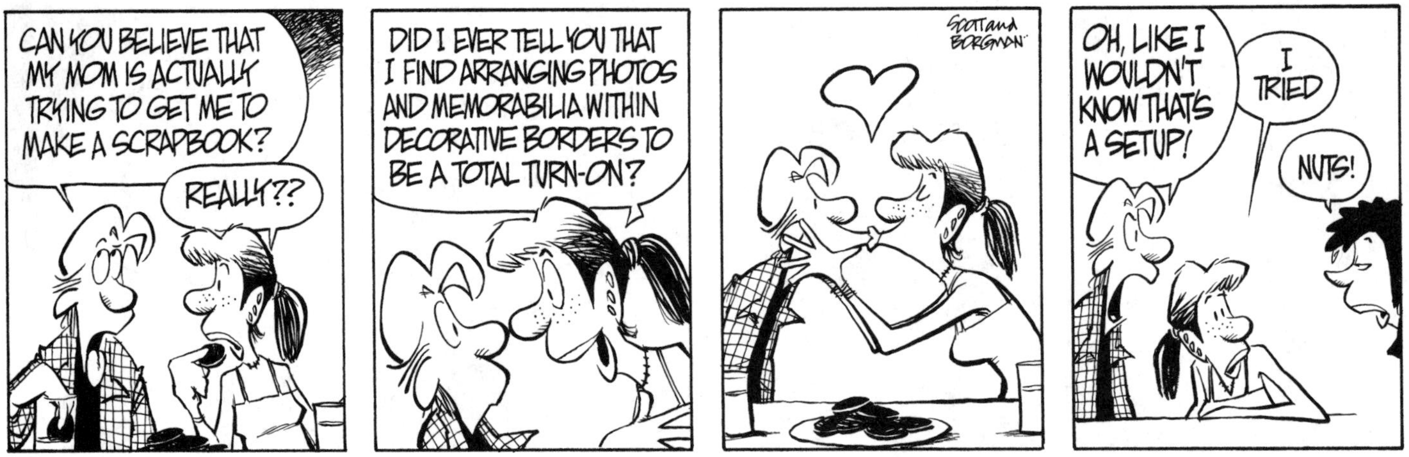
CAN YOU BELIEVE THAT MY MOM IS ACTUALLY TRYING TO GET ME TO MAKE A SCRAPBOOK?
REALLY??
DID I EVER TELL YOU THAT I FIND ARRANGING PHOTOS AND MEMORABILIA WITHIN DECORATIVE BORDERS TO BE A TOTAL TURN-ON?
SCOTT and BORGMAN
OH, LIKE I WOULDN'T KNOW THAT'S A SETUP!
I TRIED
NUTS!

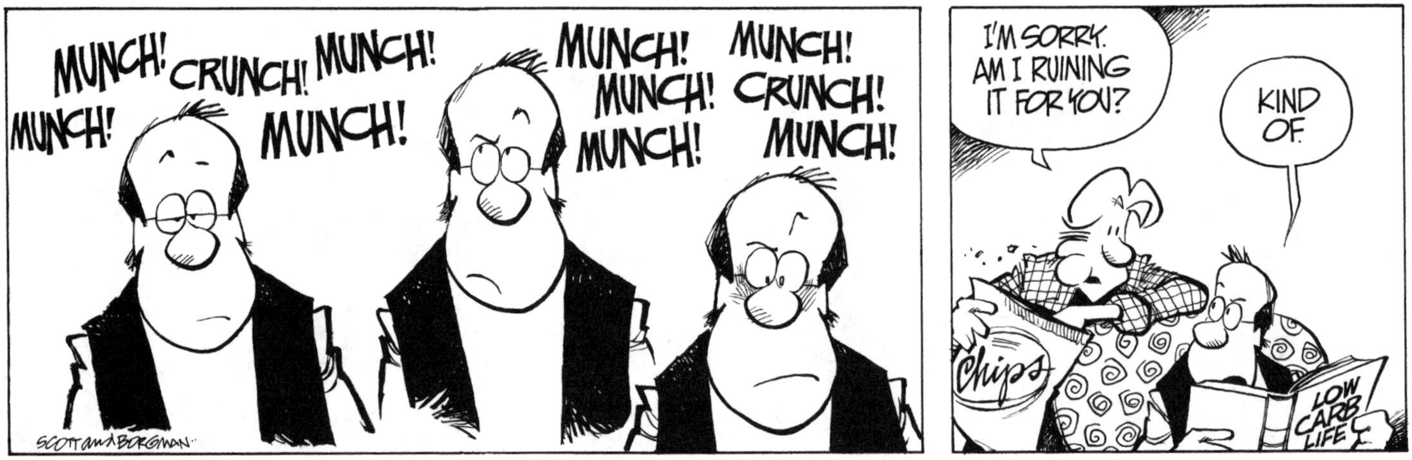
MUNCH! CRUNCH! MUNCH!
MUNCH! MUNCH!
MUNCH! MUNCH!
MUNCH! MUNCH!
CRUNCH! MUNCH!
SCOTT and BORGMAN
I'M SORRY. AM I RUINING IT FOR YOU?
KIND OF.
Chips
LOW CARB LIFE

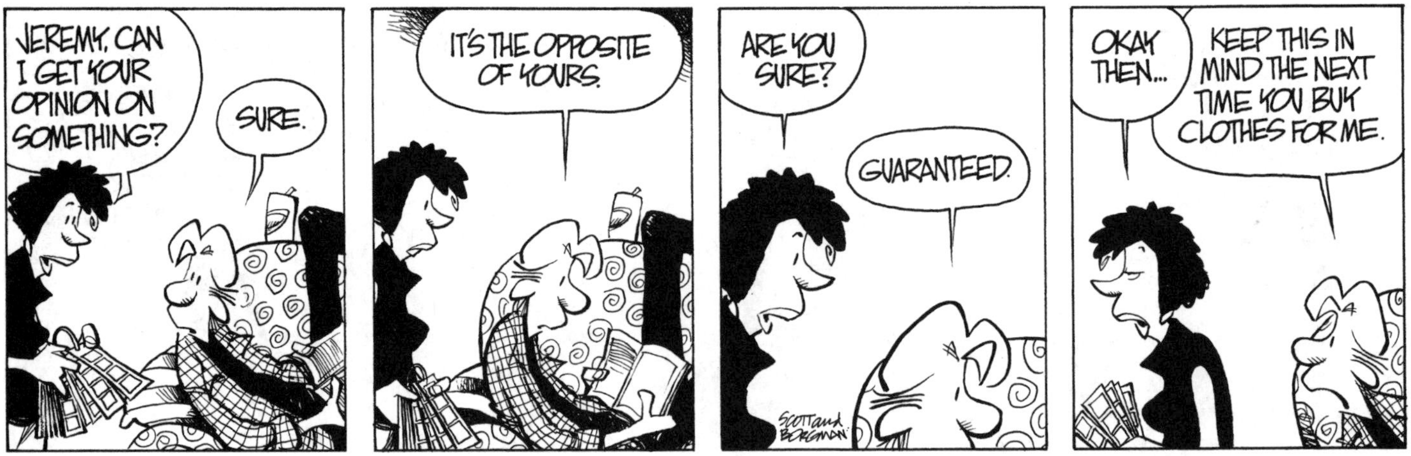
JEREMY, CAN I GET YOUR OPINION ON SOMETHING?
SURE.
IT'S THE OPPOSITE OF YOURS.
ARE YOU SURE?
GUARANTEED.
SCOTT and BORGMAN
OKAY THEN...
KEEP THIS IN MIND THE NEXT TIME YOU BUY CLOTHES FOR ME.

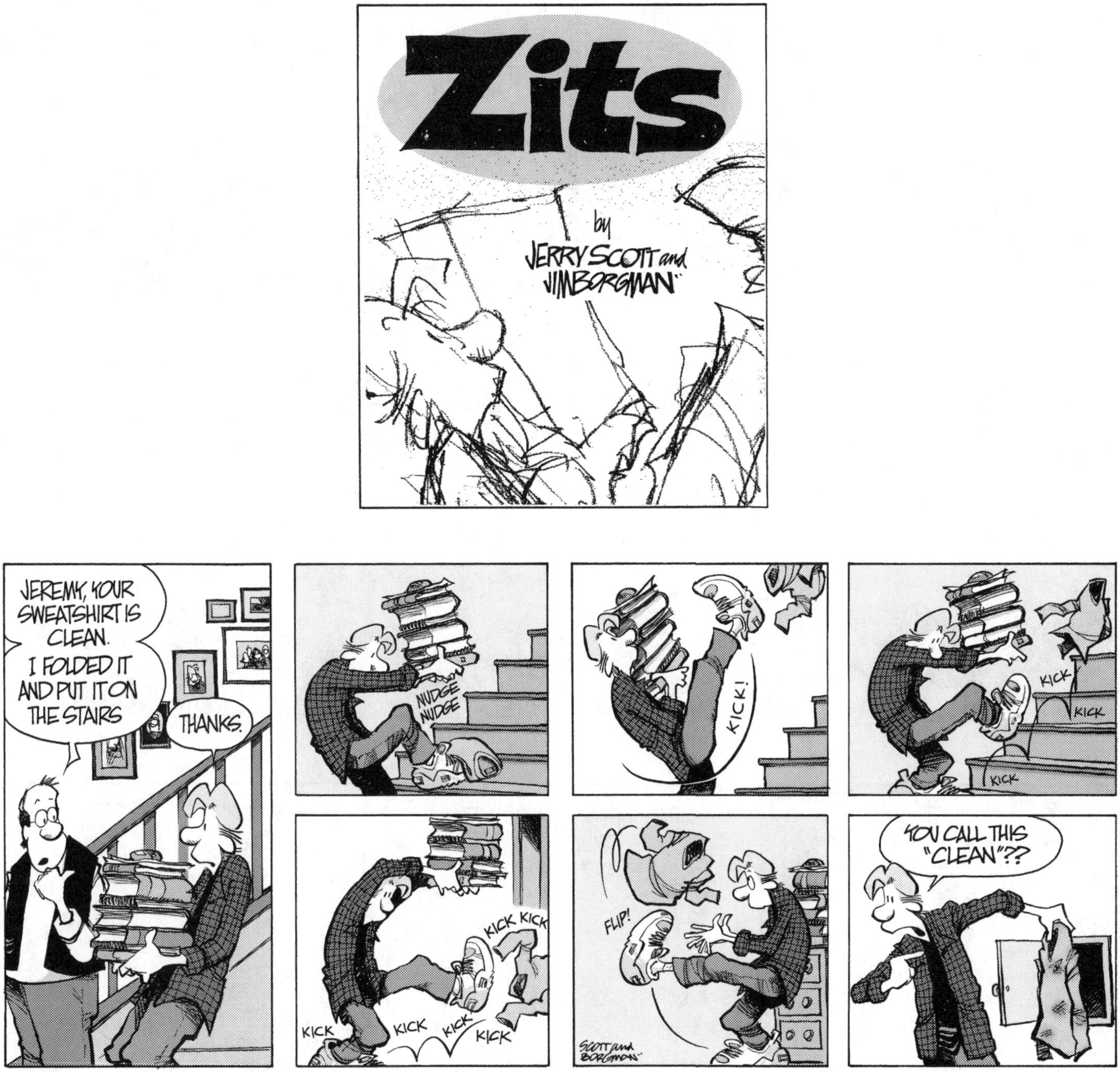
Zits
by
JERRY SCOTT and
JIM BORGMAN
JEREMY, YOUR SWEATSHIRT IS CLEAN.
I FOLDED IT AND PUT IT ON THE STAIRS
THANKS.
NUDGE NUDGE
KICK!
KICK
KICK
KICK
KICK KICK
KICK
KICK
KICK
KICK
FLIP!
SCOTT and BORGMAN
YOU CALL THIS "CLEAN"??

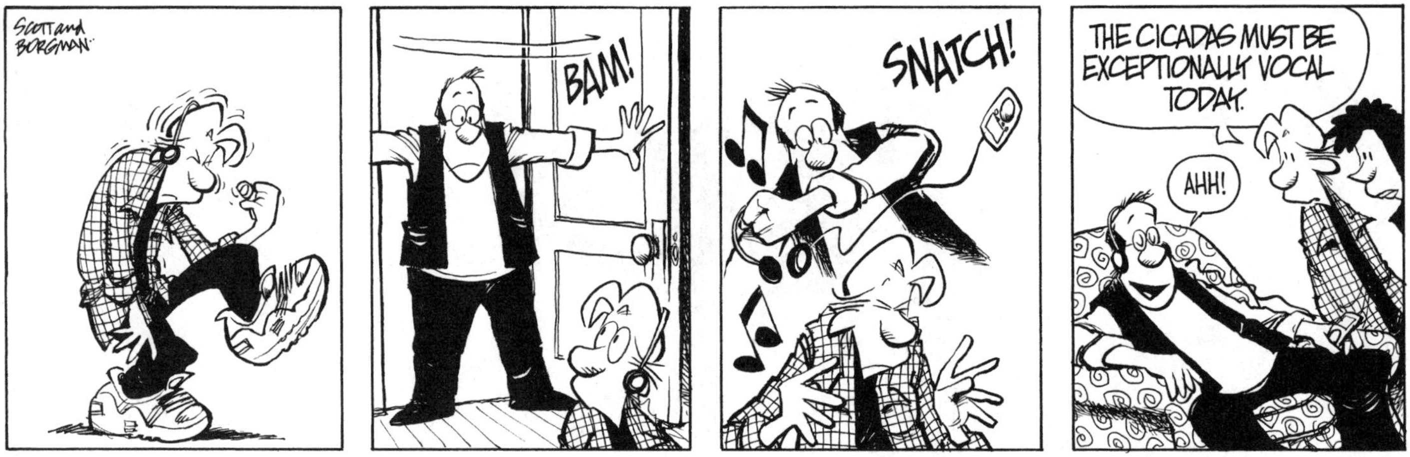
SCOTT and BORGMAN
BAM!
SNATCH!
THE CICADAS MUST BE EXCEPTIONALLY VOCAL TODAY.
AHH!

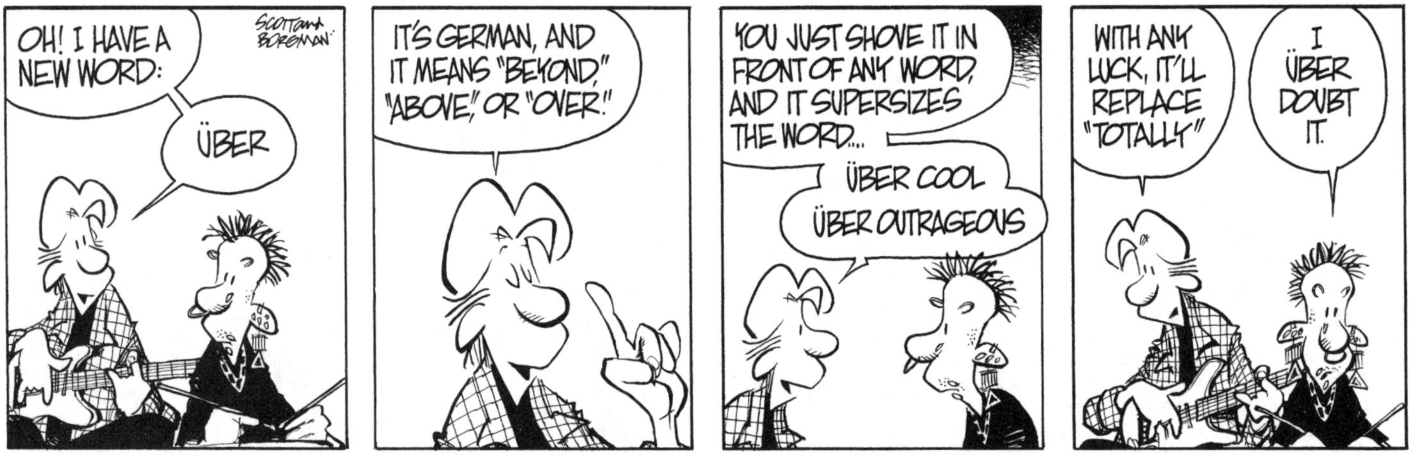
OH! I HAVE A NEW WORD:
SCOTT and BORGMAN
ÜBER
IT'S GERMAN, AND IT MEANS "BEYOND," "ABOVE," OR "OVER."
YOU JUST SHOVE IT IN FRONT OF ANY WORD, AND IT SUPERSIZES THE WORD...
ÜBER COOL
ÜBER OUTRAGEOUS
WITH ANY LUCK, IT'LL REPLACE "TOTALLY"
I ÜBER DOUBT IT.

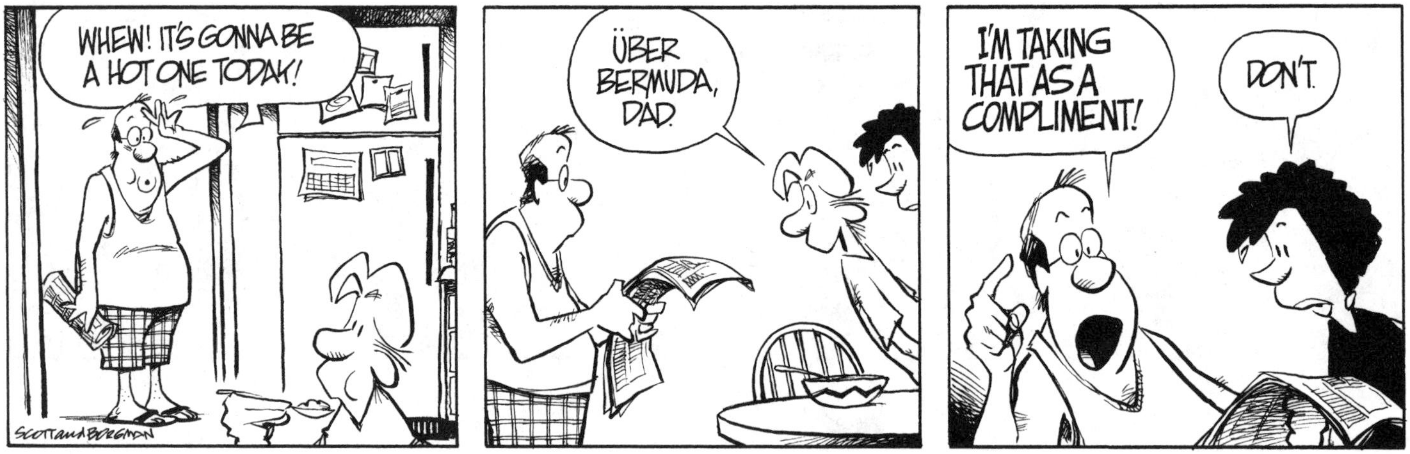
WHEW! IT'S GONNA BE A HOT ONE TODAY!
SCOTT and BORGMAN
ÜBER BERMUDA, DAD.
I'M TAKING THAT AS A COMPLIMENT!
DON'T.

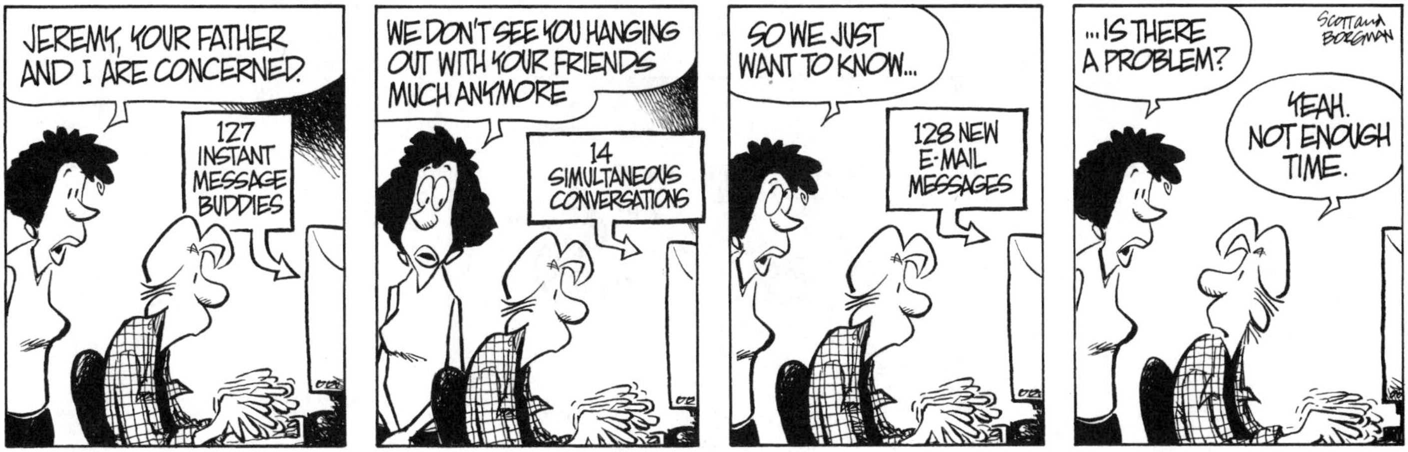
JEREMY, YOUR FATHER AND I ARE CONCERNED.
127 INSTANT MESSAGE BUDDIES
WE DON'T SEE YOU HANGING OUT WITH YOUR FRIENDS MUCH ANYMORE
14 SIMULTANEOUS CONVERSATIONS
SO WE JUST WANT TO KNOW...
128 NEW E-MAIL MESSAGES
...IS THERE A PROBLEM?
YEAH. NOT ENOUGH TIME.

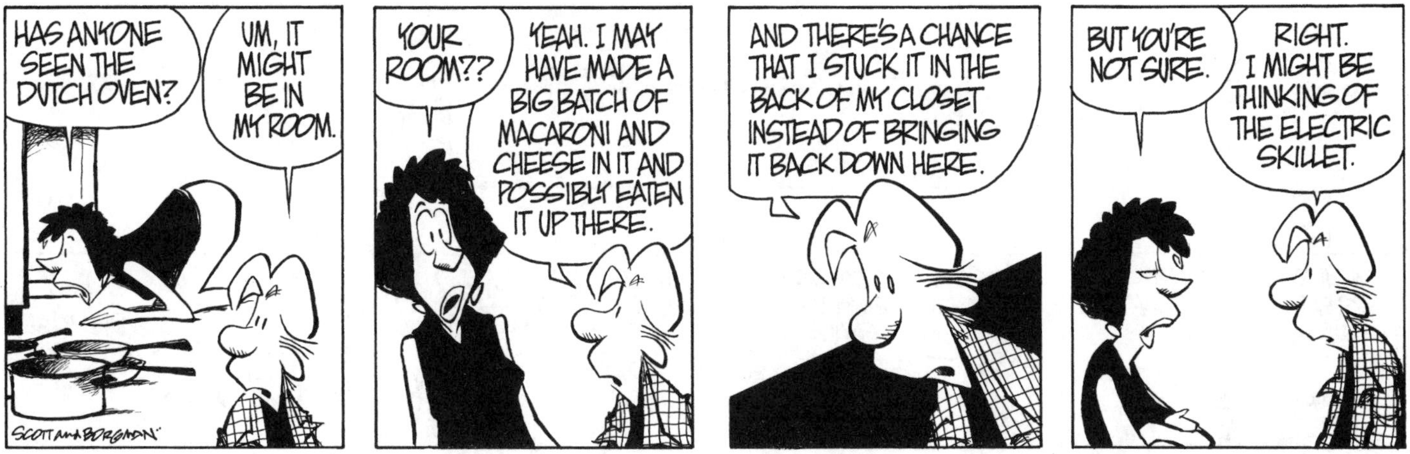
HAS ANYONE SEEN THE DUTCH OVEN?
UM, IT MIGHT BE IN MY ROOM.
YOUR ROOM??
YEAH. I MAY HAVE MADE A BIG BATCH OF MACARONI AND CHEESE IN IT AND POSSIBLY EATEN IT UP THERE.
AND THERE'S A CHANCE THAT I STUCK IT IN THE BACK OF MY CLOSET INSTEAD OF BRINGING IT BACK DOWN HERE.
BUT YOU'RE NOT SURE.
RIGHT. I MIGHT BE THINKING OF THE ELECTRIC SKILLET.

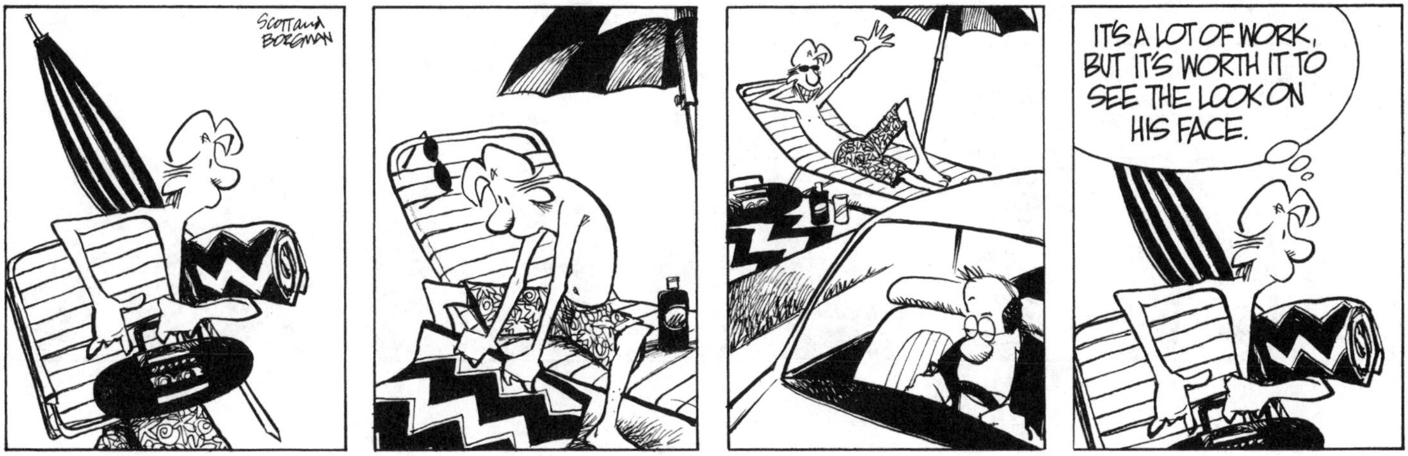
IT'S A LOT OF WORK, BUT IT'S WORTH IT TO SEE THE LOOK ON HIS FACE.

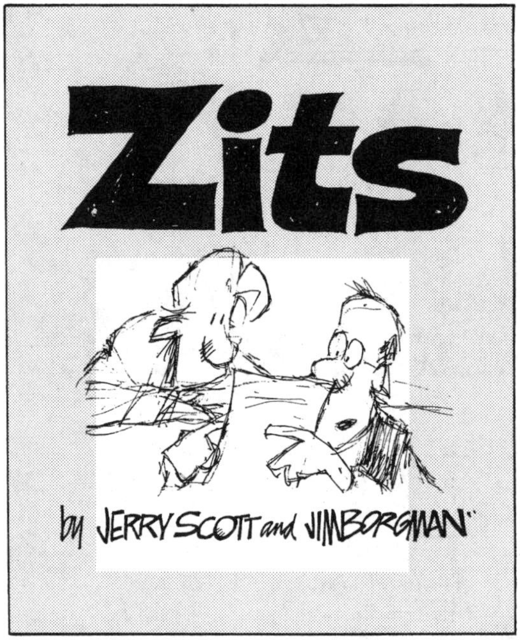
Zits
by JERRY SCOTT and JIM BORGMAN

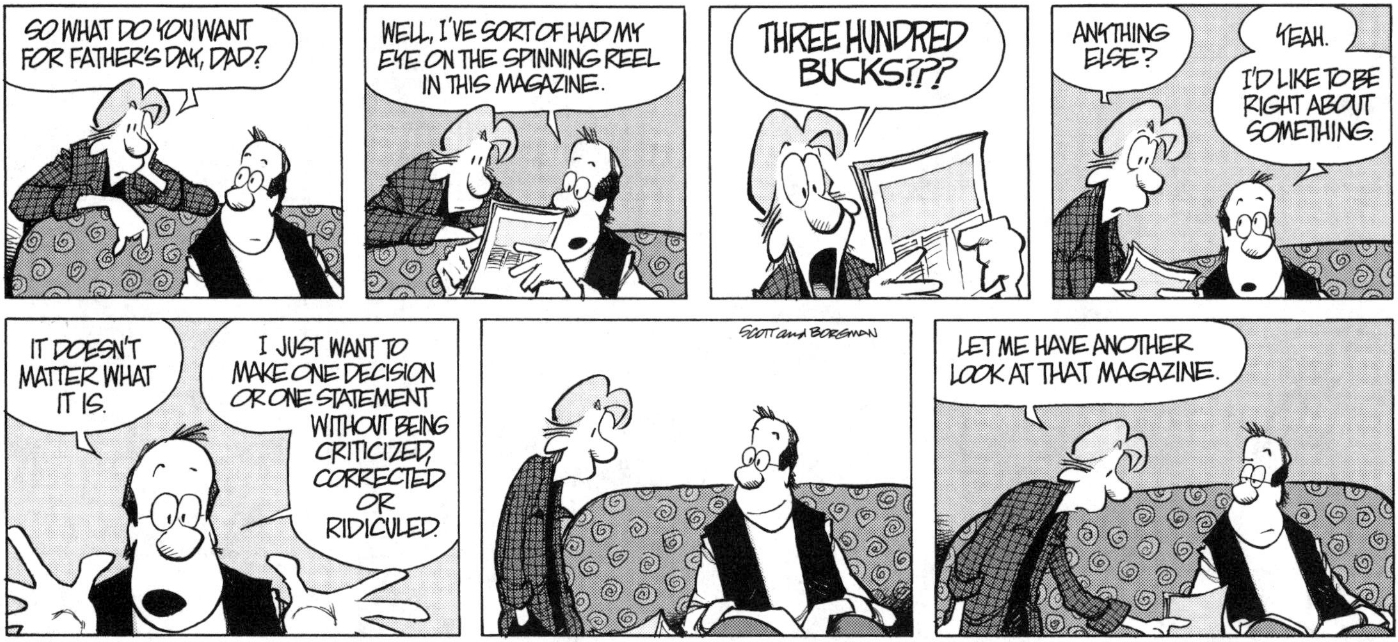
SO WHAT DO YOU WANT FOR FATHER'S DAY, DAD?
WELL, I'VE SORT OF HAD MY EYE ON THE SPINNING REEL IN THIS MAGAZINE.
THREE HUNDRED BUCKS???
ANYTHING ELSE?
YEAH.
I'D LIKE TO BE RIGHT ABOUT SOMETHING.
IT DOESN'T MATTER WHAT IT IS.
I JUST WANT TO MAKE ONE DECISION OR ONE STATEMENT WITHOUT BEING CRITICIZED, CORRECTED OR RIDICULED.
SCOTT and BORGMAN
LET ME HAVE ANOTHER LOOK AT THAT MAGAZINE.

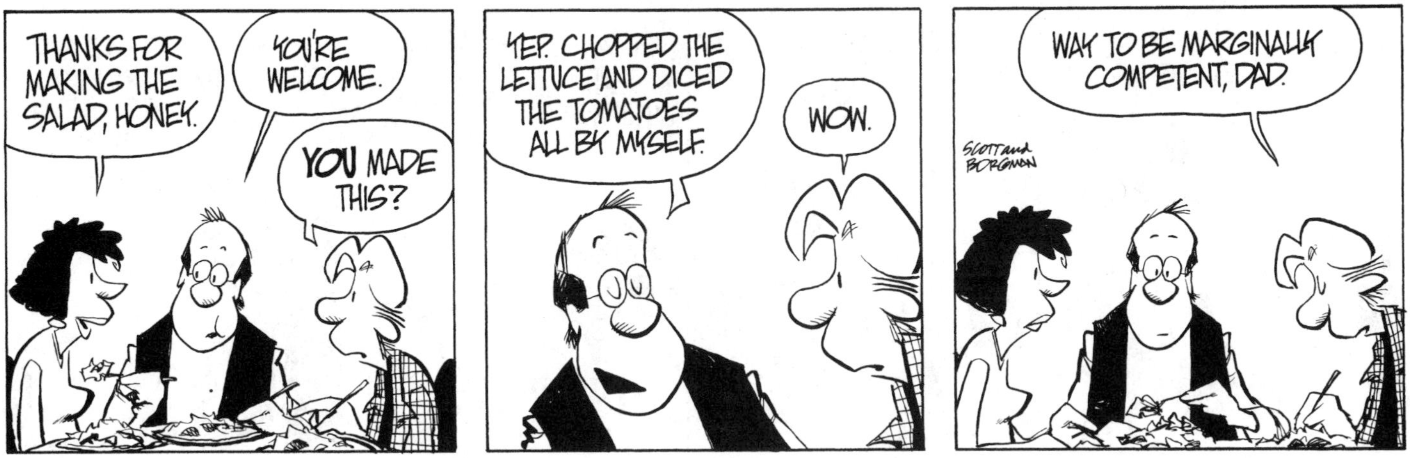
THANKS FOR MAKING THE SALAD, HONEY.
YOU'RE WELCOME.
YOU MADE THIS?
YEP. CHOPPED THE LETTUCE AND DICED THE TOMATOES ALL BY MYSELF.
WOW.
WAY TO BE MARGINALLY COMPETENT, DAD.

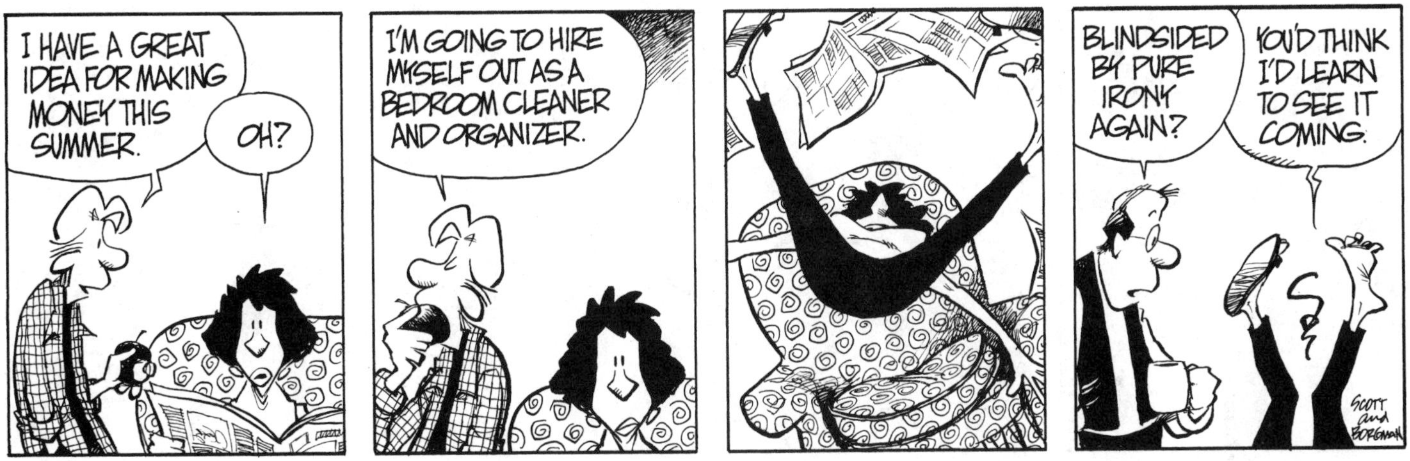
I HAVE A GREAT IDEA FOR MAKING MONEY THIS SUMMER.
OH?
I'M GOING TO HIRE MYSELF OUT AS A BEDROOM CLEANER AND ORGANIZER.
BLINDSIDED BY PURE IRONY AGAIN?
YOU'D THINK I'D LEARN TO SEE IT COMING.

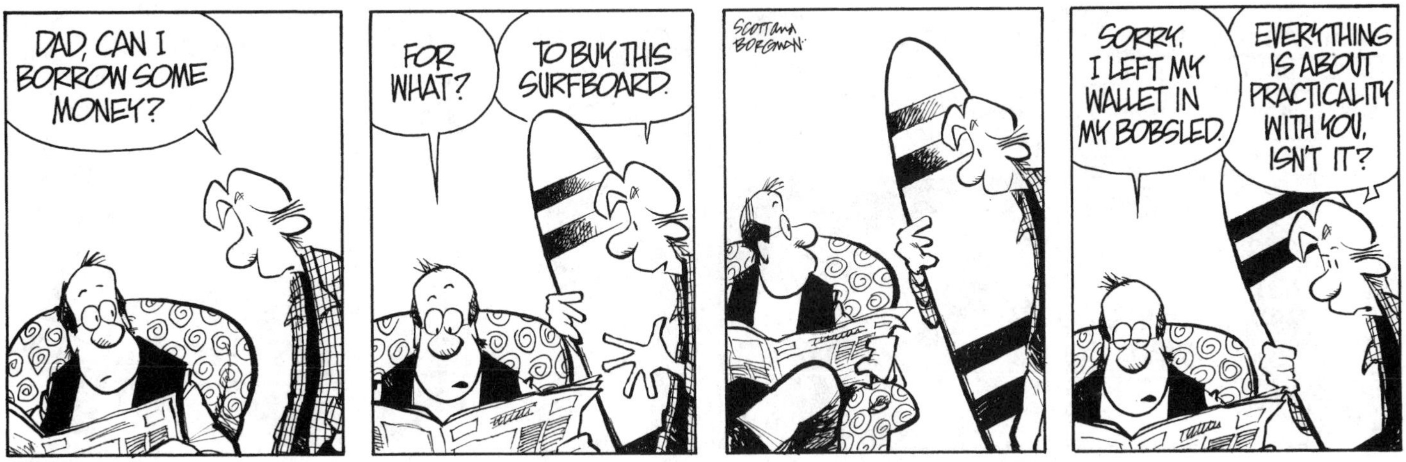
DAD, CAN I BORROW SOME MONEY?
FOR WHAT?
TO BUY THIS SURFBOARD.
SORRY. I LEFT MY WALLET IN MY BOBSLED.
EVERYTHING IS ABOUT PRACTICALITY WITH YOU, ISN'T IT?

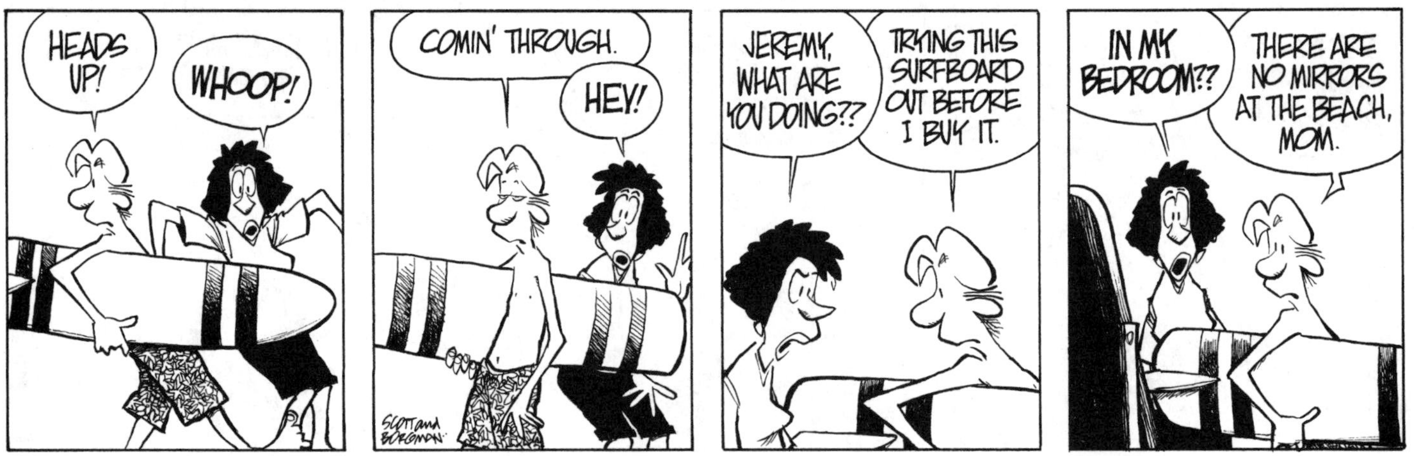
HEADS UP!
WHOOP!
COMIN' THROUGH.
HEY!
JEREMY, WHAT ARE YOU DOING??
TRYING THIS SURFBOARD OUT BEFORE I BUY IT.
IN MY BEDROOM??
THERE ARE NO MIRRORS AT THE BEACH, MOM.

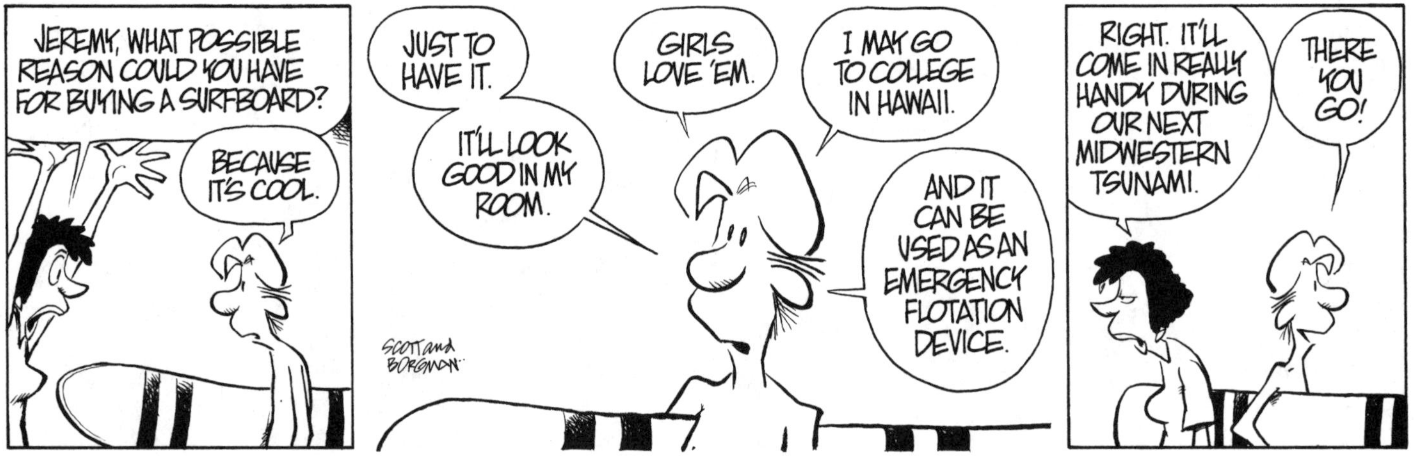
JEREMY, WHAT POSSIBLE REASON COULD YOU HAVE FOR BUYING A SURFBOARD?
BECAUSE IT'S COOL.
JUST TO HAVE IT.
IT'LL LOOK GOOD IN MY ROOM.
GIRLS LOVE 'EM.
I MAY GO TO COLLEGE IN HAWAII.
AND IT CAN BE USED AS AN EMERGENCY FLOTATION DEVICE.
RIGHT. IT'LL COME IN REALLY HANDY DURING OUR NEXT MIDWESTERN TSUNAMI.
THERE YOU GO!

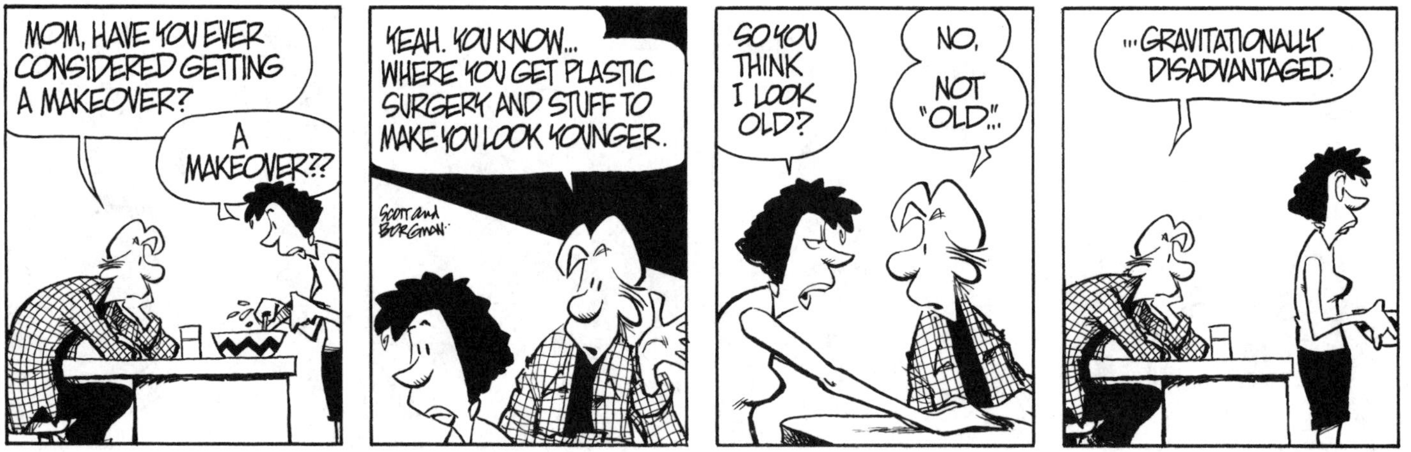
MOM, HAVE YOU EVER CONSIDERED GETTING A MAKEOVER?
A MAKEOVER??
YEAH. YOU KNOW... WHERE YOU GET PLASTIC SURGERY AND STUFF TO MAKE YOU LOOK YOUNGER.
SO YOU THINK I LOOK OLD?
NO,
NOT "OLD"...
...GRAVITATIONALLY DISADVANTAGED.

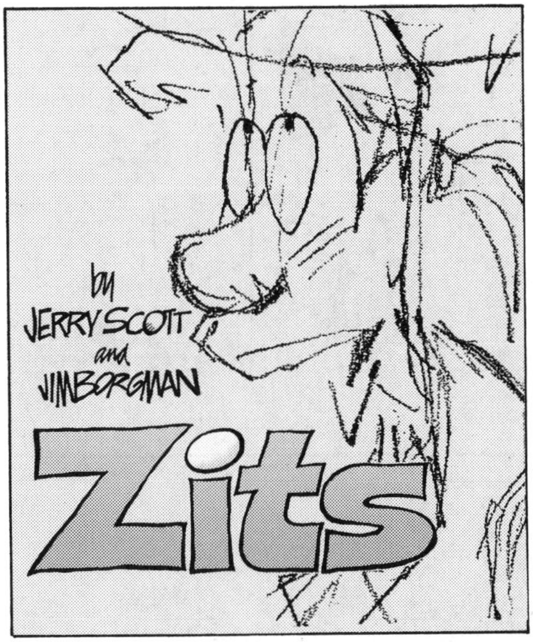
by
JERRY SCOTT
and
JIM BORGMAN
Zits

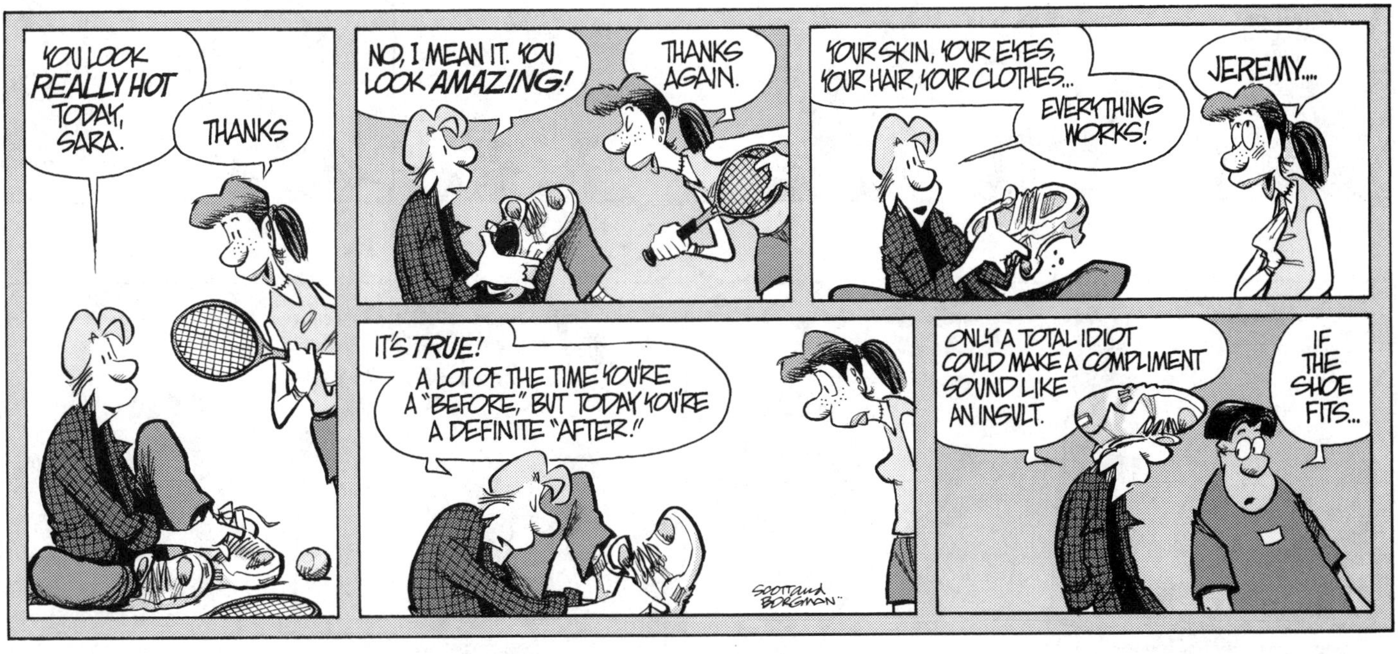
YOU LOOK REALLY HOT TODAY, SARA.
THANKS
NO, I MEAN IT. YOU LOOK AMAZING!
THANKS AGAIN.
YOUR SKIN, YOUR EYES, YOUR HAIR, YOUR CLOTHES...
EVERYTHING WORKS!
JEREMY....
IT'S TRUE!
A LOT OF THE TIME YOU'RE A "BEFORE," BUT TODAY YOU'RE A DEFINITE "AFTER."
SCOTT and BORGMAN
ONLY A TOTAL IDIOT COULD MAKE A COMPLIMENT SOUND LIKE AN INSULT.
IF THE SHOE FITS...

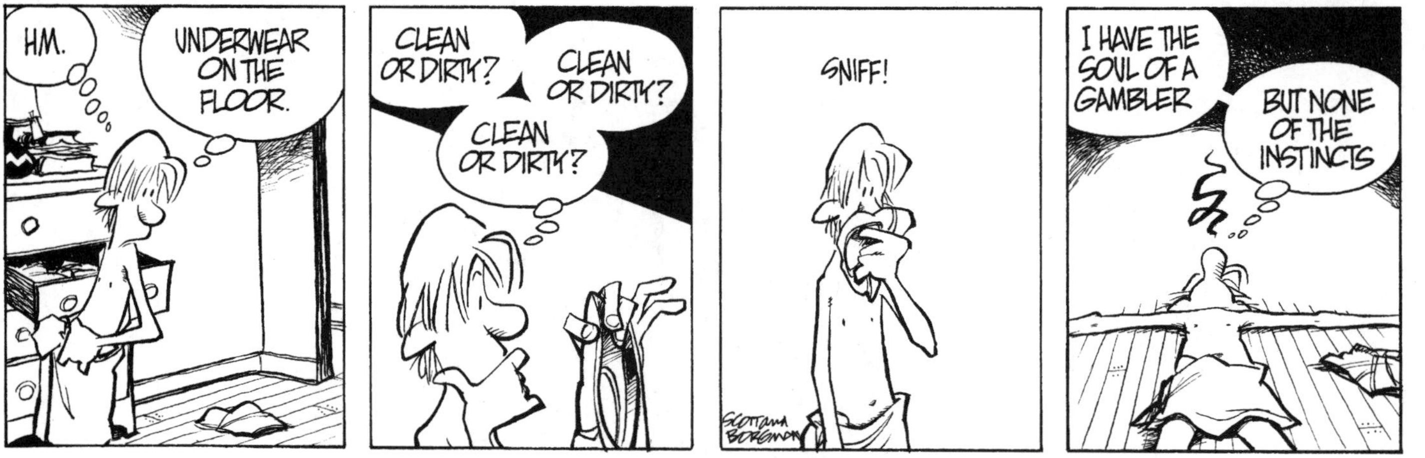
HM.
UNDERWEAR ON THE FLOOR.
CLEAN OR DIRTY?
CLEAN OR DIRTY?
CLEAN OR DIRTY?
SNIFF!
I HAVE THE SOUL OF A GAMBLER
BUT NONE OF THE INSTINCTS

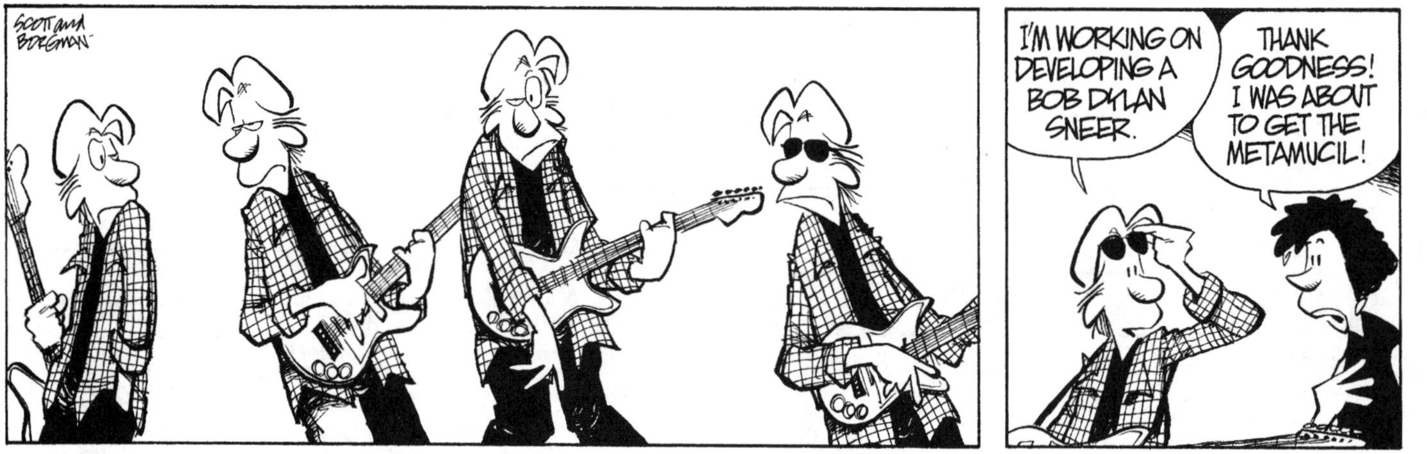
I'M WORKING ON DEVELOPING A BOB DYLAN SNEER.
THANK GOODNESS! I WAS ABOUT TO GET THE METAMUCIL!

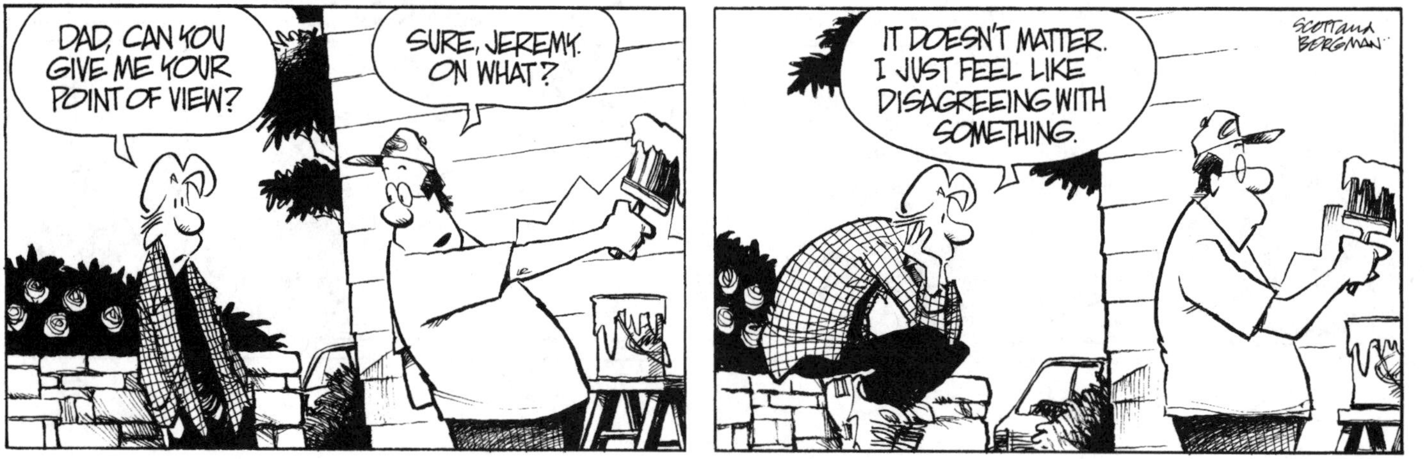
DAD, CAN YOU GIVE ME YOUR POINT OF VIEW?
SURE, JEREMY. ON WHAT?
IT DOESN'T MATTER. I JUST FEEL LIKE DISAGREEING WITH SOMETHING.

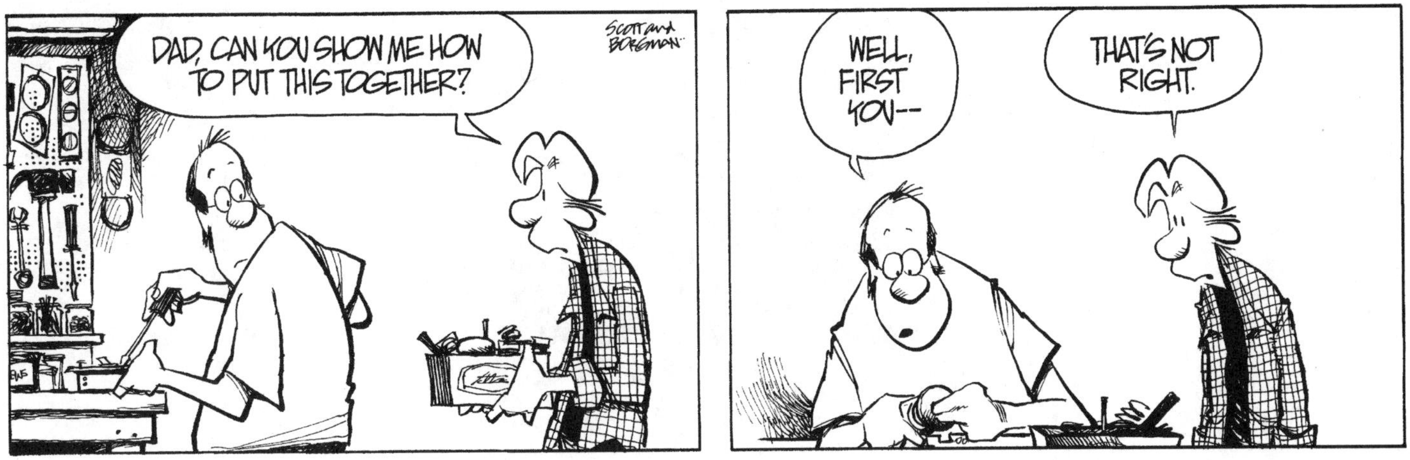
DAD, CAN YOU SHOW ME HOW TO PUT THIS TOGETHER?
WELL, FIRST YOU--
THAT'S NOT RIGHT.

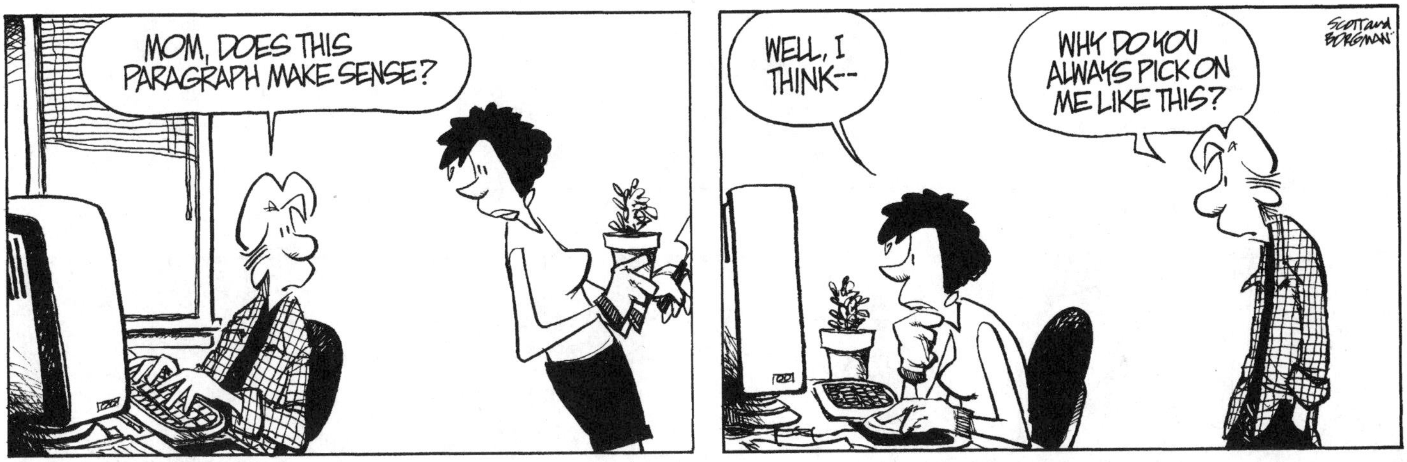
MOM, DOES THIS PARAGRAPH MAKE SENSE?
WELL, I THINK--
WHY DO YOU ALWAYS PICK ON ME LIKE THIS?

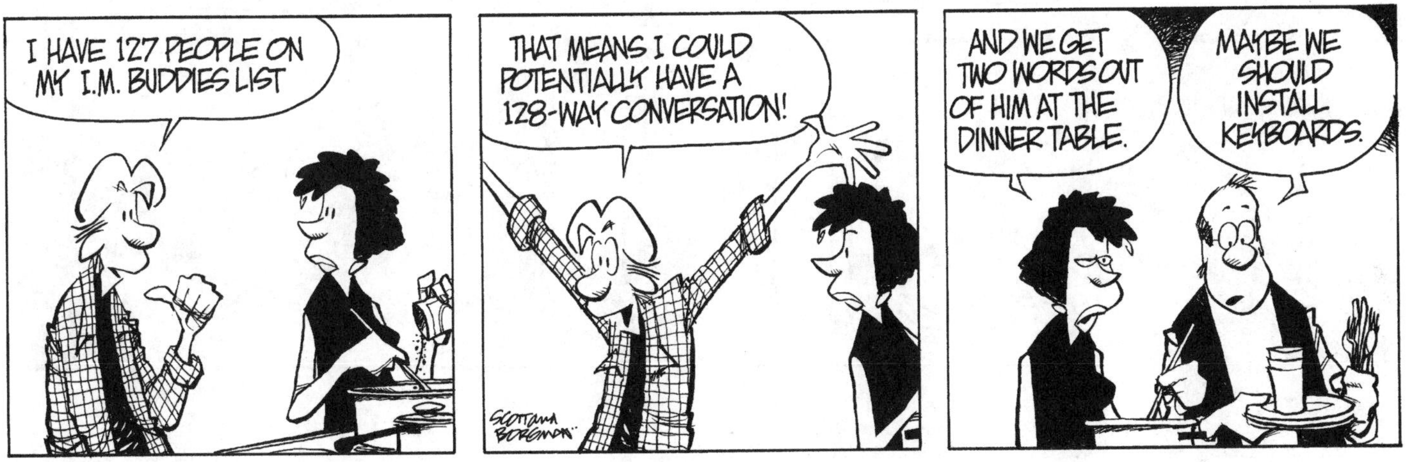
I HAVE 127 PEOPLE ON MY I.M. BUDDIES LIST
THAT MEANS I COULD POTENTIALLY HAVE A 128-WAY CONVERSATION!
AND WE GET TWO WORDS OUT OF HIM AT THE DINNER TABLE.
MAYBE WE SHOULD INSTALL KEYBOARDS.

Zits
by JERRY SCOTT and JIM BORGMAN

SCOTT and BORGMAN
ARE YOU SURE YOU DON'T HAVE ANYWHERE TO GO TODAY?
WHAT IS IT ABOUT SEEING A PERSON RELAX THAT BOTHERS YOU, MOM?

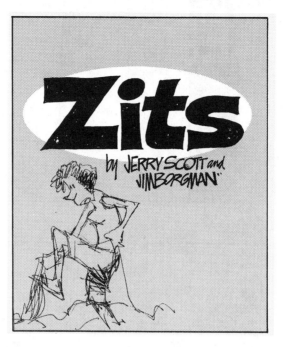

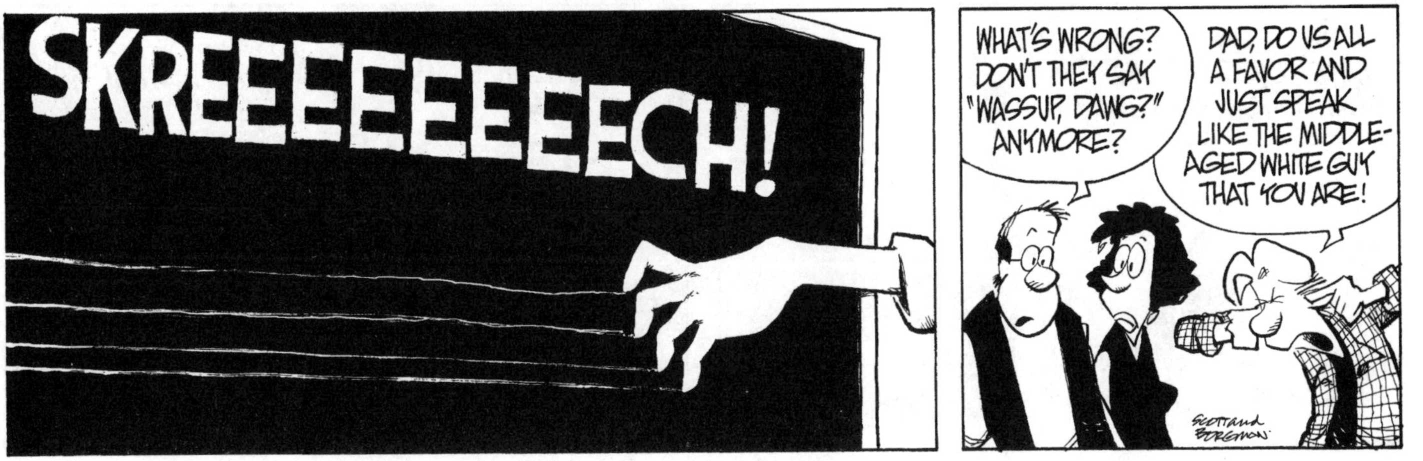
SKREEEEEEEEECH!
WHAT'S WRONG? DON'T THEY SAY "WASSUP, DAWG?" ANYMORE?
DAD, DO US ALL A FAVOR AND JUST SPEAK LIKE THE MIDDLE-AGED WHITE GUY THAT YOU ARE!
SCOTT and BORGMAN

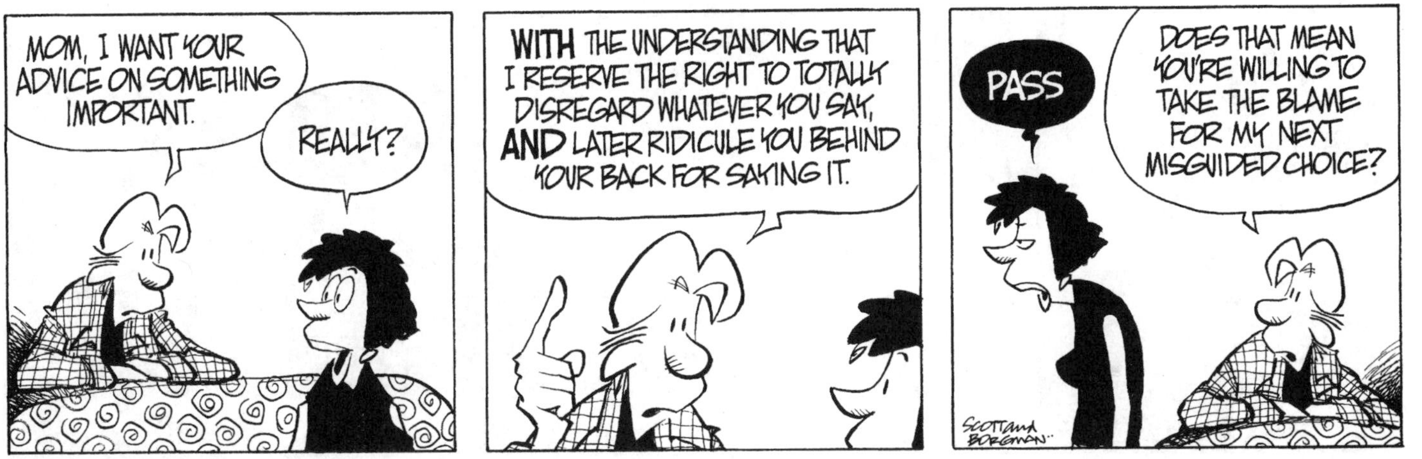
MOM, I WANT YOUR ADVICE ON SOMETHING IMPORTANT.
REALLY?
WITH THE UNDERSTANDING THAT I RESERVE THE RIGHT TO TOTALLY DISREGARD WHATEVER YOU SAY, AND LATER RIDICULE YOU BEHIND YOUR BACK FOR SAYING IT.
PASS
DOES THAT MEAN YOU'RE WILLING TO TAKE THE BLAME FOR MY NEXT MISGUIDED CHOICE?
SCOTT and BORGMAN

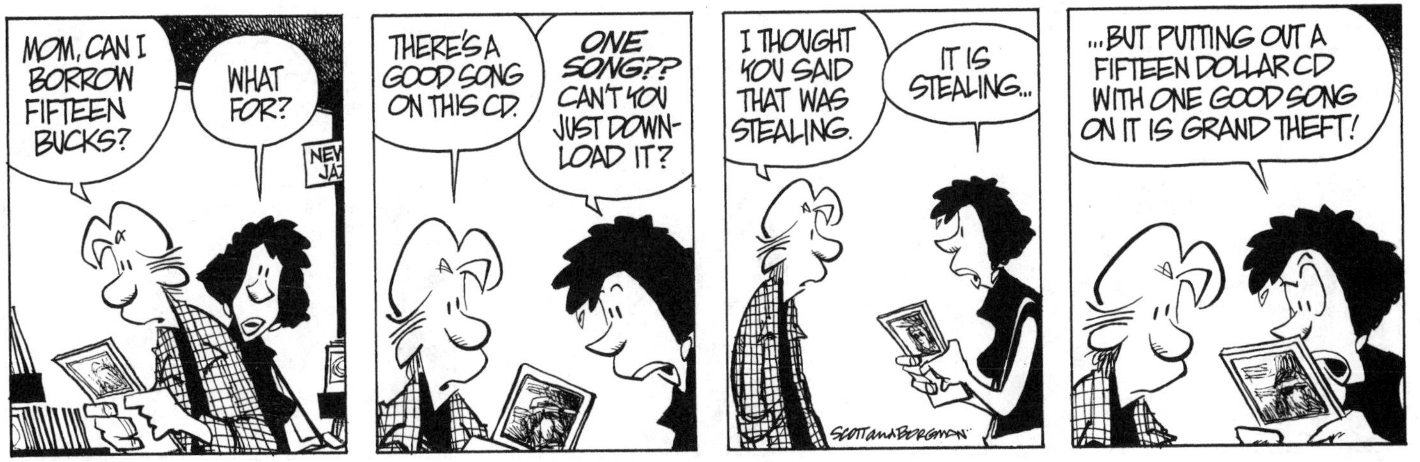
MOM, CAN I BORROW FIFTEEN BUCKS?
WHAT FOR?
THERE'S A GOOD SONG ON THIS CD.
ONE SONG?? CAN'T YOU JUST DOWNLOAD IT?
I THOUGHT YOU SAID THAT WAS STEALING.
IT IS STEALING...
...BUT PUTTING OUT A FIFTEEN DOLLAR CD WITH ONE GOOD SONG ON IT IS GRAND THEFT!
SCOTT and BORGMAN

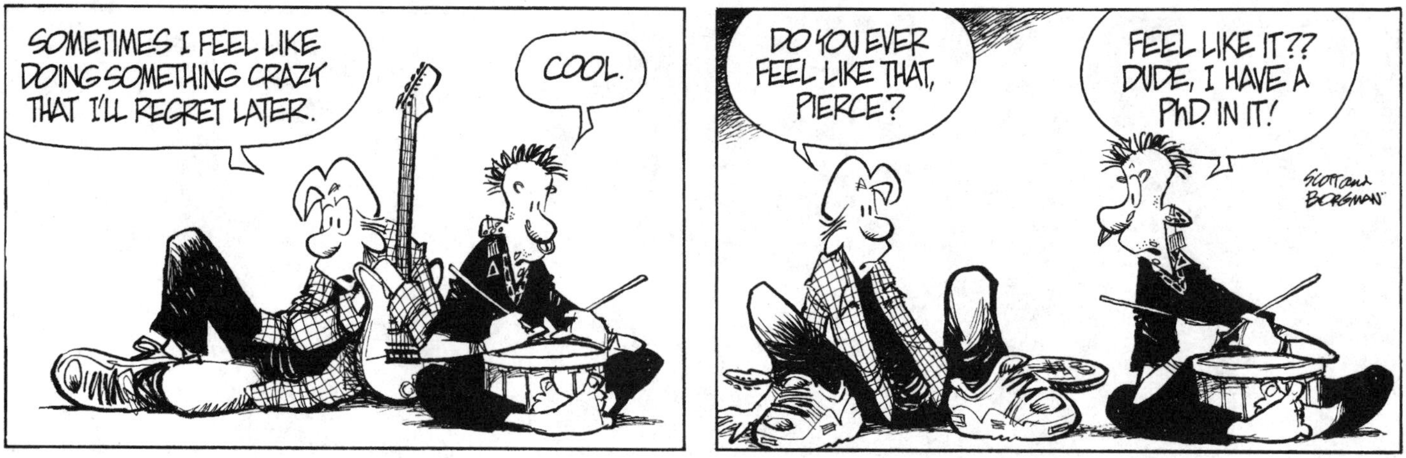
SOMETIMES I FEEL LIKE DOING SOMETHING CRAZY THAT I'LL REGRET LATER.
COOL.
DO YOU EVER FEEL LIKE THAT, PIERCE?
FEEL LIKE IT?? DUDE, I HAVE A PhD IN IT!
SCOTT and BORGMAN

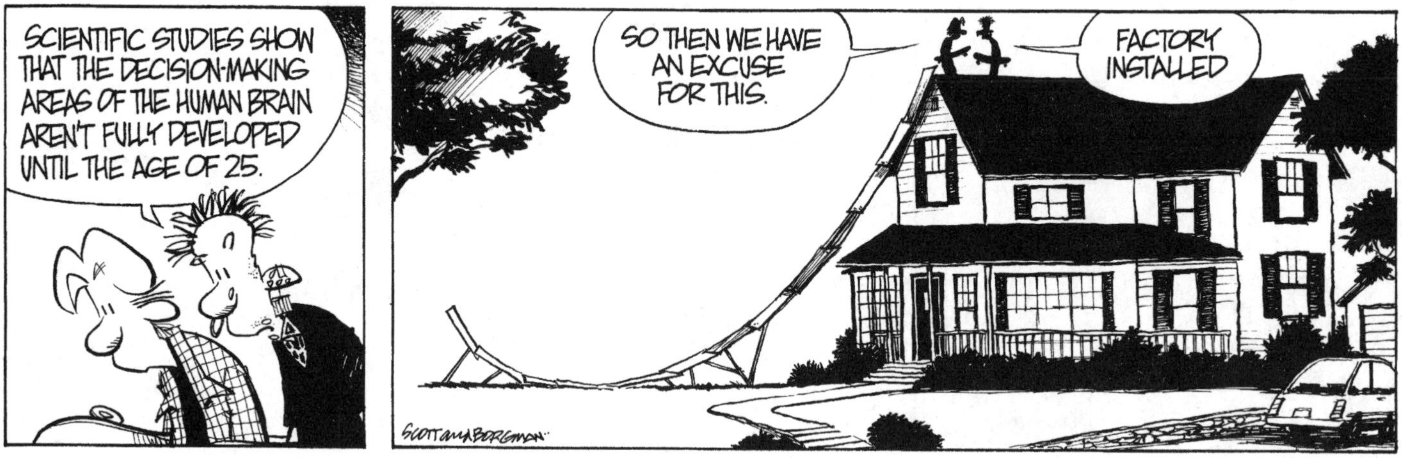
SCIENTIFIC STUDIES SHOW THAT THE DECISION-MAKING AREAS OF THE HUMAN BRAIN AREN'T FULLY DEVELOPED UNTIL THE AGE OF 25.
SO THEN WE HAVE AN EXCUSE FOR THIS.
FACTORY INSTALLED
SCOTT and BORGMAN

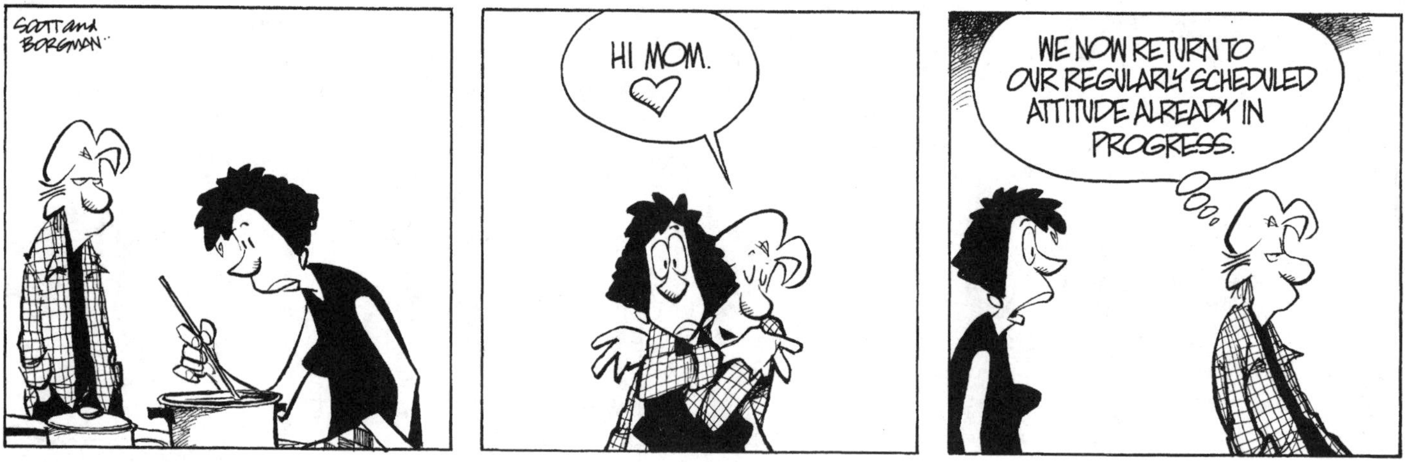
SCOTT and BORGMAN
HI MOM.
WE NOW RETURN TO OUR REGULARLY SCHEDULED ATTITUDE ALREADY IN PROGRESS.